**W9-ABY-265**

REFLECTIONS ON
LITERATURE AND CULTURE

MERIDIAN

Crossing Aesthetics

Werner Hamacher

Editor

Stanford
University
Press

Stanford,
California
2007

REFLECTIONS ON
LITERATURE AND CULTURE

Hannah Arendt

Edited and with an Introduction by

Susannah Young-ah Gottlieb

Stanford University Press
Stanford, California

Library of Congress Cataloging-in-Publication Data
Arendt, Hannah, 1906–1975.
  [Essays. English. Selections]
  Reflections on literature and culture/ Hannah Arendt ; edited and
with an Introduction by Susannah Young-ah Gottlieb.
    p. cm.
  Includes bibliographical references and index.
  ISBN-13: 978-0-8047-4498-0 (cloth : alk. paper)
  ISBN-13: 978-0-8047-4499-7 (pbk. : alk. paper)
  1. German literature—20th century—History and criticism.
2. Literature, Modern—20th century—History and criticism.
3. Civilization, Modern—20th century. 4. Arendt, Hannah, 1906–
1975—Translations into English. I. Gottlieb, Susannah Young-ah.
II. Title.

PT405.A67 2007
809—dc22

                        2006026914

Typeset by Westchester Book Group in 10.9/13 Adobe Garamond

Contents

Acknowledgments

Jerome Kohn, Trustee of the Hannah Arendt Blücher Literary Trust, and Valerie Borchardt of Georges Borchardt, Inc., have been enormously generous in helping me acquire the necessary permissions for most of the writings included in this volume. Stefan Ahrens at the Hannah-Arendt-Forschungszentrum at the Universität Oldenburg kindly facilitated the better part of my research, and the staff at the Library of Congress in Washington, D.C., also granted me access to Arendt's papers. Werner Hamacher, who first helped me conceptualize this project, and Norris Pope, who patiently ushered the volume through to publication, have been splendid guides through the editorial process. Funding from both the Northwestern University Research Grants Committee and the Northwestern Humanities Research Fund allowed me to pursue the work necessary for the completion of this volume. I am very grateful to Richard M. Buxbaum, who generously granted his permission to reproduce Carl Heidenreich's "Last Painting." Finally, I would like to thank Brent Mix for his expertise in digitalizing many of Arendt's papers, Steven Tester for his excellent research assistance, and Paul North for his superb work compiling the index.

Introduction

This volume contains almost all of the essays and reviews Hannah Arendt wrote about literary texts and the idea of culture. It also contains passages from three of her major books, each of which is principally concerned with either specific works of literature or certain general characteristics of art. A few previously unpublished lectures and lecture notes about literature and culture are also included. The texts are arranged in chronological order, so that the reader can trace the course of Arendt's thought.

Despite the fact that many of the texts included in this volume were written solely for a particular occasion and that Arendt in any case never intended to collect them in this—or any other—manner, they evince a remarkable degree of consistency, from beginning to end. The language of the essay with which this volume begins and the language of the two essays with which it concludes are, to be sure, vastly different: in the former, one finds strained German academic prose; in the latter, idiosyncratic German and idiomatic English. But despite the forty years that separate them—some of which were unprecedented in their horror—these essays are fundamentally akin: Rainer Maria Rilke explores the experience of a "being without an echo" (*Echolosigkeit*); Robert Gilbert lives the life of a poet who knows himself to be "without laurels" (*Lorbeerlos*); and W. H. Auden creates a body of poetry that does not shirk from the sober knowledge that "poetry makes nothing happen." All of these reflections then converge on one and the same problem—finding the words that would praise the world without imagining that this praise will somehow glorify the poet as well.

As the texts in this volume attest, however, Arendt subtly alters the manner in which she addresses this problem. In her earlier essays and reviews, she is especially attentive to the phenomenon of loss—the loss of a relation between the divine and human realms in her essay on Rilke; the loss of cultural continuity experienced by the "lost generations" of the 1920s and 1930s in many of her subsequent writings. For Arendt, the loss of continuity is prefigured in the development of a separate sphere of secular culture, which self-consciously compensates for the decay of religious traditions. Beginning with her inquiry into the phenomenon of the Berlin salons, Arendt's reflections on culture are drawn toward figures who recognize the illusory character of culture but do not, then, renounce it in favor of either nature worship or revived religiosity. In the texts Arendt wrote in the last decade of her life, she is again interested in poets whose experience of loss stamps their work; but instead of stressing this trait, she emphasizes—and celebrates—something else: their ability to endure all manner of misery without erecting defensive shields that would consist either in soothing condolences or in fanciful "philosophies of history" predicated on the promise that everything will work out in the end.

Literature: No Longer and Not Yet

In her never-completed work on judgment Arendt proposes that we should not look for Kant's political philosophy in the various essays he wrote on this topic; instead, we should turn to the first part of the Critique of Judgment, which is ostensibly devoted to the idea of aesthetic taste but, as she writes at the beginning of her inquiry, "actually should have become the book that otherwise is missing in Kant's great work."[1] Having stated this daring hypothesis, Arendt does not then ignore Kant's essays on political philosophy; on the contrary, the hypothesis allows her to discover the crowning achievement of "the entire critical business" in some of these late reflections, especially the section of the Conflict of the Faculties that identifies the enthusiastic spectators of the French Revolution as a "historical sign."[2] One might then ask whether a similar line of inquiry can be pursued in light of the other major thinker who hails from the Old Prussian town of Königsberg, namely, Arendt herself. Just as Kant occasionally devoted himself to political reflection without having produced a major work of political philosophy, Arendt occasionally devoted herself to literary and cultural reflection without having produced a major work of aesthetic theory. The point of posing this question is not to search among Arendt's works for a book that ostensibly concerns itself with political philosophy but "should have become" a contribution to aesthetics or cultural studies; the point is, rather, to discover a perspective from which to view some of her often-neglected reflections on literature and culture as an integral dimension—if not the crowning achievement—of her great work.

And there is good reason to pursue this line of inquiry. Arendt is justified in pursuing the suspicion that Kant drafts the outlines of a political philosophy in the guise of a "Critique of Aesthetic Judgment" only under the condition that she recognize a fundamental and, as it were, timeless affinity between political and aesthetic forms of judgment. Whoever recognizes such an affinity is automatically excused from participating in debates about the "aestheticizing of political life," which seeks to explain the roots of fascism in terms of a perverse cult of physical beauty. And Arendt, for her part, remained indifferent to these debates despite her keen interest in the works of Bertolt Brecht and Walter Benjamin.[3] If political judgment is always already akin to aesthetic judgment, then there is no sense in looking for the conditions in which politics somehow becomes aestheticized. Stating the precise nature of their "elective affinity" is by no means a simple matter, however. Fortunately, Arendt gives certain hints in this direction. In conjunction with her reading of Kant's *Conflict of the Faculties,* Arendt makes the following claim: "The judgment of the spectator creates the space without which no such objects could appear at all. The public realm is constituted by the critics and the spectators, not the actors and the makers."[4] In light of her essays on literature in particular, a corresponding thesis can thus be formulated: just as political judgment creates public space, aesthetic judgment, which suspends direct involvement in all *pragmata,* grants access to political *time.* At least one reason for this connection is not difficult to establish: as Arendt emphasizes, citing Kant, imagination is the faculty of making present what is absent,[5] and insofar as both the creation and the reception of specifically literary works are based on a highly developed use of this faculty, literature provides a particularly powerful medium for reflection on the relation between absence and presence, the "then" and the "now." From the very beginning of her career as a writer, Arendt has made her literary criticism into a forum for reflection on the nature of time, with particular attention to the uncertain breach "between past and future."

The preface to the collection of essays entitled *Between Past and Future* is exemplary in this regard. Two literary fragments guide Arendt's inquiry into "the gap between past and future": an aphorism by René Char and a parable by Franz Kafka. Char's aphorism indicates what has opened up this gap—the loss of a heritage for which there would be generally recognized documents and forms of evidence: "Our heritage is preceded by no testament." And Kafka's parable shows the resulting condition: isolated from others and even, in a sense, from its own self, an anonymous "he" is at the mercy of the combined and incongruent forces of past and future.[6] Long before she wrote this preface, Arendt had experimented with a form of literary analysis that explored a similar gap. In 1930 the twenty-four-year-old student, along with her first husband, Günther Anders, who at the time still used his original patronym (Stern), produced a complex analysis of the philosophical and religious significance of Rilke's *Duino Elegies*. The presupposition of their strenuously argued essay—which takes the form of a line-by-line commentary only because a systematic analysis would be "inappropriate to the sense of the poetry" (308)[7]—is that the *Elegies* are conscious of their total "absence of an echo" (1). Just as the *Elegies* proceed from no discernible literary heritage—and the co-authors nowhere discuss Rilke's literary predecessors—they neither hope nor expect to find readers in the future. The paradoxical situation of the poem in relation to its non-existent reception is then reflected in the equally paradoxical "mission" (*Auftrag*) of the poet: he is supposed to praise the world to an angel; but, as the opening question of the poem emphasizes—and this famous question serves as the epigraph to the essay—the poet cannot be certain that any "among the angel's orders" (quoted at 1) will hear his cry. The basic trait of the world to be praised is therefore loss, more exactly, the breakdown of any reliable relation to the divine order and the corresponding absence of a stable home that would shield both human beings and finite things from their constitutive transience. The only "rescue" or "redemption" (*Rettung*), for Rilke, lies in a transformation into "stronger existence" (*stärkeres Dasein*). Associating "stronger existence" with the Kantian sublime, the co-authors go in search of its defining characteristics: "In Rilke . . . human life does indeed hang in the air, but not because there is no God; on the contrary, it does so because the human being has been rejected and abandoned by Him. This abandonment by God and world, this belonging-nowhere, constitutes both the poetry's religious and its nihilistic character. In this way, nihilism becomes 'positive nihilism' " (23).

The essay on Rilke's *Duino Elegies* is a unique item among Arendt's literary reflections in two respects: it is the only one she co-authors, and it is the only one that is so entirely absorbed in the dynamics of the text under consideration that it foregoes any reference to the concrete historical situation of its author. Nothing, for example, is said about the difference between the elegies written before the First World War and those composed afterward, despite the enormous gap of time that separates them. A very different attitude toward the situation of the writer is evinced in Arendt's review of Hermann Broch's *Death of Virgil*. This review, which, like the book itself, appeared at the end of the Second World War, can be regarded as a characteristic example of Arendt's engagement with literary texts in the 1940s and 1950s. Its title alone indicates its principal concern: "No Longer and Not Yet." And in its opening paragraphs Arendt proposes a systematic schema of modern European literature. The schema develops, once again, out of an awareness of loss; but the nature of the loss that takes shape in the literary work has altogether changed. It does not now follow from a break in the relation between divine and human orders but, rather, from an irreparable gap in the "chain" that binds one generation to another: "In Europe such an absolute interruption of continuity occurred during and after the First World War. All the loose talk of intellectuals about the necessary decline of Western civilization or the famous lost generation, as it is usually uttered by 'reactionaries,' has its basis of truth in this break, and consequently has proved much more attractive than the corresponding triviality of the 'liberal' mind that puts before us the alternative between going ahead and going backward" (121). Two writers, then, make this temporal gap especially visible: Proust, whose massive "farewell" to the world of the nineteenth century "is written in the key of the 'no longer,'" and Kafka, who seems to have written "already from the vantage point of a distant future, as though he were or could have been at home only in a world which is 'not yet'" (122). Arendt's appraisal of Broch's achievement follows from this temporal schema. After describing *The Death of Virgil* as "something like the missing link between Proust and Kafka," she comes close to adopting its language for the purpose of depicting its definitive mission: "this book is by itself the kind of bridge with which Virgil tries to span the abyss of empty space between the no longer and the not yet. And since this abyss is very real; since it has become deeper and more frightful every single year from the fateful year of 1914 onward, until the death factories erected in the heart of Europe definitively cut the already outworn thread with which we still might have been tied to a historical entity of more than two thousand years; since we are already living in the 'empty space,' confronted with a reality which no preconceived traditional idea of the world and man can possibly illuminate—dear as this tradition may have remained to our hearts—we must be profoundly grateful for the great work of poetry which clings so desperately to this one subject" (122).

There is nothing dogmatic about Arendt's schematization of modern European literature. The point of her introductory remarks on *The Death of Virgil* does not lie in establishing, once and for all, that Proust represents the perspective of the "no longer," Kafka that of the "not yet," and Broch that of the bridge between the two. The main point of her review lies, rather, in promoting its presupposition: that reflection on certain outstanding literary works in their historical context makes visible "this gap, this opening of an abyss" (121). With few exceptions, therefore, the writers in whom she takes a direct interest belong to the generation that lost its relation to its predecessors because of the breakdown in tradition that began in 1914. And the exceptions are themselves indicative of the degree to which she is drawn to literary reflection primarily in its capacity to illuminate the dimensions of the resulting abyss. This is particularly apparent in the few earlier authors whom she chooses to discuss. Arendt shows no interest in the great novelists of the nineteenth century who explore the intricate dynamics of the social order. Of the writers who are largely indebted to this category, only Proust attracts her attention—as the one who bids farewell to the complex social world that novelists like Austen, Balzac, and Fontane lay bare. The few nineteenth-century novelists on whom she concentrates are, each in his own way, far removed from the world of society—so far removed that measuring this distance is, at least in part, the aim of her reflections on their achievements. In *Billy Budd* Melville envisages a "goodness beyond virtue," which is positively destructive to the social order, even in its most rudimentary form. In the story of the Grand Inquisitor, by contrast, Dostoevsky discovers the inverse of Melville's fable: pity for *"le peuple, les malheureux"* (Robespierre), followed to its logical conclusion, does away with the space of freedom altogether (see Chapter 26). And Adalbert Stifter provides a revealing complement to Melville and Dostoevsky, for, as Arendt writes in an unpublished review of "Rock Crystal" (an English translation of a story drawn from the wonderful collection *Stones of Many Colors*), Stifter simply wishes to pursue "his supreme desire 'to grasp the innocence of the things outside ourselves'" (110). Once again, a systematic schema is at work: Melville creates a figure of goodness beyond virtue, Dostoevsky produces images of wickedness beyond vice, and Stifter paints a motley picture of natural innocence. Despite their insuperable differences, all three novelists are united in one respect: they actively forget the social world, with all of its distracting disputes about relative status, as if an absolute break in the chain of generations had already occurred.

The question around which this schematization of moral extremity revolves can be succinctly stated as follows: how is it possible to acknowledge the claims of compassion without at the same time denying—and thereby contributing to the destruction of—the "in-between" (*Zwischenraum*) that, for Arendt, defines the world and makes it irreducible to the arithmetic sum of the people who inhabit it? Both goodness beyond virtue and wickedness beyond vice can be seen in Melville and Dostoevsky to be world-destructive, and as for natural innocence—it requires the kind of total immersion in nature that the children whom Stifter describes in "Rock Crystal" undergo (113–14). One thing is certain, moreover: this question presses itself only upon those who, despite the experience of loss, fully repudiate self-pity. And, for Arendt, one poet provides a particularly problematic answer to this question, namely, Bertolt Brecht, who not only experiments with each of the moral extremes in his writings but is also a telling representative of the "lost generations." In both of the major essays Arendt devotes to the poet, something like the following sentence establishes the context for further reflection: "Born in 1898, he belongs to the first of that 'lost generation' whose productive talents were sacrificed over and over again to private bitterness and to sentimental self-pity" (see 133 and 231). Brecht does nothing of the kind, however: he never collapses the distance that, early in his life as a poet, he established between himself and "poor B. B." But this precarious stance does not impel him in the direction of a Gottfried Benn or Louis-Ferdinand Céline, both of whom—like many other writers and intellectuals of the interwar period—take a kind of obscene pleasure in "murder, destruction, death, and decay" (138).

Brecht solves the problem of acknowledging the claim of compassion without succumbing to the anti-worldly character of pity in two conflicting manners. One of his solutions involves a self-consciously political decision; the other is the source of his greatness as a poet. On the one hand,

Brecht makes himself into an exponent of communist doctrine, with the result that he writes a play like *The Measure Taken* and, even worse, emphasizes the ultimate usefulness of "the useful one," code-name for Josef Stalin. On the other hand, drawing on the "actual anti-bourgeois element in him"—namely, his pathos of self-distance, which underlies a "Stoicism in 'dark times'" (137)—he grounds his poetry in a non-doctrinaire yet exacting conviction that those who have been defeated should never be lost to memory. What she writes of "Ballad of the Waterwheel" goes for all his best work: "The 'philosophy of history' suggested by this poem has nothing to do with either socialist realism or proletarian poetry. It deals with something much more general, which is at the same time something much more precise, namely the production of a world in which all people are equally visible, and the planning of a history that is not remembered by a few and forgotten by many, that doesn't induce forgetfulness under the pretense of remembering, that doesn't involve some while making others the instruments of history" (326).

Not only do these words capture the best of Brecht; they can be seen to reveal Arendt's own "philosophy of history"—which, as the scare quotes in the quotation immediately suggest, should not be confused with a "real" philosophy of history in the Hegelian or Marxist mode. The world can be compared to a waterwheel precisely because it never "develops." But the sober knowledge that the human species does not make "infinite progress" and that there is no such thing as "cultural development" provides no support for either pessimistic lamentations about the sorry state of humanity or Nietzschean celebrations of an "eternal return" that only the *Übermensch* can bear to contemplate. Instead, for Arendt, another aspect of the waterwheel must be emphasized: the fact that *every* paddle comes to light.

Culture: Pro and Contra

In response to Brecht's expressed rationale for abstaining from suicide— "it shouldn't look as though one had too high an opinion of oneself" (235)—Arendt has only this to add: "Above all, therefore, no pompous self-importance [Wichtigtuerei]!" (339). At the end of her essay on Kafka, she insists on a similar point: "he clearly did not want to be considered a genius" (108). A world in which everyone is equally visible is averse to claims of genius, to the extent that claims of this sort always come down to a demand that attention be paid to a few, while the many—who are, by definition, not geniuses—can be forgotten in good conscience. In order to imagine a world without pompous self-importance Brecht produced "instructional plays" (Lehrstücke) and made "absurd demands upon his 'collaborators' to learn what was beyond learning" (235). As for Kafka, who had no collaborators, he had no choice but "to anticipate the destruction of the present world" (108). For this reason—and not because he set himself up as a prophet of doom—his work is anchored in the future. As Arendt argues in the conclusion to her essay on Kafka, the last chapter of the last of his novels to enter into print reveals the source of this vision. At the beginning of this chapter, the protagonist of the novel comes across an advertisement for employment that captures, as it were, the spirit of non-pomposity: "everyone is welcome"[8]—welcome, that is, to join the "Nature Theater of Oklahoma," which not only accepts all of its applicants but also makes no demands that its actors know anything in order to play their parts. The performances of the "Nature Theater of Oklahoma" do not owe their origin to a genial author, and none of the participants in its spontaneous performances is a genial "star" whose brilliance would eclipse the visibility of a "supporting cast."

With this remark about what might be called "Kafka's last word," Arendt silently repudiates the interpretation of Kafka that Günther Anders had proposed in a lecture he delivered for the Institut d'Études Germaniques in Paris, where the couple had fled soon after the Nazi seizure of power. According to Anders, Kafka's work is firmly anchored in the past; more exactly, it derives from the decay of a religious tradition that only half-heartedly sustains itself under the hollow pretense of being "cultured." *His* conclusion about Kafka's "last word" thus runs as follows: "it formulates *the bad conscience of culture with respect to its 'ur-text'*—the self-humiliation of culture before an ur-text in which it no longer believes yet whose authenticity . . . appears to be the only thing still worth believing in."[9] The sphere of culture, in other words, cannot honestly free itself from the religious tradition against which it more or less proudly defines itself. The title of the published version of Anders' lecture captures its self-conscious ambivalence with respect to the Czech-Jewish writer: "Kafka pro and contra." One should be for Kafka, according to Anders, insofar as his work reveals the "bad conscience" of culture; one should be against him, however, insofar as he capitulates to this "bad conscience" by reaffirming the authenticity of the no-longer credible ur-text.

"In the audience of the lecture," Anders later recounts, "with the exception of Hannah Arendt and Walter Benjamin, [Kafka] was simply 'unknown.' "[10] Both Arendt and Benjamin, however, reject Anders' case against Kafka, even as they sharpen his formulation of the "pros and cons" of secular culture in general. Benjamin does so in an essay that was first published under the title "Franz Kafka, An Appreciation" on the tenth anniversary of Kafka's death.[11] Arendt follows suit in an essay that commemorates the twentieth anniversary of his death and first appeared in German under the title "Franz Kafka, Appreciated Anew." According to both Benjamin and Arendt, Kafka can be heard to assert a humble yet unyielding "no." In Benjamin's version, this "no" is directed against the uncanny forces of *forgetfulness;* but his denial of forgetfulness, it is important to add, does not arise out of a belief in the restorative power of memory. Only a certain kind of thoughtful remembrance—for which Benjamin invents the term *Eingedenken*—can thwart the distorting forces of forgetfulness.[12] In Arendt's version, by contrast, Kafka's "no" is directed against *automatic processes;* but his rejection of automation, it is equally important to add, does not arise from a belief in some natural drive or supernatural destiny that "culture" and "civilization" have somehow conspired to suppress. Only a certain kind of novelty resists the drift toward automation. In search of a name for this novelty, Arendt, too, turns to the Czech-Jewish writer, who both announced that he could spontaneously produce "perfect" (108) sentences and refused to see this ability as proof of his genius.[13]

At the center of Arendt's essay on Kafka, the basic problem of culture is lucidly presented. As the Latin term *colere* suggests, the point of all "culture" consists in gaining a certain protection from the potentially overwhelming overgrowth that simply *is* nature in its most primordial form. Furthermore, as the German term *Bildung* emphasizes—and Arendt uses this word even when she is writing in English (272)—the acquisition of culture consists in a process of "development" (*Ausbildung*). For this reason, culture can be compared to a house that protects its inhabitants from nature only insofar as they continually rebuild it: "Just as surely as a house built by men according to human laws will fall into ruin as soon as men abandon it, so surely the world fabricated by men and constituted according to human and not natural laws will once again become part of nature, and will be surrendered to catastrophic destruction when man decides to become part of nature himself—a blind but highly precise instrument of natural laws" (101). For Arendt, *The Trial* recounts the story of this surrender. It therefore becomes a peculiar kind of Bildungsroman that reveals the ironically destructive nature of *Bildung*—ironically destructive, because the aim of *Bildung,* as Arendt indicates in an early review article (Chapter 2), consists in the development of one's natural capacities under the guidance of an image (*Bild*) that derives from a secular-historical model (*Vorbild*): "As part of this development, K. is 'educated' [*gebildet*] and transformed until he is fit to assume the role forced upon him, which is to play along as best he can in a world of necessity, injustice, and lies. It is his way of adapting to existing conditions. The internal development of the protagonist finally coincides with the functioning of the machine in the last scene, namely the execution, where K. lets himself be taken away and killed without a struggle, and indeed without so much as a protest" (97).

What Kafka shows, according to Arendt, is the fallacious character of the opposition between ruin and progress. Whenever progress assumes the air of necessity, it cannot be distinguished from destruction. Assimilating oneself to whatever claims to be necessary is catastrophic—and this is true even if the necessity in question is nothing other than the natural development of one's predetermined abilities. At the center of her Kafka essay, Arendt unexpectedly quotes a manuscript that Benjamin had given her in France for safekeeping across the ocean: "Where we see a chain of events, he [the angel of history] sees a single catastrophe which unremittingly piles ruins on ruins and hurls them at his feet. He wishes he could stay to awaken the dead and to join together the fragments. But a wind blows from Paradise, gets caught in them. This wind drives him irresistibly into the future to which he turns his back, while the pile of ruins before him towers to the skies. What we call progress is *this* wind" (102).[14] Arendt does not offer an interpretation of Benjamin's now famous fragment—which appeared in print for the first time in the English version of her essay on Kafka.[15] She lets it speak for itself, without so much as a word about its author, who would have been even more "unknown" to the first readers of her essay than Kafka was to the audience Anders encountered ten years earlier. She simply suggests that Benjamin's fragment records the image of a perfectly cultured world, which is to say, a world in which there is no difference between nature and history because irrevocable and unimpeachable laws are said—and seen—to hold sway in both.

In the original version of her essay on Kafka, Arendt says nothing about his Jewishness. Indeed, readers of the essay who knew nothing else about its subject matter might wonder whether or not he was Jewish, especially since the only discussion of this question comes in the following sentence: "Kafka, an employee of a workmen's insurance company and a loyal friend of many eastern European Jews for whom he had had to obtain permits to stay in the country, had a very intimate knowledge of the political conditions of his country."[16] In another essay of 1944, however, the situation is very different. "The Jew as Pariah: A Hidden Tradition" includes a remarkable reading of Kafka's *Castle* as the story of modern Jewish existence. K. wants nothing more than to live a "normal life" (86) in the place where he happens to live—without special dispensations from the authorities above and without special attention on the part of the people below. K., who is supposed to have entered into the vicinity of the Castle for the purpose of surveying its land, thus rejects the German principle of *Bildung:* he wants to be able to live out his life in the village simply because he happens to find himself there, not because of anything he achieves, still less because of anything he represents. This is, in a sense, the unifying core of the "hidden tradition" Arendt recounts in her essay. To see Jews as pariahs is to disregard two other competing perspectives: Jews are seen neither as the subjects of a body of religious commandments nor as the proponents of a particular secular culture. "Pariah" Judaism is a "*hidden* tradition" for precisely this reason: escaping the alternative "either religious or cultured," the Jew as pariah only wants to be *un*exceptional—so much so that it would be a major mistake to say that he or she wishes to be just like everyone else insofar as this kind of likeness—achieved through a process of "assimilation"—can be a particularly blinding form of exceptionality. Kafka, whose novels and stories repeatedly expose the illusory and even self-deceptive character of *Bildung,* thus stands at the opposite end of a path Arendt begins to retrace in her reflections on the short-lived phenomenon of the Berlin salons.[17]

The salons that developed in Berlin in the late eighteenth and early nineteenth centuries in the homes and apartments of Jewish women were sites of transformation. Instead of being exceptions to society because of their religious beliefs and practices, these women wanted to be seen as exceptionally well cultured and correspondingly receptive to the purity of their own sentimental nature. At their supreme moments the salons would foster the kind of shared insulation from the "philistine" world that Arendt describes at the end of her essay on the conservative diplomat and political journalist Friedrich von Gentz: "If this 'affair' [between Gentz and Rahel Varnhagen] had ever been consummated, Gentz might have found in it the possibility of holding a second self-contained world up against the real world and so have created for himself a way to isolate himself from reality" (36). But Arendt's essay on the Berlin salons is much less interested in the salons *per se* than it is in the consequences of the "catastrophe" (50) that destroys them. Before Napoleon's invasion and occupation of Berlin in 1806, it was possible for a few Jewish women and a few members of the Prussian nobility to form an alliance with a new generation of writers and thinkers—all of whom wished to distinguish themselves from the prevailing bureaucratic-commercial norms in which their lives would otherwise be anchored. After the Napoleonic invasion, however, this fragile alliance was undone and a new idea gained widespread acceptance: the revival of a Germany of a bygone era, organized on the basis of certain eternally divided "estates" (*Stände*).[18] To be German in this context meant, above all: to fight the French, who were associated with a "superficial" Enlightenment, and to be suspicious of everything Jewish, old and new. As a direct consequence of the "catastrophe" of 1806, the organizers of the salons were therefore left with their allegiance to culture and a few unpleasant choices, which Rahel Varnhagen summarizes as follows: either become "pious" or resign oneself to being "bourgeois."

None of this is meant to suggest, however, that Arendt's essay on the Berlin salons—or any of the subsequent texts in this volume—is "against" culture. Far from attacking the salon women for having relinquished their Jewish upbringing, she views this event with a certain detachment, from which it becomes possible to grasp the historical situation in which the word *culture* becomes a term of disparagement. Of course, Arendt can also at times be highly polemical: against Stefan Zweig, for example, who believed that his literary fame should have shielded him from exposure to the unpleasantness of politics; or against Victor Lange, who indiscriminately—and disgracefully—equated a poet like Rilke with a Nazi-apologist like Rudolf Binding (126). But the object of her polemics is never culture per se; it is always only the illusion that a high degree of cultivation provides a degree of protection from political reality. Under this illusion a writer like Zweig could imagine himself secure in the world of the Austrian Empire; under a similar illusion, a literary scholar like Lange could imagine that Binding's propaganda represents the continuation of a trend begun by Rilke's *Duino Elegies*. Arendt never set herself in opposition to culture, because she recognizes that culture has something of potentially great significance to say about the sphere of politics: it can teach us what it means to forego the schematization of things into means and ends.

With this thought—which she pursues most thoroughly in "Culture and Politics" but which can be found throughout the writings collected here—Arendt refines and revises one of the foundational documents of modern German culture, namely, Friedrich Schiller's *Letters on Aesthetic Education* (1795), which argues for the establishment of an "Aesthetic State" as the prerequisite for a non-violent transition from the rule of brute force to the reign of moral freedom. "In the Aesthetic State," Schiller writes in the last of his famous letters, "everything—even the tool which serves—is a free citizen, having equal rights with the noblest; and the mind, which would force the patient mass beneath the yoke of its purpose, must here first obtain its assent."[19] As this quotation itself indicates, however, the Aesthetic State has certainly not overcome the means-end schema; on the contrary, it comes close to universalizing it. But—and this is the other famous theme Schiller pursues—the Aesthetic State is principally established for the purpose of satisfying the "play drive" (*Spieltrieb*). Unlike labor, play has no purpose beyond its sheer performance. For Arendt, the "pros" and "contras" of culture can be derived from these basic political-cultural theses. There can be no culture in the proper sense of the word unless it is free from the exigencies of biological processes. Aesthetic enjoyment, as an integral phenomenon of everything cultured, may not be "higher" than the consumption of enjoyable things; but it is categorically different. Because cultural pursuits are ends-in-themselves, they are also comparable to the mode of the *vita activa* that Aristotle calls *praxis* and Arendt translates as *action*. From the perspective of the artist, by contrast, the means-end schema is all-consuming. What Schiller affirms of the artist captures—against his own intention—the case against culture: "When the artist lays hands upon the same mass [as the artisan], he has just as little scruple in doing it violence; but he avoids showing it. For the material he is handling he has not a whit more respect than has the artisan; but the eye which would seek to protect the freedom of the material he will endeavour to deceive by a show of yielding to the latter."[20] Schiller immediately adds a word of warning that takes the form of a simple declarative sentence: "With the pedagogic or the political artist things are very different indeed. For him Man is at once the material on which he works and the goal toward which he strives"—unless, that is, the pedagogical or political artist aims for some other goal, which is far from unlikely.[21] Under these conditions the pursuit of culture is positively destructive: the production of art gives the impression that everything—including "human material"—can be used at will. The only difference between political artists and political artisans would be that the former have a talent for concealing the violence done in service of their "work."

A case for culture can be made, therefore, only when the perspective of the artist is carefully constrained. Arendt interprets a paradox at the heart of ancient Greek politics in this regard: "It was as if the Greeks could say in one and the same breath: 'He who has not seen the Zeus of Phidias at Olympia has lived in vain' *and:* 'People like Phidias, namely sculptors, really should not be granted citizenship'" (186). With this same paradox in mind, Arendt interprets a remark of Hölderlin to which Heidegger had previously drawn attention: "When Hölderlin called poetry the 'most innocent' occupation, he may have been thinking of the violence inherent in all other art forms. But, of course, the poet violates his material as well; he does not sing like the bird living in the tree" (192).[22] This paradox more or less silently traverses all of the texts in this volume. When Arendt reflects on a literary work, she is wholly absorbed in the perspective of its author: recognizing the break in the chain of generations, she reflects on the conditions under which a poet could do a peculiar kind of violence against language that results in the "coin[ing of] the words we live by" (255). When Arendt returns to the question of culture, however, she insists on turning away from the perspective of the artist. Even more innocent than the occupation of the poet is a certain kind of non-occupation—that of attending to poetry. Something similar can be said in relation to all other cultural occupations: whoever reflects on works of art is less guilty of universalizing the schema of means-ends than the artists who produce them. In this context, Arendt returns to the principal source of Schiller's plans for the establishment of an "Aesthetic State," namely, Kant's *Critique of Judgment.* In the case of the third *Critique,* however, it is quite clear that the spectator—not the artist—is at the center of attention. Indeed, critics of Kant, from Schiller onward, have complained that he neglects the perspective of the artist. For Arendt, this is all to Kant's credit. Because he wants to draw an insuperable distinction between aesthetic taste and technical skill, and because technical skill is an irreducible element of all artistic activity, including poetry, he concerns himself solely with the position of the spectator, who may know nothing about the processes by which a work of art is made. Knowledge is unimportant; only judgment or "opinion" matters. In this way, Kant inadvertently discovers a new space—that of the political: "Judgment issues from the subjectivity of a position in the world; at the same time, however, it claims that this world, in which everyone has his or her own position, is an objective fact, and thus something that we all share" (199).

The *Critique of Judgment* does not entirely ignore the perspective of the artist. As Arendt notes at the end of her Kafka essay, it includes an influential discussion of genius. But Kant's concept of genius should not be confused with its nineteenth-century counterparts: "Genius [in the nineteenth century] was no longer a gift of the gods to man, who after all remained perfectly human; the whole person became a full incarnation of genius and therefore could no longer be regarded as a mere mortal" (108). There is no question that, for Arendt, a genuine poet is different from a mere writer: "in contrast to the large class of professional writers, there are also poets, and a poet is something altogether different."[23] It is equally certain that, for Arendt, the word "poet" (*Dichter*) is not defined by formal considerations of the literary object. Broch becomes a "poet" when he writes a particularly enduring novel, *The Death of Virgil* (123). These two distinctions—between the poet and the writer, on the one hand, and between aesthetic taste and more or less indiscriminate consumption, on the other—are characteristic of what is often called "cultural elitism." And in response to Arendt's "Culture and Politics," Herbert Marcuse, for one, accuses her of seeking to resurrect the dubious distinction between "culture" and "civilization" that had assumed an important function among German cultural conservatives during the Weimar era.[24] But Marcuse's criticism misses the point: her utter rejection of the category of genius. There is doubtless a difference between poet and writer; but the poet has no *right* to greater visibility. And there is a categorical difference between aesthetic taste and mere consumption; but the eyes of the "cultured" spectator are no more capable than any other of deciding who should shine and who remain obscure. This is why Arendt is drawn to the poetry of Robert Gilbert, who is hardly considered among the great poets of the century. And this is why many of the texts in this volume are haunted by the apparition of a poetic "genius" whose work endures, even when his existence is negated. Because Heinrich Heine's "The Lorelei" stamps the character of the German language; because it coins the words by which speakers of German live—"Ich weiß nicht, was soll es bedeuten, / Daß ich so traurig bin . . . [I don't know what it means that I'm so sad]"²⁵—the Nazis could not eradicate it from the speech of German-speaking peoples, and so, despite their penchant for banning and burning books, "The Lorelei" continued to be read and recited during the Hitler years under the pretense that the name of its author was unknown.

"Stronger Existence"

Arendt and Anders close their analysis of the *Duino Elegies* by emphasizing that, in Rilke's hands, the poetic form of the elegy is no longer a "lament over what has been lost but [is], rather, the expression of loss itself" (23). Something similar can be said of all the poets to whom Arendt is attracted. At the same time, however, another Rilkean motif that she identifies in her early essay begins to give direction and provide a certain unity to her last reflections on literature: beauty is a "derivative" of "stronger existence" (10). Strength in this context has nothing to do with ruthlessness or brutality; nor is it a property of the angels to whom the *Duino Elegies* appeals. Neither a demonic nor an angelic quality, "stronger" characterizes those who unflinchingly expose themselves to creaturely misery without succumbing to the allure of self-pity—and without seeking refuge in a supposedly self-enclosed sphere of culture, which they, by virtue of their "genius," would presumably reinvigorate. Brecht's carefully delineated distance from "poor B. B." is, for this reason, an exemplary version of "stronger existence." The consistency of Arendt's reflections on literature can be gauged with reference to a writer who would otherwise appear to have little in common with either Brecht or Rilke. At the beginning of her reflection on Nathalie Sarraute, Arendt quotes the following passage from the French novelist's own analysis of the loss on which her work is predicated: " 'Since then' "—namely, since the era in which author and reader could assume that they could understand each other because the protagonist of any given novel was endowed with a sufficient number of self-evident attributes and qualities—"[the protagonist] has lost everything; his ancestors, his carefully built house, filled from cellar to garret with a variety of objects, down to the tiniest gewgaw, his sources of income and his estates, his clothes, his body, his face . . . his personality and, frequently, even his name" (213). Far from lamenting this condition of homelessness, Sarraute's novels are its exacting expression. For this reason, the end of *Fruits of Gold,* which Arendt quotes as the conclusion to her review, is a startling literary achievement. A tenuous relation between author and reader is unexpectedly restored under the rubric not now of shared experiences or generally accepted values, but of a singularly paradoxical and highly uncertain strength that consists in an uncertain recognition of common fragility: "Shortly before the end, Nathalie Sarraute turns from the 'they' and the 'I' to the 'we,' the old We of author and reader. It is the reader who speaks: 'We are so frail and they so strong. Or perhaps . . . we, you and I, are the stronger, even now'" (222).

"Stronger" is scarcely the first word one would associate with the poets whose portraits Arendt drew in the last decade of her life. She compares Randall Jarrell to a "figure from fairy land" (258), finds in Robert Gilbert's poetry the reverberations of childhood, when school was not yet compulsory (285), and concludes her discussion of W. H. Auden by describing him as an "obedient servant" of "cruel gods" (302). Loss, though, is everywhere apparent in her account of these strangely similar poets. The first book Jarrell gave to Arendt was even entitled *Losses,* and as she subtly suggests, the loss of an audience for poetry in general—"the absence of an echo" (1), to recall her essay on Rilke—can even be seen as the cause of his death. Gilbert, for his part, was expelled from "the streets of Berlin" (128) and therefore lost the only world in which his poetry could freely circulate. As for Auden, who could easily be considered an exemplary representative of the "lost generation," Arendt emphasizes something else in her commemoration of his death: "[he was] unable to do anything about the absurd circumstances that made everyday life so unbearable for him" (296). Arendt, in short, does not conceive of these poets principally in terms of the irreparable break in the chain of generations they each experienced. Still less does she attempt a systematic schematization, in which each of the three poets would represent a temporal moment or moral extremity. Arendt does not even assert that these poets, like Rilke, are able to transform lamentation over a loss into the expression of loss itself. All three of her portraits nevertheless have something in common: they summon a kind of strength that consists in sheer vulnerability. Attentive to the ever-intrusive environment of the metropolis, Gilbert captures the "nimble-witted way of thinking that will not let itself be fooled, least of all by itself" (292). Jarrell was almost wholly defenseless: "Randall . . . had nothing to protect himself against the world but his splendid laughter, and the immense naked courage behind it" (260). And in Arendt's portrait of Auden, which is the last of her literary reflections, she presents the poet as the very embodiment of "stronger existence."

The depth of Auden's vulnerability can be seen in the lines of his face. Arendt's portrait of Auden begins with a reflection on the bewildering mismatch between the starkness of his appearance and the reticence of his speech. This bewilderment is itself reflected in the peculiar syntax through which she captures the experience of renewing her acquaintance with the poet: "I did not recognize him ten years later, for now his face was marked by those famous deep wrinkles, as though life itself had delineated a kind of face-scape to make manifest 'the heart's invisible furies.' If you listened to him, nothing could seem more deceptive than this appearance" (295). As Arendt realizes, however, appearances are not deceptive in this case. Auden's battered face accurately records a form of life that exposes itself to misery of all kinds. Still, something seems to be hidden in his speech. What she calls his " 'Count your blessings' litany" (296) serves as a shelter in which the poet withdraws. But—and this is the important point—this verbal shelter offers no protection. Far from being a shield against the myriad mishaps to which his life was prone, especially in his last years, this "litany" represents a dimension of the very misery that etches the lines into his face. In the words of Arendt's reflections on Brecht, the " 'Count your blessings' litany" expresses the poet's total lack of self-pity, his distance from "poor W. H. A." And Brecht is indeed the poet in view of whom Arendt measures Auden's greatness, for, as she emphasizes—cognizant of the animosity between the two poets—they "had more in common than [Auden] was ever ready to admit" (297). Beyond the influence Brecht exerted on Auden's early work, there is a revealing affinity in their respective modes of thinking. Both were schooled in the "lost generation" of the 1920s: Brecht in its German version, with its pretense of wickedness, Auden in its English counterpart, with its air of snobbery. In both cases, moreover, their affectation of careless abandon conceals the very opposite: "an irresistible inclination toward being good and doing good" (298). And this inclination, which neither of them would admit, as though it, too, were something shameful from which they had to suffer, is the source of their turn toward politics: "What drove these profoundly apolitical poets into the chaotic political scene of our century was Robespierre's *'zèle compatissant,'* the powerful urge toward *'les malheureux,'* as distinguished from any need for action toward *public* happiness, or any desire to change the world" (298).

It is at this point that Auden parts ways with Brecht, for his *zèle compatissant* never congealed into the exposition of a political doctrine. As some of his early poems attest, "Spain 1937" in particular, Auden was doubtless tempted by the impulse that drove Brecht to write *The Measure Taken;* but in reflection on the implications of the Moscow trials and the Hitler-Stalin pact, Auden overcame this temptation. What is more: he did not then follow so many of his contemporaries and exchange an early commitment to the cause of international communism for a dogmatic affirmation of "Capitalism or Freudianism or some refined Marxism, or a sophisticated mixture of all three" (299). The reason for this reticence, according to Arendt, lies in "his complete sanity and his firm belief in sanity" (298). In this regard, Auden stands alone among his contemporaries. If he can be compared to any of the other writers and thinkers whom Arendt discusses in detail, it is perhaps only to Kant, whose attitude toward the revolutionary turmoil of his own era is similarly structured— and similarly fractured. In the *Conflict of the Faculties* Kant celebrates the spectators of the French Revolution for publicly expressing their sympathy for the revolutionaries; but he simultaneously condemns any actions or programs that aim at repeating the revolution.[26] Just as the sedentary philosopher makes a fundamental distinction between the stance of the spectator and that of the agent, the peripatetic poet draws a corresponding distinction between compassion for those who suffer and obfuscating doctrines that claim to know how all suffering can be eradicated. This, according to Arendt, is "the main thing" for Auden: "to have no illusions and to accept no thoughts—no theoretical systems—that would blind you to reality" (298). Sanity, in other words, is not a shield with which the poet protects himself from the randomness and sheer madness of life; on the contrary, it is redoubled vulnerability. Not only does Auden expose himself to misery; he also recognizes that history will not come to the rescue. In this regard, he is even saner than Kant, who turned his insight into the significance of political spectatorship into a "prophetic" prognosis that the human species is forever making progress. Auden does nothing of the kind. His "complete sanity" is thus, for Arendt, at once his greatest burden and the source of his greatness as a poet: "what made him a great poet was the unprotesting willingness with which he yielded to the 'curse' of vulnerability to 'human *un*success' on all levels of human existence—vulnerability to the crookedness of the desires, to the infidelities of the heart, to the injustices of the world" (300).

Arendt's portrait of Auden represents more than an *aesthetica in nuce;* it refutes the desperate alternatives between which much of political thought since the eighteenth-century Enlightenment has been caught: either one affirms the idea of progress, which sees in history a cure to suffering, or one embraces some kind of cultural pessimism, in which case one shields oneself from the fact of suffering by ascribing it to the eternal ways of this unhappy world. Auden, in Arendt's eyes, lives out the rejection of this alternative, for despite the misery to which he mercilessly exposes himself, the "key word" of his poetry is *praise:* "not praise of 'the best of all possible worlds'—as though it were up to the poet (or the philosopher) to justify God's creation—but praise that pitches itself against all that is most unsatisfactory in man's condition on this earth and sucks its own strength from the wound" (300). Sucking strength from the wound: perhaps nowhere does the thought of the "stronger existence" find a more exacting image—not even, dare one say, in the *Duino Elegies* themselves. Some forty years after she wrote her essay on Rilke, Arendt does something more than produce a corresponding commentary on a poet who echoes the opening lines of the last elegy: "At times, emerging at last from the violent insight / let me sing out of jubilation and praise to assenting angels" (quoted at 2).[27] She also reflects on what it means that a poet obeys the imperative of praise down to the very features of his face. As a minimum, it means that the apparently eccentric " 'Count your blessing' litany" hides nothing after all. And in the end, it means ruin. The appreciation of a grateful readership is no recompense for the ruin he experiences—still less is literary fame. Yet the portrait of Auden that Arendt draws shows that reflection on literature can "at times" do more than grant access to the uncertain time between past and future; it can let the very language of time reverberate. But it can go no further: the language of time that reverberates in literary reflection cannot be translated into a universally comprehensible discourse that would represent the cornerstone of a new "philosophy of history." A line from Auden for which Arendt could find no adequate translation into her mother tongue first convinces her of his greatness as a poet—great not only in the power of his language but also in the strength of his existence: "Time will say nothing but I told you so" (295).

REFLECTIONS ON
LITERATURE AND CULTURE

§ 1 Rilke's *Duino Elegies*[1]

by Hannah Arendt and Günther Stern

Wer, wenn ich schriee, hörte mich denn aus der Engel Ordnungen?
[Who, if I cried out, would hear me among the angel's orders?][2]

The paradoxical, ambiguous, and desperate situation from which standpoint the *Duino Elegies* may alone be understood has two characteristics:
the absence of an echo and the knowledge of futility. The conscious renunciation of the demand to be heard, the despair at not being able to be
heard, and finally the need to speak even without an answer—these are
the real reasons for the darkness, asperity, and tension of the style in
which the poetry indicates its own possibilities and its will to form.

The fundamental question arising out of a poetry that remains so fully
estranged from communication is the extent to which it wants to be understood, the extent to which it can be understood (understood by us, that
is): in other words, the extent to which interpretation is allowed. The difficulty inherent to the subject under study is shown most clearly in the Fifth
Elegy, in which it is impossible to construe any meaning, or to forge any
links from line to line, because the association of images, in their incomprehensible uniqueness and situational dependency, is wholly arbitrary.
Thus we turn to the only methodology available to us: that is, to clarify the
background of the poem's attunement, which, as if it were its musical key,
forms its sole unity. The individual lines emerge disconnected and insu-
lated from this unity; it would be perfectly conceivable to arrange them
differently. Despite this complete arbitrariness, despite the absence of a
temporally irreversible process, despite the simultaneity of the images, the
poetry does not congeal into a meaningless mass of associations. This is
because every particular element, and everything resisting connection in its
particularity, rests on the ground of what is actually to be said, the ground
that first stirs up the isolated images. The ground here is the futility on the

basis of which every image is only *one* among infinitely many images—a single image that carries others along with it, as it moves by itself.

Given the religious sense of the Elegies, the disjointed juxtaposition simultaneously signifies a lack of connection or obligation [*Unverbindlichkeit*].[3] This, together with the aforementioned absence of an echo (which, however, can only be expressed poetically), comprises the peculiarly ambiguous situation of the "Elegies." Thus, while the poetry indeed contains a religious mood, it is not a religious document. The one indication of its not being so is the remarkable fact that intermediate entities are usually substituted for "God"—the "angels" or the "dead," or, in its extreme indeterminacy, "one" ("denn man ist sehr deutlich mit uns [for one is very clear with us]," 4th Elegy). The fact that the proper religious category is left utterly indeterminate signifies the recollection of the religious as such. The power of God is indeed felt; but who and where the Almighty is—this remains in the form of a question that no longer hopes for an answer. Still, the question does not perish from lack of an answer; rather, it survives as disquietude, suddenly changing into despair at the very encounterability [*Treffbarkeit*] of God. By contrast, to every non-obligatory religiosity that, content with its own feeling, thinks that it can do without a personal God, Rilke secures a last residuum of objectivity in the indeterminacy of the "one." From this arises his singular evaluation of despair and pain, which are not (as they still are, for instance, in Kierkegaard) the danger and the "trouble"[*Ärgernis*] with religion; on the contrary, they become the religious situation as such. To be struck by God—to know it and even to proclaim it—becomes the last possible way of experiencing God.

> Daß ich dereinst, an dem Ausgang der grimmigen Einsicht,
> Jubel und Ruhm aufsinge zustimmenden Engeln.
> Daß von der klargeschlagenen Hämmern des Herzens
> keiner versage an weichen, zweifelnden oder
> reißenden Saiten. Daß mich mein strömendes Antlitz
> glänzender mache: daß das unscheinbare Weinen
> blühe. O wie werdet ihr dann, Nächte, mir lieb sein,
> gehärmte. . . . Sie (sc. Die Schmerzen) . . . sind ja
> unser winterwähriges Laub, unser dunkles Sinngrün,
> *eine* der Zeiten des heimlichen Jahres—, nicht nur
> Zeit—, sind Stelle, Siedelung, Lager, Boden, Wohnort.

> [Someday, emerging at last from the violent insight,
> let me sing out of jubilation and praise to assenting angels.

Let not even one of the clearly-struck hammers of my heart
fail to sound because of a slack, a doubtful,
or a broken string. Let my joyfully streaming face
make me more radiant; let my hidden weeping arise
and blossom. How dear you will be to me then, you nights
of anguish. Why didn't I kneel more deeply to accept you,
inconsolable sisters, and, surrendering, lose myself
in your loosened hair. How we squander our hours of pain.
How we gaze beyond them into the bitter duration
to see if they have an end. Though they are really
our winter-enduring foliage, our dark evergreen,
one season in our inner year—, not only a season
in time—, but are place and settlement, foundation and soil and home.]

10th Elegy

Despite its religious ambiguity, Rilke's world is, like every religious world, an *acoustic* world.[4] Never are "rank" or "Angel," or more generally the "stronger existence [*stärkere Dasein*]"[5] (1st Elegy), objective visions; in any case, all direct and visionary possibilities for encountering the angel are removed into an age fundamentally prior to our own and its possibilities.

. . . . Wohin sind die Tage Tobiae,
da der Strahlendsten einer stand an der einfachen Haustür,
zur Reise ein wenig verkleidet und schon nicht mehr furchtbar;
(Jüngling dem Jüngling, wie er neugierig hinaussah).
träte der Erzengel jetzt, der gefährliche, hinter den Sternen
eines Schrittes nur nieder und herwärts: hochauf-
schlagend erschlüg uns das eigene Herz. . . .

[. . . . Where are the days of Tobias,
when one of you, veiling his radiance, stood at the front door,
slightly disguised for the journey, no longer appalling;
(a young man like the one who curiously peeked through the window).
But if the archangel now, perilous, from behind the stars
took even one step down toward us: our own heart, beating
higher and higher, would beat us to death. . . .]

2nd Elegy

The sole thing that remains audible to whoever lives in futility is the "Wehende [whatever blows like the wind]" between the ranks. Listening is so little bound to an object that, on the contrary, it receives "seine ununterbrochene Nachricht, die aus Stille sich bildet [the ceaseless message that forms itself out of silence]" (1st Elegy) whenever the objects are lost and blown away: it is not a listening to a particular, articulated message; rather, it is a listening to the urgent beseeching of a heart ("Höre, mein Hertz [Listen, my heart]"), therefore a mode of being ("so waren sie hörend [such was their listening]," 1st Elegy). A beseeching of this kind does not presuppose the presence of the responding voice; nor does the beseeching of the prayer with which it is actually identical. In its intensity, however, it is independent of the voice's presence. Indeed, as a state of being, listening is already its own fulfillment, since it pays no attention to whether its beseeching may be heard.

> . . . . Höre, mein Herz, wie sonst nur
> Heilige hörten: daß sie der riesige Ruf
> aufhob vom Boden; sie aber knieten,
> Unmögliche, weiter und achteten's nicht:
> so waren sie hörend. . . .
>
> [. . . . Listen, my heart, as only
> saints have listened: until the gigantic call lifted them
> off the ground; yet they kept on, impossibly,
> kneeling and didn't notice at all:
> such was their listening. . . .]

Rilke still seeks to rescue something from the religiously alienated situation in which he "Gottes Stimme bei weitem nicht mehr ertrüge [was far from being able to endure God's voice]," in which he "verginge von seinem stärkeren Dasein [would perish from his stronger existence]." This "something" consists in an in-stance of hearing, *being-in-hearing* [*Inständigkeit des Hörens, Im-Hören-sein*]. Today, there has to be a condition and an occasion for being-in-hearing. In place of complete objectlessness, for which our heart is no longer adequate, the occasion for being-in-hearing becomes the disappearance of the object, which we pursue with our ears: the sound of the wind from the "gap" that the dying, in the transition from our existence to the "stronger" one, from one rank to another, rip in the circle of the living. What is experienced is no longer "der andere Bezug [the other relation]" (9th Elegy), but only the approach to it that we hear in missing one who has just departed. ("Es rauscht jetzt von jenen jungen Toten zu dir [It is murmuring toward you now from those who died young].")

It is from the impossibility of experiencing transcendence immediately that the dying person, in his transcending of one existence toward another, acquires a fundamentally religious meaning: he becomes one of the intermediaries and one of the preconditions for being able, not indeed to experience the "other relation," but just barely to hear from it. In this listening to the dead as they are escaping, we disappear along with them, and while we do not reach the other relation ("Und das Totsein ist mühsam und voller Nachholn, daß man allmählich ein wenig Ewigkeit spurt [And being dead is hard work and full of retrieval before one can gradually feel a trace of eternity]"), we are already estranged from our human earth and hover ambiguously between a no-longer and a not-yet:

> Freilich ist es seltsam, die Erde nicht mehr zu bewohnen,
> kaum erlernte Gebräuche nicht mehr zu üben,
> Rosen, und andern eigens versprechenden Dingen
> nicht die Bedeutung menschlicher Zukunft zu geben;
> . . .
> Seltsam, die Wünsche nicht weiterzuwünschen. Seltsam,
> alles, was sich bezog, so lose im Raume
> flattern zu sehen. . . .
>
> [Of course, it is strange to inhabit the earth no longer,
> to give up customs one barely had time to learn,
> not to see roses and other promising things
> in terms of a human future;
> . . .
> Strange no longer to desire one's own desires. Strange
> to see meanings that clung together once, floating away
> in every direction. . . .]

1st Elegy

Although human existence and human calling-out remain basically futile for Rilke, his poetry does understand itself to be a "mission [Auftrag]" (in contrast to the *Sonnets to Orpheus,* where song is called "existence [Dasein]," even though this song, too, remains futile: "Wann aber *sind* wir? [But when will we *be?*]" Orpheus I.III.) This mission is not handed down from "the Angels' hierarchies," which the "Elegies" vainly attempt to woo ("Engel, und würb ich dich auch! Du kommst nicht [Angel, and even if I were to woo you, you would not come]," 7th Elegy), nor does it come from other people; rather, it comes from things. ("Ach, wen vermögen wir denn zu brauchen? Engel nicht, Menschen nicht. . . . Es bleib uns vielleicht irgendein Baum an dem Abhang. . . . es bleibt uns die Straße von gestern. . . . [Ah, whom can we ever turn to in our need? Not angels, not humans. . . . Perhaps there remains for us some tree on a hillside. . . . there remains for us yesterday's street. . . ."], 1st Elegy). The fact that whatever remains of the relation to the world flees to what is relatively most distant—in any case does not turn to the other, to what is closest, but rather commits itself to this distant entity and claims closeness to it— shows the extent to which human existence has here been estranged from the world:

> . . . . drum zeig
> ihm das Einfache, das, von Geschlecht zu Geschlechtern gestaltet,
> als ein Unsriges lebt neben der Hand und im Blick.
> Sag ihm die Dinge. Er wird staunender stehn; wie *du* standest
> bei dem Seiler im Rom, oder beim Töpfer am Nil.
>
> [. . . . So show him
> something simple which, formed over generations,
> lives as our own, near our hand and within our gaze.
> Tell him of things. He will stand astonished; as *you* stood
> by the rope-maker in Rome or the potter along the Nile.]
>
> 9th Elegy

Things are a mission; but the fact that the human being does not belong to them in a primary way is shown both in the explicitness as well as in the belatedness of human agreement "von weit her [from far away]" (9th Elegy). For the human being actually hangs in the air, un-related to anything. In contrast to every other historically recorded estrangement from the world, this estrangement is not directly or originally determined as transcendence, nor does it escape into transcendence; it is rather characterized by the detour it makes. The detour consists in what Rilke calls "rescue" [*Rettung*]. The background to this rescue is as follows: things are transient and therefore need rescuing. Rescuing is not simply a spontaneously human act, but a task and an urge imparted by things ("drängender Auftrag [urgent mission]," 9th Elegy), and also—and herein consists the detour, and the only thing the human being can possibly achieve regarding the "other relation"—an "escape" [*Hinüberretten*] into the "stronger existence." The "other relation" is for Rilke the "unsayable," but things are capable of being said ("Sind wir vielleicht hier, um zu sagen: Haus, Brücke, Brunnen, Tor,

Krug, Obstbaum, Fenster,—[Perhaps we are here in order to say: house, bridge, fountain, gate, pitcher, fruit-tree, window,—]," 9th Elegy). Rescuing, however, is naming, in other words, preservation from destruction. In the end, naming is extolling. But being extolled does not simply mean being left in its unaltered state—and praised for this reason. Being extolled basically means being transformed into a stronger being:

> . . . . aber zu *sagen*, verstehns,
> o zu sagen, so, wie selber die Dinge niemals
> innig meinten zu sein. . . .
>
> [. . . . but to *say* them, you must understand,
> oh to say them more intensely than the things themselves
> ever dreamed of existing. . . .]
>
> 9th Elegy

It is not enough for the transformation simply to say the sayable to the angel; it endures only in repeated retelling (7th Elegy). The human being undertakes this rescue because he therein finds access to the "other relation." Things expect it of him, for

> . . . . Mehr als je
> fallen die Dinge dahin, die erlebbaren, denn,
> was sie verdrängend ersetzt, ist ein Tun ohne Bild.
>
> [. . . . More than ever
> the things that we might experience are vanishing, for
> what crowds them out and replaces them is an imageless act.]
>
> 9th Elegy

This urge and this "Zumutung [demand]" (1st Elegy) are all the more remarkable since, for Rilke, things have a higher rank in existence than do human beings; they are more permanent relative to the human being, who no longer properly belongs to the world in his extreme fleetingness, who is "endured" by things in their relative endurance, and who is merely tolerated by them:

> . . . . Siehe, die Bäume sind; die Häuser,
> die wir bewohnen, bestehn noch. Wir nur
> ziehen allem vorbei wie ein luftiger Austausch.
> Und alles ist einig, uns zu verschweigen, halb als
> Schande vielleicht und halb als unsägliche Hoffnung.

[. . . . Look: the trees exist; the houses
that we live in still stand. We alone
fly past all things, as fugitive as the wind.
And all things conspire to keep silent about us, half
out of shame, perhaps, half as unutterable hope.]

2nd Elegy

The transformation of the "visible into the invisible" is for Rilke a task springing from the contemporary situation, a task whose motivation he describes as follows: the contemporary world is only interior ("immer geringer schwindet das Außen [the exterior disappears more and more]," 7th Elegy); life is becoming an "imageless act." For this reason, things are becoming ruins, "pushed away" and "replaced" by this act. This falling into ruin also entails that no new things arise. The idea now suggests itself to understand interiority itself as a determination of transcendence. However, only as long as the interior became manifest in an exterior was the non-questioning relation to transcendence secured, and a handing-over, like praise and rescue, superfluous. Only today, because the exterior is vanishing ("Wo einmal ein dauerndes Haus war, schläg sich erdachtes Gebild vor [Where there was once an enduring building, a mental image suggests itself]," 7th Elegy)—and limiting oneself to the unsayable simply indicates a deprivation, rather than an original transcendence—we "disinherited ones" need things as our last possibility for praising and for reaching out into the other order:

Preise dem Engel die Welt, nicht die unsägliche, ihm
kannst du nicht großtun, mit herrlich Erfühltem; im Weltall,
wo er fühlender fühlt, bist du ein Neuling, drum zeig
ihm das Einfache. . . .

[Praise this world to the angel, not the unsayable one,
you cannot impress him with glorious emotion; in the universe
where he feels more powerfully, you are a novice, so show him
something simple. . . .]

9th Elegy

This privation, however, refers not only to a retreat from the world, but also—and this is what is decisive—to a "defense" against the angel:

Engel, und würb' ich dich auch! Du kommst nicht. Denn mein
Anruf ist immer voll Hinweg; wider so starke
Strömung kannst du nicht schreiten. Wie ein gestreckter

Arm ist mein Rufen. Und seine zum Greifen
oben offene Hand bleibt vor dir
offen, wie Abwehr und Warnung,
Unfaßlicher, weit auf.

[Angel, and even if I were to woo you, you would not come. For my call
is always filled with a departure; against such a powerful
current you cannot move. Like an outstretched arm
is my call. And its hand, held open and reaching up
to seize, remains in front of you, open
as if in defense and warning,
Ungraspable One, far above.]

7th Elegy

Praise only grows from the futility and despair of wooing. Only in praise is
there a being-heard [*Gehörtwerden*], namely the being-heard of what is told,
even if it has nothing to do with *being-harkened-to* [*Erhörtwerden*]. The first
impulse of the call is thus a religious impulse, the failure of which gives rise
to poetry, which contains a double ambiguity for this very reason: measured
in accordance with its religious origin, poetry is already the falsification of
that origin. As poetry, however, in other words, as expression of the interior
world, it fails to live up to its own premises.[6] "Listen, my heart, as only saints
have listened"—this is the impulse that, as is shown by what follows ("Nicht
daß du Gottes ertrügest die Stimme, bei weitem [Not that you could endure
God's voice, far from it]"), already contains the failure of listening.

The peculiar thing here consists in the fact that the echolessness of the
"andern Ordnung [other order]," which "es gelassen verschmäht, uns zu
zerstören [serenely disdains/to destroy us]" (1st Elegy), does not in fact
destroy us; rather, it suddenly changes into something positive: here arises
the concept of the beautiful.

. . . . Denn das Schöne ist nichts
als des Schrecklichen Anfang, den wir noch gerade ertragen,
und wir bewundern es so, weil es gelassen verschmäht,
uns zu zerstören. . . .

[. . . . For the beautiful is nothing
but the terrible's beginning, which we still are just able to endure,
and we marvel at it so because it serenely disdains
to destroy us.]

1st Elegy

The terrible is, therefore, the beautiful insofar as it can be endured. For its part, though, beauty in the *Duino Elegies* is not autonomous, as it presents itself in the "attic steles" of the Greeks, but is only a beginning, namely the beginning of the terrible. Thus, although this poetry does not recognize a clean separation between the beautiful and the terrible, or between divine and human competence ("diese [sc. die Greichen] Beherrschten wußten damit: soweit sind wir's, dieses ist unser, und so zu berühren; starker stemmen die Götter uns an. Doch dies ist Sache der Götter [These (namely the Greeks) self-mastered ones thereby knew: we can go this far, / this is ours, to touch one another this lightly; the gods / can press down harder upon us. But that is a matter for the gods]," 2nd Elegy), and although it is affected by the terribleness of the "stronger existence," it is still possible, since it is able to marvel at this existence as something beautiful. This poetry is thus directly grounded in futility: at the point of non-differentiation in which religious intention and religious denial are sublated, a peace and balance, hence a beauty arises that has nothing to do with religion in its origin. The secularization of the religious, which in every atheism represents a non-obligatory exploitation of religious property, arises here from a specific religious experience—the experience of futility.[7]

Futility, meanwhile, is for Rilke only an index of the human being writing the poetry, who almost always, as an embodiment of futility, stands tacitly for human existence and its situation in general. This existence, however, does not count as genuine existence. Rilke thus places the respective human situation of the poet alongside various authentic situations, or possibilities of being-in-the-world. *Situation,* here, does not refer to an ephemeral position within *a* life but, rather, to a specific life considered as a position in itself: the animal represents not a species of life, but a particular situation, a particular being-in-the-world, namely the "deathless" and futureless merging into pure presence. Thus the "hero" is not one who commits glorious deeds, but rather the situation of ongoing dying, of "von der Dauer Nicht-angefochten-seins [not-being-in-contest with permanence]" (6th Elegy), in other words, being without deadlines, thus without death; the dying person is not the human being whose life is ending, but being-in-death; put another way: not having death before one as a terminus and therefore being deathless and futureless. Thus the child refers not to an early phase in a human being's existence, but to the situation of not-yet-having-a-future, of pure presence. Thus the lover, finally, is not one bound to another human being, but is prior to every object of love, independent of it; indeed, he is being-in-love pure and simple, which the object of love can falsify.

What thus becomes clear is that there is genuine existence, for Rilke, only where it is de-substantivized and de-objectified, where it is neither bound to a personal fate, nor delimited, i.e., for him, "concealed" by an Other, whether through death, as a terminus, or through the beloved, as a singular person. Such existence refers positively to a pure presence free of opposition, a "pure occurrence" that does not contain the other temporal dimensions of human being [*menschliches Sein*]: future and past.[8] Rilke then opposes this existence to what he calls "fate" [*Schicksal*]. Fate is being temporal: being confronted by an Other and being limited by death. This being-limited by death, the terminality of human life, is the ground of time as bad duration, transience as fear of loss, and desire (cf. 8th Elegy), whose highest manifestation is wooing.

> Dieses heißt Schicksal: gegenüber sein
> und nichts als das und immer gegenüber.
>
> [This is what is called fate: to be over-against,
> and to be nothing but over-against now and forever.]
>
> 8th Elegy

Fatefulness, however, is the precondition for being a poet in the sense proposed by the *Duino Elegies,* for being over-against means nothing other than letting oneself get involved with those things, the praise of which opens the door for us to the "other relation":

> warum dann
> Menschliches müssen—und, Schicksal vermeidend,
> sich sehnen nach Schicksal?
> . . .
> Aber weil Hiersein viel ist, und weil uns scheinbar
> alles das Hiesige braucht, dieses Schwindende, das
> seltsam uns angeht. Uns, die Schwindendsten. *Einmal*
> jedes, nur *einmal. Einmal* und nicht mehr. Und wir auch
> *einmal.* Nie wieder. Aber dieses
> *einmal* gewesen zu sein, wenn auch nur *einmal:*
> irdisch gewesen zu sein, scheint nicht widerrufbar.
>
> [Why then
> have to be human—and, escaping from fate,

keep longing for fate?
. . .
But because being here is a lot; because everything here
seems to need us, this fleeting world, which in some strange way
concerns us. Us, the most fleeting of all. *Once*
for each thing, just *once. Once* and no more. And we too,
just *once.* And never again. But to have been
this *once,* even if only *once:*
to have been earthly, seems irrevocable.]

9th Elegy

Fate is therefore a provisional measure, indeed as irrevocable in its one-timeness [*Einmaligkeit*] as it is unrepeatable. This, then, constitutes the poet: taking being-provisional seriously. Yet, it seems to be bluntly contradicted by the opposing statement that characterizes being-here at another point: there it signifies the *lingering* that hides us from our one-timeness—a lingering in one's bloom (6th Elegy), for instance, or in the gratuitous breadth of time from which the hero escapes:

> . . . Dauern,
> ficht ihn nicht an. Sein Aufgang ist Dasein; beständig
> nimmt er sich fort und tritt ins veränderte Sternbild
> seiner steten Gefahr. . . .

> [. . . Permanence
> does not concern him. His ascent is existence; constantly
> moving on into the ever-changed constellation
> of his perpetual danger. . . .]

6th Elegy

Solitude arises, for Rilke, from the transience and unreliability of this world: the transient things abandon us, we "ziehen allem vorbei wie ein luftiger Austausch [fly past all things, fugitive as the wind]" (2nd Elegy). This unreliability of the world is therefore doubly determined: things abandon us, we who "nicht sehr verläßlich zu Hause sind / in der gedeutete Welt [are not very reliably at home / in our interpreted world]" (1st Elegy), and we abandon things, "denn Bleiben ist nirgends [for there is no place where we can remain]" (1st Elegy). This double abandonment, which Rilke tacitly makes into the positive quality of abandonability [*Verlaßbarkeit*], acquires an independent meaning as solitude. It is thus clear that love, for

Rilke, becomes an exemplary situation, for love is principally love of the abandoned. As a situation, love never cleaves to a single opportunity or a single beloved; these are only occasions for it. Nor is love to be understood as one feeling among others. Love overcomes and at the same time forgets the beloved, since it intends more than the accidental individual, and its horizon is obscured by the beloved's closeness ("Ach, sie verdecken sich nur miteinander ihr Los [Alas, they use each other to hide their own fate]," 1st Elegy). Love lies in this abandonment alone. Freed from the beloved into the breadth of its own horizon, it can become an organon for understanding world-relations. As an organon, it remains entirely within its abandonment and estrangement from the world. For the world that is disclosed to love is a fundamentally different world from the one that presents itself to us in our daily lives. It is a world in the cosmological-hierarchical understanding of the term, within which, according to Rilke's terminology, "ranks" and "orders" form the higher layers. Therefore, it is precisely the near world concerning us immediately that is not given in this "cognition" (*Erkennen*), and this fact once again explicitly demonstrates the estrangement from the world that is only seemingly opposed to cognition of the world. When the this-worldly sphere is surpassed, it is not for the sake of a radically other world, but for the sake of the higher layers of the world, which are not properly other-worldly despite their fundamental inaccessibility. And yet, these layers are not properly this-worldly despite the possibility that they could be experienced in the singular situation of love. They are, in sum, still parts of a hierarchically ordered Being. The ambiguity of the religious situation from which the *Duino Elegies* have grown is once again made visible in this approach, which neutralizes the crude opposition of this-worldly and otherworldly by means of a plurality of layers of being, and through the absence of any absolute transcendence radically absolving us of everything this-worldly.

Because there is no true transcendence in this ordered world, one also cannot exceed the world, but only succeed to higher ranks. This succession is actually a merging-into [*Aufgehen*] that is only accomplished purely by the lover. Merging-into, which is to say, downfall [*Untergang*], is, however, the most radical possibility of *being* ("For there is no place where we can remain"). Only in this downfall, which guarantees the self-destruction of the lover and his inclination toward the beloved, does the lover liberate himself completely from the beloved, from the inclination toward her and away from himself. In his giving-himself-up, the lover distinguishes himself from the hero, whose existence is likewise in his downfall, but "selbst der Untergang war ihm / nur ein Vorwand zu sein: seine letzte Geburt [even his downfall was / merely a pretext to be: his final birth]" (1st Elegy), and thus the last refinement and the final confirmation of his individually singular existence. This singularization of being is what the lover has just relinquished in his downfall, because there is, for Rilke, actually only *one* lover:

> Aber die Liebende nimmt die erschöpfte Natur
> in sich zurück, als wären nicht zweimal die Kräfte,
> dieses zu leisten. . . .
>
> [But nature, spent and exhausted, takes lovers back
> into herself, as if there were not enough strength
> to create them a second time. . . .]
>
> 1st Elegy

Every singular person is but the natural repetition; the bloom that is new every year and still the same. This natural repetition, however, is peculiarly uncertain, and in every case would actually have to be performed by the lover himself. Making the repetition explicit in this way is the renunciation of one's individual being, a radical de-individuation:

> . . . . das, was man war in unendlich ängstlichen Händen,
> nicht mehr zu sein, und selbst den eigenen Namen
> weglassen wie ein zerbrochenes Spielzeug.
>
> [. . . no longer to be
> what one was in infinitely anxious hands; to leave
> even one's own name behind, forgetting it
> as easily as a child abandons a broken toy.]
>
> 1st Elegy

The lover loses the specificity of his individual destiny when he compares his own fate to the identical fate of all other and earlier lovers, equates them, and finally identifies his fate with this one fate:

> . . . . Hast du der Gaspara Stampa
> denn genügügend gedacht, daß irgend Mädchen,
> dem der Geliebte entging am gesteigerten Beispiel
> dieser Liebenden fühlt: daß ich würde wie sie?

Sollen nicht endlich uns diese ältesten Schmerzen
fruchtbar warden? Ist es nicht Zeit, daß wir liebend
uns vom Geliebten befrein und es bebend bestehen:
wie der Pfeil die Sehne besteht, um gesammelt im Absprung
mehr zu sein als er selbst. . . .

> [. . . Have you imagined
> Gaspara Stampa intensely enough so that any girl
> deserted by her lover might be inspired
> by that fierce example of soaring, objectless love
> and might say to herself, "Perhaps I can be like her"?
> Shouldn't this most ancient suffering finally grow
> more fruitful for us? Isn't it time that we lovingly
> freed ourselves from the beloved and, quivering, endured:
> as the arrow endures the bowstring's tension, so that
> gathered in the snap of release it can be more than
> itself.]

1st Elegy

Love is the more loving the less it is gratified; if it wants to be loved, it flees from the abandonment of its own love into the sure protection of being loved: "Alas, they use each other to hide their own fate."

Liebende, seid ihrs dann noch? Wenn ihr einer dem andern
Euch an den Mund hebt und ansetzt—: Getränk an Getränk:
o wie entgeht dann der Trinkinde seltsam der Handlung.

[Lovers, is it still you? When you lift yourselves up
to each other's mouth and your lips join, drink against drink:
oh how strangely each drinker seeps away from his action.]

2nd Elegy

The difference between Rilke's approach and all those theories that likewise approach love as the organon of cognition (Augustine, Pascal, Kierkegaard, Scheler) becomes clear in this possibility of "using one another to hide one's fate."[9] Whereas, for these other philosophers, love is understood as a singular act, and, furthermore, the very object fixated by love becomes cognizable to the lover, here love refers primarily to the situation of objectless being-in-love, in which, conversely, the beloved person is forgotten and surpassed in favor of a transcendence: in this situation, love exceeds its supposedly immanent area of authority in order to open one's sight to world- and rank-relations, to the "other relation" and the "angels' hierarchies," which the lover not only recognizes in his abandonment, but to which he belongs:

> .... Doch selbst nur
> eine Liebende, o, allein am nächtlichen Fenster. . . .
> Reichte sie dir nicht ans Knie—?

> [. . . But even
> just one woman in love—, oh, alone at night by her window. . . .
> didn't she reach your knee—?]

7th Elegy

In love, human existence also exceeds the boundary of its own individuality in another direction. Just as it gives itself up in its abandonment and climbs into higher ranks, so it finds its way back to its roots by climbing down into the abyss of its own origin, "wo seine kleine Geburt schon überlebt war [where his little birth had already been outlived]" (3rd Elegy). This return to the "violent origin" does indeed require the beloved as an occasion:

> Zwar du erschrakst ihm das Herz; doch ältere Schrecken
> Stürzten in ihn bei dem berührenden Anstoß.

> [Yes, you did frighten his heart; but more ancient terrors
> plunged into him at the shock of that feeling.]

3rd Elegy

Her call helps him find his way back, not to her, but to

> .... seines Inneren Wildnis,
> diesen Urwald in ihm, auf dessen stummen Gestürztsein
> lightgrün sein Herz stand. . . .

> [. . . his interior wilderness,
> that primal forest inside him, where among decayed treetrunks
> his heart stood, light-green. . . .]

When he finds his way back to the abyss of his own existence, this abyss pulls him deeper over the boundaries of his authentic self, so that now the descent into the ground of his individuality descends further into the infinite pre-history of his race,

. . . . In das ältere Blut, in die Schluchten,
wo das Furchtbare lag, noch satt von den Vätern.

[. . . into more ancient blood, to ravines
where Horror lay still glutted with his fathers.]

The abyssal quality of the race (of the "verborgenen schuldigen Fluß-Gott des Bluts [hidden, guilty river-god of the blood]") is first constituted when one's own blood and the "more ancient blood" are stirred up at the same time. This does not mean that one's individual ancestors are now viewed in clear, historical sequence: "the seething multitudes" arise, the primal ground from which the individual, historical generations first emerge, and toward whose succession it remains indifferent in its absolute pastness. Everything coming later is already foreseen and overtaken in this ground, the lover as well as the beloved. This land of primeval ages, from which the "floods of ancestry" rise, belongs to the boy, since

. . . . jedes
Schreckliche kannte ihn, blinzelte, war wie verständigt.
Ja, das Entsetzliche lächelte. . . . Selten
hast du so zärtlich gelächelt, Mutter. Wie sollte
er es nicht lieben, da es ihm lächelte. . . .

[. . . every
Terror knew him, winked, as though it were advised.
Yes, atrocity smiled. . . . Seldom
had you smiled so tenderly, mother. How could he help
loving what smiled at him.]

3rd Elegy

Since he now, once again, belongs to those immemorial times that are advised about him, he has been estranged from his natural world, from his mother as from his lover: even from his mother, who only seems to be his origin and past; for in comparison with this absolute past, which as *genos* contains every future in itself, the mother is already "outlived," just like everything else in the present and in the future, and what passes away is more past than the absolute past itself.

. . . . O Mädchen,
dies: daß wir liebten *in* uns, nicht Eines, ein Künftiges, sondern
das zahllos Brauende; nicht ein einzelnes Kind,

sondern die Väter, die wie Trümmer Gebirgs
uns im Grunde beruhn; sondern das trockene Flußbett
einstiger Mütter—; sondern die ganze
lautlose Landschaft unter dem wolkigen oder
reinen Verhängnis—: *dies* kam dir, Mädchen, zuvor.

     [. . . Oh, dear girl,
this: that we loved, *inside* us, not one who would someday appear, but
the seething multitudes; not just a single child,
but also the fathers lying in our depths
like fallen mountains; also the dried-up riverbeds
of ancient mothers—; also the whole
soundless landscape under the clouded or clear
sky of its destiny—: all *this,* dear girl, preceded you.]

3rd Elegy

Love is a possibility, or guarantee of being, not only for the lovers themselves, but also indirectly for the third party, the questioner. Of course, the third party asks very different questions: for him, the lovers seem the most indubitable guarantees of human existence in general, although not guarantors of a transcendent world. If the lovers guaranteed a possibility of this-worldly existence rescued from transience,

weil die Stelle nicht schwindet, die ihr, Zärtliche,
zudeckt; weil ihr darunter das reine
Dauern verspürt. . . .

[because the place you so tenderly cover
does not vanish; because underneath it
you feel pure duration. . . .]

2nd Elegy

then the third would also be allowed a question:

Liebende, euch, ihr ineinander Genügten,
frag ich nach uns. Ihr greift euch. Habt ihr Beweise?

[Lovers, gratified in each other, I am asking you
about us. You hold each other. Do you have proof]?

A remarkable shift in aspects is thus effected through the introduction of the third: the lovers are no longer the ungratified for whom the present disappears in favor of an eschatologically determined future, but those "gratified in each other," for whom the present is absolutized and elevated to "eternity" in the fulfillment of the moment ("So versprecht ihr euch Ewigkeit fast / von der Umarmung [So you promise eternity, almost, / from the embrace]"). Time and transience are thereby paralyzed, and an existence rescued from transience is guaranteed within the fullness of love.

There are, then, three ways that Rilke sees love as the human being's authentic existence: once, as abandonment and possibility of transcendence, then as abandoning and possibility of returning to the origin, to the "mothers," and finally, as the this-worldly possibility of "pure duration." Transience is paralyzed three times in three completely different ways. Yet one thing remains the same in all three cases: love is authentic only when it is freed from every binding goal and every worldly fixation.

The estrangement from the world that is made explicit in love is, originally, not a positive human characteristic. For this reason, all of Rilke's statements about being released from the world become ambiguous and ambivalent. In its positive sense, as a benefit of love, estrangement from the world is freedom from and freedom for; in a negative sense, it is banishment from the world. This being-banished gains a characterization: "Nichtverständigtseins [not being advised about the world]." The animal is "advised," belongs to this world, its rhythm, its seasons in such a way that its participation [*Teilhaben*] in this world bespeaks nothing less than its being a part [*Teilsein*] of it. When we, by contrast, try to take part [*teilzunehmen*] in and thus try to belong to the world,

> so drängen wir uns plötzlich Winden auf
> und fallen ein auf teilnahmslosen Teich.
>
> [we force ourselves abruptly onto the wind
> and fall through onto some indifferent pond.]
>
> 4th Elegy

We thereby meet failure in the world's indifference to us, for "Wir sind nicht einig. Sind nicht wie die Zugvögel verständigt [We are not in harmony. Are not advised like the migratory birds]," who, in searching for summer, in need of experience, find their South—who, when summer comes, are summery, and when winter comes, are wintry. Because of his foreignness, however, the human being is so rhythmically unsure that not only is the summer given him in summer, and the winter in winter, but in every case there is an uncertainty with respect to both—disconnected from the world, they are non-binding possibilities: "Blühn und verdorrn ist uns zugleich bewußt [Flowering and fading come to us both at once]." The explicit dialectic that Rilke ascribes to human experience—

> Uns aber, wo wir eines meinen ganz,
> ist schon des andern Aufwand fühlbar.
>
> [But we, while we are entirely intent upon the one,
> already feel the pull of another.]—

is thus not theoretical but, rather, an index of the human being's insecurity and relative non-being-in-the-world.

From the perspective of being one with the world, the animal acquires cosmological significance for Rilke. One with this world to which it not only belongs but which it helps to comprise, the animal knows no final having-to-leave-the-world, is "frei von Tod [free of death]" (8th Elegy) and in the "pure duration" of its existence.

> . . . . Dicht sein Sein ist ihm
> unendlich, ungefaßt und ohne Blick
> auf seinen Zustand, rein, so wie sein Ausblick.
>
> [. . . But it feels its being
> as infinite, boundless, and without regard
> to its own condition: pure, like its outward gaze.]
>
> 8th Elegy

The animal is thus non-transient; it has eternity, and its existence takes its course in the mode of futurelessness and in that of the so-on-and-so-on:

> . . . . und wenn es geht, so gehts
> in Ewigkeit, so wie die Brunnen gehen.
>
> [. . . and when it moves, it moves
> already in eternity, like the fountains.]

We, however, who are fundamentally out of place because of death, never face the "open":

> Wir haben nie, nicht einen einzigen Tag,
> den reinen Raum vor uns, in den die Blumen
> unendlich aufgehn. . . .

> [Never, not for a single day, do we have
> before us that pure space into which flowers
> endlessly open. . . .]

Even the "open" is only the non-limited for us, understandable only through its opposite, which is constantly perceptible in it: "Immer ist es Welt / und niemals Nirgends ohne Nicht [Always there is world / and never nowhere without a 'no']." We are thus dependent upon an indirect possibility of seeing the "open": "Was draußen ist, wir wissens aus / des Tiers Antlitz allein [We know what is out there only from / the animal's gaze]." Otherwise only the child has a deathless existence, the child "mit Dauerndem vergnügt [gratified by what endures]" (4th Elegy), who thus lives without desires in the "reinen Vorgang [pure occurrence]" (4th Elegy). But when the child grows out of childhood, he or she grows out of being at home in the world in contrast to the animal, who does not even know this growing-out-of, or this estrangement, and is advised about the world from the beginning without needing to learn anything. We, the finally estranged, circle around the animal and place our gazes like traps around its gaze, in order to experience wide-open space and death-free existence.

> Mit allen Augen sieht die Kreatur
> das Offene. Nur unsre Augen sind
> wie umgekehrt und ganz um sie gestellt
> als Fallen, rings um ihren freien Ausgang.

> [With all its eyes the creature sees
> the Open. Only our eyes are turned
> backward and placed around them
> like traps; all around, their way out is open.]

> 8th Elegy

Although animal existence confronts human existence here as something limited, although death here, as a limit that cannot be exceeded, renders life hopelessly out of place, transience, for Rilke, still has a second meaning that is so wholly independent of this confrontation, that—as with some other terms as well—the search for a systematic lowest common denominator and for seamless self-consistency would entail an idle over-interpretation of the work inappropriate to its philosophical intention. This other version of transience nonetheless stands within the work's unified horizon of meaning; it is inconceivable without the non-objective character of the world—a world that can still be heard and tasted—and it is inconceivable without the hierarchical orders that have excluded the possibility of absolute transcendence.

This transience is not the fact of having-to-die-sometime, but constant passing and drifting away; it is not an index of the future, but life itself as it is constantly using itself up and living itself out. As passing away, however, transience bears the thither of passing away, and, as something which does not end abruptly, transience contains its possible dwelling within the very process of passing away itself. Transience, then, no longer has anything to do with that which is usually placed in radical opposition to it, namely immortality. When transience is posited as passing away, then the question arises (which is posed in Rilke without being answered), whether the thither of our transience has predestined and predetermined us, or whether it is a foreign space in which we—irrelevant to it, accidental to ourselves—drift away.

> . . . . Schmeckt denn der Weltraum,
> in den wir uns lösen, nach uns? Fangen die Engel
> wirklich nur Ihriges auf, ihnen Entströmtes,
> oder ist manchmal, wie aus Versehen, ein wenig
> unseres Wesens dabei? . . . .

> [. . . Does the world-space
> we dissolve into, taste of us then? Do the angels really
> reabsorb only what streamed out from themselves,
> or sometimes, as if by oversight, is there a trace
> of our essence as well?]

> 2nd Elegy

The fact that the *Duino Elegies* are scarcely known; the fact that they remain completely isolated among publications of the times—all of this is secondary in comparison to the echolessness that they know about themselves and from which they spring. They cannot be allotted their place in today's literary production, which either dismisses God as a matter of course, without misgivings, or exploits religious property in a non-obligatory manner, or, finally, satisfies our so-called "religious needs" with surrogates. For the impossibility of encountering God is not proof of his non-existence as far as the *Elegies* are concerned; this impossibility explicitly becomes God's distance from us—a distance that can be experienced, in its negativity, again and again, and thus becomes a religious fact. We therefore stand before a remarkable situation: the failure to encounter God, usually regarded as a neutral fact, becomes the despair of being able to encounter Him. As long as human life stood under the unquestioned determination of God, being human, as *creatum esse* [created being], as a being-before-God, meant being nothing. With the denial of the experience and existence of God, nothingness disappears as a determination of human *being:* the human being finds a natural home in the world. If the human being still understands himself as nothing, then it is not as nothing before God, but as nothing as such: his life no longer lives in nothingness, but in the meaninglessness of his being. When he admits this meaninglessness, he lives in nihilism. In Rilke, by contrast, nothingness is neither the human being's nothingness before God, nor meaninglessness (being without God); it is, rather, *being* human, insofar as a being of this kind is not at home in the world and finds no entrance into it. Here as well, human life does indeed hang in the air, but not because there is no God; on the contrary, it does so because the human being has been rejected and abandoned by Him. This abandonment by God and world, this belonging-nowhere constitutes both the poetry's religious and its nihilistic character. In this way, nihilism becomes "positive nihilism," for it despairs of its own godlessness and understands this godlessness to consist in the act of God's abandonment. Rather than being the start of, and spur to heresy, as it would be in times defined by confessional concerns, despair thus becomes the last residuum of religiousness, and elegy becomes the last literary form of religious certification—not the lament over what has been lost but, rather, the expression of loss itself.

Originally published as "Rilkes 'Duiniser Elegien'" under the co-authorship of Hannah Arendt and Günther Stern in *Neue Schweizer Rundschau* [= *Wissen und Leben*] 23 (1930): 855–71; translated by Colin Benert.

Günther Anders, originally Stern (1902–1992), studied phenomenology with Edmund Husserl and Martin Heidegger. His marriage to Arendt lasted from 1930 to 1936. Among his many later works, *Die Antiquiertheit des Menschen* (The Obsolescence of the Human Being, 1956) is perhaps the most prominent.

Rainer Maria Rilke (1875–1926), who was born in Prague, ranks among the great lyric poets in the German language. *Duino Elegies,* one of his major achievements, was begun in 1912 but not completed until 1922.—Ed.

§ 2 Review of Hans Weil, *The Emergence of the German Principle of "Bildung"*

The informative and exciting investigation of Hans Weil is important not only because of the historical thoroughness with which well-known things are reworked in entirely new ways, but especially because it can provide the historical basis for a modern discussion of "*Bildung.*"[1]

Weil shows the provenance of the German idea of *Bildung* from its beginnings in Herder's appropriation of Shaftesbury and Rousseau, through Humboldt's formulations of an "ideal" of *Bildung,* to the emergence of what he calls the "Bildungselite," in which the actual reception of the principle of *Bildung* is carried out.[2] The analysis of the reception of the *Bildung* principle, which largely consists in sociological analysis, is the most important part of the entire investigation, whereas the preceding discussions of Herder and Humboldt are mostly concerned with individual motivations. In methodological terms, the first two parts (especially the Herder chapter) combine sociological and psychological analysis. In general, the exposition is less concerned with developing an exact and thorough interpretation of a given text than in "explaining" the text in question under the presuppositions mentioned above—that it be analyzed with respect to its "personal motivations" and its "social determinants" (166).

Insofar as Weil interprets texts, he orients his investigation around an opposition that stems from pietism, namely the opposition between "worldliness and *Innigkeit.*" This *Innigkeit* is, for its part, equated with "inwardness

---

Hans Weil, *Die Entstehung des Deutschen Bildungsprinzips.* Bonn: Friedrich Cohen, 1930.

[*Innerlichkeit*]" (5).³ The two most essential possibilities of *Bildung* correspond to this opposition: 1. "*Bildung* as making into an image [*zum Bilde machen*]" and 2. *Bildung* as "the development of already given capacities [*Ausbildung vorgegebener Anlagen*]" (6). "*Bildung* as making into an image" is derived *historically* from "imagery in general" as a specifically European tradition, to the extent that it is determined in a Greek-heathen manner (22 ff.). Shaftesbury's influence owes its origin to this tradition. On the other hand, "*Bildung* as making into an image" is *sociologically* determined as a "social striving toward the noble class" (8). The meaning of "model" [*Vorbild*] belongs to both derivations, in the first case as historical model, in the second case again as the sociological one. By contrast, "*Bildung* as the development of already given capacities" represents a socially "submissive comportment" (9), insofar as it is interpreted in a sociological manner; it stems from pietistic inwardness insofar as it is understood historically.

Weil establishes a principle of interpretation that demands that any case of inwardness be understood "from the perspective of a particular kind of 'worldliness,'" since worldliness is, as it were, the more manifest side (5). In this way, everything inward is implicitly understood as dependent on a "particular kind of worldliness," and in the same way, inwardness is often only seen as compensation for a failed worldliness.⁴ By means of this—unspoken—theory of compensation, the tradition of inwardness is, to a certain extent, excluded. To be sure, Weil appeals to pietism but does not enter into an historical analysis of this phenomenon. Pietism is seen only as a personal heritage, not interpreted actually as something historically transmitted. This kind of interpretation is, in any case, almost forced to conform to the opposition "inwardness-worldliness," which is itself not interpreted. Posing questions in terms of this alternative, however, demands historical legitimation: it cannot be applied everywhere with equal right. It fails most conspicuously, in my opinion, in the analysis of Herder. Herder is understood in terms of a doubleness specific to him: the two above-mentioned tendencies of *Bildung* come together in him. Herder takes over *Bildung* as "making into an image" from Shaftesbury, and *Bildung* as "development of already given capacities" from Rousseau. Weil identifies Herder's own tradition with the pietism of his parental house and his position as Protestant minister; that is, he considers only his personal heritage; it therefore happens that the influence of Lessing is completely neglected.⁵

As Weil has shown in an excellent discussion, Shaftesbury provides Herder with the legitimacy for something he had already experienced: human inequality. By drawing an analogy between the individual human being and organic-vegetative nature, Rousseau provides Herder with the possibility of "character formation [*Charackterbildung*]" (96). True to Herder's pietistic provenance, *Bildung* as "making into an image" is thereby "interiorized." Both tendencies, according to Weil, tend toward human autonomy: "At the same time, however, the principle of *Bildung* as striving toward the beautiful image gives the individual an autonomy of spirit and personality, comparable to that change in autonomy that Luther had demonstrated to the Christian in the sphere of religion" (41).[6] This autonomy emerges through the *process* of *Bildung* whose analogy is the plant that consists "in itself, through itself, and for itself " (42). Weil then tries to show that Herder's reflections on history take their point of departure from this vegetative conception of the human being, as it proceeds from Shaftesbury's influence "by means of his aesthetically-harmonizing goal-setting," through Rousseau, and toward the "limitlessness" of the merely "natural human being."

This exposition of Herder seems to me to underestimate the significance of history and thus of extra-personal reality (as, for instance, in the ideas of "destiny" or "disaster") for both Herder himself and for his concept of *Bildung*. The isolation of the human being who is understood according to the metaphor of the plant stands in contrast to all those assertions of Herder (especially in his essay "Another Philosophy of History") which explicitly speak of the "chain of individuals" and of the "tradition" that forms the human being. Indeed, Herder directly polemicizes against such an isolated process of *Bildung,* as Weil describes it—not, to be sure, directly in a polemic against Rousseau but in the polemic against Lessing: "Assume that the human being receives everything from itself and develops whatever it receives in isolation from outer objects, then you'd certainly get a history of 'the' human being but not of *human beings,* not of the entire species" (*Ideas toward the History of Humanity,* first part, 9th book, I, 2). Through the eruption of history and thus of a reality over which the human being has no power, a destruction of human autonomy is carried out in Herder's work: the human being is only the "ant on the wheel of disaster." Accordingly, it seems questionable to me whether Herder's use of the plant metaphor should be taken with the same degree of seriousness as its use in Rousseau. In my estimation,

Weil's discussion of Herder would correspond much better to Schleiermacher's concept of individuality.[7]

For Herder, the reception of history belongs to *Bildung*. According to Weil, however, history in this sense takes place, above all, in the "feeling-related connectiveness of whoever is forming himself [*sich Bildenden*] in accordance with models that are chosen and felt." This assertion is correct but one-sided: for Herder, the "silent, eternal power of the model and of a series of models" stands in very close connection with *Bildung*; but this reception does not take place "more through 'feeling' than through 'thinking'" (68); rather, it occurs through understanding, which is completely neutral with respect to the opposition between feeling and thinking. In Herder, who knew about the irrevocable uniqueness of everything historical, this kind of understanding preserves a certain distance with respect to reality: distance not only with respect to the history it conjures up but also with respect to the history that really was, which means that it can do without pedagogical goals and connivances.[8] As I see it, this distance of understanding and, in general, its corresponding idea of understanding as an entirely new possibility of gaining access to the world and to reality has become extraordinarily effective not only for the principle of *Bildung* but also for the intellectual elite, whose "distance," according to Weil, makes it into the "judge of culture" (233).

A very illuminating analysis of Humboldt, who first made *Bildung* into an "ideal," prepares the way for the third part, which is concerned with the emergence of the German *Bildung* elite. Weil wants to conceive of Humboldt as the bearer of "transpersonal significance," in which "transpersonal significance" is essentially equated with "social significance" (95). Humboldt's biography, his origin, and so forth are all recounted in this exemplary sense—always with respect to the social and economic situation of the nobility in general. One of the best modern expositions of Humboldt emerges out of this sociologically oriented analysis.

Two things are thus emphasized: Humboldtean realism ("'intuition.' . . . as a mode whereby the opposition between 'thinking' and 'feeling' is overcome," 91–92), on the one hand, and love of one's own individuality, on the other. Humboldt is, to be sure, consigned to realism, that is, forced to work his way into the world, because he "no longer needed his own form of thought"—which he had "learned" from the bourgeois Enlightenment—"as a weapon" (101); on the other hand, his "individuality as a uniquely true possession" (103) still remains his own, for he has been fully individualized. As Weil notes in a well-formulated phrase, all of this means that "he encountered only what fascinated him" (142). But the connection between these two components is not fully clarified: how is Humboldt's realism related to the fact that he "had, in general, a relation to the world only insofar as it touched his interior?" (103). It seems to me that there is, indeed, such a connection and that it consists in a Humboldtean notion of an absolute realism, in which everything that is always remains real despite its complete anonymity. "This, for me, is an almost unshakable principle: nothing that happens to a man of goodness and greatness ever really perishes—even if it is only an immediate feeling of a single moment, recognized by no one. It stamps itself into his very being. . . . and even if no one is there, it leaves its mark, I want to say, in dead nature itself," Humboldt writes to Caroline in 1803.[9] This remarkable notion of realism seems to perform both functions: it takes seriously every event as an event, and it demands, on the other hand, that one "carefully cultivate inner existence."

If *Bildung* as a process was in Herder the expression of the belief that the "way is more important than the goal," in Humboldt "*Bildung* as a state, not as an occurrence, [is] the 'ideal' of *Bildung* as a process" (120). From Herder onward, the state of being educated [*gebildet*] has been articulated with respect to specific "ideal contents" (131), somewhat like the masculine and feminine principle. This "concentration" had the function of making a synopsis possible. (Furthermore, in my estimation, this possibility of classification saves autonomy from its Herderian destruction.) The goal of all *Bildung* is "objectivation of itself as a figure" (135), an objectivation that is first made possible by a fixating accommodation, in which the individual "knows" what he is. This accommodation of the individual—which is favored by fact that the " 'educated' [*Gebildeten*] always direct themselves toward a few models" (143)—accomplishes two things: first, "the individuation of the individual is controlled" (143), and second, the individuated individual is effectively separated off from the masses. The emergence of the German "intellectual elite" [*Geisteselite*] means both of these.

The resulting attempt to sketch a "sociology of the intellectual elite" is oriented toward three questions: "1) How is the *appurtenance* of the members of the group experienced? 2) How is the elite *sociologically* structured? 3) What are the social *foundations* of the elite and its *functions* within the entire society?"

The answers to these three questions can be given here only in a schematic fashion. The reviewer simply wishes to point out the instructive and innovative discussions contained in the book. Someone is considered part of the elite on account of a "particular mode of being," which Weil calls "representative" (154). This representation can take place as a result of an objectively determinable accomplishment, but it does not have to take place in this manner, for the only thing that, at bottom, gives legitimacy to an individual is "faith" in him (156–57), that is, the extent to which he possesses the possibility of fascination. The relative independence of the elite from objective accomplishments goes hand in hand with its "indifference with respect to outward position" (161). Decisive for the actual appurtenance of someone to the elite group is participation in "circulation," the specific kind that "preserves . . . intelligence," whose bearer is the "circle" (158). In its characteristic hovering between the esoteric and the exoteric or, otherwise stated, between intimate friendship and claims to public validity, the phenomenon of the elite stands in the closest possible connection with the "salon" (225). What distinguishes the elite from the salon is "distance" as a personal expression for being selected out. This, in turn, is documented and legitimated in "great models" (161, 185), which Herder had already recommended for *Bildung*. The relation to the models gives the elite the possibility of a "new principle of order, which plays an important role for the members of the elite, who are often so qualitatively distinct and isolated from one another" (162).

The difference between the social structure of the elite and its social function makes its members into ambiguous parts of the "middle class" (164); its kind of participation in intellectual matters allows it to be necessarily "apolitical" (164); its possible effect is only through "word and text" (169). The effectiveness of the elite depends, however, entirely on its "prestige," which determines whether "it only knows itself to be representative" or "is also actually considered representative" (171). The elite best maintains its legitimacy by means of "prestige" "when social groups . . . are grasped from a social process of circumspection" (171). As Weil explains, its social function consists in "giving an image of the world and of society, which amounts to a complete counter-image to social reality" (173). A certain kind of social alteration and postponement—which makes it possible to observe individuality more closely and to take it more seriously—favors the emergence of the intellectual elite at the end of the eighteenth and the beginning of the nineteenth centuries. The social alteration seizes the nobility most of all, for the nobility lost its old "functional meaning" within the limits of human society "as a result of the disappearance of the feudal system." At the same time, because of "free trade," there emerged moreover a grand bourgeoisie, which was not primarily interested in the state; furthermore, pietism's school for the soul appeared, which found a home among the petit bourgeoisie (192). In this upheaval, according to Weil, the traditional aristocracy was "not up to the job" (219), allowing the intellectual elite to establish itself in its place. A few members of the nobility even aided this elite (221). We find an effective opposition to the intellectual elite first in the time of romanticism, which "gave" the traditional nobility "an instrument for the intellectual justification of a patriarchal stratified-state [*Ständesstaat*]" (212).[10] In this context, Weil pays particular attention to von der Marwitz and his battle against the Enlightenment.[11] This purely sociological elucidation—for which we should offer thanks—nevertheless forgets, in our estimation, the actual historical tradition, i.e. in this case, a tradition that begins with the "petit bourgeois Herder," who writes the first "pamphlet" against the Enlightenment. And it seems to me that the words of von der Marwitz cited by Weil, which are directed against the eighteenth century, represent a surprisingly direct quotation of Herder's dictum about the very same subject: "the child grown old by way of cleverness blasphemes."

The actual limit of the welcome investigations contained in Weil's book seems to me to lie here: in the forgetting of the historical. In conclusion, it should be remarked that the citations Weil has chosen are very skillfully arranged. Not only do they make for a clear exposition, they also make it possible at every point to verify his claims.

Originally published in *Archiv für Sozialwissenschaft und Sozialpolitik* 66 (1931): 200–205; translated by Susannah Young-ah Gottlieb.
Hans Weil (1898–1972) was a scholar who specialized in the problems of pedagogy.—Ed.

§ 3 Friedrich von Gentz

On the 100th Anniversary of His Death, June 9, 1932

"He seized upon untruth with a passion for truth."
—Rahel Varnhagen

Rarely has a great writer been more thoroughly forgotten. When, in the mid-1830s, Varnhagen von Ense erected a monument to Gentz in a portrait summarizing his life and work, and when a little later Gustav Schlesier published a first selection of his writings and letters, the *Hallish Annual* opined even then that nothing Gentz had produced could rescue him from the neglect he so richly deserved.[1] It was not worthwhile to argue against him, the periodical claimed; he was passé and forgotten. And even Rudolf Haym's much more objective and fair-minded assessment found that Gentz's "combining of literary and political talents"—a combination rarely seen in Germany—was the only thing about him of significance to posterity.[2]

This neglect is all the more remarkable when we consider that Gentz was the only member of his generation and, more important, of his circle to play an active role in European politics. He was born in Breslau in 1764, studied with Kant in the 1780s, then went to Berlin to begin a career in the Prussian civil service. In Berlin, he first befriended Wilhelm von Humboldt, then joined the circle that gathered around Henriette Herz and later around Rahel Varnhagen.[3] He belonged to the generation that consciously experienced the French Revolution as the triumph of philosophy over history. More rapidly than the others of his circle, Gentz shifted his initial enthusiasm for the Revolution into a more enduring admiration for the stature and historical durability of the English constitution. He was the first to translate Burke and by doing so created the first foundations for the conservative position in Germany.[4] An open letter he wrote in 1797 to Friedrich Wilhelm III, on the occasion of Friedrich's assumption of the throne, calling for freedom of the press and the citizen's right to exercise any trade he chose, made him so unpopular in Prussia that further promotion was closed to him.[5]

Because he was not willing to spend the rest of his life in the rank of military councillor, he went to Vienna in 1802, at first as a "free-lance" writer—as a "volunteer," as he later described himself—in the service of the Austrian government. Before that he traveled to England and reinforced the ties that already bound him to English politicians. He received money from the English government for his work as a writer, and from this time on he was never able to rid himself of the reproach that he could be bought.

On his return to Austria, his major goal was to unite the European cabinets against Napoleon. All his writings from this period—especially the famous *Fragments from the Recent History of the European Balance of Power*—are only nominally addressed to the nations of Europe, but the audience he was really addressing was the cabinets to which he did not yet have any access. From 1812 on he was a loyal and devoted follower of Metternich and adherent of Austrian restoration policy.[6] He wrote justifications for government policies; he wrote the minutes of the Congress of Vienna; he was an untiring mediator there and Metternich's secret adviser. This role he continued to play at the Carlsbad Congress and the later congresses at Troppau and Laibach. He became the conservative spokesman for the status quo, the most bitter opponent of freedom of the press, the most intelligent advocate of those who wanted to see the contribution of the people to the wars of liberation forgotten in favor of cabinet politics. Metternich's policy, the policy of calm at any price, celebrated only brief triumphs. The rebellions in Spain, Italy, and Greece, and the July Revolution in France, appeared to render Gentz's life's work illusory.

When Gentz died in 1832, he knew that he had fought for a lost cause, that "the spirit of the times would prove stronger" than he and those in whose service he had placed himself, that "art is no more able than political power . . . to slow the turning of the world's wheel." The spirit of the times, which Gentz so passionately hated, was stronger than the art of the diplomat and the power of the statesman. In his defense of cabinet government, Gentz had fought against two enemies, neither of which actually emerged victorious in his lifetime, but both of which unofficially shaped the life of the times. These two were *liberalism* and *conservatism*.

Liberalism and its "insidious claim that everyone may regard his own reason as a source of law" meant anarchy to him, the end of a moral and political world order. He played against this liberalism a "feudalism, even though of a mediocre order" suggested to him in the romantic formulation of his friend Adam Müller.[7] But conservatism cannot claim him as its own either, for he used it only as a foil against anything that smacked of reform. He did not advocate it for its own sake, but used it only as a means of maintaining a "balance." He tried to perpetuate the status quo, to suspend the course of history in order to create a "stable system" in which tradition and reason would exist in equilibrium. When he gave up his life as a freelance writer to achieve specific goals in the service of a specific state, he threw in his lot with reality—and consequently against the Enlightenment and the possible "triumph of philosophy over history." But he turned just as decisively against romanticism, whose world seemed illusionistic to him. As a corrective to the arrogance of reason, he held up "human frailty," and as a corrective to conservatism, to the principle of legitimacy, he maintained that this principle was not "absolute" but had been "born in time," was "caught up in time," and had to be "modified by time." He promoted neither one principle nor the other, but devoted his efforts entirely to the "magnificent old world" whose decline he was witnessing. This "magnificent old world" was Europe. He remained untouched by patriotism, the new national feeling, that momentarily allied dying feudalism with the emerging liberal Prussian patriots.

It was no coincidence that the liberal Varnhagen was the first to argue with Gentz. Gentz's mode of argumentation was drawn from the Enlightenment; his mode of life was early romantic. Both these factors place him in the generation he seemed to be turning away from when he opted for reality, the generation of Wilhelm von Humboldt and Friedrich Schlegel.[8] And indeed he never fully turned away from his old friends— not from Humboldt any more than from Rahel Varnhagen or Pauline Wiesel.[9] Despite his friendship with Adam Müller, he did not convert to Catholicism, nor did he experience an inner change equivalent to such a step. He may have lived in the world of Viennese diplomacy, but to the extent he wanted to be understood, he had to turn to a liberal intellectual world whose political incarnation he was fighting against. As Rudolf Haym wrote, "He continued living like Mirabeau, but he began thinking like Burke."[10] His virtuosity consisted in his ability to be a different person than the cause he was advocating demanded he be. He did not understand that the life of the Enlightenment man, which he was, required an Enlightenment politics (at that time, liberal politics) as well. For him, politics was merely the art of guiding states and ruling populations, an art the liberals dabbled in as dilettantes; the romantics, as victims of their own illusions.

All the criticisms of Gentz take as their basic assumption that politics is a matter of character, of principle. That is precisely what politics for Gentz was not. Heinrich von Stein called him a man with a "rotten heart and a dried-up brain," objecting, in other words, to the very principles of his politics.[11] His friend Adam Müller, on the other hand, who was in total agreement with the principles of Austria's politics, always appealed nonetheless to "something better in him." His principles, Müller thought, could not be reconciled with his life. Gentz was regarded as the greatest egoist, as "the living principle of hedonism" (*Hallisch Annual*), and his work as available to any who would pay his price. In more objective portraits he appears sometimes as the cavalier of the eighteenth century, sometimes as "the spirit of *Lucinde* incarnate."[12] All these criticisms are directed at the ambiguity of Gentz's character, but they miss the mark because they fail to understand the reason for that ambiguity, because they do not understand that he is not a "hypocrite." Rahel Varnhagen, who stood by him despite all the personal disappointments she experienced at his hands, recognized this when she spoke repeatedly of his incredible "naïveté."

Toward the end of his life, Gentz wrote a genuine apologia for his political activities. To the challenge of Amalie Imhof, a woman with whom he had been very much in love in his youth, he responded with his "political confession."[13]

"World history," he wrote, "is a constant transition from the old to the new. In this never-ending cycle of things, everything destroys itself, and the fruit that has ripened falls from the plant that produced it. But if this cycle is not to lead to the rapid demise of everything that exists and of everything just and good as well, then there must be, along with the large and ultimately always greater number of those who work to bring in the new, a smaller number of those who try to maintain the old and to contain the freshets of the times, neither being able nor wanting to hold them back altogether, within fixed banks. In eras of great civil convulsions, such as our own, the contest between these two parties assumes a passionate, excessive, an often wild and destructive character. The principle, however, remains the same, and the better forces on both sides know how to guard against the follies and errors of their allies. In my twenty-fifth year, I made my choice. Earlier, influenced by recent German philosophy and also no doubt by some presumably new discoveries in the field of political science, which was however still very alien to me at the time, I had recognized with utter clarity from the outbreak of the French Revolution what my role would be. I had felt initially, then later had understood and known, that I, by virtue of the inclinations and abilities with which nature had equipped me, was called to be a defender of the old and an opponent of innovation."

Gentz justifies himself here by means of an appeal to the role that fell to him in reality, but at the same time, in this self-justification, he distances himself from the world in which he played a definite part. As a pure observer of the world, he assigns himself a place in it. He does not seek to render an account for any cause but only for himself or, rather, for the role he played.

Whether one can ever succeed in finding a place in the world, in reality, is one of the basic questions raised by early romanticism, which was a formative influence for Gentz's generation.

The remove of fantasy from reality, the imagination's dalliance among infinite possibilities, accounts for the wreckage of Friedrich Schlegel's life. By contrast, a genuine engagement with the world, even if only in the form of experimentation, provided Humboldt with a chance at success; for in experimenting with himself and the world Humboldt broke free from himself and his purely imaginative impulses. He gave the world the opportunity to take him by surprise. Gentz gave himself to the world immediately and directly, and it consumed him. His hedonism was only the most radical way open to him to let the world consume him; indeed, his relationship to himself was one of "enjoying his own self." Even his own ego was a reality he did not control but to which he could submit. His "greatest virtuosity" was that of "enjoying his own self." This total passivity is why he could be called "the spirit of *Lucinde* incarnate."

Gentz himself called this being-consumed-by-the-world his "unbounded receptivity." He wrote to Rahel Varnhagen: "Do you know, dear, why we developed such a grand and complete relationship? You are an *infinitely productive being;* and I am *an infinitely receptive* one. You are a great man; I am the most womanly of all women who have ever lived. I know that if I had been a woman physically, I would have had the world at my feet. . . . Consider this remarkable fact: From my own being I cannot strike even the most pathetic spark. . . . My receptivity is completely without limits. Your constantly active, constantly fruitful spirit (I don't mean your mind alone but your soul, everything) encountered this unbounded receptivity, and so we gave birth to ideas and emotions and loves and languages all never heard of before. No mortal has any inkling of what we two know." The idea that the androgynous human being is the perfect human being, an idea familiar to us from *Lucinde,* appears here in real and concrete form. If this "affair" had ever been consummated, Gentz might have found in it the possibility of holding a second self-contained world up against the real world and so have created for himself a way to isolate himself from reality.

When Friedrich Schlegel found access to a larger world by way of Catholicism, he called his relationship to the political events of his time one of "participatory co-thinking." In a similar vein, Gentz stressed his *co-knowingness* as his highest achievement. "I know *everything.* No one on earth knows what *I* know of contemporary history." This remark and others like it recur over and over again in Gentz. But he was, as he himself said, "delighted by nothing, instead very cold, blasé, scornful of the foolishness of just about everyone else and of my own, not wisdom, but perspicacity, my insight, my keen and profound understanding, and, in myself, almost fiendishly pleased that the so-called great historical events ultimately came to such a ridiculous conclusion." This blasé attitude did not leave him as long as he remained completely involved in politics. (It disappeared only in the final years of his life when he was completely possessed by his passion for the dancer Fanny Elßler.)[14] But what still kept drawing him back to the "affairs of the world" was the possibility of knowing what was going on. To take part in the world, though only in the form of knowledge, to be a witness to it, appears to be the greatest opportunity available to the romantics. Gentz sacrificed to it his philosophical outlook, his status, and his fame as a writer. His success at knowing all there really was to know left him ultimately indifferent toward the destruction of everything he had sought to achieve in his political life. From his distancing himself from everything specific—and not from any fixed conviction or determinate point of view—comes the sentence with which he closed his apologia to Amalie Imhof: *"Victrix causa deis placuit, sed victa Catoni"* (The victorious cause pleased the gods, but the defeated one pleases Cato).

Originally published as "Friedrich von Gentz: Zu seinem 100. Todestag am 9. Juni" in *Kölnische Zeitung* 308 (June 8, 1932), Unterhaltungsblatt; translated by Robert and Rita Kimber for *Essays in Understanding: 1930–1954,* ed. Jerome Kohn (New York: Harcourt Brace & Company, 1994), 50–56. I have slightly altered the translation for this volume.

Friedrich von Gentz (1764–1832) was a conservative political theorist. As the translator of Burke's *Reflections on the French Revolution* (1790), he was an advocate of the British style of checks and balances. Because he vehemently opposed Napoleon, he moved to Austria when Prussia declared its neutrality. He became a secretary to Prince von Metternich and served as secretary-general at numerous European congresses, where he supported the old regime against claims that it should be altered to new circumstances.—Ed.

§ 4 Adam Müller—Renaissance?

One of the peculiarities of the National-Socialist movement is its penchant for seeking out its ideologies and even its historical figureheads retroactively. That search has now led it to Adam Müller: the publisher A. Kröner in Leipzig has added an announcement to its selection of Müller's political writings—a book addressing a keenly felt need—to the effect that the volume constitutes the foundation for "National Socialism." Friedrich Bülow, in turn, who contributes an introduction on Müller and romanticism, confirms the relationship between the political romantics and the current theories.[1] The only common denominator he cites is the prevalence in both cases of "the self-abandonment to super-individual values, rooted in feeling and immediate lived experience." This is a rather paltry comparison; surely there is more to be said about this relationship. We should not, however, expect any more from an editor who denounces Schelling's philosophy as "empty formula" and "dead schematism" for the benefit of his personal hero.[2] In short, the introduction is beyond the pale wherever it attempts to do more than provide biographical data.

~

As what kind of figure is Adam Müller supposed to be revealed? As the *progenitor of National Socialism*, i.e. the defender of the strata-state [*Ständestaat*], the enemy of liberalism, of industrialization, of Enlightenment; the "romantic," the defender of the metaphor of the organic, the ideologue of "Ground and Earth" [*Grund und Boden*]. Is that who Adam Müller was?

It seems downright impossible to answer this question with a clear "yes" or "no." For example, when we call Müller a "defender of the strata-state," we need to be clear about the fact that he is writing first and foremost in the name of *feudal nobility*. When he is said to have been fighting *in the name of community* against what he already called an "atomizing" individualism, we should not forget that the actual model of that community was the *Catholic Church*. When he is praised as the *prophet of the national idea*, we need to keep in mind that for him it represented no contradiction to become one of the pacesetters of *Austrian Restoration*.

Who, then, was Adam Müller? Müller, born the son of a Berlin civil servant in 1779, belongs to the generation of the romantics Arnim and Brentano; this in itself means that for him the French Revolution no longer counts among the "greatest tendencies of the century" (Schlegel), and that he does not first have to give up on the revolution as Schlegel or Fichte did, but that he already finds himself born into the general European disillusionment that found its highest expression in the political theory of the Englishman Burke. Müller, at least in his early years, is an explicit student and propagator of Burke's ideas.

In a certain, non-personal sense Müller is a parvenu. Along with others of his generation, he finds himself in a paradoxical situation: since Herder, *history* has been "discovered." If it was discovered, and had to be discovered, this means that it is something other than the authoritarian tradition that still exists. History is being discovered by the bourgeoisie, which is to say, by people who are "ahistorical" for two reasons: they have no ancestors, and they do not belong to the ranks that have made history and whose history is history *per se*. The emancipation of the bourgeoisie, its self-conquest by means of a break with history and a clean start at a "new year one," evaporates with the collapse of the French Revolution. The bourgeois looks to connect with those powers that were history, those whose right is based on their existence, and not those who aspire to found their existence on a supposedly "natural" right. He is filled with *ressentiment* against the nobleman; he, who may only "have," pitted against the one who "is." "He (the bourgeois) may not ask: 'what are you,' only 'what do you have? What insight, what knowledge, what skill, how much wealth?' " (Goethe, *Wilhelm Meister's Apprenticeship*.)[3]

∽

During his student days in Göttingen, Müller is already pulled into the *conflict between natural law and historical law*—embodied by two of his teachers—that will occupy him for the rest of his life. In a sense, Müller identifies natural law with the theses of the French Revolution: it is the law that may be claimed by everybody by virtue of their humanity—a claim to rights, not a right to claims. The irreality of this merely moral claim seems to him to be a crime against the facts, namely against the sort of right that history itself has formed through its continuation: the right to privileges [*Vorrecht*]. To coin a motto for Müller's philosophy, one could resort to a variation of the famous Hegelian phrase "whatever is real, is rational"; in other words, whatever is, is legitimate.[4] The power of history is its legitimacy. The rank glorified in history, the one in which history glorified itself, has privileges. The "randomness," the "good fortune" of these privileges cannot simply be erased by adhering to the rationalist rule of equality. Randomness, which to the Enlightenment presented a scandalous threat to reason, and which even Schlegel considered "raw, unformed randomness," is here cast as *good fortune*, which determines the construction of the entire social world. Only he who is counting on that good fortune from the very first and in general (that is, who recognizes nobility as the privileged state of good fortune) is immune to singular "fortunate events." Man "must be in a position to address good fortune thus: I will let you enter into my works; I will let you create a certain apparent irregularity within my calculations, because I know that they will gain in universal and eternal validity what they stand to lose in singular and momentary precision; I will recognize the honoring of the families whom you have distinguished by letting them be the first, and by having them be present at the founding moment of a state without furthering their enterprises in any particular way; I require of their current representatives neither accomplishments, nor industriousness, nor virtuosity, nor talent; what is more, I recognize the fortunate human beings with their fortune as I do the accomplished human beings with their accomplishments . . . I make a pact with good fortune itself, and can thus weather all singular *cases of good fortune*" (1809). Müller was well aware that there is no escape from "raw and unformed" reality, which gains power over man in the form of randomness; he compacts with reality by recognizing a particular kind of historically legitimated randomness in order to remove himself from the grasp of any other kind.

The demand for *equality of human rights*, which regards all human beings only as individuals, makes no sense to Müller for yet another reason: it disregards the fact that not all human beings are individuals. (What is essential therefore is not that all are created equal, but rather that not all

are individuals.) *They only become individuals by being granted citizenship.*
The nobleman, however—and the rural nobleman in particular—is only
part of a larger whole, merely a random and current representative and
deputy of an "estate" that is more permanent than any individual. The
nobility: they are the "comrades by virtue of shared space" [*Raumgenossen*]
who spread across time; they are the element guaranteeing the connected-
ness of past, present, and future, and are thereby vouching for the whole
of a nation that is more than just a synchronous whole. The bourgeois, by
contrast, who commands neither land nor an estate, lives only in the present and therefore puts the continuity of history at risk.

The motivation behind this apology for everything that stands—which
is no less impressive in Müller than in Hegel—may be more readily recognized in the former. Social contract theory, seminally formulated in
Rousseau's *Contrat Social*, conceives the state as something produced by
human individuals.[5] Müller clearly perceived the revolutionary dangers
implied by this theory: human beings will dare to change anything they
regard as merely man-made. All that may be said to *be*, in the proper sense
of the word, is that which has grown organically and cannot be produced.
Müller's polemic is by no means directed only at individualism—that is,
the thesis that the state ultimately rests on individuals—but most of all
at the view that the state is created freely and artificially by "human fiat."
It is the very *notion of artificiality* within natural law that irritates him. He
contrasts it with an entirely different conception of nature, namely that of
the organically grown: that which is whole in the sense of a living being.
Treitschke realized with exceptional clarity that Müller employed this conception of nature for the sake of the most artificial constructions: Müller
"constructed for himself the artifice . . . of a natural social hierarchy."[6]

~~~

The "whole"—this notion (which is also the point of departure for the
Viennese sociologist Spann, who followed in Müller's footsteps) ties Müller
to German Idealism.[7] The concept of the organism—of central importance in Schelling, particularly in his *Naturphilosophie*—has here entered
the realm of political philosophy as a metaphor to the extent that man as
organism is portrayed as the outright model of the nation. Müller is not
alone in proposing this analogy during that time. Steffens and Novalis
regularly talk of nature and nation in the same breath.[8] In Müller's case,
however, the analogy takes on an ideological meaning, with a particular

objective: he wants to assert a metaphysical legitimacy for the stratification and organization of states into social ranks.

This theory of the nation has precious little to do with the nationalism of today. Müller's theses can only be understood as counter-theories—though extremely detailed ones at that—against Karl August von Hardenberg's absolutist tendencies, against "mechanistic" liberalism, and against Adam Smith, whom Müller rapturously adored and critiqued at the same time.[9] In individual cases, Müller spoke out rigorously against every kind of organic and self-motivated movement of nations. His view of the Wars of Liberation as a popular cause was an extremely skeptical one, despite his own organizational role in the Tyrolean uprising. After the Battle of Belle-Alliance, he adopted the absurd view—which had its origins among British Legitimationists—according to which one should simply abstract from Napoleon's existence. On this view, Louis XVIII supposedly had been the legitimate King of France for the last 24 years, since "otherwise the ridiculous right of the people to have a sort of will" would have to be recognized.

In addition, the *organic unity of the nation* for Adam Müller is *by no means a purely worldly* or *political* one. Its ultimate legitimacy is given through the authority of the Church. Its doctrine, to the extent that it is known in the second half of the past century, is considered thoroughly papist (*ultramontan*), and therefore not *völkisch*. Erich Przywara, who contributed an introduction to a selection of Müller's writings edited in 1924, was still in a position to say that "Adam Müller's Christian political philosophy may not have constituted the ultimate solution" but was nevertheless "on a crucial mission to enlighten his contemporaries—drunk on visions of retro-pagan nationalism as they were—about the fact that the redemption of Christ still presented a viable model for all of human life."[10] To be sure, this aspect of Müller's thought is rarely emphasized in today's rediscovery, and equally neglected are his role as philosopher—fitting poorly with the model of the National-Socialist "experiential man"—and his political career and activity, which make a mockery of every one of his own theories.

~

Like Hobbes, Rousseau, Hegel, and Marx, Müller starts out as a political philosopher with an essay on "difference," following the early Kant and Schelling in his presentation of *polarity as the foundational principle of the world*.[11] This essay on the duality of all being, which is seminal in several of its parts, will later serve him as personal legitimation and, in a sense, as the presumptive letter of apology for all of his ambiguities of character. As others will later do on his behalf, Müller explains his infamous offer to Hardenberg in 1809 to "write a journal that was ministerial and oppositional at the same time"—an offer that Hardenberg understandably refused—as a mere verification of his philosophical systematics. This justification seems all the more unlikely for the fact that Müller's life as a whole was in constant contradiction to his doctrine.

To give just one example: Müller chides the liberalist conception of the state for seeing the state as a house that one could move out of at one's own pleasure. State and birth, Müller holds, are binding, and apart from this bond the individual is nothing. For himself, however, he apparently did not consider this thesis—which in its detailed presentation anticipates much of Marx's theory of the inevitable sociality of man (not without reason Müller is often considered the first "sociologist")—to be binding; he changed his citizenship as readily as his religious affiliation and his social rank. The Protestant Prussian bourgeois died a Catholic Austrian nobleman; the advocate of Prussian rural nobility became the Austrian Knight of Rittersdorf. His entire life was a sequence of attempts—some of them successful, others futile—to make his way into higher social strata and sanctioned realms. Naturally, this kind of success was only possible because Müller became the spokesman of every group he joined. His historical function was to intellectualize the anti-bourgeois tendencies, and to introduce them into discussions with the intellectual agility that his bourgeois background afforded him. His transition to the nobility is part of the way that the nobility fended off the bourgeoisie.

After his studies, Müller moved to Berlin—not as just anybody, but already as a protégé of Friedrich von Gentz, older than Müller by a generation. Gentz, translator of Burke, long remained an admirer of the Burke-propagator Müller. Here in Berlin Müller wrote his review of Fichte's "Closed State of Economy," which he compared to Adam Smith's economic theories.[12] This piece is therefore where *English economics and German philosophical speculation* meet for the first time, those two sources necessary for the sustenance of every revolutionary, as a well-known phrase from the mid-nineteenth century has it. Indeed, this emerging doctrine of differences contains elements that will play a crucial role in later revolutionary theories by Feuerbach and Marx.[13] The way in which the restorationist Müller dissolved the Enlightenment concept of the subject is scarcely different from the manner in which the revolutionaries did the same. Feuerbach's theses to the effect that there is no such thing as "man as such" but only man and woman, and that the concept of man implicitly contains its plural, "men"—all of these dissolutions of Enlightenment abstractions are already present in Adam Müller.

~

As vehemently as Müller polemicizes against Fichte, the vigor of this polemic is matched by that directed against Adam Smith, whose economics Müller considers not a national economics, but rather a *system of private economies*. Smith turns everything into movable goods, according to Müller; the essentially immobile national goods (the estates of the nobility) and the non-material goods (the national intellectual life) are not factored in.

His series of conversions begins in the aftermath of this essay: following an invitation by Gentz, Müller goes to Catholic Vienna; he then accepts a position as a tutor on an East Elbian estate. The educational stations have thus become stages of his life. Coming to Dresden in 1806, Müller plays a major role in society, gives public lectures, and has in a sense arrived: his philosophical doctrine of difference is made manifest in the elements that have "formed" his life: "Nobility and bourgeoisie, freedom and law, tradition and letters are opposed to one another" (Bülow).

To be sure, the two elements are now no longer seen as completely equal poles; at this point Müller has already taken sides. Long since converted to Catholicism, he still remains an advocate of Prussian culture, which shows in both his literary and his moral versatility. In addition to Wieland, it is Müller who deserves credit for helping Kleist, with whom he later edited the journal *Phöbus*, to reach an audience.[14] Despite his clearly pro-Austrian leanings at this point, Müller went to Berlin—forced by political upheaval—to give lectures on Frederick the Great, the major representative of the Enlightenment. In Berlin, however, he faced a difficult situation due to Hardenberg's activities against the nobility. The critique of feudalism in Hardenberg's edicts, including the petition of the Kurmärkischen Estates, signed by Ludwig von der Marwitz, was attributed to Adam Müller.

Müller once again went to Vienna where he quickly became submerged in Austrian politics, engaged in forming alliances within Metternich's circle, and was a fixture during the Vienna Congress. His activity was eventually awarded with an appointment as Austrian Consul General in Leipzig. Concurrent with his political activity, particularly concerning the politics of the university, Müller's theologico-political writings now appeared in print, in which he not only treats God and the Church as the ultimate guarantors of politics, but even *interprets the entire hierarchy of the state in Christian terms*—which clearly puts him at odds with many of his followers today. The idea that Christ had died not only for individuals but also for nations was already introduced in his early essay. Now his detailing of the Christian interpretation of the state goes so far as to cast the respective national states of education, defense, and food supply as representations of belief, love, and hope. The hierarchy of the state, which was originally represented as organic and natural, has in the end become a symbolic institution.

~

The recourse of the National-Socialists to Adam Müller is aimed first and foremost at his theory of man within the "community." To be sure, Müller's concept of community—in part biological, historical, and religious—is difficult to grasp. In his last writings, however, it clearly designates a political representation of redemption, as Przywara rightly emphasizes. The individual is unredeemed, and only among others is he "delivered." But this deliverance into the womb of history, of "comrades by virtue of shared space" or fellow dwellers, and of the Church constitutes only the first step toward redemption in the specifically Christian sense. National-Socialism manages to turn that which is intended in a Catholic sense in Müller into something "pagan" and seemingly natural, in the words of Przywara. What remains as the lowest common denominator is a purely formal commonality, insufficient for turning Müller into the figurehead of the current movement.

Originally published as "Adam Müller-Renaissance?" in *Kölnische Zeitung* (September 13, 1932, and September 17, 1932), Unterhaltungsblatt [literary supplement]; translated by Martin Klebes. The occasion for this review was the publication of a selection of Müller's writings edited by Friedrich Bülow under the title *Vom Geiste der Gemeinschaft* (On the Spirit of Community) (Leipzig: Kröner, 1931).
Adam Müller (1779–1829) was a conservative political theorist and economist who belonged to the second generation of German romantics. Among his many writings are *Die Elemente der Staatskunst* (The Elements of the Art of the State, 1809) and *Von der Notwendigkeit einer theologischen Grundlage der gesamten Staatswissenschaften und der Staatswirtschaft insbesondere* (On the Necessity of a Theological Foundation for All Political Science and for the Science of Political Economy in Particular, 1820).—Ed.

§ 5 Berlin Salon

Je serai cet après-diné entre six et sept heures chez vous, chère et aimable Mademoiselle Lévi, pour raisonner et déraisonner avec vous pendant deux heures [I will come by this evening between six and seven, dear and lovely Mademoiselle Lévi, so that we can reason and un-reason together for a couple of hours].—I said to Gentz, that you are a moral midwife who provided one with so gentle and painless a confinement that a tender emotion remained from even the most tormenting ideas.—Until then, be well.

—Louis

Mademoiselle Lévi is Rahel Levin, known in her time as "Little Lévi," later as Rahel Varnhagen or simply Rahel.[1] And Louis is Prussian Prince Louis Ferdinand.[2] The social circle that made this intimate note and many letters possible is known by the name "Berlin Salon."

This Berlin social life had a brief genesis and a short duration. It arose from the "scholarly Berlin" of the Enlightenment, which accounts for its social neutrality. In its effective and representative form, it lasted only from the French Revolution until the outbreak of the unfortunate war.[3] The fact that this society, which was more a product of the Frederickian Enlightenment,[4] was somewhat behind the times accounts for its peculiar isolation and, consequently, its private nature. It encompasses the two classes that have a certain publicity in daily life: actors and the nobility. Those are the two extremes between which the bourgeoisie stands and from which it is in a certain sense excluded. But now an ever more powerful bourgeoisie would begin appropriating those classes to itself. That is evident in the portrayal of Wilhelm Meister, who owes his education [*Bildung*] and orientation in the world to those very two groups; and it is evident, too, in the nobility's practice of entrusting the schooling of their children to bourgeois tutors. It is therefore no coincidence that the first Berlin social circle that was headed by a woman (Henriette Herz), and could therefore rightly be termed a salon, included both Humboldts, who had been educated by the Berlin Enlightenment educator Joachim Heinrich Campe, and the Count Dohna, in whose home Friedrich Schleiermacher had been a tutor.[5]

The social neutrality of the salon corresponds to the social indeterminacy of Berlin Jewry, which could adapt itself at an uncannily rapid rate. The Jews did not now have to free themselves from all possible social ties. From the beginning, they stood entirely outside society. And although Jewish men were to some degree limited by their professions, Jewish women—once they were emancipated—were free from all convention to an extent difficult to imagine today. These Jewish houses, which could feel neither compromised nor genuinely honored, became the meeting places of the intellectual world.

The League of Virtue [*Tugendbund*], brought to life by Henriette Herz in the 1780s, was still completely a product of the Enlightenment. It included both Humboldts, Alexander von Dohna, Carl von Laroche, and Brendel Veit, who later named herself Dorothea Schlegel.[6] Except for Brendel, who was a friend of Henriette Herz's youth, they were all students of Marcus Herz and came regularly to his house for lectures. The two women played the role of older confidantes. The League was based on the pursuit of virtue and on the premise of the equality of all "good" human beings. It is important to note that this idea of the equal rights of all good human beings first gave rise to the kind of indiscretion we have come to regard as typically romantic. All the members of the League were obliged, for example, to show each other important letters, even ones from individuals not known to the rest of the group. The reason for this rule was, as we know from Caroline von Dachröden, "that those people who entrust a secret to us would just as readily entrust it to the rest of the group if they knew them as well as they know us."[7] As Wilhelm von Humboldt's fiancée, Caroline voiced strong objections to this leveling of the individual, which stems from a superficial devotion to Lessing, and she convinced Wilhelm to leave this circle of virtue venerators.[8] The circle fell apart rapidly. Dorothea went to Jena with Friedrich Schlegel; Wilhelm von Humboldt dissolved his ties to the circle as a result of his engagement; Dohna remained as a personal friend of Henriette Herz. Through him she became acquainted with Schleiermacher. What the tone of the League must have been, however, we can gather from a remark Friedrich Schlegel made years later to Caroline Schlegel: "Schleiermacher's association with Henriette Herz is ruining him in himself and for me and for our friendship. . . . They puff up each other's vanity. There is no real pride there but only a silly intoxication, as if from some barbaric punch. They preen themselves for every little exercise of virtue, no matter how paltry. Schleiermacher's mind is shriveling up. He is losing his sense for what is truly great. In short, this damned wallowing in petty emotion is driving me wild!"[9]

About four or five years after the founding of the League of Virtue, Rahel Levin's reputation began to grow. Her circle was the first to separate itself from the Enlightenment and to reveal the emerging consciousness of a new generation that was finding its own mode of expression in its reverence for Goethe. Rahel established the Goethe cult in Berlin, which was fundamentally different from that of the romantics. If it was characteristic for Jena society, at the center of which were the two Schlegel brothers and Caroline Schlegel, that every member of it considered himself and everyone else in it a genius and that Goethe was the prototype and standard of the genius, Goethe's role in the Berlin circle was only that he expressed what everyone else felt: he was their spokesman. Infused with Goethe's spirit, people of the most varied classes and personalities gathered at Rahel's. They formed a circle "for admission to which royal princes, foreign ambassadors, artists, scholars, and businessmen of every rank, countesses, and actresses all vied with the same zeal; and in which each of them acquired neither more nor less value than he himself was able to establish by virtue of his cultivated personality"—thus wrote Brinckmann, the Swedish ambassador in Berlin, to Varnhagen after Rahel's death.[10] The condition for acceptance, then, was "a cultivated personality [*gebildete Persönlichkeit*]." That excludes from the outset the idea that accomplishment or social position could qualify one for membership in the salon. If we let pass in review before us those who frequented Rahel's "attic" in the 1790s, we will see how wide the range of possibilities was and to what extent they were often all held together only by Rahel's *goût* itself. Along with the Jewish doctor David Veit there was von Burgsdorff, the Brandenburg nobleman, who passed his time with that refined dilettantism that from time immemorial had been regarded as the privilege of the aristocracy but now, as self-improvement, acquired new value.[11] Peter von Gualtieri, who belonged to the court circle, had never written anything, and offered nothing but his personal fascination—a welcome social talent.[12] Rahel numbered him among the "four vain ones." How did he find his way to her? "He was capable of experiencing a higher level of suffering than anyone I have ever known before, for he simply could not bear it." This one mark of excellence was enough. Then there was Hans Genelli, a young architect with a mixture of shyness, irony, and impeccable cleanliness that is hard to describe, withal a charm that could make the most serious things appear light and delicate.[13] And the famous actress Unzelmann, who was loved by all; and Henriette Mendelssohn of whom Schlegel said, her "beautiful soul would surely be more beautiful if it were not so exaggeratedly and exclusively beautiful"; the Bohemian Countess Josephine Pachta, who left her husband and lived with a commoner for eighteen years; Countess Karoline von Schlabrendorff, who sometimes wore men's clothes and traveled to Paris with Rahel because she was expecting an illegitimate child.[14] Then Friedrich Gentz; Pauline Wiesel, the lover of Prince Louis Ferdinand; Christel Eigensatz, the actress and lover of Gentz.[15] Friedrich Schlegel, Schleiermacher, Humboldt, Jean Paul, and other major figures sometimes appeared, too; but they were not representative of the tone and nature of this circle.[16]

To educate oneself [*Sich selbst bilden*] was necessary for those whose social traditions had been loosened. Caught up in this process of dissolution were not only the young nobility, who had been enlightened by bourgeois tutors and alienated from the ideals of their own class, yet at the same time could not identify with middle-class ones, but also the recently emancipated Jews who had still not had time enough to form a new tradition. Both were consequently thrown back on their own lives. The veneration and esteem of women that is documented in this salon is the result of taking private life seriously, a realm that appears more congenial to woman by nature than to man—and that was revealed to the public in almost shameless fashion in Schlegel's *Lucinde*.[17]

Initially, this indiscretion was guided in Henriette Herz's League of Virtue by an apparent ideal, namely virtue—even though, for Wilhelm von Humboldt, this ideal pales completely beside the interest in the "interesting human being." Now, in the 1790s, this interest became general. Everything intimate thus acquires a public character; everything public, an intimate one. (Even today, speaking in a mode at once both public and private, we refer to the women who became famous at that time by their first names: Rahel, Bettina, Caroline.)[18] One could be indiscreet because private life lacked the element of intimacy, because private life itself had acquired a public, objective quality. But what is thus forcibly removed from the sphere of intimacy is not so much the individual person and his individuality as his life. "But to me life itself was the assignment," Rahel wrote, much like Wilhelm von Humboldt, who said of himself in his autobiography that his "true sphere is life itself." From this attitude arises that personal historicity that makes one's own life, the data of which can be recorded, into a sequence of objective events, whatever those events may be. If we call this objectification of the personal with Rahel "destiny," we can see the relative modernity of this category, which we take for granted today. Destiny is where one's own life is historicized or, as Rahel says, "when one knows what kind of destiny one has." The noblest example of such a historicized life was that of Goethe, whose works are "fragments of a great confession." "Goethe and life are always one for me; I am working my way into both."

Beyond participation in life, in personal events as such, the bearer of this life is forgotten. Hence the fact that there was a complete absence of selectivity. We consequently have, for example, an extensive correspondence containing innumerable intimate details that Rahel conducted with a certain Rebecca Friedländer,[19] whom Rahel herself described as "pretentious and of an unnatural poverty of spirit."[20] But this person of poor spirit was unhappy, and her unhappiness, her pain, was as it were more real than she herself. The only "consolation" is that what has happened is preserved in the communication of it. "Consolation is dreadful!" Rahel wrote to Friedländer, "but it is your task to convey your pain to the most sympathetic heart." In this way, one can acquire a witness for oneself, a witness who can attest to one's reality when all public esteem has disappeared. "Let *this* be your consolation for the horror you have experienced: that there is a living creature who is a loving witness to our existence. . . ." Bearing witness takes the form of true sympathy with the life of the other. To be a witness to many lives and many events is the only justification for, and the true origin of, this indiscretion and thus for the sociality of the society as such.

The catastrophe of 1806 was a catastrophe for this society as well. The public events, the dimensions of the general misfortune, could no longer be absorbed into the private realm. The intimate was once again separated from the public, and what of the intimate remained "known" became gossip. The possibility of living without social status as an "imaginary romantic person, one to whom true *goût* could be given!"[21] was buried. Rahel never again succeeded in being the focal point of a representative circle without representing something other than herself. As early as 1808 Humboldt wrote from Berlin to his wife that Rahel was completely isolated. "What has become of our time," Rahel wrote to Pauline Wiesel in 1818, "when we were all together. It went under in 1806, went under like a ship, carrying life's loveliest treasures, life's greatest joys."

The salons did not simply cease to exist; they just formed around different people, people of status and name. The best known of these salons are those of Privy Councillor Stägemann, Countess Voß, and Prince Radziwill.[22] They were frequented by Adam Müller, Heinrich von Kleist, Wilhelm von Humboldt, Achim von Arnim, Ferdinand von Schill.[23] The meetings had the character of secret patriotic leagues and were therefore very exclusive. It was typical of them that together with the landed aristocracy, the higher levels of the civil service and the older generation came to the fore again. Until that time, the civil servants had not been able to compete socially with the Jewish salons of Berlin. Adam Müller set the intellectual tone for this older generation and its conservatism. Arnim, Müller, Clemens Brentano—the younger generation of the romantics, born around 1780 and ten to fifteen years younger than Rahel's circle— defined the physiognomy of Berlin society after 1809. In keeping with the pronounced political nature of the new salons, they were not content to be simply salons. They sought instead a form that could bring the members of the circle closer together. A first attempt in this direction was Zelter's Singing Circle, "in which men from all classes of respectable Berlin society came together to cultivate the art of song and further the national idea."[24] This was the origin of that odd mixture—found only in Germany—of patriotism and men's glee clubs. Originally, however, this link was only a disguise to let what was really a political club evade the censors. Wilhelm von Humboldt wrote in 1810: "I was at Zelter's Singing Circle today, but things are too serious there to permit of any singing."

The Christian-German Table Society was the direct descendant of the Singing Circle and counted some of the same figures among its members.[25] Arnim founded it. Brentano, Kleist, and Adam Müller belonged to it, along with members of the aristocracy and the upper ranks of the military and the bureaucracy. This produced a strange transitional organization in which romantic and Prussian elements came together in a brief marriage. The Table Society had established laws and was almost like a club. The romantic element was represented here by means of an unusual institution: it was a rule that at each meeting a serious story would be read that "recounted a relatively unknown incident demonstrating patriotic loyalty and courage."[26] Immediately on the heels of this story came a comic one that retold the same story but gave it an ironic or grotesque twist. This romantic impulse to treat serious attitudes ironically was still tolerated by the group. The main requirements for admission were that the candidate not be "a Jew, a Frenchman, or a philistine." The tossing to-gether of Jews, Frenchmen, and philistines seems odd at first glance. But what it indicates—apart from the predictable anti-Semitism of the aris-tocracy and the predictable hostility toward the French of the patriots—is that the three groups are representatives of the Enlightenment. Karl Au-gust von Hardenberg, because of his reform initiatives, was the prototype of the philistine; Goethe, the prototype of the non-philistine. Everything we know about the anti-philistine ideology of this society can be found in Brentano's essay "The Philistine Before, In, and After History."²⁷ There we learn that philistines "scorn old folk festivals and legends and every-thing that, somehow preserved from the impudence of modern ways, has grown gray with age," "that they constantly busy themselves with destroy-ing everything that gives their fatherland a distinctive, individual charac-ter." "They call Nature anything that falls within the sphere of their vision, or, rather, the square of their vision, because they can comprehend only four-sided things. . . . A beautiful landscape, they say, nothing but thoroughfares! They prefer Voltaire to Shakespeare, Wieland to Goethe, Ramler to Klopstock; Voss is their favorite of all time."²⁸ France was seen as the classic country of the Enlightenment, and the Jews owed entirely to the Enlightenment and its belief in equal rights for all men the arguments for social emancipation and the demand for the equality of Jews as citi-zens. Then, too, women were excluded from the Table Society, which can be read as a direct protest against the earlier salons. Altogether character-istic of the style of the meetings is that they were held at the noon meal, in contrast to the salons that came together at tea time or in the evening. It is a crucial difference whether one drinks beer or tea. For the Prussian aristocracy, this strange union of romanticism and Prussian patriotism would find its natural end in the wars of liberation, and for the romantics in the romantic conversions to Catholicism.

The Varnhagen salon of the 1820s was no longer representative of the intelligentsia. Rahel Levin, as Frau Varnhagen von Ense, became a mem-ber of society, and her social contacts were therefore essentially deter-mined for her. She was acutely aware of that. She still maintained some important friendships—Heinrich Heine was one of them—and some major figures of the time still found her fascinating. But her essentially conventional invitations no longer carried any special significance.²⁹ When Rahel died, her first salon had been scattered for twenty-five years. Some of its members had sunk into anonymity; some had gone over to the

Table Society; some had been converted; the best of them, like Prince Louis and Alexander von der Marwitz, had died in the wars.[30] The only person who remained to her from earlier times was the one who from the very beginning had stood outside any given intellectual, political, or social order: Pauline Wiesel. Nothing of the original sociality was left over—except that which had always stood outside of society.[31]

Originally published in German as "Berliner Salon" in *Deutscher Almanach für das Jahr 1932* (Leipzig: Reklam) 173–84; translation by Robert and Rita Kimber for *Essays in Understanding*, 57–65. I have slightly altered the translation for this volume.

As a postscript to her essay, Arendt published and annotated a long letter Rahel Varnhagen wrote to Pauline Wiesel on June 8, 1826 ("Brief Rahels an Pauline Wiesel," *Deutscher Almanach für das Jahr 1932*, 185–90). Some of Arendt's notes are included in the notes to this essay.—Ed.

§ 6 Review of Hans Hagen, *Rilke's Revisions*

This study provides a fairly complete set of materials for an interpretation of Rilke's revisions. Most importantly, it facilitates a quick orientation by virtue of its very detailed synopsis of earlier and later drafts.

The interpretation itself aspires to be "a contribution to the psychology of his poetic creativity." From the beginning, it analyzes the revisions as an expression of particular ways in which Rilke changed his mind. In this regard, the author disappoints the reader at the outset by devoting only one chapter to what he first defines as his task. To be sure, as Hagen already emphasizes in the introduction: "In contrast to this developmental principle, this study is based on a belief in the vital self-unfolding of Rilke the mystic, who speaks to us from all of his genuinely personal works." For an unprejudiced observer, it is equally hard to grasp what revisions are supposed to be—especially from a psychological point of view—if not symptoms of a development, and how the author understands the word *mystic*. Even though the word recurs frequently, the only thing the reader can ascertain is that the author takes Rilke to be a mystic: "Rilke just is a dyed-in-the-wool mystic," Hagen declares, hoping that the "educated" reader will be able to make something or other of this statement.

Unfortunately, the terminology becomes altogether incomprehensible when the study discusses Rodin; this is regrettable because Hagen appears at this point to come very close to grasping the root of Rilke's revisions.

Hans Wilhelm Hagen. *Rilkes Umarbeitungen.* Leipzig: Eichblatt, 1931. 138 pp.

Elucidating the significance of Rodin—and especially his imperative, "il faut travailler toujours" [it is always necessary to work]—is an absolutely crucial task for any understanding of Rilke's own work.[1] The author duti- fully notes the importance of the "il faut travailler toujours" especially for the revisions; but unfortunately, he does not go beyond this remark. After all, simply noting that "Rodin constituted Rilke's experience of artistic- psychological creation, and Cézanne . . . that of aesthetic composition" is no explanation: only the contemplation of artistic creation can be psycho- logical, not the creation itself; artistic composition, in turn, is never aes- thetic.[2]

The second chapter, which supposedly treats "The Revisions in Their Aesthetic Context," tries the reader's patience. Hagen includes a number of very beautiful poems and expresses his boundless admiration by prais- ing "how delicate [Rilke's] ability to discern rhythmic differences is," "how deep" he supposedly is, and "how infinitely delicate Rilke's eye for the whole of a collection of poems" appears. If Rilke had had no ability to discern rhythmic differences, he would have been a bad poet, and an in- terpretation of his work would have been superfluous. Hymnic praise of this sort, camouflaged as interpretation, is simply embarrassing.

The third chapter, "The Revisions in Their Psychological Context," does not offer anything that could not have been included—or wasn't already included—in the first chapter, with which it forms a thematic unity. The fourth and final chapter is ambitiously titled "The Revisions in Their Philosophical Context," and displays such a confusion of concepts and objects that even criticism seems pointless.

Originally published in *Zeitschrift für Ästhetik und allgemeine Kunstwissenschaft* 28 (1934): 111–12; translated by Martin Klebes.

Hans Wilhelm Hagen was a German historian and literary critic who was also in- volved in politics.—Ed.

§ 7 Review of Käte Hamburger, *Thomas Mann and Romanticism*

This study attempts to find a relationship between Thomas Mann and romanticism.[1] The author's prophylactically expressed concern, however, "that unrelated things are here forced together," does not in itself justify the "and" in the title. Examining both elements side by side would be legitimate only if the real, i.e. historical connections were established, and Mann were likewise presented as the intellectual heir of the romantics. Picking out historically neutral similarities is a distortion of history and thus misrepresents both elements of the comparison. The author, however, rejects the notion of an historical study. She emphasizes that her aim is not "proof of a direct influence" of romantic writings as sources for Mann; she only claims to provide "more general [proof] that the intellectual heritage and attitude bequeathed by the romantics has become such an integral part of German intellectual life that its principal problematic has been reshaped in the work of the modern writer Thomas Mann, and not in his work alone." The fact that romanticism has become part of the German tradition, and that Thomas Mann is part of that tradition, is self-evident enough for a "more general proof " to be superfluous.

The framing of the topic therefore appears to be misguided from the outset. This impression is bolstered by an entirely imprecise use of the word "romantic" that is derived only from "educated" small-talk: "visualizing the work of this . . . writer hardly gives us a romantic feeling, so to

---

Käte Hamburger, *Thomas Mann und die Romantik*. Berlin: Juncker & Dünnhaupt, 1932.

speak." Hamburger cannot expect the term to gain clarity simply by opposing it to two others, namely "chiseled" and "plastic." The "traditional problematic" common to both is identified by the author primarily as the "irresolvable connection between life and death." This connection has remained a persistent central theme over the past 3000 years, as far as we can tell; the author, however, believes that this irresolvable connection constitutes the "problem of every view of life whose orientation is primarily irrational." This is not only unclear, but an error.

Hamburger's book is not completely devoid of scholarly references. Those provided by her, however, are references in just that methodological sense rejected by her in the beginning of the book, providing proof of direct influence through sources. (See for example p. 56ff.)

Originally published in *Zeitschrift für Ästhetik und allgemeine Kunstwissenschaft* 28 (1934): 297–98; translated by Martin Klebes.
Käte Hamburger (1896–1992) was a literary critic who later achieved wide recognition for attempts to describe the "logic of poetry."—Ed.

§ 8 Stefan Zweig

Jews in the World of Yesterday

A hundred and thirty five years ago Rahel Varnhagen jotted down the following dream: she had died and gone to heaven, together with her friends Bettina von Arnim and Caroline von Humboldt. In order to relieve themselves of the burdens they acquired in their lives, the three friends assigned themselves the task of inquiring into the worst things they had experienced. Rahel thus asked: Did you know disappointed love? The other two women broke into tears, and all three thus relieved this burden from their hearts. Rahel asked further: Did you know disloyalty? Sickness? Worry? Anxiousness? Each time the women said "yes," as they cried, and once again all three were relieved of their burdens. Finally Rahel asked: did you know disgrace? As soon as this word had been spoken, there was a hushed silence, and the two friends took their distance from Rahel and looked at her in a disturbed and strange manner. Then did Rahel know that she was entirely alone and that this burden could not be taken away from her heart. And then she woke up.

Disgrace and honor are political concepts, categories of public life. In the world of culture [*Bildung*], cultural goings-on [*Kulterbetriebes*], and purely private existence, it is just as impossible to get a handle on these categories as in the life of business. Businessmen know only success or failure, and their disgrace is poverty. The literati know only fame or obscurity, and their disgrace is anonymity. Stefan Zweig was a man of

---

Occasioned by *The World of Yesterday: An Autobiography,* by Stefan Zweig (New York: The Viking Press, 1943).

letters, and in his last book he describes the world of the literati—a world in which he had once acquired *Bildung* and fame. A friendly fate protected him from poverty, a favorable star from anonymity. Concerned only with his personal dignity, he had kept himself so completely aloof from politics that, in retrospect, the catastrophe of the last ten years seemed to him like a lightning bolt from the sky, as if it were a monstrous, inconceivable natural disaster. In the midst of this disaster, he tried to safeguard his dignity and bearing as well and as long as he could. He considered it unbearably humiliating when the hitherto wealthy and respected citizens of Vienna had to go begging for visas to countries which only a few weeks before they would have been unable even to find on the map. That he himself, only yesterday so famous and welcome a guest in foreign countries, should also belong to this miserable host of the homeless and suspect was simply hell on earth. But deeply as the events of 1933 had changed his personal existence, they had no effect on his basic attitude with respect to the world and to his own life. He continued to boast of his unpolitical point of view; it never occurred to him that, politically speaking, it might be an honor for him to stand outside the law when all men were no longer equal before it.¹ What he sensed—and did not hide from himself—was that during the 1930s the better classes in Germany and elsewhere were steadily yielding to Nazi precepts and discriminating against those whom the Nazis proscribed and banned.²

Not one of his reactions during all this period was the result of political convictions; they were all dictated by his hypersensitivity to social humiliation. Instead of hating the Nazis, he just wanted to annoy them. Instead of despising those of his coterie who had been *gleichgeschaltet,* he thanked Richard Strauss for continuing to accept his libretti.³ Instead of fighting, he kept silent, happy that his books had not been immediately banned. And later, though comforted by the thought that his works were removed from German bookstores together with those of equally famous authors, this could not reconcile him to the fact that his name had been pilloried by the Nazis like that of a "criminal," and that the famous Stefan Zweig had become the Jew Zweig. Like so many of his less sensible, less talented, and less endangered colleagues, he failed to perceive that the dignified restraint, which society had so long considered a criterion of true *Bildung,* was under such circumstances tantamount to plain cowardice in public life. And he likewise failed to perceive that the distinction that had so effectively and for so long protected him from all kinds of unpleasant and embarrassing events would suddenly give rise to an endless series of humiliations that really did make his life into hell.

Before Stefan Zweig took his own life, he recorded—with the pitiless accuracy that springs from the coldness of genuine despair—what the world had given him and then done to him.[4] He records the pleasure of fame and the curse of humiliation. He tells of the paradise from which he had been banished—the paradise of cultured [*gebildeten*] enjoyment, of meetings with like-minded and equally famous people, of infinite interest in the dead geniuses of humanity; penetrating into their private lives and gathering their personal relics was the most enjoyable pursuit of an inactive existence. And then he tells of how he suddenly found himself facing a reality in which there was nothing left to enjoy, in which those as famous as himself either avoided him or pitied him, and in which cultured [*gebildete*] curiosity about the past was continuously and unbearably disturbed by the tumult of the present, the murderous thunder of bombardment, the infinite humiliation at the hands of the authorities.

Gone, destroyed forever, was that other world in which, *"frühgereift und zart und traurig"* (Hofmannsthal),[5] one had established oneself so comfortably; razed was the "reservation" for the chosen few, the living and the dead, who had taste and honored art; broken were the trellises that kept out the *profanum vulgus* of the uncultured more effectively than a Chinese wall. With that world had passed also its counterpart, that society of famous young men, among whom, astonishingly enough, one hoped to discover "real life": the bohemians. For the young son of a bourgeois household, craving escape from parental protection, the bohemians from whom he was completely separated by essential things (the bohemians, after all, only rarely combed their hair and when they did, they weren't happy about it, and anyway they could never pay for their coffee) became identified with men experienced in the adversities of life. For the arriviste, those "unarrived," who only dreamt of large editions of their works, became the symbol of unrecognized genius and the example of the dreadful fate that "real life" could prepare for hopeful young men.

Naturally, the world that Zweig depicts was anything but *the* world of yesterday; naturally, the author of this book did not actually live in the world, only on its rim. The gilded trellises of this peculiar sanctuary were very thick, depriving the inmates of every view and every insight that could disturb their enjoyment. Not once does Zweig mention the most ominous manifestations of the years after the First World War, which struck his native Austria more violently than any other European country: unemployment. But the rare value of his document is not in the least lessened by the fact that, for us today, the trellises behind which these people spent their lives and to which they owed their extraordinary feeling of security seem little different from the walls of a prison or a ghetto. It is astounding, even spooky, that there were still people living among us whose ignorance was so great and whose conscience was so pure that they could continue to look on the prewar period with the eyes of the nineteenth century and could regard the impotent pacifism of Geneva and the treacherous lull before the storm, between 1924 and 1933, as a return to normalcy. But it is admirable and gratifying that at least one of these men had the courage to record it all in detail, without hiding or prettifying anything. Zweig finally realized what fools they all had been, even if he never gained insight into the connection between their misfortune and their folly.

The same period that Zweig calls the "Golden Age of Security" was described by his contemporary Charles Péguy (shortly before he fell in the First World War) as the era in which political forms that were presumably outmoded lived on with inexplicable monotony: in Russia, anachronistic despotism; in Austria, the corrupt bureaucracy of the Habsburgs; in Germany, the militarist and stupid regime of the Junkers, hated by the liberal middle class and the workers alike; in France, the Third Republic, which was granted twenty-odd years more despite its chronic crises. The solution to the puzzle lay in the fact that Europe was much too busy expanding its economic radius for any social stratum or nation to take political questions seriously.[6] For fifty years—before the opposing economic interests burst into national conflicts, sucking the political systems of all Europe into their vortex—political representation had become a kind of theatrical performance, sometimes an operetta, of varying quality. Simultaneously, in Austria and Russia, the theater became the focus of national life for the upper ten-thousand.

During the "Golden Age of Security" a peculiar dislocation of the balance of power occurred. The enormous development of all industrial and economic potential produced the steady weakening of purely political factors, while at the same time economic forces grew dominant in the international play of power. Power became synonymous with economic potential, which could bring government to its knees. This was the real reason why governments played ever-narrowing and empty representative roles, which grew more and more obviously theatrical and operetta-like. The Jewish bourgeoisie, in sharp contrast to their German and Austrian equivalents, were uninterested in positions of power, even of the economic kind. They were content with their accumulated wealth, happy in the security and peace that their wealth seemed to guarantee. An increasing number of their sons from well-to-do homes deserted commercial life, since the empty accumulation of wealth was senseless. The consequence of this situation was that within a few decades both Germany and Austria saw a great number of their cultural enterprises, such as newspapers, publishing houses, and the theater fall into Jewish hands.

Had the Jews of western and central European countries displayed even a modicum of concern for the political realities of their times, they would have had reason enough not to feel secure. For, in Germany, the first anti-Semitic parties arose during the 1880s; Treitschke made anti-Semitism "fit for the salon." The turn of the century brought the Lueger-Schoenerer agitation in Austria, ending with the election of Lueger as mayor of Vienna. And in France the Dreyfus Affair dominated both internal and foreign policies for years.[7] Even as late as 1940 Zweig could admire Lueger as an "able leader" and a kindly person whose "official anti-Semitism never stopped him from being helpful and friendly to his former Jewish friends." Among the Jews of Vienna no one took anti-Semitism, in the amiable Austrian version Lueger represented, seriously—with the exception of the "crazy" feuilleton editor of the *Neue Freie Presse,* Theodor Herzl.[8]

At least, so it would appear at first glance. Closer examination changes the picture. After Treitschke had made anti-Semitism fit for the salon, conversion ceased to be a ticket of admission to non-Jewish circles in Germany and Austria. Just how anti-Semitic "better society" had become could not be easily ascertained by the Jewish businessmen of Austria, for they pursued only commercial interests and cared nothing about invitations to non-Jewish groups. But their children discovered soon enough that in order for a Jew to be fully accepted into society there was one and only one thing to do: become famous.

There is no better document of the Jewish situation in this period than the opening chapters of Zweig's book. They provide the most impressive evidence of how fame and the will to fame motivated the youth of his generation. Their ideal was the genius that seemed incarnate in Goethe. Every Jewish youth able to rhyme passably played the young Goethe, as everyone able to draw a line was a future Rembrandt, and every musical child was a demonic Beethoven. The more cultured the parental homes, the more coddled were these imitative *Wunderkinder*. Nor did this stop with poetry; it dominated every detail of personal life. They felt as sublime as Goethe, imitated his "Olympian" aloofness from politics; they collected rags and gewgaws that had once belonged to famous people of other periods; and they strove to come into direct touch with every living period of renown, as if a tiny reflection of fame would thus fall upon them—or as if one could prepare for fame by attending a school of notoriety.

Of course, the idolatry of genius was not restricted to the Jews. It was a gentile, Gerhardt Hauptmann, who, as is well known, carried this idolatry as far as to make himself look, if not like Goethe, at least like one of the many cheap busts of the master.[9] And if the parallel enthusiasm that the German petty bourgeoisie showed for Napoleonic splendor did not actually produce Hitler, it contributed mightily to the hysterical raptures with which this "great man" was greeted by many German and Austrian intellectuals.

Although deification of the "great man," without much consideration for what he actually achieved, was a general disease of the era, it assumed a special form among the Jews: it was particularly passionate with regard to the great men of culture. In any case, the school of fame that the Jewish youth of Vienna attended was the theater; the image of fame that they held before them was that of the actor.

Again a qualification is in order. In no other European city did the theater ever acquire the same significance that it had in Vienna during the period of political dissolution. Zweig recounts how the death of a famous court actress made his family cook, who had never heard or seen her, burst into tears. Simultaneously, as political activity began to resemble theater or operetta, the theater itself developed into a kind of national institution, the actor into a national hero. Since the world had undeniably acquired a theatrical air, the theater could appear as the world of reality. It is hard for us today to believe that even Hugo von Hofmannsthal fell under the spell of this theater hysteria and for many years believed that behind the Viennese absorption in the theater lay something of the Athenian public spirit.[10] He overlooked the fact that Athenians attended the theater for the sake of the play, its mythological content, and the grandeur of its language, through which they hoped to become masters of the passions and molders of their national destiny. The Viennese went to the theater exclusively for the actors; playwrights wrote for this or that performer; critics discussed only the actor or its parts; directors accepted or rejected plays purely on the basis of effective roles for their matinee idols. The star system, as the cinema later perfected it, was completely forecast in Vienna. What was in the making there was not a classical renaissance but Hollywood.

Whereas political conditions made this inversion of being and appearance possible, Jews were the ones who brought into existence this world of appearance, supplied the public demand, and spread the fame. And since the European world, not unjustifiably, considered Austrian backstage culture representative of the whole period, Zweig is not wrong when he proudly asserts that "nine-tenths of what the world celebrated as Viennese culture in the nineteenth century was promoted, nourished, or even created by Viennese Jewry."

A culture built around an actor or virtuoso established standards that were as novel as they were dubious. "Posterity weaves no wreaths for the mime," and so the mime requires an incredible amount of present fame and applause. His well-known vanity is, as it were, an occupational disease. To the degree that every artist dreams of leaving his mark on future generations, of transporting his period into another, the artistic impulses of virtuosi and actors are forever frustrated and require hysterical outlets. Since the actor must renounce immortality, his criterion of greatness depends altogether on contemporary success. Contemporary success was also the only criterion that remained for the "geniuses in general," who were detached from their achievements and considered only in the light of "greatness in itself." In the field of letters this took the form of biographies describing no more than the appearance, the emotions, and the demeanor of great men. This approach not only satisfied vulgar curiosity about the kind of secrets a man's valet would know; it was prompted by the belief that such idiotic abstraction would clarify the essence of greatness. In their respect for "greatness in itself" Jews and Gentiles stood side by side. That was why Jewish organizations of most cultural enterprises, and particularly of the theatrical culture of Vienna, could go on without restraint, and even become in a sense the epitome of European culture.

Stefan Zweig's thorough knowledge of history preserved him from adopting this yardstick without any qualms. Yet, despite his "connoisseurship," this knowledge could not prevent him from simply ignoring the greatest poets of the postwar period, Franz Kafka and Bertolt Brecht, neither of whom were ever great successes. Nor could it prevent him from confusing the historical significance of writers with the size of their editions: "Hofmannsthal, Arthur Schnitzler, Beer-Hofmann and Peter Altenberg gave Viennese literature European standing such as it had not possessed under Grillparzer and Stifter."[11] Precisely because Zweig was modest about himself, discreetly glossing over the uninteresting personal data in his autobiography, the repeated enumeration of famous people he met in his life or entertained at home is especially striking. It seems like exact proof that even the best of those cultured Jews could not escape the curse of their time—the worship of that great leveling idol, Success. Nothing does more harm to a highly differentiated sensibility than the comic vanity that, without any principle of selection and without any sense for differences, drops as many famous names as possible. In his guest book at Salzburg, Zweig gathered "eminent contemporaries" as passionately as he had collected the handwriting and relics of dead poets, musicians, and scientists. His own success, the benign renown of his own accomplishments, failed to sate the appetite of a vanity that could hardly have originated in his character. Presumably his character found it repulsive, but this vanity was solidly rooted in the depths of a conviction that formed its own *Weltanschauung*—the conviction that began with the search for the "born genius" or "poet made flesh" and considers life worth living only insofar as it plays itself out in the midst of an atmosphere of fame among a chosen elite.

Incomplete satisfaction in one's own success, the attempt rather to transform fame into a social atmosphere, to create a caste of famous men, to organize a society of well-known people—these were the traits that distinguished the Jews of the period and differentiated their manner from the general genius-lunacy of the times. This attempt also explains why the world of art, literature, music, and the theater fell, as it were, right into their hands. They alone were really more interested in those things than even in their own personal products or their own fame.

For, just as the Jewish generation from the time of the turn of the century achieved economic security, they acquired equal rights as a matter of course; at the same time, however, their situation in society was equally questionable, their social position equally insecure and ambiguous. Seen from the perspective of society, they were and remained pariahs as long as they failed to make themselves fit for the salon by some extraordinary means such as fame. With regard to a famous Jew, society would forget its unwritten law. Zweig's "radiant power of fame" was a very real social force, in whose aura one could move freely and could even have anti-Semites as friends, such as Richard Strauss and Karl Haushofer.[12] Fame and success offered the means for the socially homeless to create a home and an environment for themselves. Since great success transcended national borders, famous people could easily become the representatives of a nebulous international society, where national prejudice appeared to be no longer valid. In any case, a famous Austrian Jew was more apt to be accepted as an Austrian in France than in Austria. The world citizenship of this generation, this remarkable nationality that its members claimed as soon as their Jewish origin was mentioned, somewhat resembles those modern passports that grant the bearer the right of sojourn in every country except the one that issued it.

This international society of famous people was punctured for the first time in 1914 and finally buried in 1933. It is all to Zweig's credit that he never allowed himself to be fooled into participating in the universal war hysteria. He remained loyal to his principles and kept his distance from politics; he never yielded to the temptation that afflicted so many literati—the temptation of using the war to establish a place in society outside of the circle of international intelligence. It thus came about that, for him, the remnants of this pre-war society preserved itself throughout the war. And it is well-known that in the 1920s, which is to say, in the years to which Zweig owes his greatest success, the international society of fame once again functioned in Europe. After 1938 Zweig learned, however, some bitter lessons: that this international society, including the rights of its citizenry, depended on the possession of a very national passport, and that, for the stateless, there is no "international" anything.

The international society of the successful was the only one in which Jews enjoyed equal rights. Little wonder, then, that the most meager talents developed quite happily; still less that, for them, "the most beautiful odor on earth, sweeter than the rose of Schirach, [was] the smell of printers' ink." There was nothing in their lives more joyous than the printing of a book, the reviews, the complimentary copies, the translations into foreign languages. It was an always renewing ritual of placing-oneself-in-relation to a world where one gets one's name into print so as to be recognized.

The fame that gave the social pariah something like the rights to a homeland in the international elite of the successful brought another privilege, which, according to Zweig's own judgment, was at least equally important—the suspension of anonymity, the possibility of being recognized by unknown people, of being admired by strangers. Even if one fell back into anonymity for a time, fame stood like a solid suit of armor that one could mount again at any moment in order to protect oneself from the terrible effects of life. There is no question that Zweig feared nothing more than sinking back into an obscurity where, stripped of his fame, he would become again what he had been at the beginning of his life—except that now everything would be different and much worse: he would be no more than one of the many unfortunates who are confronted with the almost insuperable problem of conquering, bedazzling, and forcing oneself onto a strange, uncanny world—which is precisely how society must look to anyone who does not belong to it from birth and to all those against whom it discriminates.

Fate, in the form of a political catastrophe, eventually did almost thrust him into this very anonymity. Robbed of his fame, he knew—better than many of his colleagues—that the fame of a writer flickers out when he cannot write and publish in his own language. His collections were stolen from him, and with them, so, too, was his intimate association with the famous dead. His house in Salzburg was stolen, and with it, so, too, was his association with the famous men among the living. Stolen, finally, too, was the invaluable passport, which had not only enabled him to represent his native land in other countries but had also helped him to evade the questionable character of his civic existence in that native land itself.

And again, as during the First World War, it is to Zweig's credit that he was neither enflamed by the universal hysteria nor beguiled by his newly acquired British citizenship. He could hardly have represented England in other countries. Since, finally, the international society of the famous disappeared completely with the Second World War, this homeless man lost the only world in which he had once had the delusion of a home.

In a last article, "The Great Silence" (ONA, March 9, 1942), written shortly before his death,[13] he tried to take a political stand—for the first time in all of these years. The word Jew does not occur to him, for Zweig strove once more to represent Europe—more exactly, central Europe—now that it was shocked into silence. Had he spoken about the terrible fate of his own people, he would have been closer to all the European peoples who are today, in battle against their oppressors, struggling against the persecutors of the Jews. The European peoples know—better than did this self-appointed spokesman who had never in his whole lifetime concerned himself with their political destiny—that yesterday is not detached from today, "as if a man had been hurled down from a great height as the result of a violent blow." For, to them, yesterday was in no way that "century whose progress, whose science, whose art, and whose magnificent inventions were the pride and the faith of us all."

Without the protective clothing of fame, naked and disrobed, Stefan Zweig was confronted with the reality of the Jewish people. There had been various escapes from social pariahdom, including the ivory tower of fame. But only flight around the globe could offer salvation from political outlawry [*Außerhalb-des-Gesetzes-Stehen*]. This defamation was a disgrace to those who wanted to remain at peace with the political and social value-standards of their time. There is no doubt that this is precisely what Stefan Zweig, all his life, had trained himself for: to live at peace with the world and his surroundings; to abstain in a noble fashion from struggles and from all politics. In the mind of the world with which Zweig wanted to make his peace, it was and is a disgrace to be a Jew—a disgrace that current society does not directly punish with death but with defamation, a disgrace from which there is no longer an individual escape into international fame but, rather, only an escape into a political attitude and a struggle for the honor of the entire people.[14]

Originally published as "Stefan Zweig: Juden in der Welt von gestern," in *Sechs Essays* (Heidelberg: Schneider, 1948), 112–27; reprinted in *Die vorborgene Tradition: Acht Essays* (Frankfurt am Main: Suhrkamp, 1976), 74–87; translated by Susannah Young-ah Gottlieb. An earlier English version appeared under the title "Portrait of a Period" in *The Menorah Journal* 31 (1943): 307–14; reprinted in *The Jew as Pariah: Jewish Identity and Politics in the Modern Age*, ed. and intro. Ron H. Feldman (New York: Grove, 1978), 112–21.

Stefan Zweig (1881–1942) was a prolific Austrian-Jewish writer who achieved great literary fame in the 1920s and 1930s as a poet, novelist, dramatist, biographer, and translator. He referred to his Jewishness as an accident of birth. Among his best known works are the stories collected in *Amok;* his chess novella, *The Royal Game;* and the autobiography Arendt is here reviewing, *The World of Yesterday*. Zweig committed suicide in Brazil in 1942 along with his second wife, Charlotte Altmann.—Ed.

§ 9 The Jew as Pariah

A Hidden Tradition

When it comes to claiming its own in the field of European arts and letters, the attitude of the Jewish people may best be described as one of reckless magnanimity. With a grand gesture and without a murmur of protest it has calmly allowed the credit for its great writers and artists to go to other peoples, itself receiving in return (in punctiliously regular payments) the doubtful privilege of being acclaimed father of every notorious swindler and mountebank. True enough, there has been a tendency in recent years to compile long lists of European worthies who might conceivably claim Jewish descent, but such lists are more in the nature of mass-graves for the forgotten than of enduring monuments to the remembered and cherished. Useful as they may be for purposes of propaganda (offensive as well as defensive), they have not succeeded in reclaiming for the Jews any single writer of note unless he happened to have written specifically in Hebrew or Yiddish. Those who really did most for the spiritual dignity of their people, who were great enough to transcend the bounds of nationality and to weave the strands of their Jewish genius into the general texture of European life, have been given short shrift and perfunctory recognition. With the growing tendency to conceive of the Jewish people as a series of separate territorial units and to resolve its history into so many regional chronicles and parochial records, its great figures have been left perforce to the tender mercies of assimilationist propagandists—to be exploited only in order to bolster selfish interests or furnish alleged illustrations of dubious ideologies.

No one fares worse from this process than those bold spirits who tried to make of the emancipation of the Jews that which it really should have been—an admission of Jews *as Jews* to the ranks of humanity, rather than a permit to ape the gentiles or an opportunity to play the *parvenu*. Realizing only too well that they did not enjoy political freedom nor full admission to the life of nations, but that, instead, they had been separated from their own people and lost contact with the simple natural life of the common man, these men yet achieved liberty and popularity by the sheer forces of imagination. As individuals they started an emancipation of their own, of their own hearts and brains. Such a conception was, of course, a gross misconstruction of what emancipation had been intended to be; but it was also a vision, and out of the impassioned intensity with which it was evinced and expressed it provided the fostering soil on which Jewish creative genius could grow and contribute its products to the general spiritual life of the Western world.

That the status of the Jews in Europe has been not only that of an oppressed people but also of what Max Weber has called a "pariah people" is a fact most clearly appreciated by those who have had practical experience of just how ambiguous is the freedom which emancipation has ensured, and how treacherous the promise of equality which assimilation has held out.[1] In their own position as social outcasts such men reflect the political status of their entire people. It is therefore not surprising that out of their personal experience Jewish poets, writers, and artists should have been able to evolve the concept of the pariah as a human type—a concept of supreme importance for the evaluation of mankind in our day and one which has exerted upon the gentile world an influence in strange contrast to the spiritual and political ineffectiveness which has been the fate of these men among their own brethren. Indeed, the concept of the pariah has become traditional, even though the tradition be but tacit and latent, and its continuance automatic and unconscious. Nor need we wonder why: for over a hundred years the same basic conditions have obtained and evoked the same basic reaction.

However slender the basis out of which the concept was created and out of which it was progressively developed, it has nevertheless loomed larger in the thinking of assimilated Jews than might be inferred from standard Jewish histories. It has endured, in fact, from Salomon Maimon in the eighteenth century to Franz Kafka in the early twentieth.[2] But out of the variety of forms which it has assumed we shall here select four, in each of which it expresses an alternative portrayal of the Jewish people. Our first type will be Heinrich Heine's *schlemihl* and "lord of dreams"

(*Traumweltherrscher*); our second, Bernard Lazare's "conscious pariah";[3] our third, Charlie Chaplin's grotesque portrayal of the suspect;[4] and our fourth, Franz Kafka's poetic vision of the fate of the man of goodwill. Between these four types there is a significant connection—a link which in fact unites all genuine concepts and sound ideas when once they achieve historical actuality.

1. Heinrich Heine: The Schlemihl and Lord of Dreams

In his poem, *Princess Sabbath*, the first of his *Hebrew Melodies*, Heinrich Heine depicts for us the national background from which he sprang and which inspired his verses. He portrays his people as a fairy prince turned by witchcraft into a dog. A figure of ridicule throughout the week, every Friday night he suddenly regains his mortal shape, and freed from the preoccupations of his canine existence (*von hündischen Gedanken*), goes forth like a prince to welcome the sabbath bride and to greet her with the traditional hymeneal, *Lecha Dodi.*[5]

This poem, we are informed by Heine, was especially composed for the purpose by the people's poet—the poet who, by a stroke of fortune, escapes the grueling weekly transformation of his people and who continually leads the Sabbath-like existence which is to Heine the only positive mark of Jewish life.

Poets are characterized in greater detail in Part IV of the poem, where Heine speaks of Yehudah Halevi. They are said to be descended from "Herr Schlemihl ben Zurishaddai"—a name taken from Shelumiel ben Zurishaddai mentioned in the biblical Book of Numbers as the leader of the tribe of Simeon. Heine related his name to the word *schlemihl* by the humorous supposition that by standing too close to his brother chieftain Zimri he got himself killed accidentally when the latter was beheaded by the priest Phinehas for dallying with a Midianite woman (cf. Numbers, 25:6–15). But if they may claim Shelumiel as their ancestor, they must also claim Phinehas—the ruthless Phinehas whose

> ". . . spear is with us,
> And above our heads unpausing
> We can hear its fatal whizzing
> And the noblest hearts it pierces."
>
> (*Trans. Leland*)

History preserves to us no "deeds heroic" of those "noblest hearts." All we know is that—they were *schlemihls*.

Innocence is the hall-mark of the *schlemihl*. But it is of such innocence that a people's poets—its "lords of dreams"—are born. No heroes they and no stalwarts, they are content to seek their protection in the special tutelage of an ancient Greek deity. For did not Apollo, that "inerrable god-head of delight," proclaim himself once for all the lord of *schlemihls* on the day when—as the legend has it—he pursued the beauteous Daphne only to receive for his pains a crown of laurels? To be sure, times have changed since then, and the transformation of the ancient Olympian has been described by Heine himself in his poem *The God Apollo*. This tells of a nun who falls in love with that great divinity and gives herself up to the search for him who can play the lyre so beautifully and charm hearts so wondrously. In the end, however, after wandering far and wide, she discovers that the Apollo of her dreams exists in the world of reality as Rabbi Faibusch (a Yiddish distortion of Phoebus), cantor in a synagogue at Amsterdam, holder of the humblest office among the humblest of peoples. Nor this alone; the father is a *mohel* (ritual circumciser), and the mother peddles sour pickles and assortments of odd trousers; while the son is a good-for-nothing who makes the rounds of the annual fairs playing the clown and singing the Psalms of David to the accompaniment of a bevy of "Muses" consisting of nine buxom wenches from the Amsterdam casino.

Heine's portrayal of the Jewish people and of himself as their poet-king is, of course, poles apart from the conception entertained by the privileged wealthy Jews of the upper classes. Instead, in its gay, insouciant impudence it is characteristic of the common people. For the pariah, excluded from formal society and with no desire to be embraced within it, turns naturally to that which entertains and delights the common people. Sharing their social ostracism, he also shares their joys and sorrows, their pleasures and their tribulations. He turns, in fact, from the world of men and the fashion thereof to the open and unrestricted bounty of the earth. And this is precisely what Heine did. Stupid and undiscerning critics have called it materialism or atheism, but the truth is that there is only so much of the heathen in it that it seems irreconcilable with certain interpretations of the Christian doctrine of original sin and its consequent sense of perpetual guilt. It is, indeed, no more than that simple *joie de vivre* which one finds everywhere in children and in the common people—that passion which makes them revel in tales and romances, which finds its supreme literary expression in the ballad and which gives to the short love-song its essentially popular character. Stemming as it does from the basic affinity of the pariah to the people, it is something which neither literary criticism nor antisemitism could ever abolish. Though they dub its author "unknown," the Nazis cannot eliminate the *Lorelei* from the repertoire of German song.[6]

It is but natural that the pariah, who receives so little from the world of men that even fame (which the world has been known to bestow on even the most abandoned of her children) is accounted to him a mere sign of *schlemihldom,* should look with an air of innocent amusement, and smile to himself at the spectacle of human beings trying to compete with the divine realities of nature. The bare fact that the sun shines on all alike affords him daily proof that all men are essentially equal. In the presence of such universal things as the sun, music, trees, and children—things which Rahel Varnhagen called "the true realities" just because they are cherished most by those who have no place in the political and social world—the petty dispensations of men which create and maintain inequality must needs appear ridiculous. Confronted with the natural order of things, in which all is equally good, the fabricated order of society, with its manifold classes and ranks, must needs appear a comic, hopeless attempt of creation to throw down the gauntlet to its creator. It is no longer the outcast pariah who appears the *schlemihl,* but those who live in the ordered ranks of society and who have exchanged the generous gifts of nature for the idols of social privilege and prejudice. Especially is this true of the *parvenu* who was not even born to the system, but chose it of his own free will, and who is called upon to pay the cost meticulously and exactly, whereas others can take things in their stride. But no less are they *schlemihls* who enjoy power and high station. It needs but a poet to compare their vaunted grandeur with the real majesty of the sun, shining on king and beggarman alike, in order to demonstrate that all their pomp and circumstance is but sounding brass and a tinkling cymbal. All of these truths are old as the hills. We know them from the songs of oppressed and despised peoples who—so long as man does not aspire to halt the course of the sun—will always seek refuge in nature, hoping that beside nature all the devices of men will reveal themselves as ephemeral trifles.

It is from this shifting of the accent, from this vehement protest on the part of the pariah, from this attitude of denying the reality of the social order and of confronting it, instead, with a higher reality, that Heine's spirit of mockery really stems. It is this too which makes his scorn so pointed. Because he gauges things so consistently by the criterion of what is really and manifestly natural, he is able at once to detect the weak spot in his opponent's armour, the vulnerable point in any particular stupidity which he happens to be exposing. And it is this aloofness of the pariah from all the works of man that Heine regards as the essence of freedom. It is this aloofness that accounts for the divine laughter and the absence of bitterness in his verses. He was the first Jew to whom freedom meant more than mere "liberation from the house of bondage" and in whom it was combined, in equal measure, with the traditional Jewish passion for justice. To Heine, freedom had little to do with liberation from a just or unjust yoke. A man is born free, and he can lose his freedom only by selling himself into bondage. In line with this idea, both in his political poems and in his prose writings Heine vents his anger not only on tyrants but equally on those who put up with them.

The concept of *natural* freedom (conceived, be it noted, by an outcast able to live beyond the struggle between bondage and tyranny) turns both slaves and tyrants into equally unnatural and therefore ludicrous figures of fun. The poet's cheerful insouciance could hardly be expected from the more respectable citizen, caught as he was in the toils of practical affairs and himself partly responsible for the order of things. Even Heine, when confronted with the only social reality from which his pariah existence had not detached him—the rich Jews of his family—loses his serenity and becomes bitter and sarcastic.

To be sure, when measured by the standard of political realities, Heine's attitude of amused indifference seems remote and unreal. When one comes down to earth, one has to admit that laughter does not kill and that neither slaves nor tyrants are extinguished by mere amusement. From this standpoint, however, the pariah is always remote and unreal; whether as *schlemihl* or as "lord of dreams" he stands outside the real world and attacks it from without. Indeed, the Jewish tendency towards utopianism—a propensity most clearly in evidence in the very countries of emancipation—stems, in the last analysis, from just this lack of social roots. The only thing which saved Heine from succumbing to it, and which made him transform the political non-existence and unreality of the pariah into the effective basis of a world of art, was his creativity. Because he sought nothing more than to hold up a mirror to the political world, he was able to avoid becoming doctrinaire and to keep his passion for freedom unhampered by fetters of dogma. Similarly, because he viewed life through a long-range telescope, and not through the prism of an ideology, he was able to see further and clearer than others, and takes his place today among the shrewdest political observers of his time. The basic philosophy of this "prodigal son" who, after "herding the Hegelian swine for many years," at last became even bold enough to embrace a personal god, could always have been epitomized in his own lines:

> "Beat on the drum and blow the fife
> And kiss the *vivandière,* my boy.
> Fear nothing—that's the whole of life,
> Its deepest truth, its soundest joy.
> Beat reveille, and with a blast
> Arouse all men to valiant strife.
> Waken the world; and then, at last
> March on. . . . That is the whole of life."
>
> (*Trans. Untermeyer*)

By fearlessness and divine impudence Heine finally achieved that for which his coreligionists had vainly striven with fear and trembling, now furtively and now ostentatiously, now by preening and vaunting, and now by obsequious sycophancy. Heine is the only German Jew who could truthfully describe himself as both a German and a Jew. He is the only outstanding example of a really happy assimilation in the entire history of that process. By seeing Phoebus Apollo in the German language, he in fact put into practice that true blending of cultures of which others merely talked. One has only to remember how zealously assimilated Jews avoid the mention of a Hebrew word before Gentiles, how strenuously they pretend not to understand it if they hear one, to appreciate the true measure of Heine's accomplishment when he wrote, as pure German verse, lines like the following, praising a distinctively Jewish dish:

> "Schalet, ray of light immortal
> Schalet, daughter of Elysium!
> So had Schiller's song resounded,
> Had he ever tasted Schalet."
>
> (*Trans. Leland*)

In these words, Heine places the fare of Princess Sabbath on the table of the gods, beside nectar and ambrosia.

While the privileged wealthy Jews appealed to the sublimities of the Hebrew prophets in order to prove that they were indeed the descendants of an especially exalted people, or else—like Disraeli—sought to validate their people by endowing it with some extraordinary, mystic power,[7] Heine dispensed with all such rarefied devices and turned to the homespun Judaism of everyday life, to that which really lay in the heart and on the lips of the average Jew; and through the medium of the German language he gave it a place in general European culture. Indeed, it was the very introduction of these homely Jewish notes that helped to make Heine's works so essentially popular and human.

Heine is perhaps the first German prose writer really to embody the heritage of Lessing. In a manner least expected, he confirmed the queer notion so widely entertained by the early Prussian liberals that once the Jew was emancipated he would become more human, more free and less prejudiced than other men. That this notion involved a gross exaggeration is obvious. In its political implications, too, it was so lacking in elementary understanding as to appeal only to those Jews who imagined—as do so many today—that Jews could exist as "pure human beings" outside the range of peoples and nations. Heine was not deceived by this nonsense of "world-citizenship." He knew that separate peoples are needed to focus the genius of poets and artists; and he had no time for academic pipedreams. Just because he refused to give up his allegiance to a people of pariahs and *schlemihls,* just because he remained consistently attached to them, he takes his place among the most uncompromising of Europe's fighters for freedom—of which, alas, Germany has produced so few. Of all the poets of his time Heine was the one with the most character. And just because German bourgeois society had none of its own, and feared the explosive force of his, it concocted the slanderous legend of his characterlessness. Those who spread this legend, and who hoped thereby to dismiss Heine from serious consideration, included many Jewish journalists. They were averse to adopting the line he had suggested; they did not want to become Germans and Jews in one, because they feared that they would thereby lose their positions in the social order of German Jewry. For Heine's attitude, if only as a poet, was that by achieving emancipation the Jewish people had achieved a genuine freedom. He simply ignored the condition which had characterized emancipation everywhere in Europe—namely, that the Jew might only become a man when he ceased to be a Jew. Because he held this position he was able to do what so few of his contemporaries could—to speak the language of a free man and sing the songs of a natural one.

2. Bernard Lazare: The Conscious Pariah

If it was Heine's achievement to recognize in the figure of the *schlemihl* the essential kinship of the pariah to the poet—both alike excluded from society and never quite at home in this world—and to illustrate by this analogy the position of the Jew in the world of European culture, it was the merit of Bernard Lazare to translate the same basic fact into terms of political significance. Living in the France of the Dreyfus Affair, Lazare could appreciate at first hand the pariah quality of Jewish existence. But he knew where the solution lay: in contrast to his unemancipated brethren who accept their pariah status automatically and unconsciously, the emancipated Jew must awake to an awareness of his position and, conscious of it, become a rebel against it—the champion of an oppressed people. His fight for freedom is part and parcel of that which all the down-trodden of Europe must needs wage to achieve national and social liberation.

In this heroic effort to bring the Jewish question openly into the arena of politics Lazare was to discover certain specific, Jewish factors which Heine had overlooked and could afford to ignore. If Heine could content himself with the bare observation that "Israel is ill-served, with false friends guarding her doors from without and Folly and Dread keeping watch within," Lazare took pains to investigate the political implications of this connection between Jewish folly and gentile duplicity. As the root of the mischief he recognized that "spurious doctrine" (*doctrine bâtarde*) of assimilation, which would have the Jews "abandon all their characteristics, individual and moral alike, and give up distinguishing themselves only by an outward mark of the flesh which served but to expose them to the hatred of other faiths." He saw that what was necessary was to rouse the Jewish pariah to a fight against the Jewish *parvenu*. There was no other way to save him from the latter's own fate—inevitable destruction. Not only, he contended, has the pariah nothing but suffering to expect from the domination of the *parvenu*, but it is he who is destined sooner or later to pay the price of the whole wretched system. "I want no longer," he says in a telling passage, "to have against me not only the wealthy of my people, who exploit me and sell me, but also the rich and poor of other peoples who oppress and torture me in the name of my rich." And in these words he puts his finger squarely on that phenomenon of Jewish life which the historian Jost had so aptly characterized as "double slavery"—dependence, on the one hand, upon the hostile elements of his environment and, on the other, on his own "highly-placed brethren" who are somehow in league with them.[8] Lazare was the first Jew to perceive the connection between these two elements, both equally disastrous to the pariah. His experience of French politics had taught him that whenever the enemy seeks control, he makes a point of using some oppressed element of the population as his lackeys and henchmen, rewarding them with special privileges, as a kind of sop. It was thus that he construed the mechanism which made Jewish poverty, to which they referred whenever their own position was jeopardized. This, he divined, was the real basis of their precarious relationship with their poorer brethren—on whom they would be able, at any time it suited them, to turn their backs.

As soon as the pariah enters the arena of politics, and translates his status into political terms, he becomes perforce a rebel. Lazare's idea was, therefore, that the Jew should come out openly as the representative of the pariah, "since it is the duty of every human being to resist oppression." He demanded, that is, that the pariah relinquish once and for all the prerogative of the *schlemihl,* cut loose from the world of fancy and illusion, renounce the comfortable protection of nature, and come to grips with the world of men and women. In other words, he wanted him to feel that he was himself responsible for what society had done to him. He wanted him to stop seeking release in an attitude of superior indifference or in lofty and rarefied cogitation about the nature of man *per se.* However much the Jewish pariah might be, from the historical viewpoint, the product of an unjust dispensation ("look what you have made of the people, ye Christians and ye princes of the Jews"), politically speaking, every pariah who refused to be a rebel was partly responsible for his own position and therewith for the blot on mankind which it represented. From such shame there was no escape, either in art or in nature. For insofar as a man is more than a mere creature of nature, more than a mere product of Divine creativity, insofar will he be called to account for the things which men do to men in the world which they themselves condition.

Superficially, it might appear as though Lazare failed because of the organized opposition of the rich, privileged Jews, the nabobs and philanthropists whose leadership he had ventured to challenge and whose lust for power he had dared to denounce. Were this the case, it would be but the beginning of a tradition which might have outlived his own premature death and determined, if not the fate, at least the effective volition of the Jewish people. But it was not the case; and Lazare himself knew—to his own sorrow—the real cause of his failure. The decisive factor was not the *parvenu;* neither was it the existence of a ruling caste which—whatever complexion it might choose to assume—was still very much the same as that of any other people. Immeasurably more serious and decisive was the fact that the pariah simply refused to become a rebel. True to type, he preferred to "play the revolutionary in the society of others, but not in his own," or else to assume the role of *schnorrer* feeding on crumbs from the rich man's table, like an ancient Roman commoner ready to be fobbed off with the merest trifle that the patrician might toss at him. In either case, he mortgaged himself to the *parvenu,* protecting the latter's position in society and in turn protected by him.

However bitterly they may have attacked him, it was not the hostility of the Jewish nabobs that ruined Lazare. It was the fact that when he tried to stop the pariah from being a *schlemihl,* when he sought to give him a political significance, he encountered only the *schnorrer.* And once the pariah becomes a *schnorrer,* he is worth nothing, not because he is poor and begs, but because he begs from those whom he ought to fight, and because he appraises his poverty by the standards of those who have caused it. Once he adopts the role of *schnorrer,* the pariah becomes automatically one of the props which hold up a social order from which he is himself excluded. For just as *he* cannot live without his benefactors, so *they* cannot live without him. Indeed, it is just by this system of organized charity and alms-giving that the *parvenus* of the Jewish people have contrived to secure control over it, to determine its destinies and set its standards. The *parvenu* who fears lest he become a pariah, and the pariah who aspires to become a *parvenu,* are brothers under the skin and appropriately aware of their kinship. Small wonder, in face of this fact, that of all Lazare's efforts—unique as they were—to forge the peculiar situation of his people into a vital and significant political factor, nothing now remains. Even his memory has faded.

3. Charlie Chaplin: The Suspect

While lack of political sense and persistence in the obsolete system of making charity the basis of national unity have prevented the Jewish people from taking a positive part in the political life of our day, these very qualities, translated into dramatic forms, have inspired one of the most singular products of modern art—the films of Charlie Chaplin. In Chaplin the most unpopular people in the world inspired what was long the most popular of contemporary figures—not because he was a modern Merry Andrew, but because he represented the revival of a quality long thought to have been killed by a century of class conflict, namely, the entrancing charm of the little people.[9]

In his very first film, Chaplin portrayed the chronic plight of the little man who is incessantly harried and hectored by the guardians of law and order—the representatives of society. To be sure, he too is a *schlemihl,* but not of the old visionary type, not a secret fairy prince, a protégé of Phoebus Apollo. Chaplin's world is of the earth: earthy, grotesquely caricatured if you will, but nevertheless hard and real. It is a world from which neither nature nor art can provide escape and against whose slings and arrows the only armor is one's own wits or the kindness and humanity of casual acquaintances.

In the eyes of society, the type which Chaplin portrays is always fundamentally suspect. He may be at odds with the world in a thousand and one ways, and his conflicts with it may assume a manifold variety of forms, but always and everywhere he is under suspicion, so that it is no good arguing rights or wrongs. Long before the refugee was to become, in the guise of the "stateless," the living symbol of the pariah, long before men and women were to be forced in their thousands to depend for their bare existence on their own wits or the chance kindnesses of others, Chaplin's own childhood had taught him two things. On the one hand, it had taught him the traditional Jewish fear of the "cop"—that seeming incarnation of a hostile world; but on the other, it had taught him the time-honored Jewish truth that, other things being equal, the human ingenuity of a David can sometimes outmatch the animal strength of a Goliath.

Standing outside the pale, suspected by all the world, the pariah—as Chaplin portrays him—could not fail to arouse the sympathy of the common people, who recognized in him the image of what society had done to them. Small wonder, then, that Chaplin became the idol of the masses. If they laughed at the way he was forever falling in love at first sight, they realized at the same time that the kind of love he evinced was their kind of love—however rare it may be.

Chaplin's suspect is linked to Heine's *schlemihl* by the common element of innocence. What might have appeared incredible and untenable if presented as a matter of casuistic discussion, as the theme of high-flown talk about the persecution of the guiltless etc., becomes, in Chaplin's treatment, both warm and convincing. Chaplin's heroes are not paragons of virtue, but little men with a thousand and one little failings, forever clashing with the law. The only point that is made is that the punishment does not always fit the crime, and that for the man who is in any case suspect there is no relation between the offense he commits and the price he pays. He is always being "nabbed" for things he never did, yet somehow he can always slip through the toils of the law, where other men would be caught in them. The innocence of the suspect which Chaplin so consistently portrays in his films is, however, no more a mere trait of character, as in Heine's *schlemihl;* rather is it an expression of the dangerous incompatibility of general laws with individual misdeeds. Although in itself tragic, this incompatibility reveals its comic aspects in the case of the suspect, where it becomes patent. There is obviously no connection at all between what Chaplin does or does not do and the punishment which overtakes him. Because he is suspect, he is called upon to bear the brunt of much that he has not done. Yet at the same time, because he is beyond the pale, unhampered by the trammels of society, he is able to get away with a great deal. Out of this ambivalent situation springs an attitude both of fear and of impudence, fear of the law as if it were an inexorable natural force, and familiar, ironic impudence in the face of its minions. One can cheerfully cock a snoot at them, because one has learned to duck them, as men duck a shower by creeping into holes or under a shelter. And the smaller one is the easier it becomes. Basically, the impudence of Chaplin's suspect is of the same kind as charms us so much in Heine's *schlemihl;* but no longer is it carefree and unperturbed, no longer the divine effrontery of the poet who consorts with heavenly things and can therefore afford to thumb noses at earthly society. On the contrary, it is a worried, careworn impudence—the kind so familiar to generations of Jews, the effrontery of the poor "little Yid" who does not recognize the class order of the world because he sees in it neither order nor justice for himself.

It was in this "little Yid," poor in worldly goods but rich in human experience, that the little man of all peoples most clearly discerned his own image. After all, had he not, too, to grapple with the problem of circumventing a law which, in its sublime indifference, forbade "rich and poor to sleep under bridges or steal bread?" For a long time he could laugh good-humoredly at himself in the role of a *schlemihl*—laugh at his misfortunes and his comic, sly methods of escape. But then came unemployment, and the thing was not funny any more. He knew he had been caught by a fate which no amount of cunning and smartness could evade. Then came the change. Chaplin's popularity began rapidly to wane, not because of any mounting antisemitism, but because his underlying humanity had lost its meaning. Men had stopped seeking release in laughter; the little man had decided to be a big one.

Today it is not Chaplin, but Superman. When, in *The Dictator,* the comedian tried, by the ingenious device of doubling his role, to point up the contrast between the "little man" and the "big shot," and to show the almost brutal character of the Superman ideal, he was barely understood. And when, at the end of the film, he stepped out of character, and sought, in his own name, to reaffirm and vindicate the simple wisdom and philosophy of the "little man," his moving and impassioned plea fell, for the most part, upon unresponsive audiences. This was not the idol of the thirties.

4. Franz Kafka: The Man of Goodwill

Both Heine's *schlemihl* and Lazare's "conscious pariah" were conceived essentially as Jews, while even Chaplin's suspect betrays what are clearly Jewish traits. Quite different, however, is the case of the last and most recent typification of the pariah—that represented in the work of Franz Kafka. He appears on two occasions, once in the poet's earliest story, *Description of a Fight,* and again in one of his latest novels, entitled *The Castle.*

Description of a Fight is concerned, in a general way, with the problem of social interrelations, and advances the thesis that within the confines of society the effects of genuine or even friendly relations are invariably adverse. Society, we are told, is composed of "nobodies"—"I did wrong to nobody, nobody did wrong to me; but nobody will help me, nothing but nobodies"—and has therefore no real existence. Nevertheless, even the pariah, who is excluded from it, cannot account himself lucky, since society keeps up the pretense that it is somebody and he nobody, that it is "real" and he "unreal."[10] His conflict with it has therefore nothing to do with the question whether society treats him properly or not; the point at issue is simply whether it or he has real existence. And the greatest injury which society can and does inflict on him is to make him doubt the reality and validity of his own existence, to reduce him in his own eyes to a status of nonentity.

The reality of his existence thus assailed, the pariah of the nineteenth century had found escape in two ways, but neither could any longer commend itself to Kafka. The first way led to a society of pariahs, of people in the same situation and—so far as their opposition to society was concerned—of the same outlook. But to take this way was to end in utter detachment from reality—in a bohemian divorce from the actual world. The second way, chosen by many of the better Jews whom society had ostracized, led to an overwhelming preoccupation with the world of beauty, be it the world of nature in which all men were equal beneath an eternal sun, or the realm of art where everyone was welcome who could appreciate eternal genius. Nature and art had, in fact, long been regarded as departments of life which were proof against social or political assault; and the pariah therefore retreated to them as to a world where he might dwell unmolested. Old cities, reared in beauty and hallowed by tradition, began to attract him with their imposing buildings and spacious plazas. Projected, as it were, from the past into the present, aloof from contemporary rages and passions, they seemed in their timelessness to extend a universal welcome. The gates of the old palaces, built by kings for their own courts, seemed now to be flung open to all, and even unbelievers might pace the great cathedrals of Christ. In such a setting the despised pariah Jew, dismissed by contemporary society as a nobody, could at least share in the glories of the past, for which he often showed a more appreciative eye than the esteemed and full-fledged members of society.

But it is just this method of escape, this retreat into nature and art, against which Kafka directs his shafts in *Description of a Fight.* To his twentieth-century sense of reality, nature had lost its invulnerable superiority over man since man would not "leave it in peace." He denied, too, the living actuality of monuments which were merely inherited from the dead and abandoned to everybody—that same everybody whom contemporary society would call a "nobody." In his view, the beauties of art and nature when used as an escape mechanism by those to whom its right had been refused were merely products of society. It does no good, he says, to keep thinking of them; in time they die and lose their strength. For Kafka only those things are real whose strength is not impaired but confirmed by thinking. Neither the freedom of the *schlemihl* and poet nor the innocence of the suspect nor the escape into nature and art, but thinking is the new weapon—the only one with which, in Kafka's opinion, the pariah is endowed at birth in his vital struggle against society.

It is, indeed, the use of this contemplative faculty as an instrument of self-preservation that characterizes Kafka's conception of the pariah. Kafka's heroes face society with an attitude of outspoken aggression, poles apart from the ironic condescension and superiority of Heine's "lord of dreams" or the innocent cunning of Chaplin's perpetually harassed little man. The traditional traits of the Jewish pariah, the touching innocence and the enlivening *schlemihldom,* have alike no place in the picture. *The Castle,* the one novel in which Kafka discusses the Jewish problem, is the only one in which the hero is plainly a Jew; yet even there what characterizes him as such is not any typically Jewish trait, but the fact that he is involved in situations and perplexities distinctive of Jewish life.

K. (as the hero is called) is a stranger who can never be brought into line because he belongs neither to the common people nor to its rulers. ("You are not of the Castle and you are not of the village, you are nothing at all.") To be sure, it has something to do with the rulers that he ever came to the village in the first place, but he has no legal title to remain there. In the eyes of the minor bureaucratic officials his very existence was due merely to a bureaucratic "error," while his status as a citizen was a paper one, buried "in piles of documents forever rising and crashing" around him. He is charged continually with being superfluous, "unwanted and in everyone's way," with having, as a stranger, to depend on other people's bounty and with being tolerated only by reason of a mysterious act of grace.

K. himself is of the opinion that everything depends on his becoming "indistinguishable," and "that as soon as possible." He admits that the rulers will assuredly obstruct the process. What he seeks, namely, complete assimilation, is something which they are not prepared to recognize— even as an aspiration. In a letter from the Castle he is told distinctly that he will have to make up his mind "whether he prefers to become a village worker with a distinctive but merely apparent connection with the Castle or an ostensible village worker whose real occupation is determined through the medium of Barnabas (the court messenger)."

No better analogy could have been found to illustrate the entire dilemma of the modern would-be assimilationist Jew. He, too, is faced with the same alternative, whether to belong ostensibly to the people, but really to the rulers—as their creature and tool—or utterly and forever to renounce their protection and seek his fortune with the masses. "Official" Jewry has preferred always to cling to the rulers, and its representatives are always only "ostensible villagers." But it is with the other sort of Jew that

Kafka is concerned and whose fate he portrays. This is the Jew who chooses the alternative way—the way of goodwill, who construes the conventional parlance of assimilation literally. What Kafka depicts is the real drama of assimilation, not its distorted counterpart. He speaks for the average small-time Jew who really wants no more than his rights as a human being: home, work, family, and citizenship. He is portrayed as if he were alone on earth, the only Jew in the whole wide world—completely, desolately alone. Here, too, Kafka paints a picture true to reality and to the basic human problem which assimilation involves, if taken seriously. For insofar as the Jew seeks to become "indistinguishable" from his gentile neighbors he has to behave as if he were indeed utterly alone; he has to part company, once and for all, with all who are like him. The hero of Kafka's novel does, in fact, what the whole world wants the Jew to do. His lonely isolation merely reflects the constantly reiterated opinion that if only there were nothing but individual Jews, if only the Jews would not persist in banding together, assimilation would become a fairly simple process. Kafka makes his hero follow this "ideal" course in order to show clearly how the experiment in fact works out. To make a thorough success of it, it is, of course, necessary also that a man should renounce all distinctive Jewish traits. In Kafka's treatment, however, this renunciation assumes a significance for the whole problem of mankind, and not merely for the Jewish question. K., in his effort to become "indistinguishable," is interested only in universals, in things which are common to all mankind. His desires are directed only towards those things to which all men have a natural right. He is, in a word, the typical man of goodwill. He demands no more than that which constitutes every man's right, and he will be satisfied with no less. His entire ambition is to have "a home, a position, real work to do," to marry and "to become a member of the community." Because, as a stranger, he is not permitted to enjoy these obvious prerequisites of human existence, he cannot afford to be ambitious. He alone, he thinks (at least at the beginning of the story), must fight for the minimum—for simple human rights, as if it were something which embraced the sum total of all possible demands. And just because he seeks nothing more than his minimum human rights, he cannot consent to obtain his demands—as might otherwise have been possible—in the form of "an act of favor from the Castle." He must perforce stand on his rights.

As soon as the villagers discover that the stranger who has chanced to come into their midst really enjoys the protection of the Castle, their original mood of contemptuous indifference turns to one of respectful hostility. From then on their one desire is to cast him back upon the Castle as soon as possible; they want no truck with the "upper crust." And when K. refuses, on the grounds that he wants to be free, when he explains that he would rather be a simple but genuine villager than an ostensible one really living under the protection of the Castle, their attitude changes in turn to one of suspicion mingled with anxiety—an attitude which, for all his efforts, haunts him continually. The villagers feel uneasy not because he is a stranger, but because he refuses to accept favors. They try constantly to persuade him that his attitude is "dumb," that he lacks acquaintance with conditions as they are. They tell him all kinds of tales concerning the relations of the Castle to the villagers, and seek thereby to impart to him something of that knowledge of the world which he so obviously lacks. But all they succeed in doing is to show him, to his increasing alarm, that such things as human instinct, human rights, and plain normal life—things which he himself had taken for granted as the indisputable property of all normal human beings—had as little existence for the villagers as for the stranger.

What K. experienced in his efforts to become indistinguishable from the villagers is told in a series of grim and ghastly tales, all of them redolent of human perversity and the slow attrition of human instincts. There is the tale of the innkeeper's wife who had had the "honor" as a girl to be the short-lived mistress of some underling at the Castle, and who so far never forgot it as to turn her marriage into the merest sham. Then there is K.'s own young fiancée who had had the same experience but who, though she was able to forget it long enough to fall genuinely in love with him, could still not endure indefinitely a simple life without "high connections" and who absconded in the end with the aid of the "assistants"—two minor officials of the Castle. Last but not least, there is the weird, uncanny story of the Barnabases living under a curse, treated as lepers till they feel themselves such, merely because one of their pretty daughters once dared to reject the indecent advances of an important courtier. The plain villagers, controlled to the last detail by the ruling class, and slaves even in their thoughts to the whims of their all-powerful officials, had long since come to realize that to be in the right or to be in the wrong was for them a matter of pure "fate" which they could not alter. It is not, as K. naively assumes, the sender of an obscene letter that is exposed, but the recipient who becomes branded and tainted. This is what the villagers mean when they speak of their "fate." In K.'s view, "it's unjust and monstrous, but you're the only one in the village of that opinion."

It is the story of the Barnabases that finally makes K. see conditions as they really are. At long last he comes to understand that the realization of his designs, the achievement of basic human rights—the right to work, the right to be useful, the right to found a home and become a member of society—are in no way dependent on complete assimilation to one's *milieu*, on being "indistinguishable." The normal existence which he desires has become something exceptional, no longer to be realized by simple, natural methods. Everything natural and normal in life has been wrested out of men's hands by the prevalent regime of the village, to become a present endowed from without—or, as Kafka puts it, from "above." Whether as fate, as blessing, or as curse, it is something dark and mysterious, something which a man receives but does not create, and which he can therefore observe but never fathom. Accordingly K.'s aspiration, far from being commonplace and obvious, is, in fact, exceptional and magnificent. So long as the village remains under the control of the Castle, its inhabitants can be nothing but the passive victims of their respective "fates"; there is no place in it for any man of goodwill who wishes to determine his own existence. The simplest inquiry into right and wrong is regarded as querulous disputation; the character of the regime, the power of the Castle, are things which may not be questioned. So, when K., thoroughly indignant and outraged, bursts out with the words, "So that's what the officials are like," the whole village trembles as if some vital secret, if not indeed the whole pattern of its life, had been suddenly betrayed.

Even when he loses the innocence of the pariah, K. does not give up the fight. But unlike the hero of Kafka's last novel, *America,* he does not start dreaming of a new world and he does not end in a great "Nature Theatre" where "everyone is welcome," where "there is a place for everyone" in accordance with his talents, his bent, and his will. On the contrary, K.'s idea seems to be that much could be accomplished, if only one simple man could achieve to live his own life like a normal human being. Accordingly, he remains in the village and tries, in spite of everything, to establish himself under existent conditions. Only for a single brief moment does the old Jewish ideal stir his heart, and he dreams of the lofty freedom of the pariah—the "lord of dreams." But there is "nothing more senseless," he observes, "nothing more hopeless than this freedom, this waiting, this inviolability." All these things have no purpose and take no account of men's desire to achieve something in the here below, if it be only the sensible direction of their lives. Hence, in the end, he reconciles himself readily to the "tyranny of the teacher," takes on "the wretched post" of a school janitor and "does his utmost to get an interview with Klamm"—in a word, he takes his share in the misery and distress of the villagers.

On the face of it, all is fruitless, since K. cannot and will not divorce himself from the distinction between right and wrong and since he refuses to regard his normal human rights as privileges bestowed by the "powers that be." Because of this, the stories which he hears from the villagers fail to rouse in him that sense of haunting fear with which they take pains to invest them and which endows them with that strange poetic quality so common in the folk-tales of enslaved peoples. And since he cannot share this feeling he can never really be one of them. How baseless a feeling it is, how groundless the fear which seems by some magic to possess the entire village, is clear from the fact that nothing whatever materializes of all the dreadful fates which the villagers predict for K. himself. Nothing more serious happens to him, in fact, than that the authorities at the Castle, using a thousand and one excuses, keep holding up his application for legal title of residence.

The whole struggle remains undecided, and K. dies a perfectly natural death; he gets exhausted. What he strove to achieve was beyond the strength of any one man. But though his purpose remained unaccomplished, his life was far from being a complete failure. The very fight he had put up to obtain the few basic things which society owes to men, had opened the eyes of the villagers, or at least of some of them. His story, his behavior, had taught them both that human rights are worth fighting for and that the rule of the Castle is not divine law and, consequently, can be attacked. He had made them see, as they put it, that "men who suffered our kind of experiences, who are beset by our kind of fear . . . who tremble at every knock at the door, cannot see things straight." And they added: "How lucky are we that you came to us!"

In an epilogue to the novel Max Brod related with what enthusiasm Kafka once repeated to him the story of how Flaubert, returning from a visit to a simple, happy family of many children, had exclaimed spontaneously: *ils sont dans le vrai* ("Those folk are right").[11] A true human life cannot be led by people who feel themselves detached from the basic and simple laws of humanity nor by those who elect to live in a vacuum, even if they be led to do so by persecution. Men's lives must be nominal, not exceptional.

It was the perception of this truth that made Kafka a Zionist. In Zionism he saw a means of abolishing the "abnormal" position of the Jews, an instrument whereby they might become "a people like other peoples." Perhaps the last of Europe's great poets, he could scarcely have wished to become a nationalist. Indeed, his whole genius, his whole expression of the modern spirit, lay precisely in the fact that what he sought was to be a human being, a normal member of human society. It was not his fault that this society had ceased to be human, and that, trapped within its meshes, those of its members who were really men of goodwill were forced to function within it as something exceptional and abnormal—saints or madmen. If Western Jewry of the nineteenth century had taken assimilation seriously, had really tried to resolve the anomaly of the Jewish people and the problem of the Jewish individual by becoming "indistinguishable" from their neighbors, if they had made equality with others their ultimate objective, they would only have found in the end that they were faced with inequality and that society was slowly but surely disintegrating into a vast complex of inhuman cross-currents. They would have found, in short, the same kind of situation as Kafka portrayed in dealing with the relations of the stranger to the established patterns of village life.

So long as the Jews of Western Europe were pariahs only in a social sense they could find salvation, to a large extent, by becoming *parvenus*. Insecure as their position may have been, they could nevertheless achieve a *modus vivendi* by combining what Ahad Ha'am described as "inner slavery" with "outward freedom."[12] Moreover those who deemed the price too high could still remain mere pariahs, calmly enjoying the freedom and untouchability of outcasts. Excluded from the world of political realities, they could still retreat into their quiet corners there to preserve the illusion of liberty and unchallenged humanity. The life of the pariah, though shorn of political significance, was by no means senseless.

But today it is. Today the bottom has dropped out of the old ideology. The pariah Jew and the *parvenu* Jew are in the same boat, rowing desperately in the same angry sea. Both are branded with the same mark; both alike are outlaws. Today the truth has come home: there is no protection in heaven or earth against bare murder, and a man can be driven at any moment from the streets and broad places once open to all. At long last, it has become clear that the "senseless freedom" of the individual merely paves the way for the senseless suffering of his entire people.

Social isolation is no longer possible. You cannot stand aloof from society, whether as a *schlemihl* or as a lord of dreams. The old escape-mechanisms have broken down, and a man can no longer come to terms with a world in which the Jew cannot be a human being either as a *parvenu* using his elbows or as a *pariah* voluntarily spurning its gifts. Both the realism of the one and the idealism of the other are today utopian.

There is, however, a third course—the one that Kafka suggests, in which a man may forgo all claims to individual freedom and inviolability and modestly content himself with trying to lead a simple, decent life. But—as Kafka himself points out—this is impossible within the framework of contemporary society. For while the individual might still be allowed to make a career, he is no longer strong enough to fulfill the basic demands of human life. The man of goodwill is driven today into isolation like the Jew-stranger in the Castle. He gets lost—or dies from exhaustion. For only within the framework of a people can a man live as a man among men, without exhausting himself. And only when a people lives and functions in consort with other peoples can it contribute to the establishment upon earth of a commonly conditioned and commonly controlled humanity.

"The Jew as Pariah: A Hidden Tradition" first appeared in *Jewish Social Studies* 6 (1944): 99–122. The German version appeared under the title "Die verborgene Tradition," in *Sechs Essays* (Heidelberg: Schneider, 1948) [= Schriften der Wandlung 3], 81–111. The English version has been reprinted in *The Jew as Pariah*, 67–90.—Ed.

§ 10 Nightmare and Flight

Among recent publications, I know of very few that come so close to the experiences of modern man. Whoever wants to catch a glimpse of the post-war, post-fascism state of mind of Europe's intellectuals should not miss reading *The Devil's Share*—carefully, patiently, and (meaning no offense) with charity. The shortcomings of author and book are obvious, glaring to an irritating degree. They confuse the reader as they have confused the author. But the point is that this confusion is the direct result of experiences to which the author bears witness and from which he does not try to escape. Such experience as well as confusion will be common to all who survive and refuse to return to the deceptive security of those "keys to history" that pretended to explain everything, all trends and tendencies, and that actually could not reveal any single real event. Rougemont is speaking of the "nightmare of reality" before which our intellectual weapons have failed so miserably; and if he is confused, it is because in a desperate attempt not to be confronted with this nightmare in spiritual nakedness, he picks up from the great and beautiful arsenal of time-honored figures and images anything that seems to correspond to or to interpret the new shocks that rock the old foundations.

The reality is that "the Nazis are men like ourselves"; the nightmare is that they have shown, have proven beyond doubt what man is capable of. In other words, the problem of evil will be the fundamental question of

---

The Devil's Share. By Denis de Rougemont. Translated from the French by Haakon Chevalier. Pantheon Books. $2.50.

post-war intellectual life in Europe—as death became the fundamental problem after the last war. Rougemont knows that ascribing all evils and evil as such to any social order or to society as such is "a flight from reality." But instead of facing the music of man's genuine capacity for evil and analyzing the nature of man, he in turn ventures into a flight from reality and writes on the nature of the Devil, thereby, despite all dialectics, evading the responsibility of man for his deeds.

The flight from reality, incidentally, is not a flight to theology, as the title and repeated quotations from the Bible suggest. It is a flight into literature, and occasionally very bad literature. There are not only little parables in which the author imitates Nietzsche at his worst—like "Woman beats man"—or essays on modern human behavior which imitate Chesterton on a much less brilliant level.[1] There are such phrases as, "I like to write only dangerous books" which in their puerile vanity make it hard for the reader to take the whole thing seriously.

More serious than immaturity (Rougemont belongs to the generation which, raised between two wars, never had sufficient opportunity to mature and has something of a birthright to immaturity) is the basic confusion of the whole approach. This consists of identifying man's capacity for evil and the problem of evil as such with the "evils of our time" loosely and generally speaking. This leads to the introduction of the Devil in person who serves simply as common denominator. Although his existence is proved with a nice trick of Chestertonian logic ("Those who stick to old wives' tales—'I can't believe in a gent with red horns and a long tail'—are those who refuse to believe in the Devil because of the image they form of him which is drawn from old wives' tales"), he is nothing but a personification of Heidegger's Nothingness that already through its "begetting nothingness" was something of an acting subject. (The Devil is the "messenger of Nothingness," "serves Nothing," is "the agent of Nothingness," "tends to Nothingness," etc.)[2]

This, of course, would be simply an attempt to explain the new experiences with the categories of the nineteen-twenties. But Rougemont does not stop there; his "flight from reality" is more complicated and more interesting to watch. Much against his will and though fearing and predicting "modern gnosticism," he falls into the worst pitfalls of gnostic speculation. His ultimate consolation is his confidence that in an eternal fight between God and the Devil, the good and the evil forces, victory is already won "from the point of view of eternity," that "our misdeeds and those of the Devil change nothing in the Order of this world" and that, consequently, "what concerns us in this century is to make ourselves immediate participants in this victory." This can but lead to the conclusion that all we have to do is "sanctify ourselves" for the purpose of joining the right, the eternally winning side. It is precisely this metaphysical opportunism, this escape from reality into a cosmic fight in which man has only to join the forces of light to be saved from the forces of darkness, this confidence that the order of the world cannot be changed no matter what man does—which makes gnosticism so attractive to modern speculation and may promote it to the place of the most dangerous and wide-spread "heresy" of tomorrow.

When all this has been said, one has the duty of recommending the book anew. Whether one likes it or not, it is a true *document humain.* Whether one agrees with Denis de Rougemont or not, he belongs to those who, in his own words, "are all in the sinking ship, and at the same time . . . are all in the ship that has launched the torpedo." Those who know this, who do not want to get away from this not very comfortable position, are not numerous, and they are the only ones who matter.

Originally published in *Partisan Review* 12 (1945): 259–60; reprinted in *Essays in Understanding*, 133–35.

Denis de Rougemont (1906–1985) was a conservative Swiss essayist and social theorist, most famous for his *L'Amour et l'occident* (1939; translated as *Love in the Western World*, 1956).—Ed.

§ 11 Franz Kafka, Appreciated Anew

When Franz Kafka, a German-speaking Jew from Prague, died of consumption at the age of forty-one in the summer of 1924, only a small circle of writers and an even smaller circle of readers were familiar with his work. Since that time, his reputation has grown slowly but steadily; in the twenties he was already recognized as one of the most important avant-garde writers in Germany and Austria; in the thirties and forties his work reached the same circles of writers and readers in France, England, and America. The specific quality of his fame always remained the same, regardless of country or decade: the numbers in which his books sold never stood in any relation to the still growing amount of secondary literature written about his work, or to the influence of that work on contemporary writers—an influence still gaining depth and breadth. It is quite telling with regard to the influence of Kafka's prose that he has been claimed by various "schools." It is as though no one who considers themselves "modern" could disregard this work because there is evidently something specifically new at work here that has, to date, emerged nowhere else with the same intensity and the same radical simplicity.

This is very surprising, however, because Kafka, in contrast to other modern authors, abstained from all experiments and mannerisms. His language is clear and simple, like everyday speech cleansed of all negligence and jargon. Kafka's German is to the infinite plurality of possible linguistic styles what water is to the infinite plurality of possible beverages. His prose seems to carry no particular characteristics; it is never charming or alluring. Rather, it is communication in its purest form, and upon closer inspection, its only characteristic quality lies in the realization that what was communicated could not have been communicated any more simply, clearly, or concisely. The lack of mannerisms is pushed almost to the point of the generic, and the lack of affection for words as such almost to the point of coldness. Kafka has no favorite words, and no preferred syntactic constructions. The result of this is a new kind of perfection that appears to be equally far removed from all past styles.

The fact of Kafka's fame is among the most convincing examples in all of literary history of how misguided the theory of the "unrecognized genius" is. There is not a single line, not a single narrative construction in all of his work that is amenable to the type of reader that emerged in the course of the last century in his quest for "entertainment and education" (Broch).[1] The only thing acting in Kafka's work to lure and entice the reader is truth itself, and Kafka was successful in enticing the reader with his style-less perfection—since every "style" would be a distraction in virtue of its particular magic spell—to such an improbable degree that his stories cast their spell even if the reader does not grasp their actual truth-content right away. Kafka's true gift is to create in the reader a general and vague fascination, along with an inevitably precise recollection of particular images and events—apparently meaningless at first—that the reader endures long enough to make it a significant part of his life; at some point and due to some experience, then, the true meaning of the story may reveal itself suddenly and with all the lucidity of an incontestable piece of evidence.

~

A small library of interpretations of *Der Prozess* (The Trial) has been published in the two decades since its appearance. It is the story of K., a man who is accused without knowing what he has done, tried according to laws which he cannot discern, and finally executed without having been able to find out what all of this is really about. In his search for the real reasons for his ordeal, the first thing he learns is that the party responsible for his arrest is "a great organization. An organization that not only employs corrupt wardens, inane inspectors, and examining magistrates who are modest at best, but also has at its disposal a judicial hierarchy of high, indeed of the highest, rank, with an indispensable and numerous retinue of servants, clerks, police and other assistants, perhaps even hangmen . . . And the aim of this great organization . . . ? It is to arrest innocent people and to subject them to a meaningless and, as in my case, inconclusive juridical process."

When K. realizes that, despite their meaninglessness, such processes do not necessarily end inconclusively, he hires a lawyer, who, through long-winded explanations, details the ways in which one may adapt oneself to existing conditions, and suggests that to criticize them would not be sensible. K., who does not want to give in and therefore fires the lawyer, seeks advice from the prison-chaplain, who preaches the hidden greatness of the system and counsels him not to ask for the truth, since "one does not have to accept everything as true, one must only accept it as necessary." In other words, while the lawyer only tried to clarify the way of the world, the task of the chaplain employed by this very world is to provide proof that this is the world order [*Weltordnung*]. And since K. takes this to be a "melancholy conclusion" and replies: "It fashions the lie into the world order," it becomes clear that he will end up losing his trial. Since, however, this did not constitute "his final judgment," and since he tried to dismiss the "unfamiliar thoughts" as "unreal things" that did not really concern him, he not only loses the trial, but does so in a humiliating manner that leaves him to face his execution with nothing but his shame.

The power of the machine that grabs and kills K. lies precisely in the appearance of necessity that is caused by the way in which human beings admire necessity. The machine is set into motion because necessity is taken to be sublime, and because its automatism—interrupted only by arbitrariness—is considered an emblem of necessity. The machine is kept in motion by the lies told for the sake of necessity, with the accepted implication that a man unwilling to submit to the "world order" of this machine is thereby considered guilty of a crime against some kind of divine order. Such submission is achieved when the question of guilt or innocence is no longer asked, replaced by the determination to play the role dictated by arbitrariness in the game of necessity.

In the case of *The Trial*, submission is obtained not by force but simply through an increase in the feeling of guilt roused in the accused K. by the baseless, empty accusation against him. Of course, this feeling is based in the last instance on the fact that no man is free of guilt. And since K., a busy bank employee, has never had the time to ponder such generalities, this feeling of guilt is what dooms him more than anything; it leads him into the kind of confusion that lets him mistake the organized and malicious iniquity of the world surrounding him for some necessary expression of that universal guilt, which is harmless and even innocent when compared with the ill will that fashions "the lie into the world order," using and abusing even man's justifiable humility to this end.

The functioning of the evil bureaucratic machine in which the protagonist is unwittingly caught is thus accompanied by an internal development triggered by the feeling of guilt. As part of this development K. is "educated" [*gebildet*] and transformed until he is fit to assume the role forced upon him, which is to play along as best he can in a world of necessity, injustice, and lies. It is his way of adapting to existing conditions. The internal development of the protagonist finally coincides with the functioning of the machine in the last scene, the execution, where K. lets himself be taken away and killed without a struggle, and indeed without so much as a protest. For the sake of necessity he is to be murdered; for the sake of necessity—and in the confusion caused by the consciousness of guilt—he submits. And the only hope, which suddenly appears for a moment at the very end of the novel, is this: "It was as though the shame outlived him"—the shame, namely, that this is the order of the world and that he, Joseph K., despite being a victim of this order, is also one of its obedient members.

The fact that *The Trial* implies a critique of the pre-War Austrian bureaucratic regime, whose numerous and conflicting nationalities were governed by a homogeneous hierarchy of officials, has been recognized from the time that the novel first appeared. Kafka, an employee of a workers' insurance company and a loyal friend of many eastern European Jews for whom he had to obtain residence permits, had a very intimate knowledge of the political conditions of his country. He knew that a man caught in the bureaucratic machine is already condemned. The domination of bureaucracy implied that the interpretation of the law became an instrument of lawlessness, while the chronic inaction of the interpreters was compensated by a senseless automatism among the lower echelons of the bureaucratic hierarchy, who were entrusted with the privilege of final decision. But given the fact that in Europe the true nature of bureaucracy was not yet widely known in the twenties when the novel first appeared— and had been responsible for the demise of only a negligibly small group of people in Europe up to this point—the horror and terror expressed in the novel seemed inexplicable and somehow not adequate to its actual content. People were more frightened by the novel than by the real thing. Thus they looked for other, seemingly deeper, interpretations, and they found them, following the fashion of the day, by seeing the novel as depicting a religious reality with kabbalistic overtones—the expression, as it were, of a satanic theology.[2]

The reason for this misinterpretation—which in my opinion is as fundamental, though not as crude, a misunderstanding as the psychoanalytical variety—is naturally to be found in Kafka's work itself. Kafka really does describe a society that considers itself the representative of God on earth, and he describes men who look upon the laws of society as though they were divine laws that cannot be altered by the will of men. The evil of the world in which Kafka's protagonists are caught is precisely the world's deification, its pretense of representing a divine necessity. Kafka wants to destroy this world by delineating its hideous structure with utmost precision, and thus contrasting reality and pretense. But the reader of the twenties—fascinated by paradoxes and confused by the interplay of contrasts as such—was no longer willing to listen to reason. His interpretations of Kafka revealed more about himself than about Kafka; in his naïve admiration of a world depicted by Kafka with exaggerated emphasis as unbearably revolting, he revealed his fitness for the "world order," and demonstrated how closely the so-called elite and the avant-garde are connected in the latter. No one paid the slightest attention to Kafka's sarcastic and bitter remark about the mendacious necessity and the necessary mendacity which together constitute the "divinity" of this world order— a remark that clearly provides the key to understanding the construction of the plot of the novel.

～

Kafka's second great novel, *Das Schloss* (The Castle), brings us back to the same world; but this time it is not seen through the eyes of somebody who helplessly submits to the appearance of necessity simply because he has never bothered to think about the government of his country, or about other questions of a more general nature. Instead, the perspective of a rather different K. is presented, one who enters this world of his own free will as a stranger, and who seeks to carry out a very definite plan in it: to establish himself, to become a fellow citizen, to build a life for himself and marry, to find work, in short, to be a useful member of society. It is characteristic of the plot in *The Castle* that the protagonist is interested only in what is most general, and that he fights only for things to which all men would seem to have a birthright. But while he makes no more than the minimum demands of human existence, it is quite obvious from the beginning that he claims these as his right, and that he will accept nothing less than what he perceives to be his right. He is willing to satisfy all necessary application procedures in order to obtain his residence permit, but he does not want to receive it merely as a favor; he is willing to change his profession, but he will not accept anything other than a permanent occupation, "regular work." All of his aspirations hinge on decisions made by the Castle, and K.'s troubles begin when it turns out that the Castle grants rights only as either favors or as privileges. Since, however, K. seeks rights rather than privileges, and since he wants to become a fellow citizen of the villagers in order to be "as far removed from the lords of the Castle as possible," he declines the offers both of favor as well as of privileged relations to the Castle. This way, or so he hopes, "with one fell swoop all paths will open up for him that would have remained not only blocked but even invisible if he had relied on the lords above and their grace."

At this point the villagers step in. They are afraid that he intends simply to become one of them, a simple "village worker," and that he refuses to become part of the dominant group. They repeatedly try to persuade K. that he lacks sufficient general experience of life and the world, and does not realize that all of life essentially depends on favor and disfavor, that it is characterized by grace and disgrace, and that there is no truly important and decisive event more comprehensible, or less random, than good and bad luck. K. is unwilling to acknowledge that, for the villagers, right and wrong, or to be in the right or in the wrong, is still part of "destiny"— which one can only accept and fulfill, but which one cannot alter.

From here onward, the strangeness of the traveling surveyor K.—who is neither a villager nor a Castle bureaucrat, and therefore finds himself outside the power relations governing the world around him—emerges in its full significance. In his insistence on human rights, the stranger reveals himself to be the only one who still grasps, quite simply, what human life on earth is all about. The villagers have been taught by their own particular experiences to consider everything that makes up this life—love and work and friendship—a gift they may receive "from above," from the realm of the Castle, but which they themselves no longer control in any way. The simplest relations are thus mysteriously veiled in darkness; the role of the world order in *The Trial* is here played by destiny—a blessing or a curse to which one submits with fear and awe as one tries to interpret it. K.'s aspiration to create and obtain on legal grounds even what is simply part of human life is thus by no means obvious in this world, but rather exceptional and therefore scandalous. K. is consequently forced to fight for a minimum of human requirements as if it represented an absurd maximum of all possible human wishes; the villagers distance themselves from him because they cannot help but suspect his desire to be a sign of hubris threatening everything and everyone. K. appears strange to them not because, being a stranger, he is deprived of human rights, but because he comes and asks for them.

Despite the fear of the villagers, who expect a catastrophe to befall K. at any moment, nothing ever really happens to him. But he never really achieves anything either, and the ending, which Kafka was only able to communicate orally, had K. dying of exhaustion—a perfectly natural death. All that K. does achieve he achieves unintentionally. Simply through his attitude and his evaluation of the things going on around him, he manages to open the eyes of some of the villagers: "You have an amazing grasp of things . . . sometimes you help me with just a single word, it must be because you are from somewhere else. We, however, with our sad experiences and constant worries are startled, without so much as a defense, by every cracking sound made by the woods, and when one person is startled, so, too, is the next, without really knowing why. In this way, it's impossible to arrive at any adequate judgment. . . . How lucky we are that you came to us." K. resists taking on this role; he did not come as a "savior," he has no time and no energy to spare for helping others, and whoever asks him to do just that "would confuse his path." All he wants to do is to straighten out his own life, and to keep it straight. Unlike the K. of *The Trial,* he does not submit to any apparent necessity in the pursuit of his quest, which is why it is the villagers' remembrance of him, rather than his shame, that will outlive him.[3]

~

Without a doubt Kafka's world is a terrible one. We can probably tell more easily today than we could have done twenty years ago that it is more than just a nightmare, and that in terms of its structure it is uncannily adequate to the reality that we were forced to live through. The greatness of this art lies in its capacity to unsettle us as much today as it did then, and that the horror of "In der Strafkolonie" (In the Penal Colony) has lost none of its immediacy in the face of the reality of the gas chambers.[4]

If Kafka's writing really amounted to nothing but a prophecy of future horrors, it would be no more valuable than any of the apocalyptic predictions to which we have been subjected, for better or worse, since the beginning of the century, or rather, since about 1870. Charles Péguy, who himself enjoyed the dubious distinction of being counted among the prophets, once remarked: "Determinism as far as it can be conceived . . . is perhaps nothing but the law of residues." This sentence alludes to a profound truth. Insofar as life ultimately and inevitably leads to death, its end may always be predicted. The way of nature is always that of ruin, and a society that blindly subjects itself to the necessity of the laws it has made for itself must necessarily perish. Prophets are always prophets of ruin, and necessarily so because the catastrophe can always be predicted. It is always salvation which is the miracle, not ruin; only salvation, and not ruin, depends upon the freedom of man and his capacity to change the world and its natural course. The fatal belief—as prevalent in Kafka's time as it is in ours—that the task of man is to submit to a process predetermined by some power or other can only hasten the natural process of ruin because, propelled by such delusions, man in his freedom only assists nature in its ruinous tendency. The words of the prison-chaplain in *The Trial* reveal the secret theology and the deep faith of bureaucrats to be a faith in necessity as such, and the bureaucrats end up as the functionaries of necessity—as if functionaries were actually needed to make decline and ruin function. In his role as functionary of necessity, man adopts the role of a manifestly superfluous functionary of the natural law of transience, thereby degrading himself, since he himself is more than just a natural being, into a tool of active destruction. Just as surely as a house built by men according to human laws will fall into ruin as soon as men abandon it, so surely the world fabricated by men and constituted according to human and not natural laws will once again become part of nature, and will be surrendered to catastrophic destruction when man decides to become himself a part of nature—a blind but highly precise instrument of natural laws.

In this context it is rather immaterial whether man, obsessed with necessity, believes in ruin or in progress. If progress were really "necessary," and therefore an inevitable superhuman law that embraced all periods of history alike, and in whose meshes humanity is inescapably caught, then progress is indeed best imagined and most exactly described in the following lines from Walter Benjamin's "On the Concept of History":

> The angel of history . . . turns his face to the past. Where we see a chain of events, he sees a single catastrophe which unremittingly piles ruins on ruins and hurls them at his feet. He wishes he could stay to awaken the dead and to join together the fragments. But a wind blows from Paradise, gets caught in them. This wind drives him irresistibly into the future to which he turns his back, while the pile of ruins before him towers to the skies. What we call progress is *this* wind.⁵

The most convincing evidence to support the claim that Kafka does not belong among the more recent prophets may be the fact that we still experience a feeling of unreality upon reading his most horrific and atrocious stories, even though, by now, reality has fulfilled or even surpassed all of them. First, there are his protagonists who often do not even have a name and are frequently referred to simply by their initials. Even if this tantalizing anonymity were due only to an arbitrary incompleteness of the stories—these protagonists certainly are not real people, persons whom we could meet in the real world; despite detailed descriptions they lack precisely the numerous unique features—those small and routinely superfluous characteristics that jointly make up a real human being. They move in a society where everybody is assigned a very particular role and is defined by their job, as it were; the protagonists consider themselves distinct from this society and assume the central role in the plot only because they have no well-defined place in this world of professionals—that is, because their role is utterly indeterminate. This is to say, however, that even the incidental characters are not real people. These stories are far removed from reality in the sense given to it by realist novels.

If Kafka's world entirely relinquishes the "real" character of the realist novel, drawn from external reality, it even more radically relinquishes the "real" character of the psychological novel, drawn from internal reality. The characters among whom Kafka's protagonists circulate do not exhibit any psychological features because they simply do not exist outside of their roles, positions, and occupations; his protagonists, in turn, do not have any psychologically definable characteristics because they are possessed completely and to the greatest depth of their souls by their respective quests—to win a trial, to obtain a residence and work permit, and so forth.

This featureless, abstract nature of Kafka's characters can easily mislead readers into taking them to be the proponents of ideas, or the representatives of opinions, and all the contemporary attempts to read a theology into Kafka's work stem, in fact, from this misunderstanding. Looking at the world presented in Kafka's novels without preconceived notions, however, it is readily apparent that his characters simply have neither the time nor the opportunity to develop individual characteristics. For instance, when the question arises in the novel *America* as to whether the head porter of the hotel may not have inadvertently mistaken the protagonist for somebody else, the porter rejects the notion with the argument that he could not remain head porter if he started mistaking people's identities; the very essence of his job, he claims, is to not mistake anybody for somebody else. His alternatives are exceedingly clear: either he is a human being, subject to the fallibility of human perception and cognition, or he is a head porter, in which case he needs to at least pretend to command a sort of superhuman perfection as part of his position. Employees whom society forces to work with an infallible precision do not thereby simply become infallible. Kafka's bureaucrats, employees, workers, and functionaries are far from perfect, but they all act on the assumption of superhuman omnicompetence [*universal-kompetente Tüchtigkeit*].

What distinguishes Kafka from novelists with a more common technique is his refusal to describe the originary conflict between a functionary's private life and his function; he does not dwell on the way in which officialdom has consumed the private life of the affected as well as the affecting person, or on how his private life—the fact that he has a family, for example—has forced him into becoming inhuman, into identifying himself with his function as only an actor would do for the brief period of a performance. Kafka immediately confronts us with the result of such a development, because for him the result is all that matters. The pretense of omnicompetence, the appearance of superhuman capacities is the hidden motor that drives the destructive machinery in which Kafka's protagonists are caught, and that is responsible for the seamless functioning of what is senseless in and of itself.

The main theme of Kafka's novels is the conflict between a world depicted in terms of a seamlessly functioning machinery of this kind, and a protagonist trying to destroy it. These protagonists, in turn, are not simply men of the sort we meet everyday, but rather varying models of man as such, whose only distinctive feature is an unyielding focus on that which is universally human. His function within the plot of each novel is always the same: he discovers that the normal world and society are in fact abnormal, that the judgments of its generally accepted and respectable members are in fact insane, and that the actions complying with the rules of this game are in fact ruinous for everyone. Kafka's protagonists are not motivated by any kind of revolutionary ambitions; they are propelled only by their good will, which exposes the hidden structures of this world almost without knowing it, or wanting to.

The impression of unreality and unfamiliarity in Kafka's narrative art is in large part due to his interest in these hidden structures, and his radical disinterest in façades, mere aspects, or the purely phenomenal character of the world. It is therefore a thorough misunderstanding to count Kafka among the surrealists. While the surrealist tries to present as many contradictory aspects of, and perspectives on, reality as possible, Kafka invents such aspects freely, and in doing so never relies on reality, since his real concern is not with reality but with truth. In contrast to the surrealists' favorite technique of photomontage, Kafka's technique could best be compared to the construction of models. Just as a man who wants to build a house or evaluate its stability would draw up a blueprint of the building, Kafka practically devises the blueprints of the existing world. Compared with a real house, of course, a blueprint is a very "unreal" affair; but without it the house could not have been built, nor could one recognize the foundations and pillars that alone assure its permanence in the real world. Kafka constructs his models on the basis of this blueprint which, although it is rooted in reality, of course owes its discovery to a thought process much more than to sensory experience. In order to understand these models, the same power of imagination is demanded of the reader as went into creating them; and he can gain this understanding from the power of imagination because we are dealing here not with free fantasy, but with the very products of thought that are used as the elements of Kafka's constructions. For the first time in literary history, a writer requires his readers to engage in the very same activity that upholds both him and his work. And this is none other than the power of imagination, which, as Kant says, is "very powerful in its creation of another nature out of the material that actual nature gives it."[6] Blueprints cannot be understood except by those who are willing and able vividly to imagine the intentions of the architect and the future appearances of the building.

At every turn, what Kafka demands of his reader is this exertion of the real power of imagination. This is why the purely passive reader, molded and educated as he has been by the tradition of the novel, and active only in his identification with one of the characters, does not know what to do with Kafka. The same is true of the curious reader, who either, disappointed by his own life, is looking around for a substitute world in which things happen that would never happen in his own life, or, driven by a true thirst for knowledge, is looking to be edified. Kafka's stories will disappoint him even more than his own life does; they contain no elements of daydreaming and offer neither advice nor edification nor solace. Only the reader who, for whatever reason and however vaguely is himself on a quest for truth, will know what to do with Kafka and his models, and he will be grateful for those moments when the naked structure of perfectly banal events is suddenly thrown into relief on a single page, or even a single sentence.

The following short prose piece, dealing with a particularly simple and common occurrence, is typical for this narrative art of abstraction and reduction to essentials:

A Common Confusion

A common occurrence: to bear it, a common confusion. A. has important business to conduct with B. in H. He goes to H. for a preliminary meeting, completes the journey there and back in ten minutes each way, and upon returning home boasts of his remarkable swiftness. The next day he once again goes to H., this time to conclude his business. Since this is expected to require several hours, A. leaves very early in the morning. But although all accompanying circumstances, at least in A.'s estimation, are exactly the same as the day before, this time it takes him ten hours to reach H. When he arrives there quite exhausted in the evening, he is told that B., annoyed at his absence, had left a half-hour before to go to meet A. in his village, and that they actually should have met each other on the road. A. is advised to wait. But anxious about his business he sets off at once and hurries home.

This time he completes the trip, without particularly noticing it, practically in an instant. At home he learns that B. had actually arrived there early in the morning—immediately after A.'s departure, indeed that he had met A. on the threshold and reminded him of their business; but A. had replied that he had no time to spare then, and that he was in a hurry to leave at once. Despite this incomprehensible behavior on the part of A., however, B. had stayed on to wait for A. He had indeed asked numerous times already whether A. was not back yet, but he was still up in A.'s room. Overjoyed at still being able to see B. and explain everything to him, A. rushes upstairs. He has almost made it to the top when he stumbles, twists a sinew, and, almost fainting from the pain, incapable even of uttering a cry, merely whimpering in the dark, he hears B.—hard to make out whether at a great distance or right next to him— stomping down the stairs, enraged, and vanishing once and for all.

Kafka's technique here is strikingly clear. All of the essential factors that tend to be involved in botched appointments are brought into play: overzealousness (A. leaves too early and still manages to overlook B. on the threshold); impatience (A. perceives his journey as being incredibly long, which causes him to worry more about the length of the journey than about his purpose, which is to meet B.); fear and nervousness (which induce A. to hurry back in a mindless rush, while he could perfectly well have waited for B. to return); all of these pave the way for that well-known will of their own which objects are apt to display as they accompany utter failure, and which both indicates and finalizes the irremediable rift between the exasperated individual and the world. Kafka constructs the occurrence out of these general factors, and not out of the experience of any specific event. With no reality interceding, as it were, to soften the impact of the construction, the individual elements are free to appear in the comically colossal dimension inherent in them, so that at first sight the story reads like one of those fantastic yarns sailors love to tell one another. The impression of exaggeration disappears only when we consider the story not as the report of an actual occurrence, or even of an event triggered by a confusion, but rather as a model of confusion itself, whose grandiose logic our own limited experiences with events of confusion seem desperate to emulate. In contrast to a tradition reaching back thousands of years, this exceedingly bold reversal of original and imitation suddenly casts what is narrated as the original, with reality appearing as an imitation called on to defend itself; this is one of the essential sources of Kafka's humor, and it makes this story so incredibly amusing that it is almost able to console us for all of the appointments we have ever missed, or will ever miss, in our life. This is because Kafka's laughter is an immediate expression of the kind of human freedom and serenity that understands man to be more than just his failures, if only because he is able to conceive of a confusion more confounding than any actual one.

~

From what has been said so far, it should be evident that Kafka was no novelist in the classical, nineteenth-century sense of the word. The basis for the classical novel was an approach to life that fundamentally accepted the world and society, that submitted to life as given, and that perceived the greatness of destiny to be beyond good and evil. The development of the classical novel corresponded to the slow decline of the citizen, who had attempted—during the French Revolution and in Kant's philosophy—to govern the world with human laws for the first time. Its peak coincided with the full self-realization of the bourgeois individual, for whom life and the world presented events as if on a stage, and who desired to "experience" more sensations and occurrences than the typically narrow and secure framework of his own life had to offer him. All of these novelists found themselves in constant competition with reality, whether they realistically copied the world or dreamed up fantastic other worlds. The classical novel of this type has led to the current form of documentary novel that is particularly well developed in America—which makes perfect sense considering that fantasy no longer appears to stand a chance of competing with the reality of current events and destinies.

The counterpart to the quiet security of the bourgeois world in which the individual expected his fair share of events and sensations from life, but never quite got enough of either, was that of great men—the geniuses and exceptional cases who in the eyes of those same bourgeois individuals represented the glorious and mysterious incarnation of something superhuman, which could be called destiny (as in the case of Napoleon), or history (as in the case of Hegel), or God's will (as in the case of Kierkegaard, who believed that God had chosen him to serve as an example), or necessity (as in the case of Nietzsche, who declared himself to be "a necessity"). The highest sensation of the individual thirsting for experience was that of destiny itself, and the highest type of man was therefore the man with a destiny, a mission, or a calling—a calling that he alone served, or whose fulfillment he himself embodied. Greatness was therefore no longer an attribute of a work or an achievement; it was the person himself who became great, namely as the incarnation of something superhuman. Genius was no longer a gift of the gods to man, who after all remained perfectly human; the whole person became a full incarnation of genius and therefore could no longer be regarded as a mere mortal. Kant's definition of genius clearly reflects the fact that this conception of the genius as a sort of superhuman monster was characteristic of the nineteenth century, and not of any prior period. For him genius is the gift "through which nature gives the rule to art."[7] This conception may seem questionable nowadays, and one could take the opposing view that genius is the disposition through which mankind itself "gives the rule to art." What is crucial, however, is that this eighteenth-century definition does not yet display any signs of that empty greatness which would rear its head, immediately after Kant, among the romantics.

What makes Kafka, for one, appear so modern and at the same time so strange, both among his contemporaries and in his own milieu of writers in Prague and Vienna, is that he clearly did not want to be considered a genius, or the incarnation of any objective entity, while at the same time he refused so passionately to simply submit to any kind of destiny. He was no longer infatuated in any way with the world as it is presented to us, and even nature, he thought, was only superior to man as long as he "leaves it in peace." Kafka envisioned a possible world that human beings would construct in which the actions of man depend on nothing but himself and his spontaneity, and in which human society is governed by laws prescribed by man himself rather than by mysterious forces, whether they be interpreted as emanating from above or from below. And in such a world—one to be immediately constructed and no longer simply dreamed of—Kafka by no means intended to be an exceptional case, but rather a fellow citizen, a "member of the community."

This does not mean, of course, as is sometimes supposed, that Kafka was modest. After all, he once noted in his diaries with genuine astonishment that every sentence he randomly wrote down was already perfect—which is quite simply true. Kafka was not modest, but humble.

In order, at least in theory, to become a fellow citizen of such a world freed from all bloody apparitions and murderous magic—as he tentatively tried to describe it at the end, the happy ending, of *America*[8]—he necessarily had to anticipate the destruction of the present world. His novels are just this anticipated destruction, and through its ruins he carries the image of man as a model of good will who can truly move mountains and construct worlds, who can bear the destruction of all misconstructions and the rubble of all ruins because the gods have given him an indestructible heart, if only his will is good. And given that these protagonists created by Kafka are not real persons, that it would amount to hubris to identify with them, and that they are only models left in anonymity even where their names are mentioned, it seems to us as though every one of us were being addressed and called. After all, this man of good will may be anybody and everybody, perhaps even you and I.

Originally published as "Kafka, von neuem gewürdigt," *Die Wandlung* 1 (December 1946): 1050–62; revised under the title "Franz Kafka" for *Sechs Essays*, 128–49; reprinted in *Die vorborgene Tradition: Acht Essays* (Frankfurt am Main: Suhrkamp, 1976), 88–107; translated by Martin Klebes.

An English version had previously been published under the title "Franz Kafka: A Revaluation (On the occasion of the twentieth anniversary of his death)," *The Partisan Review* 11 (1944): 412–22; reprinted in *Essays in Understanding*, 69–80. While working at Schocken Books in New York, Arendt helped with the publication of Kafka's *Diaries.*—Ed.

§ 12 Great Friend of Reality

Adalbert Stifter

The work of Adalbert Stifter, who was one of the very few great novelists in German literature, can be compared to no other writer of the nineteenth century in pure happiness, wisdom, and beauty. The novel in its classical form, with its three great themes—society and love and destiny—is not very well represented in first-class German literature; instead, and oddly enough from its very beginning in the eighteenth century (that is, since *Anton Reiser*), it developed a special kind of novel (the so-called Bildungsroman) in which society and love became elements of the education of the hero and in which education and individual development replace in a curious and somewhat innocent way the tragic majesty of destiny and passion.[1] (The only great exception to this rule is Goethe's *Wahlverwandtschaften* [Elective Affinities].)[2]

Stifter's novels—*Indian Summer* as well as *Witiko*—belong entirely to this German tradition. What could be more natural for the only true heir of Goethe's prose for whom *Wilhelm Meister* probably was the always-present model. Still, under the direct impact of the master's great example—Stifter was born in the first decade of the nineteenth century—he followed him loyally when he speaks of his great friendship for reality, of his supreme desire "to grasp the innocence of the things outside ourselves," and of his admiration for the natural sciences "which are so much more palpable than the humanities because the objects of nature can be considered

---

Adalbert Stifter, *Rock Crystal*. Translated by Elizabeth Mayer and Marianne Moore. Pantheon Books Inc. $2.75 pp. 94.

outside one's own self while the objects of humanity are hidden from us through ourselves." All of this was a conscious and very Goethean rebuke of the romantic fashion of his times, which found nothing interesting but the self. Stifter again shares with Goethe a distrust of generalities, of the very quality of an abstract word—and this to such a degree that, for him, the word *horse* is already too much of an abstraction. He will never write of a rider on a horse but rather of a certain well-described man on a dapple-gray.

This extraordinary precision, which never becomes pedantry, has its source in the intimate and altogether happy relationship with reality. It never becomes boring because it springs from an overwhelming, never-ending gratitude for everything that is. Out of this grateful devotion, Stifter became the greatest landscape-painter in literature (and in this he is doubtless even greater than Goethe): someone who possesses the magic wand to transform all visible things into words and all visible movements—the movement of the horse as well as that of the river or of the road—into sentences. One knows the gardens and rocks and mountains and rivers and forests of Stifter's novels even if one has never seen the Bohemian forest through which Witiko rode or the rose-gardens and hills and roads on which the young man walked to the hospitable friend in *Indian Summer*.

One of the reasons for Stifter's true greatness is that he has brought into the open the last implications of the philosophy of man that underlies the German educational novel. For Stifter, reality actually means nature and, for him, man is but one of its most perfect products. Again and again, he describes the slow, steady, and blessed process of the growth of a human being as it lives and blossoms and dies together with the trees and flowers of which it takes care during its lifetime. The individual story remains happy because it is seen, like history itself, surrounded by a greater and mightier history: "the history of the earth, the most meaningful, the most fascinating history there is, a history in which man's story is only an insertion, and who knows how small an insertion, as it may be followed by other histories of perhaps higher beings." How characteristic it is that the very idea of the end of mankind, which was to play such a sinister role in the poetry of the late nineteenth century, does not disturb Stifter's calm confidence in nature and in the inherent goodness of all its laws.

Indian Summer and *Witiko* alike are centered around the development of the individual, who should grow up into "the complete fulfillment of his forces, in accordance with the law of his own nature." In both cases, the novel starts with a young man riding away from home into the world in which he has to make his place according to his inclinations and natural gifts. His greatest sin would be to go against the law of nature as it reveals itself in his own self and to "choose life exclusively . . . with a view to serving mankind." In both cases the story comes to an end with the marriage of the hero, a marriage that coincides with his getting full disposition of his property. For whatever he owns—the house he builds and the garden he tends and the things of the past he collects and whose beauty he loves—are intimate parts of his personality, his individual homeland. "We are surrounded by (our property) as by a friend who never wavers and never breaks his loyalty." The individual person who builds his house and founds a family is the natural center of a wider circle, which one hesitates to call "society," so little has Stifter's society (where the neighbor is essentially the man "whom I advise and from whose words I learn") in common with society as an independent entity with which the individual finds himself confronted. Society does not exist in Stifter's novels because nature reigns everywhere. As long as man is "right"—one of Stifter's favorite words—he obeys natural laws in the same way as he obeys the innate laws of the wood and the stone when he builds a house. For "the real masters everywhere are the values of nature."

～

The highest value for man is the development of human nature, and the highest virtue, the prerequisite for this development, is confidence. This theme is magnificently unfolded in *Indian Summer,* where the acting persons, as well as the reader, are in complete ignorance up to the end of the story as to their names and social standings. The hero even gets engaged to a woman whose real name he learns only much later. The contrasting background story of the novel is again the story of a tragedy that occurs because, for one moment, the woman, in an unfortunate misunderstanding, had lost confidence in her lover's love, and this lover respects her too much to suspect it and therefore becomes unable to mend the break. The reconciliation that leads to the Indian summer of two people who had had no summer is brought about through confidence, the sudden insight that their love had remained intact despite all appearances, despite a whole life in which both had "sinned against the pure laws of nature" by marrying "without love and inclination." The touching beauty of this story lies in the fact that nothing in its tragic and happy events depends upon any other factor but love itself, that both people obey no other law than the law of love—dangerous, confusing, and exposed to misunderstandings as this law may have proved to be.

These few paragraphs certainly cannot reveal the great beauty and the strange innocent wisdom of Stifter's work. But they may be enough to help realize how great a risk the publishers have run in translating even one of the short stories. For nothing either in our time or in the non-German literary tradition, which hardly knows any equivalent to the Bildungsroman, meets this work half-way. Our sense of homelessness in society and of alienation in nature, whose laws we feel will function only as long as we leave it alone (as Kafka once put it), are constantly contradicted by Stifter. The publishers, in other words, must have pinned their hopes on some reading public whose feeling for beauty and pure human values is more consistent than modern or modernistic attitudes.

The choice of story and the translation are perfect in the opinion of this reviewer. "Rock Crystal," taken from the collection of stories, *Colored Stones,* is a wonderful—though not the greatest—example of Stifter's peculiar qualities. It is the tale of two children who lose their way among the icefields of a glacier. They are saved through their fearless confidence in the very nature of ice and rock and mountain, which so obviously threaten them with death. Their innocence fits so well in the sublime majesty of the mountain that they can patiently wait till the village comes to their rescue. This story is told against a larger background from which it derives part of its meaning. When the children lost their path, they were on their way back from a neighboring village beyond the mountain, where they had visited their grandparents. Their father, by marrying a beautiful girl outside his hometown, had aroused the villagers' distrust of anything foreign. The rescue party, organized by both villages from both sides of the mountain and directed to the mountain and the lost children (both of which the two hostile villages somehow always had in common), brought this alienation of the family from the village to an end. "Only from that day on were the children really felt to belong to the village, and not to be outsiders. Thenceforth they were regarded as natives whom the people had brought back to themselves from the mountain." The children, on the other hand, had been confronted with the real nature and the real danger of the mountain with which they will have to pass their lives. "The children, however, can never forget the mountain, and earnestly fix their gaze upon it when in the garden, when as in times past the sun is out bright and warm, the linden diffuses its fragrance, the bees are humming, and the mountain looks down upon them as serene and blue as the sky above."

Unpublished review. A few infelicities in the manuscript have been silently corrected.

Adalbert Stifter (1805–1868) exercised a profound influence on Friedrich Nietzsche, Franz Kafka, Martin Heidegger, and Walter Benjamin, among others. As Arendt notes, however, Stifter's work is poorly known outside the German-speaking world. This is perhaps the reason the review was never published. Born in Bohemia, Stifter studied law in Vienna and was often engaged as a tutor to the Austrian aristocracy. Among his major works are *Bunte Steine* (Colored Stones, 1853, from which the story "Rock Crystal" is drawn and from whose preface Arendt quotes in the course of her review), *Der Nachsommer* (Indian Summer, 1857), and *Witiko* (1865–1867).—Ed.

§ 13 French Existentialism

A lecture on philosophy provokes a riot, with hundreds crowding in and thousands turned away. Books on philosophical problems preaching no cheap creed and offering no panacea but, on the contrary, so difficult as to require actual thinking sell like detective stories. Plays in which the action is a matter of words, not of plot, and which offer a dialogue of reflections and ideas run for months and are attended by enthusiastic crowds. Analyses of the situation of man in the world, of the fundaments of human relationship, of Being and the Void not only give rise to a new literary movement but also figure as possible guides for a fresh political orientation. Philosophers become newspapermen, playwrights, novelists. They are not members of university faculties but "bohemians" who stay at hotels and live in the cafe—leading a public life to the point of renouncing privacy. And not even success, or so it seems, can turn them into respectable bores.

This is what is happening, from all reports, in Paris. If the Resistance has not achieved the European revolution, it seems to have brought about, at least in France, a genuine rebellion of the intellectuals, whose docility in relation to modern society was one of the saddest aspects of the sad spectacle of Europe between wars. And the French people, for the time being, appear to consider the arguments of their philosophers more important than the talk and the quarrels of their politicians. This may reflect, of course, a desire to escape from political action into some theory which merely talks about action, that is, into activism; but it may also signify that in the face of the spiritual bankruptcy of the left and the sterility of the old revolutionary élite—which have led to the desperate efforts at restoration of all political parties—more people than we might imagine have a feeling that the responsibility for political action is too heavy to assume until new foundations, ethical as well as political, are laid down, and that the old tradition of philosophy which is deeply imbedded even in the least philosophical individual is actually an impediment to new political thought.

The name of the new movement is "Existentialism," and its chief exponents are Jean-Paul Sartre and Albert Camus, but the term Existentialism has given rise to so many misunderstandings that Camus has already publicly stated why he is "not an Existentialist."[1] The term comes from the modern German philosophy which had a revival immediately after the First World War and has strongly influenced French thought for more than a decade; but it would be irrelevant to trace and define the sources of Existentialism in national terms for the simple reason that both the German and the French manifestations came out of an identical period and a more or less identical cultural heritage.

The French Existentialists, though they differ widely among themselves, are united on two main lines of rebellion: first, the rigorous repudiation of what they call the *esprit sérieux;* and, second, the angry refusal to accept the world as it is as the natural, predestined milieu of man.

L'esprit sérieux, which is the original sin according to the new philosophy, may be equated with respectability. The "serious" man is one who thinks of himself *as* president of his business, *as* a member of the Legion of Honor, *as* a member of the faculty, but also *as* father, *as* husband, or as any other half-natural, half-social function. For by so doing he agrees to the identification of himself with an arbitrary function which society has bestowed. *L'esprit sérieux* is the very negation of freedom, because it leads man to agree to and accept the necessary deformation which every human being must undergo when he is fitted into society. Since everyone knows well enough in his own heart that he is not identical with his function, *l'esprit sérieux* indicates also bad faith in the sense of pretending. Kafka has already shown, in *America,* how ridiculous and dangerous is the hollow dignity which grows out of identifying oneself with one's function: In that book the most dignified person in the hotel, upon whose word the hero's job and daily bread depend, rules out the possibility that he can make an error by invoking the argument of the "serious" man: "how could I go on being the head porter if I mistook one person for another?"

This matter of *l'esprit sérieux* was first touched upon in Sartre's novel, *La*

Nausée, in a delightful description of a gallery of portraits of the town's respectable citizens, *les salauds* [the hypocrites]. It then became the central topic of Camus's novel *L'Etranger.* The hero of the book, the stranger, is an average man who simply refuses to submit to the serious-mindedness of society, who refuses to live as any of his allotted functions. He does not behave as a son at his mother's funeral—he does not weep; he does not behave as a husband—he declines to take marriage seriously even at the moment of his engagement. Because he does not pretend, he is a stranger whom no one understands, and he pays with his life for his affront to society. Since he refuses to play the game, he is isolated from his fellow-men to the point of incomprehensibility and isolated from himself to the point of becoming inarticulate. Only in a last scene, immediately before his death, does the hero arrive at some kind of explanation which conveys the impression that for him life itself was such a mystery and in its terrible way so beautiful that he did not see any necessity for "improving" upon it with the trimmings of good behavior and hollow pretensions.

Sartre's brilliant play *Huis Clos* [*No Exit*] belongs to the same category. The play opens in hell, appropriately furnished in the style of the Second Empire. The three persons gathered in the room—"Hell is the Others"— set the diabolical torture in motion by trying to pretend. Since, however, their lives are closed and since "you are your life and nothing else," pretense no longer works, and we see what would go on behind closed doors if people actually were stripped of the sheltering cover of functions derived from society.

Both Sartre's play and Camus's novel deny the possibility of a genuine fellowship between men, of any relationship which would be direct, innocent, free of pretense. Love in Sartre's philosophy is the will to be loved, the need for a supreme confirmation of one's own existence. For Camus love is a somewhat awkward and hopeless attempt to break through the isolation of the individual,

The way out of pretense and serious-mindedness is to play at being what one really is. Again Kafka indicated in the last chapter of *America* a new possibility of authentic life. The great "Nature Theater" where everyone is welcome and where everybody's unhappiness is resolved is not by accident a theater. Here everybody is invited to choose his role, to play at what he is or would like to be. The chosen role is the solution of the conflict between mere functioning and mere being, as well as between mere ambition and mere reality.

The new "ideal" becomes, in this context, the actor whose very profession is pretending, who constantly changes his role, and thus can never take any of his roles seriously. By playing at what one is, one guards one's freedom as a human being from the pretenses of one's functions; moreover, only by playing at what he really is, is man able to affirm that he is never identical with himself as a thing is identical with itself. An inkpot is always an inkpot. Man is his life and his actions, which are never finished until the very moment of his death. He *is* his existence.

The second common element of French Existentialism, the insistence upon the basic homelessness of man in the world, is the topic of Camus's *Le Mythe de Sisyphe; essay sur l'absurde,* and of Sartre's *La Nausée.* For Camus man is essentially the stranger because the world in general and man as man are not fitted for each other; that they are together in existence makes the human condition an absurdity. Man is the only "thing" in the world which obviously does not belong in it, for only man does not exist simply as a man among men in the way animals exist among animals and trees among trees—all of which necessarily exist, so to speak, in the plural. Man is basically alone with his "revolt" and his "clairvoyance," that is, with his reasoning, which makes him ridiculous because the gift of reason was bestowed upon him in a world "where everything is given and nothing ever explained."

Sartre's notion of the absurdity, the contingency of existence is best represented in the chapter of *La Nausée* which appears in the current issue of the *Partisan Review* under the title "The Root of the Chestnut Tree." Whatever exists, so far as we can see, has not the slightest reason for its existence. It is simply *de trop,* superfluous. The fact that I can't even imagine a world in which, instead of many too many things, there would be nothing only shows the hopelessness and senselessness of man's being eternally entangled in existence.

Here Sartre and Camus part company, if we may judge from the few works of theirs which have reached this country. The absurdity of existence and the repudiation of *l'esprit sérieux* are only points of departure for each. Camus seems to have gone on to a philosophy of absurdity, whereas Sartre seems to be working toward some new positive philosophy and even a new humanism.

Camus has probably protested against being called an Existentialist because for him the absurdity does not lie in man as such or in the world as such but only in their being thrown together. Since man's life, being laid in the world, is absurd, it must be lived as absurdity—lived, that is, in a kind of proud defiance which insists on reason despite the experience of reason's failure to explain anything; insists on despair since man's pride will not allow him the hope of discovering a sense he cannot figure out by means of reason; insists, finally, that reason and human dignity, in spite of their senselessness, remain the supreme values. The absurd life then consists in constantly rebelling against all its conditions and in constantly refusing consolations. "This revolt is the price of life. Spread over the whole of an existence, it restores its grandeur." All that remains, all that one can say yes to, is chance itself, the *hazard roi* which has apparently played at putting man and world together. " 'I judge that everything is well,' said Oedipus, and this word is sacred. It resounds in the ferocious universe which is the limit of man . . . It makes of destiny an affair of men which should be settled among men." This is precisely the point where Camus, without giving much explanation, leaves behind all modernistic attitudes and comes to insights which are genuinely modern, the insight, for instance, that the moment may have arrived "when creation is no longer taken tragically; it is only taken seriously."

For Sartre, absurdity is of the essence of things as well as of man. Anything that exists is absurd simply because it exists. The salient difference between the things of the world and the human being is that things are unequivocally identical with themselves, whereas man—because he sees and knows that he sees, believes and knows that he believes—bears within his consciousness a negation which makes it impossible for him ever to become one with himself. In this single respect—in respect of his consciousness, which has the germ of negation in it—man is a creator. For this is of man's own making and not merely given, as the world and his existence are given. If man becomes aware of his own consciousness and its tremendous creative possibilities, and renounces the longing to be identical with himself as a thing is, he realizes that he depends upon nothing and nobody outside himself and that he can be free, the master of his own destiny. This seems to be the essential meaning of Sartre's novel *Les Mouches* (The Flies), in which Orestes, by taking upon himself the responsibility for the necessary killing of which the town is afraid, liberates the town and takes the Flies—the Erinyes of bad conscience and of the dark fear of revenge—with him. He himself is immune because he does not feel guilty and regrets nothing.

It would be a cheap error to mistake this new trend in philosophy and literature for just another fashion of the day because its exponents refuse

the respectability of institutions and do not even pretend to that seriousness which regards every achievement as a step in a career. Nor should we
be put off by the loud journalistic success with which their work has been
accompanied. This success, equivocal as it may be in itself, is nevertheless
due to the quality of the work. It is also due to a definite modernity of attitude which does not try to hide the depth of the break in Western tradition. Camus especially has the courage not even to look for connections,
for predecessors and the like. The good thing about Sartre and Camus is
that they apparently suffer no longer from nostalgia for the good old days,
even though they may know that in an abstract sense those days were actually better than ours. They do not believe in the magic of the old, and
they are honest in that they make no compromises whatever.

Yet if the revolutionary élan of these writers is not broken by success, if,
symbolically speaking, they stick to their hotel rooms and their cafes, the
time may come when it will be necessary to point out "seriously" those aspects of their philosophy which indicate that they are still dangerously involved in old concepts. The nihilistic elements, which are obvious in spite
of all protests to the contrary, are not the consequences of new insights
but of some very old ideas.[2]

Originally published in *The Nation* 162 (February 23, 1946): 226–28. Reprinted in
One Hundred Years of "The Nation": A Critical Anthology, ed. Henry Christman
(New York: Macmillan, 1965), 253–58; *Essays in Understanding,* 188–93.—Ed.

§ 14 No Longer and Not Yet

Hume once remarked that the whole of human civilization depends upon the fact that "one generation does not go off the stage at once and another succeed, as is the case with silkworms and butterflies."[1] At some turning-points of history, however, at some heights of crisis, a fate similar to that of silkworms and butterflies may befall a generation of men. For the decline of the old, the birth of the new, is not necessarily an affair of continuity; between the generations, between those who for some reason or other still belong to the old and those who either feel the catastrophe in their very bones or have already grown up with it, the chain is broken and an "empty space," a kind of historical no man's land, comes to the surface which can be described only in terms of "no longer and not yet." In Europe such an absolute interruption of continuity occurred during and after the First World War. All the loose talk of intellectuals about the necessary decline of Western civilization or the famous lost generation, as it is usually uttered by "reactionaries," has its basis of truth in this break, and consequently has proved much more attractive than the corresponding triviality of the "liberal" mind that puts before us the alternative between going ahead and going backward, an alternative which appears so devoid of sense precisely because it still presupposes an unbroken chain of continuity.

Speaking merely in terms of European literature, this gap, this opening of an abyss of empty space and empty time, is most clearly visible in the

---

The Death of Virgil. By Hermann Broch. Translated by Jean Starr Untermeyer. Pantheon Books. $6.50.

disparity between the two greatest masters of our time, Marcel Proust and Franz Kafka. Proust is the last and the most beautiful farewell to the world of the nineteenth century, and we return to his work, written in the key of the "no longer," again and again when the mood of farewell and of sorrow overwhelms us. Kafka, on the other hand, is our contemporary only to a limited extent. It is as though he wrote already from the vantage point of a distant future, as though he were or could have been at home only in a world which is "not yet." This puts us at a certain distance whenever we are to read and discuss his work, a distance which will not grow smaller, even though we may know that his art is the expression of some future world which is our future, too—if we are to have any future at all.

All other great European novelists and poets find their place and their standard of measurement somewhere in between these dead masters. But Hermann Broch's book falls in a different category from the rest. That he has in common with Proust the form of the inner monologue and with Kafka the utter and radical renunciation of entertainment, as well as a pre-occupation with metaphysics; that he shares with Proust a deep fondness for the world as it is given to us, and that he shares with Kafka the belief that the "hero" of the novel is no longer a character with certain well-defined qualities but rather man as such (for the real life of the man and poet Virgil is no more than an occasion for Broch's philosophical speculations)—all this is true, and the histories of literature may say it later.

What is more important, at least at this moment, is that Broch's work—through its subject matter and through its entirely original and magnificent poetic diction—has become something like the missing link between Proust and Kafka, between a past which we have irretrievably lost and a future which is not yet at hand. In other words, this book is by itself the kind of bridge with which Virgil tries to span the abyss of empty space between the no longer and the not yet. And since this abyss is very real; since it has become deeper and more frightful every single year from the fateful year of 1914 onward, until the death factories erected in the heart of Europe definitely cut the already outworn thread with which we still might have been tied to a historical entity of more than two thousand years; since we are already living in the "empty space," confronted with a reality which no preconceived traditional idea of the world and man can possibly illuminate—dear as this tradition may have remained to our hearts—we must be profoundly grateful for the great work of poetry which clings so desperately to this one subject.

Curiously enough, very little in Broch's earlier work indicates the future author of the *Death of Virgil. The Sleepwalkers*, apart from its qualities as a novel, shows only that its author is fed up with story-telling, thoroughly impatient with his own work: he tells his readers that they had better find for themselves the end of the story, and neglects character and plot in order to squeeze into his book long speculations about the nature of history. Up to a certain date Broch was a good, playful, amusing story-teller, not a great poet.

The date which made of Broch a poet seems to have coincided with the last stage of darkening in Europe. When the night arrived, Broch woke up. He awoke to a reality which so overwhelmed him that he translated it immediately into a dream, as is fitting for a man roused in night. This dream is *The Death of Virgil*.

Critics have said that the book is written in lyrical prose, but this is not quite correct. The style, unique in its concentrated tension, bears more of a resemblance to those invocations of the Homeric hymns in which the God is summoned over and over again, each time with another residence, another mythological setting, another place of worship—as though the worshiper had to make sure, absolutely sure, that he could not miss the God. In the same way Broch invokes Life, or Death, or Love, or Time, or Space, as if he wanted to make sure, absolutely sure, that he would not miss the mark. This gives the monologue its passionate urgency, and brings out the tense, concentrated action of all true speculation.

In the "O's" of the invocations are imbedded the exciting descriptions, the extensive landscape painting in which the work is so very rich. These read like a long and tender song of farewell to all Western painters, and they transcend through their form of invocation these described objects, as though they embraced all that is beautiful or all that is ugly, all that is green or all earthly dustiness, all nobility or all vulgarity.

The subject of Broch's book, as the title indicates, is the last twenty-four hours of Virgil's life. But death is treated not merely as an event but as the ultimate achievement of man—whether in the sense that moments of dying are one's last and only chance for knowing what life was all about or in the sense that it is then one passes judgment upon one's own life. This judgment is not self-accusation, for it is too late for that, nor self-justification, for it is, in a way, too early for that; it is the ultimate effort to find the truth, the last definitive word for the whole story. This makes of the last judgment a human affair, to be settled by man himself, though at the limits of his forces and possibilities—as if he wanted to spare God this whole trouble. The "no longer and not yet" on this level means the no longer alive and the not yet dead; and the task is the conscious achievement of judgment and truth.

This grandiose concept of death as an ultimate task instead of as an ultimate calamity prevents Broch's speculations from falling into the trap of modern death-philosophy, for which life has in itself the germ of death and for which, consequently, the moment of death appears as the "goal of life." If death is the last task of the living man, then life has been given, not as a death-infected gift, but rather under certain conditions—that we forever "stand on the bridge that is spanned between invisibility and invisibility and nevertheless . . . are caught in the stream."

The actual subject matter of the book is the position of the artist in the world and in history: of the man who does not "do" like human beings but "creates" like God—though in appearance only. The artist is forever excluded from reality, and banished into the "empty province of beauty." His playing at eternity—and this bewitching game that we call beauty—turns into the "laughter that destroys reality," the laughter that springs from the terrible intuition that the Creation itself, and not merely man's playing at creating, can be destroyed. With this laughter the poet "descends to the mob-patterns," to the cynical, debased vulgarity over which he had been carried on his litter through the slums of Brundisium.[2] Mob and artist alike are greedy with self-idolatry, caring only for themselves, and excluded from all true community, which is based on helpfulness. "Intoxicated with loneliness," from which spring in equal part "the intoxication of blood, the intoxication of death, and . . . the intoxication of beauty," they are both equally treacherous, equally unconcerned with truth, therefore entirely unreliable and in need of forgetting reality, by means of beauty or circus games; both are intoxicated with "empty forms and empty words."

Because the "no longer and not yet" cannot be bridged with the rainbow of beauty, the poet is bound to fall "into vulgarity . . . where vulgarity is at its worst, into literarity." From this insight rises the decision which becomes the central plot of the story, the decision to burn the *Aeneid,* to have the work "consumed by the fire of reality." This deed, this sacrifice, suddenly appears as the only escape left from the "empty province of beauty," the only door through which, even when dying and in the very last moment, the poet may still perceive the promised land of reality and human fellowship.

It is at this moment that the friends enter the scene, trying to prevent what clearly are mere fever delusions of the dying man. There follows the long dialogue between Virgil and Octavian—one of the most truthful and impressive pieces of writing in all historical fiction—which ends with the abandonment of this sacrifice. The sacrifice, after all, would have been made only for the salvation of soul, out of anxiety about the self, for the sake of the symbol—while the abandonment of the plan and the gift of the manuscript win from the face of the imperial friend a last happy smile.

Then comes death, the boat ride down to the depths of the elements when gently, one after another, the friends disappear, and man returns in peace from the long voyage of freedom into the quiet waiting of an inarticulate universe. His death seemed to him a happy death: for he had found the bridge with which to span the abyss that yawns between the "no longer and not yet" of history, between the "no longer" of the old laws and the "not yet" of the new saving word, between life and death: "Not quite here but yet at hand; that is how it has sounded and how it would sound."

The book is written in a very beautiful and extremely complicated German; the achievement of the translator is beyond praise.

Originally published in *The Nation* 1963 (September 14, 1946): 300–302; reprinted in *Essays in Understanding,* 158–62.
Hermann Broch (1886–1951) was an Austrian novelist and philosopher, whose most famous work, *Der Tod des Vergil* (*The Death of Virgil*), first appeared in English translation in 1945 and forms the subject of Arendt's review. In addition to "The Achievement of Hermann Broch" (Chapter 20), Arendt also wrote a lengthy introduction to the volumes of Broch's complete works devoted to his essays; this introduction was translated under the title "Hermann Broch, 1886–1951" for inclusion in *Men in Dark Times* (New York: Harcourt Brace Jovanovich, 1983), 111–51.—Ed.

§ 15 Proof Positive

Histories of art and literature are the step-children of the historical sciences because their subjects cannot be dealt with adequately without that quality called taste, and taste does not necessarily belong to the scholar's scale of virtues. This unfortunate state of affairs is already well-known, and there was no need for Victor Lange to prove the point.

Nevertheless, he has proved it in almost exemplary fashion in his volume, *Modern German Literature, 1870–1940* (Cornell, $2.50). If anyone wishes to know how not to write a history of literature he has only to be given this book. Every author, no matter how obscure, is mentioned at least once, and no distinctions whatever are made. Third-grade writers like Raabe are set side by side with first-rate poets like Stifter.[1] The twentieth century, for which judgments are not yet established, fares even worse. To give one single instance taken at random: "The poetry of the later Rilke, or Binding and Carossa, of Rudolf Borchardt and Rudolf Alexander Schröder, of Oskar Lörke and Agnes Miegel, and the singularly impressive epic poems of Albrecht Schäffer are all indicative of a palpable shift from expressionist abandon to the austerity of a disciplined idiom."[2] The point is that Binding, Lörke, and Agnes Miegel are indicative of nothing except very mediocre poetry; that the others may be "indicative" but of widely differing trends; and that only Borchardt and Schröder have anything in common at all.

The only proof that this book was written by a real person and is not a filing system which through some magic got into print lies in occasional omissions—of Mörike and Kleist in the first part, of Hans Blüher and the last beautiful novel-fragment of Hofmannsthal ("Andreas") in the second.[3] But for these omissions one feels rather grateful.

There would not be much sense in reviewing such a book if it were not for the, let us hope, imaginary danger that it should become a textbook. It would cause the intelligent student to shy away from German literature, while it might give to the more feeble-minded a terrific arsenal of cheap catchwords which have not the slightest relation to the respective authors and their work.

"Proof Positive" appeared in *The Nation* 162 (January 5, 1946): 22.
Victor Lange (1908–1996) was a professor of German at Cornell University when he published the book under review.—Ed.

§ 16 The Streets of Berlin

Robert Gilbert was well known in Germany, but his songs were known even better than their author's name. Now he has published in this country a book of German verses, *Meine Reime Deine Reime* (Peter Thomas Fisher, $2.75), which is unique among the works of German literature in exile. Gilbert's songs, though some of them are great poetry, are not at all "literature"; most of them are written in the dialect of Berlin, and they communicate a sense of closeness to the people, to the man in the street, that makes it difficult to realize that they actually were composed during twelve years of exile. Gilbert's "Stempellied," a song of the unemployed, was sung all over Germany during the early thirties, though he himself was not numbered among the celebrities. Such things happen only in cases of direct popularity of the sort which made it possible, for instance, for the Nazis to pretend that the author of the "Lorelei" was unknown.

These verses are a vivid reminder that Berlin was not the Reich, though the Reich certainly conquered and destroyed Berlin. For they recapture the dialect—a language with its own peculiar humor and full of strange, indirect, involved patterns of speech—and the mentality which formed it—extreme skepticism and keenness of mind together with simple kindness and great fear of sentimentality. If Berlin's streets rise again these songs will be a part of them; if not, they exist in these songs.

Gilbert writes with a delightful facility and is quite unpretentious. He does not hesitate to print, along with a number of perfect verses, less perfect songs so long as he feels that their subject matter is important. He even dares to touch the borderline of *Kitsch* and to skirt the gutter—being safe against both as only a genuine poet can be. This wonderful carelessness had great precedents in German poetry. Gilbert has inherited the carelessness and, incidentally, the convincing inner goodness of Heine, the happiness and decency of Liliencron, the political passion and the courage of Arno Holz.¹ Whether this tradition will ever revive in Germany we cannot yet know; but at least it has again found a voice in the German language.

Originally published in *The Nation* 162 (March 23, 1946): 350–51.

Robert Gilbert, originally Robert Winterfeld (1899–1978), born in Berlin, was a German poet, writer, and composer. A close and longtime friend of Arendt's second husband Heinrich Blücher (1899–1970), he went into exile in 1938. The book under review, *Meine Reime, deine Reime: Berliner, Wiener u. a. Gedichte* (*My Rhyme, Your Rhyme: Berlinese, Viennese and Other Poems*), was published in New York in 1946. Gilbert wrote four other volumes of poetry, including one for which Arendt provides the afterword (Chapter 33).—Ed.

§ 17 The Too Ambitious Reporter

Without a doubt Koestler belongs among the best reporters of our time. He has shown an extraordinary ability to seize and transmit the general feeling and thinking of a whole country during a critical period (civil-war Spain in *Dialogue with Death;* defeated France in *Scum of the Earth*). His flair for atmosphere, his sensitivity to fluctuating moods make him the ideal reporter of those events which, though never front-page news, are necessary to the understanding of front-page news. Put into any given country, he acts—or rather reacts—like a thermometer: he will produce that country's correct temperature after only ten months' stay.

"The intelligentsia," confesses Koestler, "is a kind of sensitive porous membrane stretched between media of different properties." This definition reminds one of Aristotle's statement that the best medium is a person with an empty mind and an exaggerated sensitivity. But whatever the intelligentsia, taken as a definite class, may have become, it has not yet sunk to the level of mere reactivity. On the other hand, good reporters, if they are really good, do belong in a rather dubious realm between the intellectual and the merely sensitive. Koestler himself is an excellent example. Because of his personal decency and the good fortune he has had to live through this period as a Jewish anti-fascist, he could *over*-develop his natural gifts to the point of complete identification, not simply with a given situation, but with

---

Twilight Bar. By Arthur Koestler. New York, The Macmillan Company, 1945. 104 pp. $2.00. *The Yogi and the Commissar.* By Arthur Koestler. New York, The Macmillan Company, 1945. 247 pp. $2.75.

a general state of mind. And it is our good luck that Koestler's trajectory has taken him into the bosom of the intelligentsia, whose destinies he now will share and about whom he will report. The point is that no one who really belonged to this "class" would ever have been able to report it.

Useful as this identification with the intelligentsia may prove for reportage, its more immediate consequences are disconcerting. Koestler has become ambitious, and he has written some rather bad novels and one rather nice play.

Twilight Bar is indeed almost as much "without presumptions" as the author insists. Its four acts deal good-humoredly with two characters who arrive from a star to investigate this poor planet's situation with regard to happiness; they threaten mankind with immediate death if its quotient of happiness is not raised within three days' time. This succeeds in frightening people into a state of superlative if slightly childish felicity (the point might have been made here that only children are capable of intense happiness; Koestler does not make it). But finally the two investigators land in jail as "suspicious" strangers. Whereupon everybody grows up again and becomes as unhappy as anyone could possibly be.

The theme and even more the style of this drama remind one of Shaw's minor plays, except that Shaw's supreme sense of drama, plot, and action is lacking.[1] What is left is wit that springs just as much from a foundation of banality as from the gift for repartee. This suffices, at any rate, to entertain, and makes the play much more enjoyable than Koestler's tremendously "serious" novels.

The Yogi and the Commissar is by far the most ambitious of Koestler's books because here he ventures beyond his experiments in bad fiction into something that in appearance only is individual thought. His sensitivity has communicated to him a notion of the fundamental restlessness of modern intellectuals who know that the basis of their mental activity is no longer safe. The trouble here is that Koestler tries to take part in the discussion itself instead of merely reporting its mental climate, with the result that he comes dangerously and—I am sorry to say—ridiculously close to assuming a mission. He talks about freedom, for instance, as though nobody before him had ever taken it seriously. His somewhat innocent emptiness—expressed in contemplations that always move between arbitrary polarities—is the price he, as a good reporter, has to pay for the gift of over-sensitiveness. In his first and final chapters, in which the intellectual is seen eternally swinging between the opposite extremes of "yogi" personal mysticism and "commissar" authoritarian practicality, this emptiness is particularly shocking.

All these superficial chapters actually show is that European intellectuals are apparently fed up with the myths of materialism. The remaining chapters, on the other hand, take us back to good and sometimes excellent reportage. Thus the essay on the death of the English poet and flyer, Richard Hillary, imparts something of the "mental climate of the war" in which (according to another English poet) they "who lived by honest dreams defend the bad against the worst."[2] Here are the desperate integrity and that despairing struggle for "some kind of fellowship" of which T. E. Lawrence already gave so eloquent testimony, and which is evidence to what an extent Lawrence's general attitude toward society, culture, and politics anticipated the present generation.[3]

The members of this generation, before the war, still "balanced precariously and with irritability between a despised world they had come out of and a despising world they couldn't get into"—all the while living under the dangerous illusion that somehow the despised bourgeoisie and the despising labor class were right and at home in this world and only they were out of place. While actually they were the only ones, apparently, to sense that the whole was going to pieces. Then came the war and with it the new pride in not forgetting that it was the bad they had to defend against the worse. Then came death and with it the old and saddening experience that it is Patroclus who gets killed and Thersites who sails safely home.[4] Then, finally, came the shame, the general irrational feeling of humiliation at being alive, at having survived—as though mere survival were already desertion and betrayal.

There are many more pages worth reading. The chapter on Soviet Russia gives some very valuable statistical data on a state of affairs which in its general aspect and implications is only too real. "Scum of the Earth— 1942" is a welcome and necessary supplement to the earlier reports on France. And even "Anatomy of a Myth," though again impaired by superficial brilliancies and naïve sophistication, gives a good insight into the sad story of the disillusioning of the European left.

Originally published in *Commentary* 1 (1945–46): 94–95.
Arthur Koestler, originally Kösztler (1905–1983), was a Hungarian-Jewish novelist, activist, and political theorist. He is best known for *Darkness at Noon* (1940), a novel about the Soviet show trials.—Ed.

§ 18 Beyond Personal Frustration

The Poetry of Bertolt Brecht

Poetry has played a lesser role in modern German literature than prose. Bertolt Brecht, beyond a doubt the greatest living German poet and possibly the greatest living European playwright, is the only poet one can place in the same category of relevance as Kafka and Broch in German, Joyce in English, and Proust in French literature. Born in 1898, he is of T. E. Lawrence's generation—the first generation, that is, of what one is tempted to call the "three lost generations," hoping by this pluralization somewhat to mitigate the self-pitying attitude to political reality expressed in the usual phrase. Yet this sentimentality contains more than a grain of truth. If productivity depends upon a "placid pure development" (Hebbel's *ruhige reine Entwicklung*),[1] then every generation of our century has been equally "lost"; the first, because its initial experience was the battlefields of the First World War; the second, because the effective lesson of inflation and unemployment at once taught it the instability of whatever had been left intact after preliminary destruction, as it were, of the European world; the third had the choice of being educated by Nazism, or the Spanish Civil War, or the Moscow trials. Finally, all three generations went into the Second World War: as soldiers, as refugees and exiles, as resistants, as inmates of concentration camps, or as civilians under a rain of bombs. This last experience, the Second World War, was a potent aid to reconciling the age differences between the generations. They are today all in the same situation; and if they attempt to look

---

Bertolt Brecht, *Selected Poems*, trans. H. R. Hays. Reynal & Hitchcock, 1947. $3.50.

at themselves, their lives, and their possibilities with the eyes of the nineteenth century, they invariably produce a literature where individuals complain of psychological deformation and social torture, personal frustration and general disillusion.

This essentially individualistic attitude—individualistic though it frequently has as its subject the decomposition of the individual—never entered into anything that Brecht wrote. At an early date he was more struck by the misfortunes of the time than his own unhappiness and solved all personal problems by adopting a stoic attitude with respect to everything that might happen to himself. The first startling thing in the present selection (which gives a fair insight into the best of all his periods) is the consistency of this attitude. The first poem, "Concerning Poor B. B.," and the last, "To Posterity," are separated by more than twenty years; yet they read like two consecutive pieces. Brecht, in the early twenties, wrote:

> Von diesen Städten wird bleiben: der durch sie hindurchging, der Wind!
> Fröhlich machet das Haus den Esser: er leert es.
> Wir wissen, daß wir Vorläufige sind
> Und nach uns wird kommen: nichts Nennenswertes.
>
> Bei den Erdbeben, die kommen werden, werde ich hoffentlich
> Meine Virginia nicht ausgehen lassen durch Bitterkeit,
> Ich, Bertold Brecht, in die Asphaltstädte verschlagen
> Aus den schwarzen Wäldern in meiner Mutter in früher Zeit.

The translator's English for this is:

> There shall remain of these cities but the wind that blew through them!
> The house maketh the feaster merry: it is emptied out.
> We know that we are makeshift
> And after us will come—practically nought.
>
> In the earthquakes to come it is to be hoped
> I shan't allow bitterness to quench my cigar's glow,
> I, Bertolt Brecht, astray in cement cities
> Brought from the woods in my mother long ago.

And he only sums it up in one of his latest poems, perhaps the most beautiful one in this present selection:

> Wirklich, ich lebe in finsteren Zeiten!
> Das arglose Wort is töricht. Eine glatte Stirn

Deutet auf Unempfindlichkeit hin. Der Lachende
Hat die furchtbare Nachricht
Nur noch nicht empfangen.
. . .
In die Städte kam ich zu der Zeit der Unordnung,
Als da Hunger herrschte.
Unter die Menschen kam ich zu der Zeit des Aufruhrs
Und ich empörte mich mit ihnen.
So verging meine Zeit
Die auf Erden mir gegeben war.
. . .
Ihr, die ihr auftauchen werdet aus der Flut
In der wir untergegangen sind,
Gedenkt
Wenn ihr von unsern Schwächen sprecht
Auch der finsteren Zeit
Der ihr entronnen seid.
. . . .
Gedenkt unsrer
Mit Nachsicht.[2]

Which is translated:

Indeed I live in the dark ages!
A guileless word is an absurdity. A smooth forehead betokens
A hard heart. He who laughs
Has not yet heard
The terrible tidings.
. . . .
I came to the cities in a time of disorder
When hunger ruled.
I came among men in a time of uprising
And I revolted with them.
So the time passed away
Which on earth was given me.
. . . .
You, who shall emerge from the flood
In which we are sinking,
Think—
When you speak of our weaknesses,
Also of the dark time

That brought them forth.
. . . .
Do not judge us
Too harshly.

Before going on, I should like to justify my quotation of the German original together with Hays's translation. It is, of course, needless to insist upon the fact that poetry defies translation if the translator is not the equal of the poet he is translating. (Who would dare to translate Hölderlin? and how many, alas, have dared to translate Goethe!)[3] Hays certainly has done his best, yet accuracy and Brecht's peculiar precision are so often sacrificed to not very successful English verse that one wonders whether a good prose translation would not have been more useful in a bi-lingual edition.[4] The translation problem has an especially sad aspect in Brecht's case. There is not only the fact that he has remained, as the jacket rightly states, "one of the least known" figures in contemporary literature, overshadowed by dozens of mediocrities and a few good writers who yet are of lesser relevance; this inevitable fate of the poet was formerly compensated for to a certain degree by the existence of an educated audience fluent in two or three languages in addition to its own. This audience no longer exists; multi-lingual people of today have learnt their languages when forced by events, as Brecht says, to change their "country more often than (their) shoes"; and though they may carry an understanding of foreign literatures along with them, such an itinerant audience is never an adequate substitute for an appreciation rooted in its own soil. As far as Brecht is concerned, there is the further unhappy irony that no other writer has so consistently attempted to reach an international audience. Brecht has eagerly borrowed from English and French poetry (once to the point of being accused, stupidly, of plagiarism), from the formalism of Japanese drama, and from Chinese sayings. The "moon of Alabama," the "Island of Manhattan," "Lake Erie," the "wet Ohio," the "City Mahagonny," the "ricebarge coolies" are not the backdrop of cheap romanticism; they are the precise expression of his conviction that the experiences and conclusions of the men of this century are roughly the same everywhere, that "man needs help from every creature born," and that this borrowing is one of the necessary preparations "to lay the foundations of kindness" until "at last it comes to pass that man can help his fellow man."

Brecht's personal stoicism, based on the profound insight that "if my luck leaves me I am lost," corresponds to his general view of human life as having the meaning of a task in the world. What for others was the feeling of belonging to a "lost generation," for him is simply life in "dark times" when "street led to the quicksand, speech betrayed me to the slaughterer," so that "there was little I could do." He is lost because the task is too big; if he feels himself sinking in the flood, he appeals to those who will emerge from it, and does not glance longingly backward at those who are not yet endangered. There is not the slightest trace in him of envy of the past, nor even irritation at the great crowd of happy fools who have "not yet heard the terrible tidings." Brecht escapes all the temptations of mere psychology by realizing that it would be deadly, as well as ridiculous, to measure the flood of events in which he is caught up by the yardstick of individual aspirations—to meet, for instance, the international catastrophe of unemployment with the bourgeois concept of success or failure in a job, or the catastrophe of war with the ideal of a well-rounded personality, or exile with a complaint about lost fame.

This anti-psychological insistence upon the events themselves is the chief reason for Brecht's employing the poetic forms he does: the ballad (as contrasted with the lyric) in poetry, and the "epic theatre" (as contrasted with tragedy) in drama. His plays break with a tradition that insisted on the conflict or development of one character in the world; they concentrate on a logical course of events in which men, abstracted into types, under circumstances which the audience is supposed to recognize immediately as their own, behave rightly or wrongly and are judged by the objective requirements of the events themselves; or, as in the *Dreigroschenoper* [*Threepenny Opera*], they lay bare the functioning of a world in which businessmen behave like criminals, by showing a dramatic world in which criminals behave like businessmen. The exception to the rule is Galileo (in the play *Galileo*), who is less of a type and more of a character, who loves the world and its goods more than any of Brecht's very puritanical heroes ever could afford, who can't resist "an old wine and a new thought" simply because he is genuinely fond of both and not because he wants to put forth a few anti-hypocritical reflections on the "invigorating power of money." *Galileo* is more mature, more relaxed, so to speak, than anything Brecht ever wrote. (America may have had this effect upon his work; it is after all no small matter to live for years in a country where you only hear of starving children overseas but don't meet them every other day around the corner.) But Galileo is also a type, though a new one, in Brecht's repertoire; he is the type of the man who is concerned only with truth, a truth that has become the active ingredient in the whole structure of life and the world. And strange as it may seem in a poet, there are any number of indications that a passion for truth is the central passion of the "wissensdurstigen [knowledge-thirsty] Brecht."

A similar insistence on events is evident in Brecht's poetry, which avoids individual moods and their lyrical transformation into all-fascinating, all-convincing modes of existence of everything that is. In his ballads Brecht takes some single momentous event and shows men not as types who act upon the world, but as sufferers of some extremity, some natural or man-made catastrophe. Man's virtue is invariably a mixture of half-cynical courage, stoic pride, and curiosity in the face of gruesome and destructive forces. It is obvious that this form owes its revival to the authentic experience of the First World War, which indeed was mainly an experience of helplessness. The ballad with its folk tradition of great sadness and the un-happy ending fitted this experience so well that the ballad form survived all the merely experimental modernistic efforts of post-war German poetry. The heroes of the early pieces of the *Hauspostille* [Domestic Breviary] are adventurers, pirates, professional soldiers, but also mothers who murdered their children, or children who murdered their parents. Brecht's sympathy for them had at that time hardly a social note; it did not yet need justifica-tion, it was a matter of course to side with the "Mördern, denen viel Leides geschah" ("murderers sorely afflicted with grief").

Preoccupation with murder, destruction, death and decay was a com-mon characteristic of the time and in Brecht's case is easily misunder-stood. Its most prominent literary exponents, Gottfried Benn in Germany and Céline in France (both later enthusiastic admirers of Nazism),[5] with their bitter, resentful, and half-pathological glorification of decay for its own sake, have little if anything in common with Brecht's wild and beau-tiful songs full of a glorious and triumphant vitality.

> Von Sonne krank und ganz von Regen zerfressen
> Geraubten Lorbeer im zerrauften Haar
> Hat er seine ganze Jugend, nur nicht ihre Träume vergessen
> Lange das Dach, nie den Himmel, der drüber war.[6]

("Sick from sun, by rainy weather battered, / With stolen laurels, his fierce hair torn, / His youth, not its dreams, he has forgotten, / The roof, not the sky, under which he was born.") Brecht's early violent cynicism was a rather belated reaction to the overwhelming discovery that, as Nietzsche had said, "God was dead"—and man was free to live and love howsoever he pleased, thanking whomsoever he pleased for the existence of the world. Brecht's pirates and adventurers have the hellish pride of absolutely carefree men, men who will yield only to catastrophic forces but never to the daily worries of a respectable life nor to the higher worries concerning a future eternity. He realized that in Nietzsche's dictum there might be contained the possibility of a radical liberation from fear; at any rate he obviously thought (in the "Grand Chorale of Thanksgiving") that anything would be preferable to hoping for paradise and fearing hell.

> Lobet die Kälte, die Finsternis und das Verderben!
> Schauet hinan:
> Es kommt nicht auf euch an
> Und ihr könnt unbesorgt sterben.[7]

("Praise ye the cold, the darkness and ruin! Look into the heaven: You don't matter. And you may die without fear.")

The intimate relationship long perceived between the experience of war and slaughter and this peculiar glorification of life amidst death and darkness has recently been very well explained by Sartre: "When the instruments are broken and unusable, when plans are blasted and effort is useless, the world appears with a childlike and terrible freshness, without support, without paths" ("What Is Literature," *Partisan Review,* January 1948). To this quality of "terrible freshness" with which the world emerged after the slaughter, corresponded the horrible innocence (best represented in the ballad, "Apfelboeck, or the Lily of the Field") of men who had lost all past tasks and had not yet found new ones. Compared to this jubilant cynicism, all poetry that simply went along the beaten paths of a rich tradition, taking part in what one used to call the "inventory sale of all values," was not only inadequate but immediately sounded like mere literature.

This does not mean that Brecht had no sense of tradition; he simply did not believe in it any longer. His masterful, elaborate parodies (see "Litany of Breath" and "Grand Chorale of Thanksgiving" in this selection and the choruses in the play *Die Heilige Johanna der Schlachthöfe* [Saint Joan of the Stockyards]) would defeat their own purpose if they were simply parody. Brecht's travesty has many meanings and many purposes: it forces open the old forms by adapting them to a new, revolutionary content, and thereby not only destroys but also preserves; it shows by its very mastery that every poet worthy of the name must, as a matter of craftsmanship, know how to handle the traditional forms; but it also contains a definite destructive element: the new content given traditional forms is meant to expose the old poets, to reveal what they did not say, to unmask their silence. Thus, in "The Litany of Breath," Brecht uses Goethe's "Über allen Gipfeln ist Ruh" [Above All Hilltops There's Rest] in order to show that this is also the quiet of those who look quietly on while an old woman starves; and that the silence of the birds—"die Vöglein schweigen im Walde" [The Birds Are Silent in the Forest][8]—is also that same silence in which people watch one man who did not keep quiet and was killed. In other words, Brecht's very effective rebellion against classical forms and tradition never is the rebellion of the up-to-date against the outdated and is never prompted by a desire to express a new kind of sensibility. It simply claims that beauty has also beautified a hideous reality. Respect and reverence for the undeniable greatness of tradition is paid very delicately by the purity and poetically irreproachable quality of the parody itself.

The deepest motive underlying Brecht's break with tradition, however, is neither the cause of social justice nor, certainly, his dialectical-materialist approach to history. Much more genuine in him is a passionate anger at the course of the world, where it has always been only the victors who have chosen what is to be recorded and remembered by mankind. His poetry is written not only for the underprivileged, but for all those, living or dead, whose voice has never been heard on earth.

> Denn die Einen stehn im Dunklen
> Und die andern stehn im Licht;
> Und man sieht nur die ins Lichte,
> Die im Dunklen sieht man nicht.

This is translated by Martin Greenberg:

> For some stand in the shadow
> And others in the light;
> You don't see those in the shadow—
> Only those standing in the light.[9]

Brecht's whole philosophy, in so far as it bears on his poetry, is formulated in these four lines from the *Dreigroschenoper*. The same theme recurs in the "Ballad of the Waterwheel." These are not songs of "social significance," not plaidoyers for the poor, but the expression of a passionate longing for a world in which all can be seen and heard, the passionate wrath against a history that remembered a few and forgot so many, a history that under the pretense of remembering caused us to forget. And here too lies the most valid reason for his choice of the ballad, which in German tradition had always been the folk form of poetry, the tradition of unrecorded poetry, in which the people, condemned to darkness and oblivion, attempted to record their own history and create their own poetical eternity.[10]

~

It is only natural that the limitations of a poetry so intimately tied up with a very precise and intelligent way of thinking should be limitations of understanding. It is entirely to Brecht's credit that he writes badly when he does not see the truth—however distressing it may occasionally be to see how badly he can write. Here the conscious loss of sensibility has taken its revenge.

One is tempted to draw up a list of the subjects which Brecht understands, and a list of those which he misses. In the first category belong all pre-war phenomena, such as hypocrisy, exploitation, and poverty; all war phenomena, such as senseless violence and the ridiculous helpfulness of the individual; all post-war phenomena such as unemployment, rebellion, and exile. In the second category belong all fascist and totalitarian events, such as terror, concentration camps, anti-Semitism. (The last instance is well illustrated in "The Jew, A Misfortune for the People," where he tries to explode an antisemitic argument by a *reductio ad absurdum* and produces an argument which, to an anti-Semite, is highly plausible: "Since all misfortunes are produced by Jews, it must be that the Regime is a product of the Jews. Is this not obvious!" There are quite a few anti-Semites in Germany and elsewhere who have discovered that Hitler was a Jew or the product of a Jewish conspiracy.) During the thirties when Hitler had eliminated unemployment and the standard of living of all classes had considerably risen, Brecht wrote against Nazism in terms of hunger and unemployment. It speaks for the present selection and the literary judgment of its editor that only a few songs of this period have been included. Of these, the "Burial of the Agitator in a Zinc Coffin" is most representative. The mutilated corpses of the people who died in concentration camps were shipped home to their families for burial in sealed zinc coffins. The sealed zinc coffin was obviously intended to conceal and reveal at the same time, and is a perfect example of those hide-and-show tactics of which the Nazis were masters. In addition to thus officially publicizing something whose mere mention was punished as *Greuelmärchenpropaganda* [horror-story propaganda], the zinc coffin was an effective warning to the population: Look what might happen to you! It has to be hidden in a zinc coffin because no one could stand the sight of it! Brecht deals with this subject as though it were simply the case of an agitator who "has agitated in favor of many things: for eating-your-fill, for a-roof-over-your-head, for feeding-your-children," etc. The point is, that an agitator with such slogans would have been so ridiculous in 1936 that nobody would have needed to put him out of the way. Moreover, the real horror, the way he died, is completely overlooked, and the reader is left with the impression that the agitator's fate was only slightly worse than the fate an opponent of any other form of government would undergo. This meant in practice that Nazism was made harmless and almost respectable.

In the meantime, however, or since the *Svendborger Gedichte* [Swedenborg Poems], Brecht has moved steadily away from mere propaganda slogans, and in the *Galileo* he is again dealing with one of the major predicaments of our time: the search for truth in freedom.

Originally published in *The Kenyon Review* 10 (1948): 304–12. Under review is Bertolt Brecht, *Selected Poems,* trans. H. R. Hays (New York: Reynal & Hitchcock, 1947), which Arendt obviously considered inadequate. Arendt slightly expanded the German version of this essay, which appears under the title "Der Dichter Bertolt Brecht" in *Die neue Rundschau* 61 (1950): 53–67; a shortened version of this essay, translated by Jeffrey Sammons, appeared in *Brecht: A Collection of Critical Essays,* ed. Peter Demetz (Englewood Cliffs, NJ: Prentice-Hall, 1962), 43–50.

The origin of Arendt's reflections on the political-poetic case of Bertolt Brecht (1898–1956) can apparently be found in a discussion with Karl Jaspers that took place shortly after the war. In the course of this discussion Arendt sought to defend her conviction that "a good line of verse is a good line of verse" (see Hannah Arendt and Karl Jaspers, *Correspondence, 1926–1960,* ed. Lotte Kohler and Hans Saner, trans. Robert and Rita Kimber [New York: Harcourt Brace Jovanovich, 1992], 607, translation modified; see also Hannah Arendt, *Ich will verstehen: Selbstauskünfte zu Leben und Werk,* ed. Ursula Ludz [Munich: Piper, 1996], 112–13). In other words, according to Arendt, the moral character of poets should exercise no lasting effect on our judgment of the quality of their poems. Jaspers expressed certain reservations about this conviction, which seemed to have driven Arendt to develop the thoughts that lead from "Beyond Personal Frustration" to "What Is Permitted to Jove . . ." (Chapter 28).—Ed.

§ 19 Preface to Bernard Lazare,
Job's Dungheap

Nîmes, where Bernard Lazare was born in 1865, is one of the ancient French settlements in the Languedoc where Jewish communities can trace their history back to Roman antiquity. Bernard Lazare came from a type of assimilated Sephardic family that still preserved certain traditions but did not trouble to give its children any special Jewish training. At the age of 21 he went to Paris, traditionally the meeting place for gifted young Frenchmen from the southern provinces. A modest income from his father, a small dealer in ready-made clothes, enabled him to study religious history.

He soon became well known in the literary world. Lazare was invited to attend the famous Tuesdays of Stéphane Mallarmé and shortly thereafter joined the ranks of the Symbolists.[1] After 1890 he regularly contributed literary and cultural criticism to the *Entretiens politiques et littéraires,* official organ of the Symbolists.

His political education began in a Paris that had recently witnessed Boulanger's attempt to overthrow the Republic, the Panama scandal with its revelation of the degeneration of parliamentary life, and the rapid growth of the Socialist party.[2] Lazare joined a circle of dissident socialist intellectuals who represented a curious mixture of symbolist tendencies in art and anarchist tendencies in politics.

Nothing in this—and, in fact, nothing in his early writings—would have justified one in predicting a destiny for Bernard Lazare essentially different from that of the group of intellectuals to whom he belonged at that moment. What made him different and what raised his writings above the mere expression of the spirit of his time and milieu was his early recognition of the importance of the Jewish question and his consistent courage in making this recognition the central fact of his life.

Anti-Semitic agitation first became significant in politics in France about 1884. With the Panama scandal, in which a number of Jews were compromised, anti-Semitism attained the status, for one decade, of a full-blown political movement. What was more important for Jewish intellectuals like Bernard Lazare was the fact that French anti-Semitism had been linked with various socialist tendencies, so that Lazare was confronted in his own circle not only with vague anti-Jewish feelings but with articulate anti-Semitic doctrines.

His first reaction to the Jewish question was a decision to take anti-Semitism seriously. In 1894 he published a two-volume history of anti-Semitism, *L'Antisémitisme, son histoire et ses causes.* He began with the question: Why is it that the Jews have met with so universal a hostility at all times and in all countries since their dispersal? He found the answer in the exclusiveness of the Jews themselves, who wanted to survive at any price as "a nation among nations," although they constituted a peculiar kind of nation that "had outlived and survived its nationality." At this time Lazare still believed that the Jewish question, since it was a national question, would automatically solve itself in the general process of the denationalization of the nations: with the evolution of a universal humanity the Jews would cease to be Jewish in the same way that Frenchmen would cease to be French.

The Dreyfus Affair was for Bernard Lazare—as it was for Theodor Herzl—the turning point. Captain Alfred Dreyfus, a Jewish officer in the French army, was arrested in 1894 and charged with espionage on behalf of the German army. In the same year he was convicted by a military court-martial, sentenced to life imprisonment, and interned on Devil's Island, off the coast of French Guiana. Dreyfus had consistently protested his innocence from the beginning. In the months that followed, certain developments within the French General Staff cast suspicion on the sentence in the eyes of a considerably larger circle of interested persons than the Dreyfus family, until it finally became apparent that the trial and condemnation had been prompted by political reasons—as a move against the French Republic, on the one hand, and toward the establishment of anti-Semitism as a political movement, on the other. Bernard Lazare, working as a legal counsel for the Dreyfus family, was the first to denounce the "judicial error" and to insist on its political implications. His pamphlet, *Une erreur judiciare; la vérité sur l'affaire Dreyfus,* published in 1896, succeeded in convincing Clémenceau, Zola, some of the socialists, among them Jean Jaurès, and others not only of Dreyfus' innocence but of the existence of a plot on the part of the Army against the Republic.[3] Henceforth the Dreyfus Affair was a battle for justice and the Republic against the Army and the anti-Semitic reactionary parties. By concerted effort the *Dreyfusards* secured the annulment of the original sentence and a revision trial in 1899. The second trial ended with a ten-year sentence for Dreyfus, whom the military court again judged guilty, but "with extenuating circumstances." Thereupon the President of the Republic pardoned Dreyfus. Dreyfus, upon the request of his family and his Jewish advisors (with the exception of Lazare), accepted the pardon. It was this pardon which split the ranks of the *Dreyfusards.* Jaurès and the Socialist party, together with the official representatives of French Jewry, wanted to stop the Affair at any price and welcomed the pardon, whereas Clémenceau, Zola, Bernard Lazare, and a few intellectuals around Charles Péguy wanted an unambiguous reversal of the original sentence.[4]

In 1906, three years after Lazare's death, when Clémenceau had become Premier, the Court of Appeals—the highest judicial body of France—exercised its power to review the decisions of all other judicial bodies and annulled the sentence passed at the end of the revision trial. It went one step further, however. Afraid of the outcome of a second revision trial before a military court, it acquitted Dreyfus of all the charges that had been proffered against him, despite the fact that the Court of Appeals has no authority in law to issue a decision of its own but can only order the revision of a particular trial.

In the course of the fight for the acquittal of Dreyfus, Lazare came to know the Jewish people and the Jews of France as well as the enemies of the Jewish people. The conclusion he drew from these experiences was that Zionism offers the only possible solution to the Jewish question. This Zionism, as may be seen in the essays that follow, retained a strong social-revolutionary character.

Bernard Lazare's activities within the Zionist movement were of a limited scope only. Until 1899, to be a *Dreyfusard* was not to be employed part time, particularly if one was almost the only Jew in this movement for the liberation of a Jew. His many articles were printed in two Zionist magazines: *Zion,* a multilingual publication whose French section was under Lazare's editorship, and the *Echo Sioniste.* In 1899 he founded his own monthly, *Le Flambeau*, an "organ of Zionist and social Judaism," only a few numbers of which appeared.

The second major event in Lazare's political development occurred in 1899. A year before he had attended the Second Zionist Congress at Basle, where he had been warmly received by Max Nordau as one of the few Jews in France who had dared defend and fight publicly for another Jew.[5] Lazare was elected to the Actions Committee. It was at this point that Lazare separated himself from the official Zionist movement. In an open letter to Herzl (published in *Le Flambeau*, 1899) he explained his resignation from the Zionist Actions Committee. He accused the Committee of being "a sort of autocratic government [that] seeks to direct the Jewish masses as though they were ignorant children." His apprehensions, based on the larger issues of general "tendencies, procedures, and actions," arose out of the discussion of a Jewish Colonial Bank as it had been planned by Herzl at the time and in which Bernard Lazare saw a "tool" for the "oppression and demoralization" of the Jewish people. "It is not what the prophets formerly dreamed of and the humble folk who wrote the Psalms."

Bernard Lazare had hoped that "if I cut myself off from you, I do not cut myself off from the Jewish people . . . I will continue to labor for its freedom, even though it be by means which are not yours." But in fact he was now completely isolated, since he had separated himself previously from all other Jewish organizations and institutions. The few friends who remained loyal to him and among whom he still exerted a certain influence were of the non-Jewish literary milieu of *Les Cahiers de la Quinzaine*, the only magazine that continued to print his articles. It was here that his long essay on the condition of the Jews in Rumania was published.

Bernard Lazare died in 1903 at the age of 38. French Zionism lost in him "the only French Jew of distinction which it had ever attracted" (Baruch Hagani, *Bernard Lazare*, Paris, 1919).

~

The essay that forms an introduction to this volume was taken from Charles Péguy's *Notre Jeunesse*, first published in 1910 in *Les Cahiers de la Quinzaine*.

Charles Péguy (1874–1914), the French writer and poet, belonged to that generation of French intellectuals for which the Dreyfus Affair constituted the central political experience of its life. Péguy joined the

Dreyfusards as a socialist and fought together with Georges Sorel, Bernard Lazare, and Jean Jaurès for the rehabilitation of Dreyfus.[6] Under the impact of Bergson's philosophy and the profound disillusion caused by the tactics and ambiguities of the French Socialist party during the Affair, he became a bitter enemy of all official socialism and in 1900 founded his own magazine, *Les Cahiers de la Quinzaine,* until the outbreak of the First World War the principal literary organ for writers of Left Wing tendencies and without Marxist orthodoxy.[7] Romain Rolland, Georges Sorel, Daniel Halévy, and Bernard Lazare appeared side by side in its pages, and even on occasion—reprinted from German socialist papers—Rosa Luxemburg.[8] During these years Péguy developed a Catholic socialist philosophy which was violently critical of all existing social, political, and religious institutions and showed definite tendencies toward a mystical nationalism.

The central theme of *Notre Jeunesse* is the description of the political and intellectual controversies that raged around the Dreyfus Affair, controversies at whose center, according to Péguy, stood the figure of Bernard Lazare. The essay is also, in sort, a reply to an earlier attempt by Daniel Halévy (*Apologie pour notre Passé*) to pass critical judgment on the activities and beliefs of this generation.

Originally published as an untitled preface to Bernard Lazare, *Job's Dungheap: Essays on Jewish Nationalism and Social Revolution,* trans. Harry Lorin Binsse (New York: Schocken, 1948). The volume includes a "Portrait of Bernard Lazare" by Charles Péguy and notes by Arendt.
Bernard Lazare (1865–1903) was a French social philosopher, journalist, anarchist, and early Zionist.—Ed.

§ 20 The Achievement of Hermann Broch

Hermann Broch belongs in that tradition of great twentieth-century novelists who have transformed, almost beyond recognition, one of the classic art-forms of the nineteenth century. The modern novel no longer serves as "entertainment and instruction" (Broch) and its authors no longer relate the unusual, unheard-of "incident" (Goethe) or tell a story from which the reader will get "advice" (W. Benjamin).[1] It rather confronts him with problems and perplexities in which the reader must be prepared to engage himself if he is to understand it at all. The result of this transformation has been that the most accessible and popular art has become one of the most difficult and esoteric. The medium of suspense has disappeared and with it the possibility of passive fascination; the novelist's ambition to create the illusion of a higher reality or to accomplish the transfiguration of the real together with the revelation of its manifold significance has yielded to the intention to involve the reader in something which is at least as much a process of thought as of artistic invention.

The novels of Proust, Joyce, and Broch (as well as those of Kafka and Faulkner who, however, each in his own way is in a class by himself) show a conspicuous and curious affinity with poetry on one hand and to philosophy on the other.[2] Consequently, the greatest modern novelists have begun to share the poets' and philosophers' confinement to a relatively small,

---

The Sleepwalkers, by Hermann Broch. Translated by Willa and Edwin Muir. Pantheon Books. 1948. $5.00. *The Death of Virgil,* translated by Jean Starr Untermeyer. Pantheon Books. 1945. $5.50.

select circle of readers. In this respect, the tiny editions of the greatest works and the huge editions of good second-rate books are equally significant. A gift for story-telling which half a century ago could be found only among the great is today frequently the common equipment of good but essentially mediocre writers. Good second-rate production, which is as far removed from *kitsch* as it is from great art, satisfies fully the demands of the educated and art-loving public and has more effectively estranged the great masters from their audience than the much-feared mass culture. More important for the artist himself is that a widespread possession of skill and craftsmanship and a tremendous rise in the general level of performance have made him suspicious of facility and mere talent.

The significance of *The Sleepwalkers* trilogy (whose German original appeared in 1931) is that it admits the reader to the laboratory of the novelist in the midst of this crisis so that he may watch the transformation of the art-form itself. Reaching back into three crucial years—1888, when *The Romantic* finds himself in the not yet visible decay of the old world; 1903, when *The Anarchist* gets entangled in the prewar confusion of values; 1918, when *The Realist* becomes the undisputed master of a nihilistic society—Broch seems to start in the first volume as an ordinary storyteller in order to reveal himself in the last as a poet whose main concern is judgment and not reporting, and as a philosopher who wants not just to portray the course of events but to discover and demonstrate logically the laws of movement governing the "disintegration of values."

The first part, which consciously imitates the prose style of the 'eighties, is so skilfully told that one begins to understand the extent of sacrifice made by those great narrative talents who suddenly refused to continue telling tales about the world because they had realized that this world was going to pieces. The story stops abruptly with an unconsummated wedding night, and the author asks the reader to figure out the rest for himself, thereby upsetting the illusion of a created reality in which the author controls all events and the reader is admitted only as a passive observer. The fiction itself is expressly depreciated, its validity is set at an ironical and historical distance. The story is over not when the characters' private invented destinies have been played out, but when the historical essentials of the given period are established.

Thus one of the chief attractions of novel reading, the reader's identification with the hero, is consciously destroyed, and the daydreaming element, which always had brought the novel so suspiciously close to *kitsch*, is eliminated. *The Sleepwalkers* is of course a historical novel, but the point is that Broch is never engrossed in, and never permits the reader to become absorbed by, the story itself.

The first part of *The Sleepwalkers* describes the world of the Junker von Pasenow, whose youth is spent in military duty in Berlin, years of honor and boredom brightened only by the usual affair with some sweet girl below his own class and therefore beyond responsibility, whom, however, against all rules, the lieutenant Pasenow seems to love truly, a fact which he himself realizes dimly through the fog of inarticulate class prejudices and under the shock of his unhappy wedding night. To the world in Berlin belongs Pasenow's friend, Eduard von Bertrand, who is about to desert the narrowness of Prussian aristocracy, has resigned from the army and set out on a civilian career as an industrialist. The world at home is made up of the landed nobility with their estates, the horses and fields and the servants, and their constant fight against emptiness, boredom, and financial worries. Pasenow marries the "pure" daughter of his neighbors on the adjoining estate—just as it should be and just as everybody had expected.

Broch does not picture this world from the outside; even fifty years later when, simply because of contrast, one was easily impressed and fooled by its façade of stability, he did not trust its obvious indications. Instead he uses the technique of the stream of consciousness novel whose radical subjectivization allows him to present events and feelings only insofar as they are objects of consciousness, which, however, gains in significance what it has lost in objectivity by picturing the full meaning of each experience within its proper framework of biographical reference. This enables him to show the frightening discrepancy between the open dialogue which respects the conventional forms and the always panic-ridden thoughts that accompany speech and actions with the obsessive insistence of compulsive imaginations. This discrepancy reveals the fundamental fragility of the time, the insecurity and convulsiveness of those who were its representatives. It turns out that behind the façade of still strong prejudices is a complete incapacity for orientation and that the clichés that impress society because they seem to reflect principles are the only remnants of former nobility and glory. The discrepancy dissolves and a unity of character is established when the father of Pasenow sinks into a senile insanity which gives him the privilege of saying what he thinks and acting as compulsively as he pleases.

The second part retains only a few rudimentary examples of this technique. Its principal character, the bookkeeper Esch of petty-bourgeois origin, feels no need for pretenses and is therefore even more helpless, more openly confused, and at the mercy of the general decay. The idea of justice possesses him like a hallucination of a bookkeeper who wants to keep his accounts in good order. A man of "impetuous actions," he spends his life settling imaginary accounts. The climax of this volume is a dream-like dialogue between Esch and Bertrand (from the first volume) after Esch, in his confused fanaticism, decided to denounce the beloved president of a shipping line for homosexuality. Bertrand's role in both volumes is the same: he appears as the only superior personality who is the master of his life and not a driven victim of events. As such he is the human yardstick against which the shady and shifty doings of the others are measured.

While the first part seemed to follow the tradition of the psychological novel, the second part seems to be realistic. Everything, except for the dialogue between Esch and Bertrand, happens on the tangible surface of reality. Yet this reality is no more fully and objectively presented than the psychology of the figures of the first part was objectively stated. The world of 1903 is a shadowy, sketchily drawn backdrop against which people act without any true contact between themselves so that their behavior becomes most compulsive when it seems most impetuous. Since the compulsive actions of the characters can find no common ground they constantly destroy or at least undermine the reality of the common world. Like the first, the second volume ends when the marriage of its hero seems to assure a normal, reasonably safe future. If only these two parts of the work existed, one might be left with the impression that the banality of everyday life eventually overcomes human perplexity and resolves confusion into some kind of middle-class normalcy.

The third part deals with the end of the First World War and the actual breakdown of a world which had held together and retained its right senses not by any "values," but only by the automatism of habits and clichés. The two heroes of the preceding volumes reappear: the lieutenant and Junker Pasenow, returned to active duty during the war, has become a major and military commander of a small town in Western Germany; the former bookkeeper Esch is now editor of the town's newspaper. These too, the Romantic and the Anarchist, unite and become friends across all differences in class and education against the protagonist of the third volume, the Realist Huguenau who, after deserting the army, begins his successful career as a businessman. It is Huguenau's "realism," his consistent application of business standards to all fields of life, his emancipation from every value and every passion, which eventually demonstrate the Romantic's and the Anarchist's unfitness for life: for "objective" reasons, that is for reasons of his own logical self-interest, he slanders the Major, murders the editor, and winds up a respected member of bourgeois society.

The technique of the narrative has again changed entirely. The story that binds together the heroes of the three volumes is broken by a wealth of episodes whose figures cross each other occasionally and which are woven and synchronized into the development of the main action. The most magnificent of these is the story of Goedecke of the Landwehr who had been buried alive and whom two comrades, on a wager, brought back to life. How the single organs and functions that were once the man Ludwig Goedecke slowly and piecemeal return to balance, how out of the decaying, doomed pieces a man rises up again who can speak and walk and laugh, how this "resurrection from the dead" resembles a second creation whose terrifying wonder lies in the animation and individualization of matter—this already foreshadows in its forcefulness of vision and language the most beautiful passages in *The Death of Virgil*.

The episodes that break into the narrative from all sides give the principal story—the story of the Romantic who believes in honor, of the Anarchist who seeks a new faith, and of the Realist who destroys them both—a somewhat episodic character. This impression is even strengthened through the introduction of two more levels of an entirely different kind, the lyrical parts of "The Story of the Salvation Army Girl" and the philosophical speculations about the "disintegration of values," which somehow bring the eternal to the historical narrative plane. Neither the lyrical nor the philosophical parts have anything to do with the story itself, although it is suggested that Bertrand reappears as the narrator of the love story of the Salvation Army girl and a Polish Jew whom the war has driven to Berlin. The point is that this story is a purely lyrical interlude, frequently in verses, and the reflections truly logical discourses.

In other words, the novel at its end breaks into lyricism on one side and philosophy on the other. This is indeed like a symbol of what was happening generally to the novel as a form of art. Neither the passions which lent the traditional novel its suspense, nor the universal and spiritual which illuminated it, could any longer be preserved in the narrative. The transparency of the world for the universal and the passionate affection of the individual have disappeared through "the disintegration of values," which consists in the collapse of an integrated view and way of life and the consequent radical atomization of its various spheres, each of which claims that its relative values are absolute. The universal and the rational on one side, the individual passion and the "irrational" on the other, have established themselves as the independent regions of philosophy and poetry.

The Death of Virgil, one of the truly great works in German literature, is unique in its kind. The uninterrupted flow of lyrical speculation leading through the last twenty-four hours of the dying poet begins when the ship that, in accordance with his imperial friend's desire, should carry him back from Athens to Rome, lies in at the port of Brundisium, and ends with the journey into death, when Virgil has left the feverish, over-articulated clarity of a conscious farewell to life and lets himself be led through all its remembered stages, over childhood and birth back into the calm darkness of chaos before and beyond creation. The journey leads into nothingness; but since it is an inverted story of creation, tracing all stages of world and man back to their creation out of nothingness, the journey also leads into the universe: "The nothing filled the emptiness and it became the universe."

The plot is dying itself in the sense that it is the story "of a man who feels the most significant thing of his life approaching and is full of anxiety lest he miss it." Apart from the introductory paragraph which describes the entry of the ship into the harbor, and which—comparable to the portrayal of Bohemia in the first pages of Stifter's *Witiko*—stands among the greatest literary landscapes in the German language, nothing is reported or perceived but what penetrates the invisible web woven of sensual data, fever visions, and speculations which death has already spread over its victim.[3] The richness of association produced through fever is used not only to transform one thing into another in an endless chain of association, but to bring each floating bit of memory into full actuality and to illuminate it in its universally interrelated meaningfulness, so that the contours of the concrete and the particular are at once brought into sharper relief *and* merged into a universal, dreamlike symbol pattern.

The philosophical content itself resembles a Spinozistic Cosmos- and Logos-speculation in which all things we know to be separate and particular appear as the ever-changing aspects of an eternal One, so that the manifold is understood as the merely temporary individualization of an all-comprehensive whole.[4] The philosophical basis of Broch's speculations on the all-meaningfulness of all things that exist or happen lies in a truly pantheistic and panlogical hope of redemption in which eventually beginning and end, the "no thing" and the "universe" will prove to be identical. This hope illuminates the composition just as dying, understood as a conscious action, articulates it. The magnificent, fascinating rhythm of Broch's prose, which in the form of invocation reiterates constantly and always more insistently the fundamental themes of the work, is consistent with the gesture of farewell which yearns to save what is necessarily doomed as well as with an enthusiastic drunkenness with the universal being that can express itself only in exclamations.

In this sense, the theme of the book is truth, but a truth that, like a mathematical formula, should become manifest in *one* word in order to be fully expressed at all. The repeating insistence on words like Life, Death, Time, Space, Love, Help, Oath, Solitude, Friendship, is like the speculative attempt to penetrate to the *one* word in which from the beginning the universe and man and life have been "dissolved and acquitted," "contained and preserved," "destroyed and recreated forever," to the Word of God that was in the beginning and is "beyond speech."

The prose rhythm reflects the movement of philosophical speculation, somewhat as music reflects the movements of the soul. As distinguished from *The Sleepwalkers* suspense and tension are not thwarted and broken; the suspense and the tension are those of philosophical speculation insofar as it is, independent of all philosophical techniques, the still inarticulate passionate affection by the philosophical subject itself. And just as one who has been seized by the passion for philosophy is not simply haunted by one particular problem, just as the passionate tension of speculation is not relieved by results, the reader of this book is drawn into the tenseness of a movement which is beyond the suspense caused by a plot and carries him, like Virgil himself, through all its episodes and visions to the solution of eternal rest.

The reader is expected to surrender himself to this movement and to read the novel as though it were a poem. Suspended between life and death, between the "no longer" and "not yet," life reveals itself in that all-meaningful richness which becomes visible only against the dark background of death. At the same time, the "no longer and not yet" which permeates the work like a leitmotif signifies the turning point in history, the crisis between the no longer of antiquity and the not yet of Christianity, and its obvious parallel to the present. The philosophical significance of the crisis has a resemblance to the situation of farewell: a time which despairs of everything, touches every possible problem with its questions, and asks redemption from every possible need.

"No longer and not yet," "not yet and yet close at hand," have replaced as a general frame of reference Broch's earlier insistence on the "disintegration of values." With the insight into this crisis, this turning point in history, Virgil despairs of poetry and tries to destroy the manuscript of the *Aeneid.* In the hour of his death, the poet reaches a higher, more valid region than art and beauty. Beauty, irresponsible in and excluded from reality, pretends a spurious eternity; the artist's productivity pretends to be creation, that is, it arrogates to man what is the privilege of God. Whatever the nature and level of this make-believe, circus-games for the Roman populace or masterpieces of artists for the refined, it always satisfies on different levels the same vulgar ingratitude of men who will not admit their non-human origin, and it appeases their vulgar desire to escape reality and responsibility into "the unity of the world established by beauty." "Art's . . . despairing attempt to build up the imperishable from things that perish" makes the artist treacherous, self-seeking, unreliable, and oblivious of the essentially human.

Seen within the framework of literary history, *The Death of Virgil* solves the problem of the new form and content of the novel that *The Sleepwalkers* raised. There the novel seemed to have reached an impasse between philosophy and lyricism, precisely because pure story-telling, entertainment and instruction, had been taken care of by extraordinary but second-rate talents. The historical significance of *The Death of Virgil* is the creation in both of a unity in which a new specifically modern element of suspense could materialize. It is as though only now those purely artistic elements which always gave the traditional novel its literary validity, the lyrical passion and the transfiguration of reality through the universal, have emancipated themselves from the merely informative and found a new and valid form.

Originally published in *The Kenyon Review* 11 (1949): 476–83; an abbreviated form was reprinted as the preface to Hermann Broch, *The Sleepwalkers: A Trilogy,* trans. Willa and Edwin Muir (New York: Grosset & Dunlap, 1964), v–x. As indicated in its sole note, this is a review of *The Sleepwalkers* and *The Death of Virgil.* A slightly different German version of this essay appeared under the title "Hermann Broch und der moderne Roman" (Hermann Broch and the Modern Novel) in *Der Monat* 1 (1948–49): 147–51.—Ed.

§ 21 Between Vice and Crime (On Proust)

Paris has rightly been called *la capitale du dixneuvième siècle* (Walter Benjamin).[1] Full of promise, the nineteenth century had started with the French Revolution, for more than one hundred years witnessed the vain struggle against the degeneration of the *citoyen* into the *bourgeois,* reached its nadir in the Dreyfus Affair, and was given another fourteen years of morbid respite.[2] The First World War could still be won by the Jacobin appeal of Clemenceau, France's last son of the Revolution, but the glorious century of the *nation par excellence* was at an end[3] and Paris was left, without political significance and social splendor, to the intellectual avant-garde of all countries. France played a very small part in the twentieth century, which started, immediately after Disraeli's death, with the scramble for Africa and the competition for imperialist domination in Europe. Her decline, therefore, caused partly by the economic expansion of other nations, and partly by internal disintegration, could assume forms and follow laws which seemed inherent in the nation-state.

To a certain extent, what happened in France in the eighties and nineties happened thirty and forty years later in all European nation-states. Despite chronological distances, the Weimar and Austrian Republics had much in common historically with the Third Republic, and certain political and social patterns in the Germany and Austria of the twenties and thirties seemed almost consciously to follow the model of France's *fin-de-siècle.*

Nineteenth-century antisemitism, at any rate, reached its climax in France and was defeated because it remained a national domestic issue without contact with imperialist trends, which did not exist there. The main features of this kind of antisemitism reappeared in Germany and

Austria after the First World War, and its social effect on the respective Jewries was almost the same, although less sharp, less extreme, and more disturbed by other influences.⁴

The chief reason, however, for the choice of the salons of the Faubourg Saint-Germain as an example of the role of Jews in non-Jewish society is that nowhere else is there an equally grand society or a more truthful record of it. When Marcel Proust, himself half Jewish and in emergencies ready to identify himself as a Jew, set out to search for "things past," he actually wrote what one of his admiring critics has called an *apologia pro vita sua*. The life of this greatest writer of twentieth-century France was spent exclusively in society; all events appeared to him as they are reflected in society and reconsidered by the individual, so that reflections and reconsiderations constitute the specific reality and texture of Proust's world.⁵ Throughout the *Remembrance of Things Past*, the individual and his reconsiderations belong to society, even when he retires into the mute and uncommunicative solitude in which Proust himself finally disappeared when he had decided to write his work. There his inner life, which insisted on transforming all worldly happenings into inner experience, became like a mirror in whose reflection truth might appear. The contemplator of inner experience resembles the onlooker in society insofar as neither has an immediate approach to life but perceives reality only if it is reflected. Proust, born on the fringe of society, but still rightfully belonging to it though an outsider, enlarged this inner experience until it included the whole range of aspects as they appeared to and were reflected by all members of society.

There is no better witness, indeed, of this period when society had emancipated itself completely from public concerns, and when politics itself was becoming a part of social life. The victory of bourgeois values over the citizen's sense of responsibility meant the decomposition of political issues into their dazzling, fascinating reflections in society. It must be added that Proust himself was a true exponent of this society, for he was involved in both of its most fashionable "vices," which he, "the greatest witness of dejudaized Judaism" interconnected in the "darkest comparison which ever has been made on behalf of Western Judaism":⁶ the "vice" of Jewishness and the "vice" of homosexuality, and which in their reflection and individual reconsideration became very much alike indeed.⁷

It was Disraeli who had discovered that vice is but the corresponding reflection of crime in society. Human wickedness, if accepted by society, is changed from an act of will into an inherent, psychological quality which man cannot choose or reject but which is imposed upon him from without, and which rules him as compulsively as the drug rules the addict. In assimilating crime and transforming it into vice, society denies all responsibility and establishes a world of fatalities in which men find themselves entangled. The moralistic judgment as a crime of every departure from the norm, which fashionable circles used to consider narrow and philistine, if demonstrative of inferior psychological understanding, at least showed greater respect for human dignity. If crime is understood to be a kind of fatality, natural or economic, everybody will finally be suspected of some special predestination to it. "Punishment is the right of the criminal," of which he is deprived if (in the words of Proust) "judges assume and are more inclined to pardon murder in inverts and treason in Jews for reasons derived from . . . racial predestination." It is an attraction to murder and treason which hides behind such perverted tolerance, for in a moment it can switch to a decision to liquidate not only all actual criminals but all who are "racially" predestined to commit certain crimes. Such changes take place whenever the legal and political machine is not separated from society so that social standards can penetrate into it and become political and legal rules. The seeming broad-mindedness that equates crime and vice, if allowed to establish its own code of law, will invariably prove more cruel and inhuman than laws, no matter how severe, which respect and recognize man's independent responsibility for his behavior.

The Faubourg Saint-Germain, however, as Proust depicts it, was in the early stages of this development. It admitted inverts because it felt attracted by what it judged to be a vice. Proust describes how Monsieur de Charlus, who had formerly been tolerated, "notwithstanding his vice," for his personal charm and old name, now rose to social heights. He no longer needed to lead a double life and hide his dubious acquaintances, but was encouraged to bring them into the fashionable houses. Topics of conversation which he formerly would have avoided—love, beauty, jealousy—lest somebody suspect his anomaly, were now welcomed avidly "in view of the experience, strange, secret, refined and monstrous upon which he founded" his views.[8]

Something very similar happened to the Jews. Individual exceptions, ennobled Jews, had been tolerated and even welcomed in the society of the Second Empire, but now Jews as such were becoming increasingly popular. In both cases, society was far from being prompted by a revision of prejudices. They did not doubt that homosexuals were "criminals" or that Jews were "traitors"; they only revised their attitude toward crime and treason. The trouble with their new broadmindedness, of course, was not that they were no longer horrified by inverts but that they were no longer horrified by crime. They did not in the least doubt the conventional judgment. The best-hidden disease of the nineteenth century, its terrible boredom and general weariness, had burst like an abscess. The outcasts and the pariahs upon whom society called in its predicament were, whatever else they might have been, at least not plagued by ennui and, if we are to trust Proust's judgment, were the only ones in *fin-de-siècle* society who were still capable of passion. Proust leads us through the labyrinth of social connections and ambitions only by the thread of man's capacity for love, which is presented in the perverted passion of Monsieur de Charlus for Morel, in the devastating loyalty of the Jew Swann to his courtesan and in the author's own desperate jealousy of Albertine, herself the personification of vice in the novel. Proust made it very clear that he regarded the outsiders and new-comers, the inhabitants of *"Sodome et Gomorrhe,"* not only as more human but as more normal.

The difference between the Faubourg Saint-Germain, which had suddenly discovered the attractiveness of Jews and inverts, and the mob which cried "Death to the Jews" was that the salons had not yet associated themselves openly with crime. This meant that on the one hand they did not yet want to participate actively in the killing, and on the other, still professed openly an antipathy toward Jews and a horror of inverts. This in turn resulted in that typically equivocal situation in which the new members could not confess their identity openly, and yet could not hide it either. Such were the conditions from which arose the complicated game of exposure and concealment, of half-confessions and lying distortions, of exaggerated humility and exaggerated arrogance, all of which were consequences of the fact that only one's Jewishness (or homosexuality) had opened the doors of the exclusive salons, while at the same time they made one's position extremely insecure. In this equivocal situation, Jewishness was for the individual Jew at once a physical stain and a mysterious personal privilege, both inherent in a "racial predestination."

Proust describes at great length how society, constantly on the lookout for the strange, the exotic, the dangerous, finally identifies the refined with the monstrous and gets ready to admit monstrosities—real or fancied—such as the strange, unfamiliar "Russian or Japanese play performed by native actors";[9] the "painted, paunchy, tightly buttoned personage [of the invert], reminding one of a box of exotic and dubious origin from which escapes the curious odor of fruits the mere thought of tasting which stirs the heart";[10] the "man of genius" who is supposed to emanate a "sense of the super-natural" and around whom society will "gather as though around a turning-table, to learn the secret of the Infinite."[11] In the atmosphere of this "necromancy," a Jewish gentleman or a Turkish lady might appear "as if they really were creatures evoked by the effort of a medium."[12]

Obviously the role of the exotic, the strange, and the monstrous could not be played by those individual "exception Jews" who, for almost a century, had been admitted and tolerated as "foreign upstarts" and on "whose friendship nobody would ever have dreamed of priding himself."[13] Much better suited of course were those whom nobody had ever known, who, in the first stage of their assimilation, were not identified with, and were not representative of, the Jewish community, for such identification with well-known bodies would have limited severely society's imagination and expectations. Those who, like Swann, had an unaccountable flair for society and taste in general were admitted; but more enthusiastically embraced were those who, like Bloch, belonged to "a family of little repute, [and] had to support, as on the floor of the ocean, the incalculable pressure of what was imposed on him not only by the Christians upon the surface but by all the intervening layers of Jewish castes superior to his own, each of them crushing with its contempt the one that was immediately beneath it." Society's willingness to receive the utterly alien and, as it thought, utterly vicious, cut short that climb of several generations by which newcomers had "to carve their way through to the open air by raising themselves from Jewish family to Jewish family."[14] It was no accident that this happened shortly after native French Jewry, during the Panama scandal, had given way before the initiative and unscrupulousness of some German Jewish adventurers; the individual exceptions, with or without title, who more than ever before sought the society of antisemitic and monarchist salons where they could dream of the good old days of the Second Empire, found themselves in the same category as Jews whom they would never have invited to their houses. If Jewishness as exceptionalness was the reason for admitting Jews, then those were preferred who were clearly "a solid troop, homogeneous within itself and utterly dissimilar to the people who watched them go past," those who had not yet "reached the same stage of assimilation" as their upstart brethren.[15]

Although Benjamin Disraeli was still one of those Jews who were admitted to society because they were exceptions, his secularized self-representation as a "chosen man of the chosen race" foreshadowed and outlined the lines along which Jewish self-interpretation was to take place. If this, fantastic and crude as it was, had not been so oddly similar to what society expected of Jews, Jews would never have been able to play their dubious role. Not, of course, that they consciously adopted Disraeli's convictions or purposely elaborated the first timid, perverted self-interpretation of their Prussian predecessors of the beginning of the century; most of them were blissfully ignorant of all Jewish history. But wherever Jews were educated, secularized, and assimilated under the ambiguous conditions of society and state in Western and Central Europe, they lost that measure of political responsibility which their origin implied and which the Jewish notables had still felt, albeit in the form of privilege and rulership. Jewish origin, without religious and political connotation, became everywhere a psychological quality, was changed into "Jewishness," and from then on could be considered only in the categories of virtue or vice. If it is true that "Jewishness" could not have been perverted into an interesting vice without a prejudice which considered it a crime, it is also true that such perversion was made possible by those Jews who considered it an innate virtue.

∼

Assimilated Jewry has been reproached with alienation from Judaism, and the final catastrophe brought upon it is frequently thought to have been a suffering as senseless as it was horrible, since it had lost the old value of martyrdom. This argument overlooks the fact that as far as the old ways of faith and life are concerned, "alienation" was equally apparent in Eastern European countries. But the usual notion of the Jews of Western Europe as "dejudaized" is misleading for another reason. Proust's picture, in contrast to the all too obviously interested utterances of official Judaism, shows that never did the fact of Jewish birth play such a decisive role in private life and everyday existence as among the assimilated Jews. The Jewish reformer who changed a national religion into a religious denomination with the understanding that religion is a private affair, the

Jewish revolutionary who pretended to be a world citizen in order to rid himself of Jewish nationality, the educated Jew, "a man in the street and a Jew at home"—each one of these succeeded in converting a national quality into a private affair. The result was that their private lives, their decisions and sentiments, became the very center of their "Jewishness." And the more the fact of Jewish birth lost its religious, national, and social-economic significance, the more obsessive Jewishness became; Jews were obsessed by it as one may be by a physical defect or advantage, and addicted to it as one may be to a vice.

Proust's "innate disposition" is nothing but this personal, private obsession, which was so greatly justified by a society where success and failure depended upon the fact of Jewish birth. Proust mistook it for "racial predestination," because he saw and depicted only its social aspect and individual reconsiderations. And it is true that to the recording onlooker the behavior of the Jewish clique showed the same obsession as the behavior patterns followed by inverts. Both felt either superior or inferior, but in any case proudly different from other normal beings; both believed their difference to be a natural fact acquired by birth; both were constantly justifying, not what they did, but what they were; and both, finally, always wavered between such apologetic attitudes and sudden, provocative claims that they were an elite. As though their social position were forever frozen by nature, neither could move from one clique into another. The need to belong existed in other members of society too—"the question is not as for Hamlet, to be or not to be, but to belong or not to belong"[16]—but not to the same extent. A society disintegrating into cliques and no longer tolerating outsiders, Jews or inverts, as individuals but because of the special circumstances of their admission, looked like the embodiment of this clannishness.

Each society demands of its members a certain amount of acting, the ability to present, represent, and act what one actually is. When society disintegrates into cliques such demands are no longer made of the individual but of members of cliques. Behavior then is controlled by silent demands and not by individual capacities, exactly as an actor's performance must fit into the ensemble of all other roles in the play. The salons of the Faubourg Saint-Germain consisted of such an ensemble of cliques, each of which presented an extreme behavior pattern. The role of the inverts was to show their abnormality, of the Jews to represent black magic ("necromancy"), of the artists to manifest another form of supranatural and superhuman contact, of the aristocrats to show that they were not like ordinary ("bourgeois") people. Despite their clannishness, it is true, as Proust observed, that "save on the days of general disaster when the majority rally round the victim as the Jews rallied round Dreyfus," all these newcomers shunned intercourse with their own kind. The reason was that all marks of distinction were determined only by the ensemble of the cliques, so that Jews or inverts felt that they would lose their distinctive character in a society of Jews or inverts, where Jewishness or homosexuality would be the most natural, the most uninteresting, and the most banal thing in the world. The same, however, held true of their hosts who also needed an ensemble of counterparts before whom they could be different, nonaristocrats who would admire aristocrats as these admired the Jews or the homosexuals.

Although these cliques had no consistency in themselves and dissolved as soon as no members of other cliques were around, their members used a mysterious sign-language as though they needed something strange by which to recognize each other. Proust reports at length the importance of such signs, especially for newcomers. While, however, the inverts, masters at sign-language, had at least a real secret, the Jews used this language only to create the expected atmosphere of mystery. Their signs mysteriously and ridiculously indicated something universally known: that in the corner of the salon of the Princess So-and-So sat another Jew who was not allowed openly to admit his identity but who without this meaningless quality would never have been able to climb into that corner.

It is noteworthy that the new mixed society at the end of the nineteenth century, like the first Jewish salons in Berlin, again centered around nobility. Aristocracy by now had all but lost its eagerness for culture and its curiosity about "new specimens of humanity," but it retained its old scorn of bourgeois society. An urge for social distinction was its answer to political equality and the loss of political position and privilege which had been affirmed with the establishment of the Third Republic. After a short and artificial rise during the Second Empire, French aristocracy maintained itself only by social clannishness and half-hearted attempts to reserve the higher positions in the army for its sons. Much stronger than political ambition was an aggressive contempt for middle-class standards, which undoubtedly was one of the strongest motives for the admission of individuals and whole groups of people who had belonged to socially unacceptable classes. The same motive that had enabled

Prussian aristocrats to meet socially with actors and Jews finally led in France to the social prestige of inverts. The middle classes, on the other hand, had not acquired social self-respect, although they had in the meantime risen to wealth and power. The absence of a political hierarchy in the nation-state and the victory of equality rendered "society secretly more hierarchical as it became outwardly more democratic."[17] Since the principle of hierarchy was embodied in the exclusive social circles of the Faubourg Saint-Germain, each society in France "reproduced the characteristics more or less modified, more or less in caricature of the society of the Faubourg Saint-Germain which it sometimes pretended . . . to hold in contempt, no matter what status or what political ideas its members might hold." Aristocratic society was a thing of the past in appearance only; actually it pervaded the whole social body (and not only of the people of France) by imposing "the key and the grammar of fashionable social life."[18] When Proust felt the need for an *apologia pro vita sua* and reconsidered his own life spent in aristocratic circles, he gave an analysis of society as such.

The main point about the role of Jews in this *fin-de-siècle* society is that it was the antisemitism of the Dreyfus Affair which opened society's doors to Jews, and that it was the end of the Affair, or rather the discovery of Dreyfus' innocence, that put an end to their social glory.[19] In other words, no matter what the Jews thought of themselves or of Dreyfus, they could play the role society had assigned them only as long as this same society was convinced that they belonged to a race of traitors. When the traitor was discovered to be the rather stupid victim of an ordinary frame-up, and the innocence of the Jews was established, social interest in Jews subsided as quickly as did political antisemitism. Jews were again looked upon as ordinary mortals and fell into the insignificance from which the supposed crime of one of their own had raised them temporarily.

It was essentially the same kind of social glory that the Jews of Germany and Austria enjoyed under much more severe circumstances immediately after the First World War. Their supposed crime then was that they had been guilty of the war, a crime which, no longer identified with a single act of a single individual, could not be refuted, so that the mob's evaluation of Jewishness as a crime remained undisturbed and society could continue to be delighted and fascinated by its Jews up to the very end. If there is any psychological truth in the scapegoat theory, it is as the effect of this social attitude toward Jews; for when antisemitic legislation forced society to oust the Jews, these "philosemites" felt as though they had to purge themselves of secret viciousness, to cleanse themselves of a stigma which they had mysteriously and wickedly loved. This psychology, to be sure, hardly explains why these "admirers" of Jews finally became their murderers, and it may even be doubted that they were prominent among those who ran the death factories, although the percentage of the so-called educated classes among the actual killers is amazing. But it does explain the incredible disloyalty of precisely those strata of society which had known Jews most intimately and had been most delighted and charmed by Jewish friends.

As far as the Jews were concerned, the transformation of the "crime" of Judaism into the fashionable "vice" of Jewishness was dangerous in the extreme. Jews had been able to escape from Judaism into conversion; from Jewishness there was no escape. A crime, moreover, is met with punishment; a vice can only be exterminated. The interpretation given by society to the fact of Jewish birth and the role played by Jews in the framework of social life are intimately connected with the catastrophic thoroughness with which antisemitic devices could be put to work. The Nazi brand of antisemitism had its roots in these social conditions as well as in political circumstances. And though the concept of race had other and more immediately political purposes and functions, its application to the Jewish question in its most sinister aspect owed much of its success to social phenomena and convictions which virtually constituted a consent by public opinion.

The deciding forces in the Jews' fateful journey to the storm center of events were without doubt political; but the reactions of society to antisemitism and the psychological reflections of the Jewish question in the individual had something to do with the specific cruelty, the organized and calculated assault upon every single individual of Jewish origin, that was already characteristic of the antisemitism of the Dreyfus Affair. This passion-driven hunt of the "Jew in general," the "Jew everywhere and nowhere," cannot be understood if one considers the history of antisemitism as an entity in itself, as a mere political movement. Social factors, unaccounted for in political or economic history, hidden under the surface of events, never perceived by the historian and recorded only by the more penetrating and passionate force of poets or novelists (men whom society had driven into the desperate solitude and loneliness of the *apologia pro vita sua*) changed the course that mere political antisemitism would have taken if left to itself, and which might have resulted in anti-Jewish legislation and even mass expulsion but hardly in wholesale extermination.

Ever since the Dreyfus Affair and its political threat to the rights of French Jewry had produced a social situation in which Jews enjoyed an ambiguous glory, antisemitism appeared in Europe as an insoluble mixture of political motives and social elements. Society always reacted first to a strong antisemitic movement with marked preference for Jews, so that Disraeli's remark that "there is no race at this present . . . that so much delights and fascinates and elevates and ennobles Europe as the Jewish," became particularly true in times of danger. Social "philosemitism" always ended by adding to political antisemitism that mysterious fanaticism without which antisemitism could hardly have become the best slogan for organizing the masses. All the *déclassés* of capitalist society were finally ready to unite and establish mob organizations of their own; their propaganda and their attraction rested on the assumption that a society which had shown its willingness to incorporate crime in the form of vice into its very structure would by now be ready to cleanse itself of viciousness by openly admitting criminals and by publicly committing crimes.

Originally published under the subtitle "Between Vice and Crime," in *The Origins of Totalitarianism,* rev. ed. (New York: Harcourt Brace Jovanovich, 1951), 79–88.

Marcel Proust (1871–1922) was a French novelist, whose seven-volume *À la recherche du temps perdu* (*In Search of Lost Time*, often translated as *Remembrance of Things Past*), appeared between 1913 and 1927. Arendt is particularly attentive to the volume entitled *Sodome et Gomorrhe* (Sodom and Gomorrah, sometimes translated as *Cities of the Plain*).—Ed.

§ 22 The Imperialist Character (On Kipling)

Of the two main political devices of imperialist rule, race was discovered in South Africa and bureaucracy in Algeria, Egypt, and India; the former was originally the barely conscious reaction to tribes of whose humanity European man was ashamed and frightened, whereas the latter was a consequence of that administration by which Europeans had tried to rule foreign peoples whom they felt to be hopelessly their inferiors and at the same time in need of their special protection. Race, in other words, was an escape into an irresponsibility where nothing human could any longer exist, and bureaucracy was the result of a responsibility that no man can bear for his fellow-man and no people for another people.

The exaggerated sense of responsibility in the British administrators of India who succeeded Burke's "breakers of law" had its material basis in the fact that the British Empire had actually been acquired in a "fit of absent mindedness."[1] Those, therefore, who were confronted with the accomplished fact and the job of keeping what had become theirs through an accident, had to find an interpretation that could change the accident into a kind of willed act. Such historical changes of fact have been carried through by legends since ancient times, and legends dreamed up by the British intelligentsia have played a decisive role in the formation of the bureaucrat and the secret agent of the British services.

~

Legends have always played a powerful role in the making of history. Man, who has not been granted the gift of undoing, who is always an unconsulted heir of other men's deeds, and who is always burdened with a responsibility that appears to be the consequence of an unending chain of events rather than conscious acts, demands an explanation and interpretation of the past in which the mysterious key to his future destiny seems to be concealed. Legends were the spiritual foundations of every ancient city, empire, people, promising safe guidance through the limitless spaces of the future. Without ever relating facts reliably, yet always expressing their true significance, they offered a truth beyond realities, a remembrance beyond memories.

Legendary explanations of history always served as belated corrections of facts and real events, which were needed precisely because history itself would hold man responsible for deeds he had not done and for consequences he had never foreseen. The truth of the ancient legends—what gives them their fascinating actuality many centuries after the cities and empires and peoples they served have crumbled to dust—was nothing but the form in which past events were made to fit the human condition in general and political aspirations in particular. Only in the frankly invented tale about events did man consent to assume his responsibility for them, and to consider past events *his* past. Legends made him master of what he had not done, and capable of dealing with what he could not undo. In this sense, legends are not only among the first memories of mankind, but actually the true beginning of human history.

The flourishing of historical and political legends came to a rather abrupt end with the birth of Christianity. Its interpretation of history, from the days of Adam to the Last Judgment, as one single road to redemption and salvation, offered the most powerful and all-inclusive legendary explanation of human destiny. Only after the spiritual unity of Christian peoples gave way to the plurality of nations, when the road to salvation became an uncertain article of individual faith rather than a universal theory applicable to all happenings, did new kinds of historical explanations emerge. The nineteenth century has offered us the curious spectacle of an almost simultaneous birth of the most varying and contradictory ideologies, each of which claimed to know the hidden truth about otherwise incomprehensible facts. Legends, however, are not ideologies; they do not aim at universal explanation but are always concerned with concrete facts. It seems rather significant that the growth of national bodies was nowhere accompanied by a foundation legend, and that a first unique attempt in modern times was made precisely when the decline of the national body had become obvious and imperialism seemed to take the place of old-fashioned nationalism.

The author of the imperialist legend is Rudyard Kipling, its topic is the British Empire, its result the imperialist character (imperialism was the only school of character in modern politics). And while the legend of the British Empire has little to do with the realities of British imperialism, it forced or deluded into its services the best sons of England. For legends attract the very best in our times, just as ideologies attract the average, and the whispered tales of gruesome secret powers behind the scenes attract the very worst. No doubt, no political structure could have been more evocative of legendary tales and justifications than the British Empire, than the British people's drifting from the conscious founding of colonies into ruling and dominating foreign peoples all over the world.

The foundation legend, as Kipling tells it, starts from the fundamental reality of the people of the British Isles.[2] Surrounded by the sea, they need and win the help of the three elements of Water, Wind, and Sun through the invention of the Ship. The ship made the always dangerous alliance with the elements possible and made the Englishman master of the world. "You'll win the world," says Kipling, "without anyone *caring* how you did it: you'll keep the world without anyone *knowing* how you did it: and you'll carry the world on your backs without anyone *seeing* how you did it. But neither you nor your sons will get anything out of that little job except Four Gifts—one for the Sea, one for the Wind, one for the Sun and one for the Ship that carries you. . . . For, winning the world, and keeping the world, and carrying the world on their backs—on land, or on sea, or in the air—your sons will always have the Four Gifts. Long-headed and slow-spoken and heavy—damned heavy—in the hand, will they be; and always a little bit to wind-ward of every enemy—that they may be a safe-guard to all who pass on the seas on their lawful occasions."

What brings the little tale of the "First Sailor" so close to ancient foundation legends is that it presents the British as the only politically mature people, caring for law and burdened with the welfare of the world, in the midst of barbarian tribes who neither care nor know what keeps the world together. Unfortunately this presentation lacked the innate truth of ancient legends; the world cared and knew and saw how they did it and no such tale could ever have convinced the world that they did not "get anything out of that little job." Yet there was a certain reality in England herself which corresponded to Kipling's legend and made it at all possible, and that was the existence of such virtues as chivalry, nobility, bravery, even though they were utterly out of place in a political reality ruled by Cecil Rhodes or Lord Curzon.[3]

The fact that the "white man's burden" is either hypocrisy or racism has not prevented a few of the best Englishmen from shouldering the burden in earnest and making themselves the tragic and quixotic fools of imperialism. As real in England as the tradition of hypocrisy is another less obvious one which one is tempted to call a tradition of dragon-slayers who went enthusiastically into far and curious lands to strange and naïve peoples to slay the numerous dragons that had plagued them for centuries. There is more than a grain of truth in Kipling's other tale, "The Tomb of His Ancestor,"[4] in which the Chinn family "serve India generation after generation, as dolphins follow in line across the open sea." They shoot the deer that steals the poor man's crop, teach him the mysteries of better agricultural methods, free him from some of his more harmful superstitions and kill lions and tigers in grand style. Their only reward is indeed a "tomb of ancestors" and a family legend, believed by the whole Indian tribe, according to which "the revered ancestor . . . has a tiger of his own—a saddle tiger that he rides round the country whenever he feels inclined." Unfortunately, this riding around the countryside is "a sure sign of war or pestilence or—or something," and in this particular case it is a sign of vaccination. So that Chinn the Youngest, a not very important underling in the hierarchy of the Army Services, but all-important as far as the Indian tribe is concerned, has to shoot the beast of his ancestor so that people can be vaccinated without fear of "war or pestilence or something."

As modern life goes, the Chinns indeed "are luckier than most folks." Their chance is that they were born into a career that gently and naturally leads them to the realization of the best dreams of youth. When other boys have to forget "noble dreams," they happen to be just old enough to translate them into action. And when after thirty years of service they retire, their steamer will pass "the outward bound troopship, carrying his son eastward to the family duty," so that the power of old Mr. Chinn's existence as a government-appointed and army-paid dragon-slayer can be imparted to the next generation. No doubt, the British government pays them for their services, but it is not at all clear in whose service they eventually land. There is a strong possibility that they really serve this particular Indian tribe, generation after generation, and it is consoling all around that at least the tribe itself is convinced of this. The fact that the higher services know hardly anything of little Lieutenant Chinn's strange duties and adventures, that they are hardly aware of his being a successful reincarnation of his grandfather, gives his dreamlike double existence an undisturbed basis in reality. He is simply at home in two worlds, separated by water- and gossip-tight walls. Born in "the heart of the scrubby tigerish country" and educated among his own people in peaceful, well-balanced, ill-informed England, he is ready to live permanently with two peoples and is rooted in and well acquainted with the tradition, language, superstition, and prejudices of both. At a moment's notice he can change from the obedient underling of one of His Majesty's soldiers into an exciting and noble figure in the natives' world, a well-beloved protector of the weak, the dragon-slayer of old tales.

The point is that these queer quixotic protectors of the weak who played their role behind the scenes of official British rule were not so much the product of a primitive people's naïve imagination as of dreams which contained the best of European and Christian traditions, even when they had already deteriorated into the futility of boyhood ideals. It was neither His Majesty's soldier nor the British higher official who could teach the natives something of the greatness of the Western world. Only those who had never been able to outgrow their boyhood ideals and therefore had enlisted in the colonial services were fit for the task. Imperialism to them was nothing but an accidental opportunity to escape a society in which a man had to forget his youth if he wanted to grow up. English society was only too glad to see them depart to faraway countries, a circumstance which permitted the toleration and even the furtherance of boyhood ideals in the public school system; the colonial services took them away from England and prevented, so to speak, their converting the ideals of their boyhood into the mature ideas of men. Strange and curious lands attracted the best of England's youth since the end of the nineteenth century, deprived her society of the most honest and the most dangerous elements, and guaranteed, in addition to this bliss, a certain conservation, or perhaps petrification, of boyhood noblesse which preserved *and* infantilized Western moral standards.

Originally published under the subtitle "The Imperialist Character" in *The Origins of Totalitarianism*, 207–11.
Rudyard Kipling (1865–1936) was a British novelist and imperialist who is most famous for his stories set in British-controlled India, especially *The Jungle Book* (1894) and *Kim* (1901). He won the Nobel Prize for Literature in 1907.—Ed.

§ 23 The Permanence of the World and the Work of Art

Among the things that give the human artifice the stability without which it could never be a reliable home for men are a number of objects which are strictly without any utility whatsoever and which, moreover, because they are unique, are not exchangeable and therefore defy equalization through a common denominator such as money; if they enter the exchange market, they can only be arbitrarily priced. Moreover, the proper intercourse with a work of art is certainly not "using" it; on the contrary, it must be removed carefully from the whole context of ordinary use objects to attain its proper place in the world. By the same token, it must be removed from the exigencies and wants of daily life, with which it has less contact than any other thing. Whether this uselessness of art objects has always pertained or whether art formerly served the so-called religious needs of men as ordinary use objects serve more ordinary needs does not enter the argument. Even if the historical origin of art were of an exclusively religious or mythological character, the fact is that art has survived gloriously its severance from religion, magic, and myth.

Because of their outstanding permanence, works of art are the most intensely worldly of all tangible things; their durability is almost untouched by the corroding effect of natural processes, since they are not subject to the use of living creatures, a use which, indeed, far from actualizing their own inherent purpose—as the purpose of a chair is actualized when it is sat upon—can only destroy them. Thus, their durability is of a higher order than that which all things need in order to exist at all; it can attain permanence throughout the ages. In this permanence, the very stability of the human artifice, which, being inhabited and used by mortals, can never be absolute, achieves a representation of its own. Nowhere else does the sheer durability of the world of things appear in such purity and clarity, nowhere else therefore does this thing-world reveal itself so spectacularly as the non-mortal home for mortal beings. It is as though worldly stability had become transparent in the permanence of art, so that a premonition of immortality, not the immortality of the soul or of life but of something immortal achieved by mortal hands, has become tangibly present, to shine and to be seen, to sound and to be heard, to speak and to be read.

The immediate source of the art work is the human capacity for thought, as man's "propensity to truck and barter" is the source of exchange objects, and as his ability to use is the source of use things. These are capacities of man and not mere attributes of the human animal like feelings, wants, and needs, to which they are related and which often constitute their content. Such human properties are as unrelated to the world which man creates as his home on earth as the corresponding properties of other animal species, and if they were to constitute a man-made environment for the human animal, this would be a non-world, the product of emanation rather than of creation. Thought is related to feeling and transforms its mute and inarticulate despondency, as exchange transforms the naked greed of desire and usage transforms the desperate longing of needs—until they all are fit to enter the world and to be transformed into things, to become reified. In each instance, a human capacity which by its very nature is world-open and communicative transcends and releases into the world a passionate intensity from its imprisonment within the self.

In the case of art works, reification is more than mere transformation; it is transfiguration, a veritable metamorphosis in which it is as though the course of nature which wills that all fire burn to ashes is reverted and even dust can burst into flames.[1] Works of art are thought things, but this does not prevent their being things. The thought process by itself no more produces and fabricates tangible things, such as books, paintings, sculptures, or compositions, than usage by itself produces and fabricates houses and furniture. The reification which occurs in writing something down, painting an image, modeling a figure, or composing a melody is of course related to the thought which preceded it, but what actually makes the thought a reality and fabricates things of thought is the same workmanship which, through the primordial instrument of human hands, builds the other durable things of the human artifice.

We mentioned before that this reification and materialization, without which no thought can become a tangible thing, is always paid for, and that the price is life itself: it is always the "dead letter" in which the "living spirit" must survive, a deadness from which it can be rescued only when the dead letter comes again into contact with a life willing to resurrect it, although this resurrection of the dead shares with all living things that it, too, will die again. This deadness, however, though somehow present in all art and indicating, as it were, the distance between thought's original home in the heart or head of man and its eventual destination in the world, varies in the different arts. In music and poetry, the least "materialistic" of the arts because their "material" consists of sounds and words, reification and the workmanship it demands are kept to a minimum. The young poet and the musical child prodigy can attain a perfection without much training and experience—a phenomenon hardly matched in painting, sculpture, or architecture.

Poetry, whose material is language, is perhaps the most human and least worldly of the arts, the one in which the end product remains closest to the thought that inspired it. The durability of a poem is produced through condensation, so that it is as though language spoken in utmost density and concentration were poetic in itself. Here, remembrance, *Mnēmosynē*, the mother of the muses, is directly transformed into memory, and the poet's means to achieve the transformation is rhythm, through which the poem becomes fixed in the recollection almost by itself. It is this closeness to living recollection that enables the poem to remain, to retain its durability, outside the printed or the written page, and though the "quality" of a poem may be subject to a variety of standards, its "memorability" will inevitably determine its durability, that is, its chance to be permanently fixed in the recollection of humanity. Of all things of thought, poetry is closest to thought, and a poem is less a thing than any other work of art; yet even a poem, no matter how long it existed as a living spoken word in the recollection of the bard and those who listened to him, will eventually be "made," that is, written down and transformed into a tangible thing among things, because remembrance and the gift of recollection, from which all desire for imperishability springs, need tangible things to remind them, lest they perish themselves.[2]

Thought and cognition are not the same. Thought, the source of art works, is manifest without transformation or transfiguration in all great philosophy, whereas the chief manifestation of the cognitive processes, by which we acquire and store up knowledge, is the sciences. Cognition always pursues a definite aim, which can be set by practical considerations as well as by "idle curiosity"; but once this aim is reached, the cognitive process has come to an end. Thought, on the contrary, has neither an end nor an aim outside itself, and it does not even produce results; not only the utilitarian philosophy of *homo faber* but also the men of action and the lovers of results in the sciences have never tired of pointing out how entirely "useless" thought is—as useless, indeed, as the works of art it inspires. And not even to these useless products can thought lay claim, for they as well as the great philosophic systems can hardly be called the results of pure thinking, strictly speaking, since it is precisely the thought process which the artist or writing philosopher must interrupt and transform for the materializing reification of his work. The activity of thinking is as relentless and repetitive as life itself, and the question whether thought has any meaning at all constitutes the same unanswerable riddle as the question for the meaning of life; its processes permeate the whole of human existence so intimately that its beginning and end coincide with the beginning and end of human life itself. Thought, therefore, although it inspires the highest worldly productivity of *homo faber,* is by no means his prerogative; it begins to assert itself as his source of inspiration only where he overreaches himself, as it were, and begins to produce useless things, objects which are unrelated to material or intellectual wants, to man's physical needs no less than to his thirst for knowledge. Cognition, on the other hand, belongs to all, and not only to intellectual or artistic work processes; like fabrication itself, it is a process with a beginning and end, whose usefulness can be tested, and which, if it produces no results, has failed, like a carpenter's workmanship has failed when he fabricates a two-legged table. The cognitive processes in the sciences are basically not different from the function of cognition in fabrication; scientific results produced through cognition are added to the human artifice like all other things.

Both thought and cognition, furthermore, must be distinguished from the power of logical reasoning which is manifest in such operations as deductions from axiomatic or self-evident statements, subsumption of particular occurrences under general rules, or the techniques of spinning out consistent chains of conclusions. In these human faculties we are actually confronted with a sort of brain power which in more than one respect resembles nothing so much as the labor power the human animal develops in its metabolism with nature. The mental processes which feed on brain power we usually call intelligence, and this intelligence can indeed be measured by intelligence tests as bodily strength can be measured by other devices. Their laws, the laws of logic, can be discovered like other laws of nature because they are ultimately rooted in the structure of the human brain, and they possess, for the normally healthy individual, the same force of compulsion as the driving necessity which regulates the other functions of our bodies. It is in the structure of the human brain to be compelled to admit that two and two equal four. If it were true that man is an *animal rationale* in the sense in which the modern age understood the term, namely, an animal species which differs from other animals in that it is endowed with superior brain power, then the newly invented electronic machines, which, sometimes to the dismay and sometimes to the confusion of their inventors, are so spectacularly more "intelligent" than human beings, would indeed be *homunculi*. As it is, they are, like all machines, mere substitutes and artificial improvers of human labor power, following the time-honored device of all division of labor to break down every operation into its simplest constituent motions, substituting, for instance, repeated addition for multiplication. The superior power of the machine is manifest in its speed, which is far greater than that of human brain power; because of this superior speed, the machine can dispense with multiplication, which is the pre-electronic technical device to speed up addition. All that the giant computers prove is that the modern age was wrong to believe with Hobbes that rationality, in the sense of "reckoning with consequences," is the highest and most human of man's capacities, and that the life and labor philosophers, Marx or Bergson or Nietzsche, were right to see in this type of intelligence, which they mistook for reason, a mere function of the life process itself or, as Hume put it, a mere "slave of the passions." Obviously, this brain power and the compelling logical processes it generates are not capable of erecting a world, are as worldless as the compulsory processes of life, labor, and consumption.

One of the striking discrepancies in classical economics is that the same theorists who prided themselves on the consistency of their utilitarian outlook frequently took a very dim view of sheer utility. As a rule, they were well aware that the specific productivity of work lies less in its usefulness than in its capacity for producing durability. By this discrepancy, they tacitly admit the lack of realism in their own utilitarian philosophy. For although the durability of ordinary things is but a feeble reflection of the permanence of which the most worldly of all things, works of art, are capable, something of this quality—which to Plato was divine because it approaches immortality—is inherent in every thing as a thing, and it is precisely this quality or the lack of it that shines forth in its shape and makes it beautiful or ugly. To be sure, an ordinary use object is not and should not be intended to be beautiful; yet whatever has a shape at all and is seen cannot help being either beautiful, ugly, or something in-between. Everything that is, must appear, and nothing can appear without a shape of its own; hence there is in fact no thing that does not in some way transcend its functional use, and its transcendence, its beauty or ugliness, is identical with appearing publicly and being seen. By the same token, namely, in its sheer worldly existence, every thing also transcends the sphere of pure instrumentality once it is completed. The standard by which a thing's excellence is judged is never mere usefulness, as though an ugly table will fulfill the same function as a handsome one, but its adequacy or inadequacy to what it should look like, and this is, in Platonic language, nothing but its adequacy or inadequacy to the *eidos* or *idea,* the mental image, or rather the image seen by the inner eye, that preceded its coming into the world and survives its potential destruction. In other words, even use objects are judged not only according to the subjective needs of men but by the objective standards of the world where they will find their place, to last, to be seen, and to be used.

The man-made world of things, the human artifice erected by *homo faber,* becomes a home for mortal men, whose stability will endure and outlast the ever-changing movement of their lives and actions, only insomuch as it transcends both the sheer functionalism of things produced for consumption and the sheer utility of objects produced for use. Life in its non-biological sense, the span of time each man has between birth and death, manifests itself in action and speech, both of which share with life its essential futility. The "doing of great deeds and the speaking of great words" will leave no trace, no product that might endure after the moment of action and the spoken word has passed. If the *animal laborans* needs the help of *homo faber* to ease his labor and remove his pain, and if mortals need his help to erect a home on earth, acting and speaking men need the help of *homo faber* in his highest capacity, that is, the help of the artist, of poets and historiographers, of monument-builders or writers, because without them the only product of their activity, the story they enact and tell, would not survive at all. In order to be what the world is always meant to be, a home for men during their life on earth, the human artifice must be a place fit for action and speech, for activities not only entirely useless for the necessities of life but of an entirely different nature from the manifold activities of fabrication by which the world itself and all things in it are produced. We need not choose here between Plato and Protagoras, or decide whether man or a god should be the measure of all things; what is certain is that the measure can be neither the driving necessity of biological life and labor nor the utilitarian instrumentalism of fabrication and usage.[3]

Originally published as chapter 23 in *The Human Condition* (Chicago: University of Chicago Press, 1958), 167–74.—Ed.

§ 24 Culture and Politics

I

Whatever it may be that we take to be culture, it is no longer something that we take for granted without question, or with gratitude.[1] The word itself has become cause for discomfort, not only among intellectuals but also among those who create the objects that, taken as a whole, constitute culture. I am afraid that not taking into account this discomfort, which we are presently all aware of, would mean missing both that which is, as well as that which could be.

Culture did not become suspect only yesterday. In Germany the suspicion probably started with the emergence of the "cultural philistinism" [*Bildungsphilisterium*] first described by Clemens Brentano about 150 years ago.[2] For the philistine, culture had become a matter of social prestige and social advancement that became devalued in its eyes precisely because it gained some sort of social utility. We are quite familiar with this dynamic up to the present time: people usually call it the "bargain sale of values" [*Ausverkauf der Werte*], without recognizing that the "bargain sale" began when modern society first discovered the "value" of culture, which is to say, the usefulness of appropriating cultural objects and transforming them into values. The cultural or educated philistine may be a specifically German type; but the socialization of culture—its devaluation in the form of social values—is a more generally modern phenomenon. The philistine in Germany corresponds to the snob in Britain, to the high-brow intellectual in the United States, and perhaps to the *bienpensant* in France, where Rousseau discovered the phenomenon for the first time in the eighteenth-century salons. In Europe these days, those things should be more or less a thing of the past, something to which no one need pay much attention; matters are somewhat different in the United States, where the cultural snobbism of the high-brows is a reaction to mass society. The "bargain sale of values" has been, above all, a "bargain sale" of educational values, and the demand for these values has barely outlasted their declining supply.

The phenomenon of socialization is something else altogether. That which we call "mass culture" is nothing other than the socialization of culture that started in the salons. It is just that the sphere of the social, which first took hold of the upper classes and social ranks, now extends to practically all strata and has thus become a mass phenomenon. All of the features, however, that mass psychology has by now identified as typical of man in mass society: his abandonment [*Verlassenheit*] (and this abandonment is neither isolation nor solitude), along with his utmost adaptability; his irritability and lack of support; his extraordinary capacity for consumption (if not gluttony), along with his utter inability to judge qualities or even to discern them; but most of all his egocentrism and the fatal alienation from the world that he mistakes for self-alienation (this, too, dates back to Rousseau)—all of this first manifested itself in "good society," which does not have a mass character. The first people of the new mass society, one might say, constituted a mass to such a small degree (in a quantitative sense) that they were actually able to consider themselves an elite.

Nevertheless, there are considerable differences between the latest phase in the process whereby culture became socialized and the earlier one that produced cultural philistinism. The phenomenon of the entertainment industry may provide the best and most ready example of these differences, for it is the object that by far concerns the educated philistine and the cultural snob the most. The philistine took hold of the cultural as cultural value, by means of which he secured a higher social position for himself—higher, that is, than the one he occupied, in his own estimation, naturally or by birth. Cultural values were thus what they always are, namely exchange values, and the devaluation that set in almost as a matter of course consisted in the fact that culture was being used or abused for social purposes. By being passed around, cultural values lost their luster and thus the potential—once indigenous to all cultural facts—to captivate in and of themselves. These cultural objects that were denatured to become values were not, however, consumed; even in their most depleted form, they remained a worldly-objective set of things.

Matters are quite different with those objects manufactured by the entertainment industry. They serve to pass the time, as we say; but this means that they serve the life-process of society, which consumes them in the same manner it consumes other objects of consumption. The empty time thus consumed is biological time—the time that remains when labor and sleep are accounted for. In the case of the laboring human being, whose only activity consists in maintaining his own vital process and that of his family, and strengthening it through increased consumption and a raised standard of living, pleasure occupies those parts of life where the biologically determined labor cycle—"the metabolism between man and nature" (Marx)—has created a hiatus. The easier laboring becomes and the less time is taken up by the sustaining of life, the greater the recreational hiatus. The fact that ever more time is freed up that must be filled by pleasure, however, takes nothing away from pleasure being just as much an essential part of the biological process of life as labor and sleep. Biological life, in turn, is always a metabolism that nourishes itself through the ingestion of things, whether it labors or is at rest, whether it consumes or amuses itself. The things offered by the entertainment industry are not values to be used and exchanged; rather, they are objects of consumption as apt to be depleted as any other such object. *Panem et circenses* [bread and circuses]— these two do indeed go together: both are necessary for the life-process, for its sustenance and its recovery; both are also swallowed up in this process, that is to say, they both have to be produced and performed time and again if this process is not to come to an eventual halt.

This is all well and good, as long as the entertainment industry produces its own objects of consumption, and one could reproach this industry no more than one could reproach a bakery for creating products of such limited durability that these have to be depleted in the instant of their creation, lest they should spoil. If, however, the entertainment industry lays claim to products of culture—and this is exactly what happens within mass culture—the immense danger arises that the life-process of society, which, like all life-processes, insatiably incorporates everything it is offered into the biological circulation of its metabolism, begins literally to devour the products of culture. Of course, this does not happen when cultural products—books or images—are thrown into the market in the form of cheap reproductions and are as a result sold in large numbers; but it certainly does happen when the products of culture are being altered—rewritten, condensed, popularized, transformed into kitsch by means of reproduction—so that they may be used by the entertainment industry. It is not the entertainment industry that is a sign of what we call "mass culture," and what should more precisely be called the deterioration of culture. And it is not that this deterioration begins when everyone can buy the dialogues of Plato for pocket change. Rather, it begins when these products are changed to such an extent as to facilitate their mass retailing—a mass retailing that would otherwise be impossible. And those who further this deterioration are not the composers of popular music but the members of the habitually well-read and well-informed intellectual proletariat that is currently attempting to organize and spread culture all over the globe and, in addition, to make this culture palatable to those who actually want nothing to do with it.

Culture relates to objects and is a phenomenon of the world, and pleasure relates to people and is a phenomenon of life.[3] If life is no longer satisfied with the pleasure derived from the ingestive metabolism established between man and nature—a pleasure that always accompanies struggle and labor because human vital energy can no longer exhaust itself in this process of circulation—then it is free to reach for objects in the world, to appropriate them, and to consume them. Life will then seek to prepare these objects of the world or of culture so that they may become suitable for consumption; that is, it will treat them as if they were objects of nature, which, after all, must also be prepared before they may be merged with the human metabolism. The objects of nature are unaffected by being consumed in this way; they continually renew themselves, since man—as long as he lives and labors, struggles and recovers—is also a natural being whose biological circulation is fitted to the larger circulation in which everything natural is moving. But the things of the world produced by man, insofar as he is a worldly and not just a natural being, do not renew themselves. They simply disappear when life appropriates them and consumes them for pleasure. And this disappearance, which first emerges in the context of a mass society founded on alternating labor and consumption, is surely something other than what happens when things wear out within society by circulating as exchange values until their original texture is barely recognizable anymore.

To explain these two processes that are destroying culture in historical or sociological terms, the devaluation of the products of culture within cultural philistinism may be said to exemplify the typical danger of a commercial society, the most important public space of which was the market for goods and exchange; the disappearance of culture within mass society, in turn, may be attributed to a society of laborers who, as laborers, neither know nor need a public, worldly space existing independently of their life-process, while, as persons, they of course need such a space and would be able to construct it as soon as any other human being under other temporal circumstances. A laboring society—which by no means needs to be the same thing as a society of laborers—is, in any event, characterized by understanding and interpreting everything in terms of the function of the individual or social life process. One thing, however, is shared by these anti-cultural processes that are rather different in and of themselves: both are set into motion when all objects produced in the world are brought into a relation with a society that either uses and exchanges them, evaluates and applies them, or else consumes and ingests them. In both cases, we are dealing with a socialization of the world. The rather common view that democracy is opposed to culture, and that culture may flourish only within aristocracies, is correct insofar as democracy is taken to signify the socialization of man and world—which is by no means how it must necessarily be understood. In any case, it is the phenomenon of society, and that of good society no less than that of mass society, which is threatening to culture.

II

Given that our uneasiness with respect to culture stems from the anti-cultural phenomena of cultural philistinism and of mass culture—both of which appeared in this century as a result of an all-pervasive socialization—it is of very recent vintage.[4] There is another kind of distrust with respect to culture, however, which is considerably older but perhaps no less relevant. In the context of a reflection on culture, moreover, it has a definitive advantage: instead of being a response to certain degenerative appearances of cultural matters, it was sparked by the very opposite, namely the eminence of culture and the corresponding fear that it might become too overpowering. This distrust is rooted in the political sphere; it is also not unfamiliar to us if we think of our own discomfort with the notion of aesthetic culturedness, or about compound constructions such as *Kulturpolitik*. In either case we become conscious of a tension and a possible conflict between politics and culture, which the aesthete seeks to resolve in favor of culture (clueless as he is about the exigencies of politics), and the politician (unfamiliar with the necessities of cultural production) in favor of politics, that is to say: cultural politics. Our discomfort with such attempts at conflict resolution is, of course, conditioned by modern experiences. The aesthete reminds us of the cultural philistine who likewise believed that that which is supposedly "higher," namely, cultural "values," could only be sullied and degraded by being pulled down into what he believed to be the vulgar and lowly sphere of the political. Even the most liberal cultural politics will recall to us the dreadful experiences with which we have been faced in recent years under a totalitarian regime, where the thing called "politics" has all but annihilated the thing that is generally taken to be culture.

For the purposes of these reflections, I would like to set such typically modern associations aside for the moment and propose to consider a different historical model. Political science cannot operate without such historical models, not only because it is history that supplies it with its objects of study, but also because it is only with the aid of historically sedimented experiences of such things as "politics" and "culture" that we may attempt to broaden our own horizon of experience—forever limited as it is—in order to gain a perspective on general phenomena such as the relationship between culture and politics. As a matter of fact, my proposal to move away from modernity simply acknowledges that the politico-public sphere was of an unparalleled dignity and of much more relevance for people in the life of antiquity. What this implies for political science is that particular elementary phenomena and problems emerge and may be shown much more clearly against this historical backdrop than against that of any subsequent period. With respect to the specific issue before us, the Middle Ages may anyway be disregarded, since its public space in particular was not shaped by primarily secular, earthly forces. Today, the question of the relation between culture and politics is a secular question (which it is not at all times) and therefore cannot be decided from the religious point of view. Modernity, however, poses nearly insurmountable problems to any clarification of political phenomena, since in this period a new sphere has opened up between the familiar spaces of the private and the public, in which the public sphere is in the process of being made private, and its private counterpart is in the process of being made public. The distortion and disfiguration common to all political problems reflected and studied in the medium of society cannot be discussed here. I only wanted to mention it in order to justify my reference to such a distant past. I would thus ask you to recall that, especially during the classical period both Greek and Roman antiquity, harbored such deep suspicion, if not against culture as such, then at least against all those who produced cultural objects—that is, the artisans and artists—that the prevailing opinion was that people of this sort should not really be considered full citizens. The Romans, for example, resolved the conflict between culture and politics in such a clearly one-sided manner in favor of politics that culture ended up appearing in Rome as a Greek import. (Mommsen writes that "singer and poet were lined up right alongside tightrope walkers and jesters," and, as far as the plastic arts were concerned, "even Varro ridiculed the masses and their desire for puppets and icons.")[5] One indicator of this is the fact that the word culture, which is, after all, of Roman origin, actually denotes "care," which suggests that, in this entire sphere, the Romans adopted the role not of producers and creators but of caretakers and guardians. This is basically the same attitude that also characterized them politically, namely the equally caring retention of beginnings grounded in the past and hallowed by tradition: the founding of the city was to politics what the Greek tradition was to spiritual-intellectual [*geistig*] matters. This attitude may be typical for an agricultural people; it certainly became most productive for the Romans wherever it merged with the incomparably ardent relationship this people had to nature, which is to say: in the shaping of the Roman landscape. Real art, or so it seemed to them, should develop as naturally as the landscape; it should be cultivated nature, and they regarded as the oldest song "the one sung by the leaves to themselves in the green solitude of the woods" (Mommsen). The notion that even agriculture could "yoke" the earth and subject it to violence, and that such violence was evidence of the uncanny greatness of man, as Sophocles tells it in the famous choir lines from *Antigone*—"Numberless wonders / Terrible wonders walk the world but none the match for man"[6]—that is in exact opposition to what the Romans believed. In short, one could say that the Greeks conceived even of agriculture in terms of *technē* and *poiesis,* while the Romans conversely experienced even the cultural, world-producing activities of man in terms of the model of labor in which nature is carefully tended to become culture in order to provide man as a natural being with food and a home.

Even though in our use of the word *culture* Roman associations are still present, the Roman model of the relationship between culture and politics is not particularly fruitful. The Romans did not take the cultural seriously until it was ready to become an object of care for them, and thus a part of the *res publica*. In early times they simply stopped artists and poets in their tracks because they believed that such childish play did not conform to *gravitas,* the solemnity and dignity befitting a citizen. They did not think that this kind of productivity would give rise to an activity equal—or perhaps even threatening—to the sphere of the political. The fruitfulness of the Greek model, by comparison, may be gleaned from the fact that, at least in Athens, the conflict between politics and culture never clearly benefited one side or the other, but was also not mediated to the point that either sphere became indifferent to the other. It was as if the Greeks could say in one and the same breath: "He who has not seen the Zeus of Phidias at Olympia has lived in vain" *and:* People like Phidias, namely sculptors, really should not be granted citizenship.[7]

Thucydides reports a famous saying by Pericles, in which the politically founded suspicion of culture is expressed in an indirect but nevertheless strikingly characteristic way.[8] I am referring to the phrase, all but impossible to translate, *philosophoumen aneu malakias kai philokaloumen met' euteleias.*[9] Here we can clearly hear that it is the polis, the political, which limits the love for wisdom and the love for beauty (both of which are understood, however—and that is what makes the phrase untranslatable—not as states but rather as activities); for it is *euteleia,* the accuracy preventing excess, that is a political virtue, whereas *malakia,* as reported by Aristotle, was considered a barbaric vice; the primary thing, however, which the Greeks believed elevated them above the barbarians was the polis and the political. In other words, by no means did the Greeks believe that it was their higher form of culture that distinguished them from the barbarians. Quite the contrary, it was the fact that, among them, the polis limited whatever was essentially cultural. It is difficult for us to grasp this rather simple point of Pericles's words because we tend to believe much more easily—because our tradition has repressed and submerged the political experiences of the West and its world-view in favor of philosophical experiences—that they speak of the familiar conflicts between truth and beauty, on the one hand, and of thought and action, on the other. Our naïve understanding is conditioned by the narrative of the history of philosophy, according to which Plato and the philosophers preceding him wanted to ban Homer and the poets from the republic for telling lies. As it turns out, however, the philosopher Plato was not the only one who felt impelled to put "Homer and their ilk" in their place; the politician Pericles did the same thing, in the same eulogy, while citing very different reasons. He explicitly says that part of the very greatness of Athens consisted in not needing Homer and the poets in order to make those things that are said and done—which constitutes the essence of the political—immortal. The power of this polis, he thought, was great enough for the monuments to its fame to grow directly out of action, and thus out of the political itself; great enough, that is, to be able to do without the professional producers of fame: the artists and poets, who objectify the living word and the living deed, turning them into things in order to ensure the permanence necessary for their immortal fame.

I believe that the Greek tendency to keep artists and artisans from having any influence on the polis has often been thoroughly misunderstood because it was thought that this tendency could readily be equated with a contempt for the physical labor necessary for the sustaining of life. This contempt is likewise of an originally political nature: no one can be free who is being forced by life, whose activities are dictated by the necessities of life. The life of the free man within the polis is only possible if he has mastered the necessities of life, which means: he has become a master commanding a household of slaves. The labor that is necessary for bare life, however, stands outside the political and cannot, therefore, come into conflict with it; after all, such labor is not performed in the public sphere but, rather, in the private realm of the family and the household. Those who are excluded from the public sphere and confined to the sphere of the private household—the Greek *oiketai* (those belonging to the house) and the Roman *familiares* (those belonging to the family)—are as fundamentally distinct from the craftsmen (who, as their name *demiourgoi* indicates, by no means remain at home but, rather, go out among the people to do their work), as they are distinct from the artists, the *poietai,* whose works serve to educate and to decorate the public space in which political life is situated. A conflict between the political and the cultural can arise only because the activities (acting and producing) and the products of each (the deeds and the works of people) all have their place in public space. The question to be decided regarding this conflict is simply that of which standards should in the end apply in this public space created and inhabited by people: the standards common to acting, or else to producing; those that are political in the basic sense of the word, or those that are specifically cultural.

III

We have determined that the conflict between culture and politics is situated in the public sphere, and that this conflict is about whether the public space we all share should be governed by the standards of those who have erected it—that is, by man insofar as he is *homo faber*—or whether its standards should be directly derived from interactions between people, manifested in the world in deeds, words, and events. As we all know, the Greeks chose the latter alternative—and for a good reason, it seems to me. This decision manifests itself everywhere. If one wanted to discover it in the usual way that things are evaluated, one could say that the standard of size was primary, compared to all other standards of judgment. If one wanted to see it in terms of political organization, one would do well to remember the phrase, "Wherever you may be you will constitute a polis"—a phrase that was told to all departing exiles, implying that the very organization of the polis was so utterly independent of the singular physiognomy that had been achieved at home that it could be summarily left behind and exchanged as long as the far less tangible relationship established through acting and speaking among human beings remained intact.

The nature of this decision is not only *not* to resolve, once and for all, the conflict between culture and politics—the fight over whether the producing person or the acting person should be privileged—but, rather, to fan its flames even more. The greatness of man, after all, on which the whole question turns, is taken to consist in the human ability to do things and to speak words that are deserving of immortality—that is, worthy of eternal remembrance—despite the fact that human beings are mortal. This exclusively human and purely earthly immortality to which greatness lays claim is called "fame." And the purpose of fame is not only to keep word and deed—which are even more transient and fleeting than mortal human beings—from their immediate disappearance, but even to lend them an immortal permanence. The question posed by Pericles in the citation above really amounts to this: Who is better suited to doing that? The organization of the polis that secures the public space in which greatness may appear and may communicate, and in which a permanent presence of people who see and are seen, who speak and hear and may be heard, thus assures a permanent remembrance? Or else the poets and artists—and more generally, the world-creating, world-producing activities, which obviously provide a considerably better guarantee of fame than acting and political organization, since they consist in the making-permanent and the making-imperishable of that which is by its very nature of the most perishable and the most fleeting kind? It was poetry that taught the Greeks, whose educator was Homer, what fame was and what it was capable of being. And even if poetry, together with music, may be the least materially bound art, it still is a form of production, and it achieves a kind of objectification, the absence of which would make permanence, let alone imperishability, inconceivable.

Furthermore, the dependence of acting upon producing is not limited to that of the "hero" and his fame upon the poet—which is the example mentioned by Pericles. Artistic objectification in general grows out of, and remains beholden to, an already existing world of objects without which the artwork would have no place to exist. This world of objects cannot simply be traced back to the life-necessities of man; it is not necessary for bare survival, as the nomadic tribes, the tents and huts of primitive peoples demonstrate. Rather, it derives from a desire to erect a dam against one's own mortality, to place something between the perishability of man and the imperishability of nature that serves as the yardstick for mortals to measure their mortality. What occupies this place is the man-made world that is not immortal but nevertheless considerably more durable and lasting than the life of human beings. All of culture begins with this kind of world-making, which in Aristotelian terms is already an *athanatidzein,* a making-immortal. Outside of such a world—that is to say, outside of what we call "culture" in the broadest sense—acting may not be strictly impossible, but it would leave no trace; no history and no "one thousand stones dug from the bosom of the earth would testify by speaking."[10]

Among the objects of the world we have come to distinguish between things that are used and works of art. Both are alike in that they are objects; that is, they occur not in nature but only in the man-made world, and they are characterized by a certain permanence that extends from the durability of the common object of use to the potential immortality of the artwork. In this way, both are distinct from consumer goods, on the one hand, the earthly lifespan of which hardly exceeds the time required for their production, and products of action, on the other hand—in other words, events, deeds, words, and eventually the stories to be derived from them, all of which are themselves so fleeting that they would barely survive the hour or the day of their emergence if memory and the productive capacities of people did not come to their aid. If one looks at objects in the world from the perspective of their durability, it is clear that artworks are superior to all other objects. Even after millennia they have the ability to shine for us, as they did on the day that brought them into the world. That is why they are the most worldly of all things. They are the only ones that are produced for a world supposed to outlast each mortal human being, and that therefore have no function whatsoever in the life-process of human society. Not only are they not being consumed like consumer goods, or used up like objects of use; they have to be lifted out of this process of use and consumption altogether; they must be explicitly sealed, so to speak, against the biological necessities of human beings. This may happen in various ways, but culture in the specific sense is only found where it does happen.

I have no idea whether or not it is part of human nature to be a worldly or world-making being. There are worldless peoples, just as there are worldless individuals; and human life requires a world only insofar as it needs a home on earth for the duration of its presence. To be sure, every world serves those living in it as an earthly home, but that does not mean that every kind of human making-oneself-at-home amounts to world-making. The earthly home becomes a world only when objects as a whole are produced and organized in such a way that they may withstand the consumptive life-process of human beings living among them—and may outlive human beings, who are mortal. We speak of culture only where this outliving is assured, and we speak of artworks only where we are confronted with objects that are always present in their facticity and their quality, independently of all functional or utilitarian aspects.

For these reasons, it seems to me, any reflection on culture would do well to take as its point of departure the phenomenon of the artwork. This is particularly true of our present attempt, which tries to investigate the relation between culture and politics with reference to the Greek approach to these things. Artworks in and of themselves have a closer relationship to politics than other objects, and their mode of production has a closer relationship to acting than to any other type of occupation. For one thing, it is a fact that only artworks need the public sphere in order to gain recognition; a similar affinity is expressed in the fact that artworks are spiritual-intellectual objects. In Greek terms, *Mnēmosynē*—remembering and remembrance—is the mother of the muses, which is to say that it is through thinking and remembering that reality is revaluated. This revaluation makes it possible to arrest and objectify the intangible, namely events and deeds and words and stories. Artistic objectification has its root in thought, just like the artisanal kind has its root in use. An event does not become eternal simply by being remembered; but this remembrance prepares it for potential immortality, which is then carried out through artistic objectification. For the Greeks, however, it was potential immortality that was the highest and most profound goal of all politics, and of their very own form of political organization—the polis—in particular. What they sought was not the immortality of the artwork itself but, rather, the potential imperishability, the potentially eternal persistence in memory of great words and deeds: the kind of immortal fame that could be assured by poets through productive objectification, and by the polis through ceaseless narrative commemoration.

IV

Given that Greek thought, especially in its political aspects, was directed so exclusively at the potential immortality of mortals, and thus at the imperishability of what is most perishable, it would seem that no human faculty would have been deemed more important than the productive and art-making one, which is to say, the poetic faculty in the Greek sense of the word *poesis*. And if we recall the formidable—and formidably rapid—development of Greek art that begins with a masterwork in order to move from one masterwork to the next in the span of only a few centuries, what is particularly evident is the extraordinary, specifically cultural force sparked by this politically rooted belief in immortality.

Without a doubt, the Greek suspicion of production in all its forms, their suspicion of the danger that supposedly threatened the polis and the political from within the realm of the produced and cultural world, concerns not so much the cultural objects themselves as the attitudes on which production is based—attitudes that typify whoever does nothing but produce things. The suspicion is directed against a generalization of the standards of producers and against their ways of thinking, which intrude upon the political sphere. This explains what may initially be surprising to us, namely that someone could display the greatest receptivity for art and the most ardent admiration of artworks—which, as we know from plentiful anecdotal evidence, was matched by an altogether remarkable self-assuredness on the part of the artists—and yet be constantly considering whether or not artists as persons should be excluded from the political community. The same suspicion is evident in the tendency to regard what were essentially political activities—if, like legislative work or urban planning, these had even the least bit to do with producing—only as pre-political conditions of the political, and thus to exclude them from the polis itself, which is to say, from the realm of essential political activities for which citizenship was required.

This suspicion of production is justified for two factual reasons, both of which may be directly derived from the nature of this activity. First, the latter is essentially impossible without the application of force: In order to produce a table, a tree must be felled, and the wood of the felled tree must in turn be violated to emerge in the form of a table. (When Hölderlin called poetry the "most innocent" activity, he may have been thinking of the violence inherent in all other art forms. But, of course, the poet violates his material as well; he does not sing like the bird living in the tree.) Second, production is always situated within the category of means-ends relations, the only truly legitimate place of which is the sphere of production and fabrication. The process of production has a clearly discernible purpose, namely the end product, for the benefit of which everything that is part of it—the material, the tools, the activity itself, and even the persons involved—becomes a mere means. As the end, the work justifies all means; most of all, it justifies the violence without which those means could never be secured. The producers cannot but regard all objects as means to their ends, and must judge all objects according to their specific utility. If generalized and extended to areas other than that of fabrication, this attitude characterizes *Banausen* [ignoramuses] to this day, one of the few German words borrowed from the Greek that has barely changed its original meaning. The suspicion directed at them stems from the sphere of the political and at one time suggested the desire to keep both the violence and the utilitarian attitude of means-ends-rationality out of the public political space of human community.

Even the most cursory look at the history of political theories or the usual definitions of political action readily reveals that this suspicion has not had the least bit of influence on our tradition of political thought, and that it disappeared just as quickly from the scene, so to speak, as it had emerged in the history of political experiences. Nothing seems more natural to us today than the notion that politics is exactly that space where violence may be legitimate, and this space is usually defined by ruling and being ruled. We cannot even imagine that action could be something other than an activity that pursues a set end by appropriate means, whereby it goes without saying that these means are justified by the given ends. Much to our misfortune we have by now experienced the practical, political consequences of such a belief in the universality of the *banausische* [ignorant] attitude. In any case, what has happened is exactly that which the Greek suspicion of culture sought to avoid—namely, that the political sphere should be overwhelmed and suffused with the categories and the mentality of production. Even though it was never the means, but originally the in-order-to of production, the political lost its independence, and the public sphere, in which human beings, politically organized, act and talk to one another—that is, the ready-made world—was subsumed under the same categories that are first of all necessary to bring that world into existence.

We know from experience how capable a utilitarian means-ends-rationality is of giving politics over to inhuman behavior. Still it strikes us as very strange that such inhuman behavior should arise out of the cultural sphere in particular, and that the humanizing element should be the one assigned to the political sphere. This is due to the fact that no matter how much knowledge of, or appreciation for, Greek culture we may possess, our understanding of culture is essentially determined by the Romans, who conceived of this sphere not from the standpoint of the producer of culture but, rather, from that of the loving and careful keeper of the natural and the inherited. To grasp the altogether different Greek view, we need to remember that their discovery of the political rested on the earnest attempt to keep violence out of the community, and that within Greek democracy only the power of *peithō*—the art of convincing and of talking with one another—was considered a legitimate mode of interaction. We must also not lose sight of the fact that the political really refers only to the circumstances internal to the polis. Only because violence as such was considered apolitical and thus beyond the bounds of the polis could the wars among the Greek republics be so terribly devastating. Whatever lay outside of the polis was beyond the law and was thus completely given over to violence; here it really was the case that the strong did what they could, and the weak suffered what they had to.

One of the reasons why we find it so difficult to discover an element of violence within culture is that thinking in categories of production has become a given for us, so much so that we take these categories to be universal. In accordance with these categories, we act violently everywhere and in all areas; we then try to stave off the worst by means of laws and agreements. For this reason, however, the domain where these categories are really at home and where indeed nothing comes to light but their own configurations appears to us to be the most harmless domain of all—and rightly so. In comparison with the violence that men inflict on one other, the violence they inflict on nature in order to engage in world-making is doubtless innocent. This is why we believe the real danger of the cultural to be enfeeblement, and translate Pericles's mention of *malakia* that was cited above in this sense. But the unmanliness implied by this word, which seemed barbaric to the Greeks, excludes violence no more than it excludes resorting to all attainable means in order to reach the end one is seeking. We who have so often witnessed how a so-called "cultural elite of artists and the educated" may be won over for a politics of brutality, and how that elite is in awe of the latter for finally having left behind all "never-ending chatter"—that is, reciprocal sharing of convictions—we may be somewhat more attuned to these things, and may come to see in them more than a mere "trahison des clercs."[11] To believe in the violence of politics is by no means the sole privilege of brutality. The basis for this belief may also be what the French call a *déformation professionelle,* an aberration among producers and sponsors of culture that is preformed by their line of work.

The suspicion of means-ends thinking, which in its origins is political as well, hits closer to home. The objection, of course, that may be raised by politics against this type of thinking—necessary as it is for production—is that the end justifies the means, and that perfectly appealing ends may engender altogether terrifying and destructive means. If we follow this line of thinking, which in our century has become all but commonplace, we find that acting in and of itself knows of no ends, or at least is unable ever to realize any end in the way it has been conceptualized. For all acting is situated in a web of relations in which anything intended by individuals is immediately transformed, and is thus prevented from being brought about as a set goal, such as a program, for example. This is to say that in politics the means are always more important than the ends; the same thing could be expressed by saying to oneself, as I did at one time: Every good deed for an evil cause factually makes the world a better place, while every bad deed for a good cause factually makes it worse. But pronouncements like these rely on paradoxes produced by the category of means-ends relations, and in fact convey only that this category is just not relevant to acting. The kind of thinking associated with it assumes a sovereignty that only the producer but not the acting person possesses—a sovereignty in dealing with the purposes one sets for oneself, in dealing with the means necessary for one's own realization of these purposes, or in dealing with other people whom one has to command, so they may simply execute orders to fabricate a preconceived end product. Only the producer can be the master; he is sovereign and may take possession of all things as means and tools to his end. The acting person always remains in a relation to, and dependent upon, other acting persons; he is never truly sovereign. What directly derives from this is the well-known fact of the irreversibility of historical processes, namely those that are rooted in action; this impossibility of reversing that which has been done by no means applies to processes of production, in which the producer may always intervene destructively—that is, reverse the process of production—if he so chooses.

What the Greeks found to be so suspicious about the *Banausen* was this sovereignty inherent to producing displayed by *homo faber,* to whom what we would call a generally utilitarian approach—an estimation of things as means to an end—comes naturally, because he produces things intended for use, and always requires certain things in order to produce others. They supposed, with good reason, that, whenever it is generalized, this way of thinking would necessarily lead to a devaluation of things *qua* things, and that this devaluation would extend to natural objects not produced by man and essentially independent of him. In other words, they feared that the sovereignty and mastery of *homo faber* would end in hubris if this kind of human being were given access to the political sphere. And they further believed that such a "victory" of culture would end in barbarism, because hubris was considered a barbarian vice just as much as *malakia.* At this point I would like to remind you once again of the famous chorus from Antigone: *polla ta deina k'ouden anthrōpou deinoteron pelei*[12]—because it captures in a singular manner the peculiar split in the Greek evaluation of the productive faculties, which inspired them with the highest awe and the most resounding fear at the same time. These faculties remained frightening to them because the hubris they contained threatened the very existence of nature and of the world.

V

The worry about the preservation of the world primarily burdens man insofar as he is not only a producing but also a political being. As such, he needs to be able to depend on production, so that it may provide lasting shelter for acting and speaking in their transience—and for the perishability of mortal life in its perishability. Politics is thus in need of culture, and acting is in need of production for the purpose of stability; but it still needs to protect both the political and the readily produced world from culture and production, since all production is at the same time destruction.

Insofar as it is culture, the world is supposed to guarantee permanence, and it does so in its purest and most unencumbered form in those objects that we call artworks—objects of culture in an emphatic sense. To fulfill their "purpose," they must be carefully protected from all purposive declarations and existential interests, from being used and consumed; in the present context it is irrelevant whether this protection is assured by putting artworks in sacred places—in temples and churches—or by entrusting them to the care of museums and preservationists. In either case, they need the public sphere and find their proper place only in the shared world. They do not gain recognition if hidden among private possessions, and they have to be protected against private interests. It is only under the protection of the public that they may emerge as what they are. And whatever emerges in them—which we usually call beauty—is imperishable from the standpoint of the political sphere and its activities, which is the standpoint of acting and speaking in their very transience. Politically speaking, beauty guarantees that even the most transient and perishable things—the deeds and words of mortal human beings—may gain earthly shelter in the human world.

Culture, however, is no less dependent on politics than politics is dependent on culture. Beauty requires the publicity of a political space protected by acting human beings because the public is the space of appearance *par excellence,* in contrast to the private, which is reserved for concealment and security. But beauty itself is not a political phenomenon; it essentially belongs to the sphere of production and is a criterion of the latter, because all objects have an aspect and a shape that is peculiar to their own status as objects. In this way, beauty remains a criterion even for objects of use—not because "functional" objects could ever be beautiful but, on the contrary, because no object, including objects of use, is ever exhausted by its functionality. Functionality, for its part, is not the aspect in which the object appears; rather, the aspect in which something appears is its form and shape. The functionality of things, by contrast, is that in virtue of which they once again disappear by being used up and consumed. In order to evaluate an object only in terms of its use value and not also in terms of its appearance—namely, whether it is beautiful, or ugly, or something in between—we would first have to put out our own eyes.

Culture and politics are thus dependent on each other, and they have something in common: they are both phenomena of the public world. Even though, as we shall see, this commonality, in the end, outweighs all conflicts and oppositions between the two spheres, what they hold in common concerns only the objects of culture, on the one hand, and acting, political human beings, on the other. This commonality has nothing to do with the producing artist. For *homo faber* does not, after all, stand in the same self-evident relationship to the public sphere that characterizes the objects he has given shape and brought to light. In order to keep adding such objects to the world, he himself must be isolated and hidden from the public, whereas political activities—acting and speaking—are all but impossible to perform without the presence of others and therefore without the public sphere of a space constituted by the many. The activities of the artist as well as the craftsman are subject to very different conditions than those that are political. And it is all but self-evident that *homo faber*—as soon as he raises his voice in order to let his opinion of the value of the political be known—will be as suspicious of the political sphere as the polis is suspicious of the mentality and conditions of production.

This side of the coin can only be hinted at here, namely how properly political activities are perceived by the producers of culture with concern and suspicion. What is more important in our present context, however, is that we take notice of one human activity that suggests the common character of culture and politics. I am taking this suggestion from the first part of Kant's *Critique of Judgment,* which contains what is in my opinion the greatest and most original aspect of Kant's political philosophy.[13]

You will recall that Kant's political philosophy in the *Critique of Practical Reason* posits the legislative faculty of reason, and it assumes that the principle of legislation as it is determined by the "categorical imperative" rests on an agreement of rational judgment with itself—which is to say, in Kantian terms, that if I do not want to contradict myself, I must desire only those conditions that could, in principle, also be a general law. The principle of self-agreement is very old. One of its forms, which is analogous to Kant's, can be already found in Socrates, whose central doctrine, in its Platonic formulation, reads as follows: "Since I am one, it is better for me to be in contradiction with the world than to be self-contradictory." This proposition has formed the basis for Western conceptions of ethics and logic, with their emphases on conscience and the law of non-contradiction respectively.

Under the heading "Maxims of Common Sense" in the *Critique of Judgment,* Kant now adds to the principle of agreement with oneself the principle of an "enlarged way of thinking," which submits that I can "think from the standpoint of everyone else." The agreement with oneself is thus joined by a potential agreement with others. The power of judgment rests on this enlarged way of thinking, and judging thereupon derives its proper power of legitimacy. This means, in the negative, that it may disregard its own "subjective private conditions." In positive terms, it means that it cannot function or prevail without the existence of others from whose standpoint it would think. The presence of the self is to the law of non-contradiction in logic, and the no less formal law of non-contradiction in conscience-based ethics, what the presence of others is to judgment. A certain concrete universality accrues to judgment—a universality [*Allgemeingültigkeit*] that is altogether different than universal validity [*universale Gültigkeit*]. The claim to validity can never reach further than other claims, from whose standpoint things are thought in common. Judgment, as Kant says, applies to "every judging person," which means that it does not apply to people who do not participate in the process of judgment and who are not present in the public sphere, where the objects to be judged ultimately appear.

To be sure, the insight that the power of judgment is a *political* faculty in the specific sense of the word is almost as old as articulated political experience itself—a political faculty, that is, in exactly the way in which Kant determines it, namely as the faculty of seeing things not only from one's own perspective but from that of all others who are also present. In this way, judgment is perhaps the basic faculty; it enables man to orient himself in the public-political sphere and therefore in the world held in common. It is all the more surprising, therefore, that no philosopher before or after Kant has ever made it the object of his inquiry; and the reason for this surprising fact may be found in the antipathy towards politics in our philosophical tradition, although this antipathy cannot be discussed here. The Greeks, for one, called this faculty *phronēsis,* and Aristotle's decision to contrast this cardinal ability of the politician with the *sophia* of the philosophers (who are most concerned with truth), is consistent with public opinion in the Athenian polis, as are his political writings generally. Today, we mostly mistake this ability for a "healthy mindset" [*gesunden Menschenverstand*], which at one time used to be called "Gemeinsinn" in German, and was thus identical with the kind of *common sense* or *sens commun* that the French simply call *le bon sens*—and which could also straightforwardly be called a sense of the world [*Weltsinn*]. It alone deserves credit for the fact that our private and "subjective" five senses and their data are fitted to a non-subjective, "objectively" common world that we may share and evaluate together with others.

Kant's definitions are altogether remarkable: he discovered judgment in all its glory, as he came upon the phenomena of taste and the judgment of taste. He objected to the supposed arbitrariness and subjective nature of *de gustibus non disputandum est* because this arbitrariness was incompatible with his sense of politics. In contrast to these common prejudices, he insisted that taste actually "assumes that others experience the same pleasure" and that judgments of taste "suggest everyone's agreement." He therefore understands that taste, like the common sense [*Gemeinsinn*] from which it is derived, is the exact opposite of a "private feeling," even if the two are almost always mistaken for each other.

Discussing all of this in detail would take us too far afield. Even our brief treatment reveals, however, that the specifically cultural behavior of human beings is here understood as political activity in an emphatic sense. Both judgments of taste and political judgments are decisions. As decisions, they have a "foundation that cannot but be subjective." Nevertheless, they must remain independent of all subjective interests. Judgment issues from the subjectivity of a position in the world; at the same time, however, it claims that this world, in which everyone has his or her own position, is an objective fact, and thus something that we all share.

Taste decides what the world *qua* world is supposed to look and sound like, how it is supposed to be looked at and listened to, independently of its usefulness or our existential interests in it. Taste evaluates the world according to its worldliness. Instead of concerning itself with either the sensual life or with the moral self, it opposes both and proposes a pure, "disinterested" interest in the world. It is the world that is primary for the judgment of taste, not man—neither his life nor his self.

The judgment of taste is also like political judgment in that it carries no obligations and—in contrast to the cognitive judgment—cannot prove anything conclusively. All that the judging person can do, as Kant nicely puts it, is "to court everyone's agreement" and to hope to arrive at a common point of view. This courting is nothing other than what the Greeks called *peithein,* which is to say, the kind of rhetoric of persuasion that was valued in the polis as the preferred means of conducting political dialogue. *Peithein* was not only opposed to the physical violence they despised; it was also clearly distinguished from the properly philosophical *dialeghestai,* precisely because the latter was concerned with cognition, which, like the search for truth, required conclusive proof. In the cultural and political spheres—which constitutes the entire sphere of public life— it is not cognition and truth, but judging and deciding that are crucial: the normative evaluation and discussion of the shared world, on the one hand, and the decision concerning what the world is supposed to look like and what sort of actions should be taken in it, on the other.

What speaks for this categorization of taste among the political faculties of man, which may perhaps seem odd, is the well-known but little recognized fact that taste commands an organizational power of peculiar strength. We all know that there is nothing comparable to the discovery of agreement in questions concerning likes and dislikes to help human beings recognize one another—and then to feel irrevocably bound to one another. It is as though taste decided not only what the world should look like, but also who belongs together in the world. It is probably not wrong to see this feeling of common belonging, in political terms, as an essentially aristocratic principle of organization. But its political potential may go even further. The belonging-together of persons—this is what gets decided in judgments about a common world. And what the individual manifests in its judgments is a singular "being-thus-and-not-otherwise," which characterizes everything personal and which gains legitimacy to the degree that it distances itself from whatever is merely idiosyncratic. But the political, in speech and action, has precisely to do with such personhood—the "who" one is, regardless of one's talents or qualities. For this reason, the political finds itself opposed to the cultural, where quality is always ultimately the decisive factor—the quality, above all, of the produced object, which, under the supposition that something personal is expressed in it, points back to individual talents and qualities rather than the "who" of that very person. The judgment of taste, however, does not simply decide matters of quality; on the contrary, these matters are necessarily evident—even if, in times of cultural decline, only a few should be susceptible to evidence of this kind. Taste decides *among* qualities, and can fully develop only where a sense of quality—the ability to discern evidence of the beautiful—is generally present. Once that is the case, it is solely up to taste, with its ever-active judgment of things in the world, to establish boundaries and provide a human meaning for the cultural realm. All of this is to say: its task consists in de-barbarizing culture.

It is well-known that the term *humanity* is of Roman origin, and that no word corresponding to the Latin *humanitas* could be found in Greek. For this reason, I would consider it appropriate to resort to a Roman example to illustrate the way in which taste is the political faculty by means of which culture is humanized. Recall the ancient saying that is Platonic in both its content and its meaning: *amicus Socrates, amicus Plato, sed magis aestimanda veritas* [I love Socrates, I love Plato, but hold truth in higher esteem]. This fundamentally apolitical and inhuman principle, which explicitly rejects persons and friendship in the name of truth, should be contrasted with a less well-known statement by Cicero, who once said the following in the context of a disagreement: *Errare malo cum Platone quam cum istis (sc. Pythagoraeis) vera sentire* [I would rather be in error with Plato than experience the truth with that other one]. Granted, this pronouncement is highly ambiguous. It could mean: I would rather err using Platonic reason than to "feel" the truth using Pythagorean non-reason. But if emphasis is put on *sentire,* the phrase means, instead: It is a question of taste to prefer the company of Plato to that of other people, even if he should be the reason for my error. Assuming that the latter reading is correct, one might object that neither scientists nor philosophers would ever be able to say such things. It is, however, the way a thoroughly political and cultured human being—in the sense of the Roman *humanitas*—would speak. Most certainly, it is what one would expect to hear from someone who is free in all respects, and for whom the question of freedom is also the most important question in philosophy. Such a person would say: I will not let myself be forced in my interactions with both people and objects—not even if the force happens to be truth.

In the realm of the cultural, freedom is manifested in taste because the judgment of taste contains and communicates more than an "objective" judgment about quality. As a judging activity, taste brings together culture and politics, which already share the open space of the public realm. And taste likewise equalizes the tension between them—a tension that stems from the internal conflict between action and production. Without the freedom of the political, culture remains lifeless: the slow death of the political and the withering away of judgment are the preconditions for the socialization and devaluation of culture with which this essay began. Without, however, the beauty of cultural things and without the radiant splendor in which a politically articulated permanence and a potential imperishability of the world manifest themselves, the political as a whole could not last.

Originally published as "Kultur und Politik," *Merkur* 12 (1959): 1122–45; reprinted in *Untergang oder Übergang: 1. Internationaler Kulturkritikerkongress in München, 1958,* ed. Alfred Machionini (Munich: Banaschewski, 1959), 35–66; translated by Martin Klebes.
The original German essay was delivered as part of the commemoration of the 800th anniversary of the founding of the city of Munich, which included a forum on "culture-critique." An English version of this essay was prepared but never published. Arendt wrote a similar essay under the title "Society and Culture," *Daedalus* 89 (1960): 278–87, which was then reworked as "The Crisis in Culture: Its Social and Its Political Significance," in *Between Past and Future: Six Exercises in Political Thought* (New York: Viking, 1961), 197–226.—Ed.

§ 25 Foreword to Carl Heidenreich's Exhibition Catalog

Carl Heidenreich's work had won an easy and early recognition in pre-Hitler Germany where it had been shown in Berlin, in Hamburg, in Munich years before he had to leave the country in November 1934. The fate of modern art during the Third Reich is well known; Heidenreich's paintings belonged to the "degenerate art" which was removed from the museums, and together with these works, which to a large part disappeared only for a time and only from Germany, many pictures went forever, those that were still unpainted and now fated never to see the light of day; others never returned and many, painted outside the German borders, have never been exhibited in Germany.

The same fate that made modern German art homeless made the painter Heidenreich homeless and, for a long time, stateless, driving him half-way around the globe until he could settle down in New York. During the long years of exile, he never ceased to paint, but now always under the conditions of exile—foreignness, lack of recognition—and during long periods under the pressure of great poverty and the struggle for the daily necessities of life. These conditions did not affect his work and his development as a painter at all, nor did they change the intensely personal character of his art.

During the thirty years that he was away from Germany he remained a specifically German painter. He was able to preserve that quality of *Innigkeit*—a word impossible to translate in any other language and perhaps best described (not defined) as an intense inwardness—which inspired the very best of German lyric poetry. This quality is, I think, manifest even in his most "modern" works, all of which belong to the German tradition from Caspar David Friedrich to Lovis Corinth and Emil Nolde.[1] Loyal to this tradition, or rather to its poetical inspiration, Heidenreich became a loner who never succumbed to the fashions of the day, hence never could become fashionable. Instead, he became one of the few entirely autonomous, independent painters of modern art. He understood and knew how to use Juan Gris' great statement: ". . . if I am not in possession of the abstract, with what am I to control the concrete? . . . if I am not in possession of the concrete, with what am I to control the abstract?"[2]

The largest part of Heidenreich's work consists of landscapes. He has an extraordinary feeling for the earth and for man as an inhabitant of this earth. In his youth he was an excellent portraitist, of the same quality as Modigliani; he did not continue—perhaps because modern people were not earth-bound, not natural enough for his taste, too interested in the expressions of their so-called inner life, too sophisticated as it were.[3] At any rate, the work he created in thirty years of relentless, single-minded devotion to nothing but his art and craft shows us an extensive series of faces of the earth as he discovered them wherever his wanderings happened to take him—to Spain, France, New York, Mexico, Alaska, the Pacific, and so on. These paintings and watercolors are all developed out of the basic colors as they are characteristic and conspicuous in the various parts of the world. The ability to see and represent these basic elements, the fundamental chord, as it were, with all its modulations, is manifest in every picture.

It is good to think that this entirely independent and altogether poetic talent has found its loyal and admiring audience in New York. The friends of Carl Heidenreich's paintings know how marvelous it is to live with them and that as they hang on one's walls they become ever more beautiful.

Originally a foreword to the exhibition catalog *Carl Heidenreich: Gemälde und Aquarelle* (Frankfurt am Main: Karmeliterkloster, 1964). An English version was published under the supervision of the Goethe House, New York, for an exhibition in 1972. The Library of Congress gives 1962 as the date for the original English typescript.

Carl Heidenreich (1901–1965) was a German painter who went into exile when the Nazis seized power, because of his association with a branch of the German Communist Party. In 1934 he fled to Spain, was expelled to France, and returned to fight in the Spanish Civil War, during which time he was imprisoned and tortured—and painted pictures of his prison. He arrived in New York in 1941 and became friends with a number of German émigrés, including Arendt and Blücher.—Ed.

Carl Heidenreich, "Last Picture" (1965). Oil on canvas, 24″ × 20″. Courtesy of Richard M. Buxbaum.

§ 26 The Social Question
(On Melville and Dostoevski)

Whatever theoretically the explanations and consequences of Rousseau's teachings might be, the point of the matter is that the actual experiences underlying Rousseau's selflessness and Robespierre's "terror of virtue" cannot be understood without taking into account the crucial role compassion had come to play in the minds and hearts of those who prepared and of those who acted in the course of the French Revolution.[1] To Robespierre, it was obvious that the one force which could and must unite the different classes of society into one nation was the compassion of those who did not suffer with those who were *malheureux* [miserable], of the higher classes with the low people. The goodness of man in a state of nature had become axiomatic for Rousseau because he found compassion to be the most natural human reaction to the suffering of others, and therefore the very foundation of all authentic "natural" human intercourse. Not that Rousseau, or Robespierre for that matter, had ever experienced the innate goodness of natural man outside society; they deduced his existence from the corruption of society, much as one who has intimate knowledge of rotten apples may account for their rottenness by assuming the original existence of healthy ones. What they knew from inner experience was the eternal play between reason and the passions, on one side, the inner dialogue of thought in which man converses with himself, on the other. And since they identified thought with reason, they concluded that reason interfered with passion and compassion alike, that it "turns man's mind back upon itself, and divides him from everything that could disturb or afflict him." Reason makes man selfish; it prevents nature "from identifying itself with the unfortunate sufferer"; or, in the words of Saint-Just: "Il faut ramener toutes les définitions à la conscience; l'esprit est un sophiste qui conduit toutes les vertus à l'échafaud [It is necessary to bring all definitions to consciousness; the mind is a sophist that leads all virtues to the scaffold]."[2]

We are so used to ascribing the rebellion against reason to the early romanticism of the nineteenth century and to understanding, in contrast, the eighteenth century in terms of an "enlightened" rationalism, with the Temple of Reason as its somewhat grotesque symbol, that we are likely to overlook or to underestimate the strength of these early pleas for passion, for the heart, for the soul, and especially for the soul torn into two, for Rousseau's *âme déchirée* [tattered soul]. It is as though Rousseau, in his rebellion against reason, had put a soul, torn into two, into the place of the two-in-one that manifests itself in the silent dialogue of the mind with itself which we call thinking. And since the two-in-one of the soul is a conflict and not a dialogue, it engenders passion in its twofold sense of intense suffering and of intense passionateness. It was this capacity for suffering that Rousseau had pitted against the selfishness of society on one side, against the undisturbed solitude of the mind, engaged in a dialogue with itself, on the other. And it was to this emphasis on suffering, more than to any other part of his teachings, that he owed the enormous, predominant influence over the minds of the men who were to make the Revolution and who found themselves confronted with the overwhelming sufferings of the poor to whom they had opened the doors to the public realm and its light for the first time in history. What counted here, in this great effort of a general human solidarization, was selflessness, the capacity to lose oneself in the sufferings of others, rather than active goodness, and what appeared most odious and even most dangerous was selfishness rather than wickedness. These men, moreover, were much better acquainted with vice than they were with evil; they had seen the vices of the rich and their incredible selfishness, and they concluded that virtue must be "the appanage of misfortune and the patrimony" of the poor. They had watched how "the charms of pleasure were escorted by crime," and they argued that the torments of misery must engender goodness.[3] The magic of compassion was that it opened the heart of the sufferer to the sufferings of others, whereby it established and confirmed the "natural" bond between men which only the rich had lost. Where passion, the capacity for suffering, and compassion, the capacity for suffering with others, ended, vice began. Selfishness was a kind of "natural" depravity. If

Rousseau had introduced compassion into political theory, it was Robespierre who brought it on to the market-place with the vehemence of his great revolutionary oratory.

It was perhaps unavoidable that the problem of good and evil, of their impact upon the course of human destinies, in its stark, unsophisticated simplicity should have haunted the minds of men at the very moment when they were asserting or reasserting human dignity without any resort to institutionalized religion. But the depth of this problem could hardly be sounded by those who mistook for goodness the natural, "innate repugnance of man to see his fellow creatures suffer" (Rousseau), and who thought that selfishness and hypocrisy were the epitome of wickedness. More importantly even, the terrifying question of good and evil could not even be posed, at least not in the framework of Western traditions, without taking into account the only completely valid, completely convincing experience Western mankind had ever had with active love of goodness as the inspiring principle of all actions, that is, without consideration of the person of Jesus of Nazareth. This consideration came to pass in the aftermath of the Revolution, and while it is true that neither Rousseau nor Robespierre had been able to measure up to the questions which the teachings of the one and the acts of the other had brought onto the agenda of the following generations, it may also be true that without them and without the French Revolution neither Melville nor Dostoevski would have dared to undo the haloed transformation of Jesus of Nazareth into Christ, to make him return to the world of men—the one in *Billy Budd,* and the other in "The Grand Inquisitor"—and to show openly and concretely, though of course poetically and metaphorically, upon what tragic and self-defeating enterprise the men of the French Revolution had embarked almost without knowing it. If we want to know what absolute goodness would signify for the course of human affairs (as distinguished from the course of divine matters), we had better turn to the poets, and we can do it safely enough as long as we remember that "the poet but embodies in verse those exaltations of sentiment that a nature like Nelson's, the opportunity being given, vitalizes into acts" (Melville). At least we can learn from them that absolute goodness is hardly any less dangerous than absolute evil, that it does not consist in selflessness, for surely the Grand Inquisitor is selfless enough, and that it is beyond virtue, even the virtue of Captain Vere. Neither Rousseau nor Robespierre was capable of dreaming of a goodness beyond virtue, just as they were unable to imagine that radical evil would "partake nothing of the sordid or sensual" (Melville), that there could be wickedness beyond vice.

That the men of the French Revolution should have been unable to think in these terms and therefore never really touched the heart of the matter which their own actions had brought to the fore, is actually almost a matter of course. Obviously, they knew at most the principles that inspired their acts, but hardly the meaning of the story which eventually was to result from them. Melville and Dostoevski, at any rate, even if they had not been the great writers and thinkers they actually both were, certainly were in a better position to know what it all had been about. Melville especially, since he could draw from a much richer range of political experience than Dostoevski, knew how to talk back directly to the men of the French Revolution and to their proposition that man is good in a state of nature and becomes wicked in society. This he did in *Billy Budd*, where it is as though he said: Let us assume you are right and your "natural man," born outside the ranks of society, a "foundling" endowed with nothing but a "barbarian" innocence and goodness, were to walk the earth again—for surely it would be a return, a second coming; you certainly remember that this happened before; you can't have forgotten the story which became the foundation legend of Christian civilization. But in case you have forgotten, let me retell you the story in the context of your own circumstances and even in your own terminology.

Compassion and goodness may be related phenomena, but they are not the same. Compassion plays a role, even an important one, in *Billy Budd*, but its topic is goodness beyond virtue and evil beyond vice, and the plot of the story consists in confronting these two. Goodness beyond virtue is natural goodness and wickedness beyond vice is "a depravity according to nature" which "partakes nothing of the sordid or sensual." Both are outside society, and the two men who embody them come, socially speaking, from nowhere. Not only is Billy Budd a foundling; Claggart, his antagonist, is likewise a man whose origin is unknown. In the confrontation itself there is nothing tragic; natural goodness, though it "stammers" and cannot make itself heard and understood, is stronger than wickedness because wickedness is nature's depravity, and "natural" nature is stronger than depraved and perverted nature. The greatness of this part of the story lies in that goodness, because it is part of "nature," does not act meekly but asserts itself forcefully and, indeed, violently so that we are convinced: only the violent act with which Billy Budd strikes dead the man who bore false witness against him is adequate, it eliminates nature's "depravity." This, however, is not the end but the beginning of the story. The story unfolds after "nature" has run its course, with the result that the wicked man is dead and the good man has prevailed. The trouble now is that the good man, because he encountered evil, has become a wrong-doer too, and this even if we assume that Billy Budd did not lose his innocence, that he remained "an angel of God." It is at this point that "virtue" in the person of Captain Vere is introduced into the conflict between absolute good and absolute evil, and here the tragedy begins. Virtue—which perhaps is less than goodness but still alone is capable "of embodiment in lasting institutions"—must prevail at the expense of the good man as well; absolute, natural innocence, because it can only act violently, is "at war with the peace of the world and the true welfare of mankind," so that virtue finally interferes not to prevent the crime of evil but to punish the violence of absolute innocence. Claggart was "struck by an angel of God! Yet the angel must hang!" The tragedy is that the law is made for men, and neither for angels nor for devils. Laws and all "lasting institutions" break down not only under the onslaught of elemental evil but under the impact of absolute innocence as well. The law, moving between crime and virtue, cannot recognize what is beyond it, and while it has no punishment to mete out to elemental evil, it cannot but punish elemental goodness even if the virtuous man, Captain Vere, recognizes that only the violence of this goodness is adequate to the depraved power of evil. The absolute—and to Melville an absolute was incorporated in the Rights of Man—spells doom to everyone when it is introduced into the political realm.

We noted before that the passion of compassion was singularly absent from the minds and hearts of the men who made the American Revolution. Who would doubt that John Adams was right when he wrote: "The envy and rancor of the multitude against the rich is universal and restrained only by fear or necessity. A beggar can never comprehend the reason why another should ride in a coach while he has no bread"; and still no one familiar with misery can fail to be shocked by the peculiar coldness and indifferent "objectivity" of his judgment.[4] Because he was an American, Melville knew better how to talk back to the theoretical proposition of the men of the French Revolution—that man is good by nature—than how to take into account the crucial passionate concern which lay behind their theories, the concern with the suffering multitude. Envy in *Billy Budd,* characteristically, is not envy of the poor for the rich but of "depraved nature" for natural integrity—it is Claggart who is envious of Billy Budd—and compassion is not the suffering of the one who is spared with the man who is stricken in the flesh; on the contrary, it is Billy Budd, the victim, who feels compassion for Captain Vere, for the man who sends him to his doom.

The classical story of the other, non-theoretical side of the French Revolution, the story of the motivation behind the words and deeds of its main actors, is "The Grand Inquisitor," in which Dostoevski contrasts the mute compassion of Jesus with the eloquent pity of the Inquisitor. For compassion, to be stricken with the suffering of someone else as though it were contagious, and pity, to be sorry without being touched in the flesh, are not only not the same, they may not even be related. Compassion, by its very nature, cannot be touched off by the sufferings of a whole class or a people, or, least of all, mankind as a whole. It cannot reach out farther than what is suffered by one person and still remain what it is supposed to be, co-suffering. Its strength hinges on the strength of passion itself, which, in contrast to reason, can comprehend only the particular, but has no notion of the general and no capacity for generalization. The sin of the Grand Inquisitor was that he, like Robespierre, was "attracted toward *les hommes faibles*," not only because such attraction was indistinguishable from lust for power, but also because he had depersonalized the sufferers, lumped them together into an aggregate—the people *toujours malheureux,* the suffering masses, et cetera. To Dostoevski, the sign of Jesus's divinity clearly was his ability to have compassion with all men in their singularity, that is, without lumping them together into some such entity as one suffering mankind. The greatness of the story, apart from its theological implications, lies in that we are made to feel how false the idealistic, high-flown phrases of the most exquisite pity sound the moment they are confronted with compassion.

Closely connected with this inability to generalize is the curious muteness or, at least, awkwardness with words that, in contrast to the eloquence of virtue, is the sign of goodness, as it is the sign of compassion in contrast to the loquacity of pity. Passion and compassion are not speechless, but their language consists in gestures and expressions of countenance rather than in words. It is because he listens to the Grand Inquisitor's speech with compassion, and not for lack of arguments, that Jesus remains silent, struck, as it were, by the suffering which lay behind the easy flow of his opponent's great monologue. The intensity of this listening transforms the monologue into a dialogue, but it can be ended only by a gesture, the gesture of the kiss, not by words. It is upon the same note of compassion—this time the compassion of the doomed man with the compassionate suffering felt for him by the man who doomed him—that Billy Budd ends his life, and, by the same token, the argument over the Captain's sentence, and his "God bless Captain Vere!" is certainly closer to a gesture than to a speech. Compassion, in this respect not unlike love, abolishes the distance, the in-between which always exists in human intercourse, and if virtue will always be ready to assert that it is better to suffer wrong than to do wrong, compassion will transcend this by stating in complete and even naïve sincerity that it is easier to suffer than to see others suffer.

Because compassion abolishes the distance, the worldly space between men where political matters, the whole realm of human affairs, are located, it remains, politically speaking, irrelevant and without consequence. In the words of Melville, it is incapable of establishing "lasting institutions." Jesus's silence in "The Grand Inquisitor" and Billy Budd's stammer indicate the same, namely their incapacity (or unwillingness) for all kinds of predicative or argumentative speech, in which someone talks *to* somebody *about* something that is of interest to both because it *inter-est,* it is between them. Such talkative and argumentative interest in the world is entirely alien to compassion, which is directed solely, and with passionate intensity, towards suffering man himself; compassion speaks only to the extent that it has to reply directly to the sheer expressionist sound and gestures through which suffering becomes audible and visible in the world. As a rule, it is not compassion which sets out to change worldly conditions in order to ease human suffering, but if it does, it will shun the drawn-out wearisome processes of persuasion, negotiation, and compromise, which are the processes of law and politics, and lend its voice to the suffering itself, which must claim for swift and direct action, that is, for action with the means of violence.

Here again, the relatedness of the phenomena of goodness and compassion is manifest. For goodness that is beyond virtue, and hence beyond temptation, ignorant of the argumentative reasoning by which man fends off temptations and, by this very process, comes to know the ways of wickedness, is also incapable of learning the arts of persuading and arguing. The great maxim of all civilized legal systems, that the burden of proof must always rest with the accuser, sprang from the insight that only guilt can be irrefutably proved. Innocence, on the contrary, to the extent that it is more than "not guilty," cannot be proved but must be accepted on faith, whereby the trouble is that this faith cannot be supported by the given word, which can be a lie. Billy Budd could have spoken with the tongues of angels, and yet would not have been able to refute the accusations of the "elemental evil" that confronted him; he could only raise his hand and strike the accuser dead.

Clearly, Melville reversed the primordial legendary crime, Cain slew Abel,[5] which has played such an enormous role in our tradition of political thought, but this reversal was not arbitrary; it followed from the reversal the men of the French Revolution had made of the proposition of original sin, which they had replaced by the proposition of original goodness. Melville states the guiding question of his story himself in the Preface: How was it possible that after "the rectification of the Old World's hereditary wrongs . . . straightway the Revolution itself became a wrong-doer, one more oppressive than the Kings?" He found the answer—surprisingly enough if one considers the common equations of goodness with meekness and weakness—in that goodness is strong, stronger perhaps even than wickedness, but that it shares with "elemental evil" the elementary violence inherent in all strength and detrimental to all forms of political organization. It is as though he said: Let us suppose that from now on the foundation stone of our political life will be that Abel slew Cain. Don't you see that from this deed of violence the same chain of wrongdoing will follow, only that now mankind will not even have the consolation that the violence it must call crime is indeed characteristic of evil men only?

Originally published as the second part of chapter 3 of "The Social Question" in *On Revolution* (New York: Viking, 1963), 79–88.

Herman Melville (1819–1891) was a great American writer. Among his many works are the novels *Moby-Dick* (1851), *Pierre* (1852), and *The Confidence Man* (1857), his stories "Bartleby the Scrivener" (1853), "Benito Cereno" (1856), and *Clarel: A Poem and Pilgrimage in the Holy Land* (1876). In later life, unable to earn a living from his writing, he relied on his wife's family. His last novel, *Billy Budd*, was probably finished shortly before his death and was posthumously published in 1924.

Fyodor Dostoevski (1821–1881) was a great Russian novelist. Among his many works are *Notes from Underground* (1854), *Crime and Punishment* (1866), and *The Possessed* (1872). (For Arendt's lecture notes on the latter, see Chapter 31.) *The Brothers Karamazov* (1879–1880) includes a chapter entitled "The Grand Inquisitor." He died soon after this novel was completed.—Ed.

§ 27 Review of Nathalie Sarraute,
The Golden Fruits

With the exception of the early *Tropismes,* all of Nathalie Sarraute's books are now available in English. Thanks are due to her publisher and to Maria Jolas who, to quote Janet Flanner in *The New Yorker,* has put her work "into English of such verisimilitude that it seems merely orchestrated in another key." Novels are rarely masterpieces, and this is as it should be; it is even rarer to find a translation that is perfect, and this, perhaps, is not as it should or could be.

When Nathalie Sarraute published her first novel, *Portrait of a Man Unknown,* in 1948, Sartre, in an Introduction, placed her with such authors of "entirely negative works" as Nabokov, Evelyn Waugh, and the Gide of *Les Faux-Monnayeurs,* and called the whole genre "anti-novel."[1] In the Fifties, the anti-novel became the New Novel and Sarraute its originator. All these classifications are somewhat artificial and, if applied to Mme. Sarraute, difficult to account for. She has herself pointed out her ancestors, Dostoevsky (especially the *Notes from Underground*) and Kafka in whom she sees Dostoevsky's legitimate heir. But this much is true: She wrote at least her first pair of novels, the *Portrait* and *Martereau* (1953), against the assumptions of the classical novel of the nineteenth century, where author and reader move in a common world of well-known entities and where easily identifiable characters can be understood through the qualities and possessions bestowed upon them. "Since then," she writes in

---

Nathalie Sarraute, *The Golden Fruits,* trans. Maria Jolas (New York: Braziller, 1964). 177 pages, $4.00.

her book of essays, *The Age of Suspicion,* "[this character] has lost every-thing; his ancestors, his carefully built house, filled from cellar to garret with a variety of objects, down to the tiniest gewgaw, his sources of in-come and his estates, his clothes, his body, his face . . . his personality and, frequently, even his name." Man as such is or has become unknown so that it matters little to the novelist whom he chooses as his "hero" and less into what kind of surrounding he puts him. And since "the character occupied the place of honor between reader and novelist," since he was "the object of their common devotion," this arbitrariness of choice indi-cates a serious break-down in communication.

In order to recover some of this lost common ground, Nathalie Sar-raute very ingeniously took the nineteenth-century novel, supposedly the common cultural heritage of author and reader, as her point of departure and began by choosing her "characters" from this richly populated world. She fished them right out of Balzac and Stendhal, stripped them of all those secondary qualities—customs, morals, possessions—by which they could be dated, and retained only those bare essentials by which we re-member them: avarice—the stingy father living with his homely, penny-pinching spinster daughter, the plot turning about her numerous illnesses, fancied or real, as in *Portrait;* hatred and boredom—the closely-knit fam-ily unit which still survives in France, the "dark entirely closed world" of mother, father, daughter, and nephew in *Martereau,* where the plot turns about the "stranger" who swindles the father out of the money he had wanted to save from the income tax collector; even the hero of the later work, *The Planetarium,* personified ambition (the plot is a familiar one describing his ruthless "rise in social space").[2]

Sarraute has cracked open the "smooth and hard" surface of these tra-ditional characters ("nothing but well-made dolls") in order to discover the endless vibrations of moods and sentiments which, though hardly per-ceptible in the macrocosm of the outward world, are like the tremors of a never-ending series of earthquakes in the microcosm of the self. This in-ner life—what she calls "the psychological"—is no less hidden from "the surface world" of appearances than the physiological life process that goes on in the inner organs beneath the skin of bodily appearance. Neither shows itself of its own accord. And just as the physiological process an-nounces itself naturally only through the symptoms of a disease (the tiny pimple, to use her own image, which is the sign of the plague), but needs a special instrument—the surgical knife or X rays—to become visible, so these psychological movements cause the outbreak of symptoms only in case of great disaster and need the novelist's magnifying lenses of suspicion to be explored. To choose the intimacy of family life, this "semi-darkness" behind closed curtains with its Strindbergian overtones, as a laboratory for this kind of psychological vivisection, instead of the couch, was a sheer stroke of genius, for here "the fluctuating frontier that [ordinarily] separates conversation from sub-conversation" breaks down most frequently so that the inner life of the self can explode onto the surface in what is commonly called "scenes."[3] No doubt these scenes are the only distraction in the infinite boredom of a world entirely bent upon itself, and yet they also constitute the life-beat of a hell in which we are condemned to going "eternally round and round," where all appearances are penetrated but no firm ground is ever reached. Behind the lies and the pretenses, there is nothing but the vibrations of an ever-present irritation—a "chaos in which a thousand possibilities clash," a morass where every step makes you sink deeper into perdition.

Nathalie Sarraute had become a master of this tumultuous, explosive inner life of an "all-powerful I" before she began her second series of novels, *The Planetarium* (1959) and *The Golden Fruits* (1963), which, despite similarity of technique and style, belong to a different genre. In her essays, written during the first period and published in 1956, as well as in interviews and in numerous passages in the novels themselves, she has explained her intentions with great lucidity, and the reviewer finds it tempting indeed to echo her own insights. She thus has spoken with great abandon of the "psychological movements" which "constitute, in fact, the principal element of my research"; she also has mentioned, though with more restraint, her hope to break through to some domain of the authentically *real,* not Goethe's "the beautiful, the good, the true," but just some tiny, undiluted, undistorted factual matter. Perhaps it will turn out to be "nothing, or almost nothing,"—"the first blade of grass . . . a crocus not yet open . . . a child's hand nestling in the hollow of my own." But "believe me, that's all that counts." Finally, she quotes a famous line from *The Brothers Karamazov,* which could well be placed as a motto over her whole work: " 'Master, what must I do to gain eternal life?' The Staretz comes a little nearer: 'Above all, do not lie to yourself.' " (In this, as in other respects, she has more in common with Mary McCarthy than with almost any other living writer.)[4]

In an author who has gone to such lengths to explain what she is doing, conspicuous elements she has not mentioned may be all the more noteworthy. First, there is the entirely negative character of her discoveries, which Sartre found so striking. Nothing in either her method or subject matter explains the catastrophic nature of the inner life, the complete or almost complete absence of love, generosity, magnanimity, and the like in her work. Every word, if it is not meant to deceive, is a "weapon," all thoughts are "assembled like a large and powerful army behind its banners . . . about to roll forward." The imagery of warfare is all-pervasive. Even in Kafka, as she herself has noted—let alone in Dostoevsky or in Proust and Joyce, the earlier masters of the inner monologue—there are still these "moments of sincerity, these states of grace," which are absent from her own work. There is, second, and more surprisingly, the fact that she has never elaborated on her enormously effective use of the "they"—what "they say," the commonplace, the cliché, the merely idiomatic turn of the phrase—emphasized by many of her reviewers and admirers. "They" made their first appearance in the *Portrait,* moved into the center of the plot in *The Planetarium,* and become the "hero" of *The Golden Fruits.*

In the *Portrait*—which like a Greek tragedy has three main characters: Father, Daughter, and Watcher, the old Messenger in new disguise, who tells the story—"they" form the chorus. Both Father and Daughter are surrounded and supported by a "protective cohort" from the outside world, the father by his "old cronies" whom he meets regularly in a tavern, the daughter by the ceaselessly gossiping elderly women in the doorways of the big apartment houses, who had gathered around her ever since she lay in the cradle, "wagging their heads . . . like the wicked godmothers in fairy tales." Singing out their ageless platitudes, the choruses support the main figures ("children never show any gratitude, believe me") and they form a "firm rampart" of ordinariness behind the fighting line to which the characters betake themselves to regain "density, and weight, steadiness," and to become "somebodies" again. And peace comes when the daughter, having finally found a commonplace husband, looks forward to joining the chorus: "Piously, I shall mingle my voice with theirs."

This relationship between "I" and "They" is sometimes reversed in the later novels. In both *The Planetarium* and *The Golden Fruits* "they" often appear as the incarnation of the enemy, the cause of all disasters suffered by the "I"—at the first moment of inattention, "they" will come and "apprehend, snatch" you without pity, "like dogs that smell in every corner to discover the prey they're going to carry away between their teeth and which, in a little while, they will lay, all warm and quivering, at the feet" of whomever they happen to recognize as their master at that particular moment.

There is finally the "metamorphosis," the moment of truth, around which each novel is centered, as Greek tragedy is centered around the moment of recognition. This is what gives Nathalie Sarraute's writing a dramatic quality which is, I think, unique in contemporary fiction. (She probably borrowed the word from Kafka's famous story—in the *Portrait* she even uses the original image: Father and Daughter confront each other like "two giant insects, two enormous dung beetles.")[5] The metamorphosis occurs in the rare moments when "sub-conversation" and "sub-conversation" confront each other, that is, at the moment of descent from the daylight world of seeming down to "the bottom of a well" where naked, "clasped to each other," slipping and fighting in a nether world, as private and incommunicable as the world of dreams and nightmares, the characters meet in a murderous intimacy that will conceal nothing.

In their ferocious pursuit of truth (this is how you are, do not lie to yourself) the first two novels leave the reader with Strindberg's compassion for the whole species: "Oh, for the pity of men." The family after all is the most natural human community, and what is revealed in its setting seems to indicate something about "human nature." The setting of the two later novels is Society, which is "artificial" in comparison to the family and even more artificial in this case as it is the society of the literary clique. (The Planetarium "is not the real sky but an artificial sky," as Mme. Sarraute explained in an interview with François Bondy in *Der Monat*, December 1963.) Strangely enough, the result of the different settings is that on the one hand conversation and sub-conversation are more closely interrelated, and, on the other, everything which has been so desperately sad, almost tragic, in the earlier work now turns into sheer, hilarious comedy. Here, in the sphere of the social, there is "nothing sacred. . . . No holy places. No taboos," that can be violated; here "we are all the same, all human beings . . . all alike" and do not need any intimacy to call each other's bluff; every distinction or even mere difference, "that's an accident, a curious excrescence, that's a sickness," perhaps even "a little miracle" if it turns out to materialize into an object, some work of art "that can't be explained . . . but as for the rest, what a resemblance." (From *The Golden Fruits*.)

The Planetarium still retains a number of "characters," taken from the family—father, aunt, and in-laws—who are by no means "all alike," and it has two main characters, Julien Sorel and Mme. de Rênal in modern disguise: the young *ambitieux* has become an ordinary social climber, "a little scoundrel . . . When he wants something, nothing can stop him, there's nothing he wouldn't do," and the *femme passionée* of good society has become a literary celebrity. They have no affair, there is no passion left in this society; they are not true protagonists, but more like members of a chorus that has lost its protagonist, the almost accidentally chosen figures of the "they."

The story tells how the newly-wed couple-on-the-make obtain the apartment of the young man's aunt (they have an apartment to live in, but they need a new one "to entertain"), who to her own great grief had installed in it a brand-new door in "bad taste," and most of the story's complexities turn about furniture and the unfortunate door. The metamorphosis takes place near the end of the book and, delightfully, concerns the same door: The young man takes the celebrity around for whom he had gone to all the trouble. He is in agony because of the door, but he is saved: While the celebrity is looking around, "in one second, the most amazing, the most marvelous metamorphosis takes place. As though touched by a fairy wand, the door which, as soon as he had set eyes on it, had been surrounded by the thin papier-maché walls, the hideous cement of suburban houses . . . reverts to its original aspect, when, resplendent with life, it had appeared framed in the walls of an old convent cloister." Alas, the poor door is not permitted to remain for long in its state of re-found grace; there is another embarrassing object in the apartment, a Gothic virgin marred on one side by a restored arm, and the celebrity, oh horror, does not detect it: she "stares fixedly at the shoulder, the arm, she swallows them stolidly, her strong stomach digests them easily, her eyes maintain the calm, indifferent impression of a cow's eyes." This is the moment of truth when everything comes apart in "a breach, a sudden cleavage:" she loses her power to perform miracles and back comes "the oval door . . . floating, uncertain, suspended in limbo . . . massive old convent door or that of a cheap bungalow . . ." to haunt him forever after.

This is one of the most exquisitely funny passages that I know in contemporary literature: it is of course the comedy of our American "other-directedness" or of the "inauthentic" in French parlance. But how feeble and pedantic these words sound compared to the miserably grotesque reality of the thing itself! What makes it so comical is that it all takes place in the milieu of the presumably "inner-directed" élite of "good taste" and refinement, among intellectuals boasting of the highest standards, who pretend to care about nothing, certainly talk about nothing but things of the highest spiritual order. When asked to portray themselves they appear as "highly sensitive and frail beings at odds with a dark and hostile world," as the *New York Times Book Review,* as though asked to compound the fraud that *The Planetarium* exposes, said in high praise. But this is perhaps as it must be, for the truth of the matter is that *The Planetarium* and *The Golden Fruits* taken together constitute the severest indictment ever meted out to the "intellectuals." It is as though Sarraute said: *Le Trahison des Clercs?* Don't make me laugh. What have these creatures got that they could betray to begin with?

The comedy is at its purest in *The Golden Fruits.* Here, "they" are among themselves, undisturbed by any "characters" from outside the literary clique. The book tells the story of another book, a novel just published and called "The Golden Fruits," from its initial spectacular success to its quiet downfall into oblivion, and it ends with an outlook into the book's uncertain future. (Its first reception in France, I am told, was not enthusiastic, perhaps because the reviewers asked themselves how they could possibly consider a work in which every phrase, every turn of smart or idiotic praise or blame has been anticipated and revealed as mere talk.) We never learn anything about the book itself—the author is mentioned because he belongs to the literary clique—for this is the story of Everybook that has the misfortune to fall into the hands of the literate Everybody, whose whispers and shouts last until Everything has been said.

And indeed everybody is present: The critic; the *maître:* and the admiring ladies; "the culprit" who once had "fallen from grace" by offending impeccable taste, but has been "disinfected long ago"; the husband who is suspected of not having discovered "The Golden Fruits" by himself, but he has, he has, says his wife; the provincial who far from "them" had found the novel full of platitudes (but it was done "on purpose," and he is convinced); the scholars ("heads heavy with learning") who, having grouped the dead "according to category, lesser, average, great," find a place for the newest arrival; even the doubter, "mad, exalted creature who goes about the world, barefooted and in rags" disturbing its peace; even "the foreigner, the pariah" (but "you are one of us," there "can be no question of excluding you"). As they exhaust all aspects, all arguments and outdo each other with superlatives until they all know: "There will be those who came before and those who came after 'The Golden Fruits'." There occurs in each one of them this mysterious, delicious process of being "emptied of himself—an empty recipient that will be entirely filled with what they are going to put into it."

And who are "they"? Each one of them is the same "all-powerful I" whose catastrophic inner life was the subject-matter of the earlier novels. Each one of them has come out of hell and is afraid of being returned there, remembering only too well how it was when he was still alone, a "poor devil, obscure little fellow, unknown author," always trying to be admitted and invariably beaten down. What would have happened to him had he not clung fast to "another image [of himself] . . . with gigantic proportions, more and more enormous, spreading out on every side"? This is why "they" are all alike and have found in each other's company the medium in which "the weakest vibration is communicated immediately," and "becomes amplified in ever-increasing waves." This kind of society is the macrocosm of the "I," the "I" writ large. Or, perhaps, it is the other way round and the "psychological" inner life, whose trembling fluctuations Sarraute explored, is only the "inner" life of those egomaniacs who, seemingly "outer-directed," are in fact interested in no one and nothing but themselves. Nothing at any rate resembles more closely the disastrous instability of teeming and swarming emotions—from which all loyalty, faithfulness, steadfastness must be absent by definition—than the ups and downs, the tidal waves of fashionable taste by which "they" are thrown hither and thither.

The tide, to be sure, turns, its rise is followed by its fall, and everything quickly crumbles away "you never know exactly how." All you know is that from one day to the other everything is in reverse—we hear the same people, the same critic, the same ever-loving wife whose husband now "from the beginning was never taken in," and all the rest of "them," until finally the book is given the *coup de grâce*—"You're still with . . . 'The Golden Fruits'?" "They," to be sure, are not disturbed by this *volte-face,* they remain in the same medium, the same company, they are hardly aware of what happened. And should any one of them ever be beset by doubts, he will be told to evoke History, the goddess of change, by which "they [are] borne along . . . as by a superb ocean liner."

This is comedy and like all good comedy concerned with something deadly serious. The falsity of the intellectual "they" is particularly painful, because it touches one of the most delicate and, at the same time, indispensable elements of human relationships, the element of common taste for which indeed "no criterion of values" exists. Taste decides not only about how the world should look, it also determines the "elective affinities" of those who belong together in it. The "secret signs" by which we recognize each other, what else do they say but, "We are brothers, aren't we . . . I offer you this holy bread. I welcome you to my table." This feeling of natural kinship in the midst of a world, to which we all come as strangers, is monstrously distorted in the society of the "refined" who have made passwords and talismans, means of social organization, out of a common world of objects. But have they really succeeded in ruining it? Shortly before the end, Nathalie Sarraute turns from the "they" and the "I" to the "we," the old We of author and reader. It is the reader who speaks: "We are so frail and they so strong. Or perhaps . . . we, you and I, are the stronger, even now."

Originally published in *The New York Review of Books* 2 (March 5, 1964): 5–6. A German version, translated by Wolfgang von Einseidel, was published as an afterword to the German translation of Sarraute's novel, *The Planetarium* (Munich: dtv, 1965).

Born in Russia, Nathalie Sarraute (1900–1999) moved to France when she was nine, where she later studied and practiced law. At the beginning of the Second World War she quit her law practice and devoted herself to the writing of fiction, becoming one of the leading representatives of the so-called *nouveau roman.*—Ed.

§ 28 What Is Permitted to Jove . . .

Reflections on the Poet Bertolt Brecht and His Relation to Politics

You hope, yes,
> your books will excuse you,
save you from hell:
> nevertheless,
without looking sad,
> without in any way
seeming to blame
> (He doesn't need to,
knowing well
> what a lover of art
like yourself pays heed to),
> God may reduce you
on Judgment Day
> to tears of shame,
reciting by heart
> the poems you would
have written, had
> your life been good.

> —W. H. Auden[1]

I

When Bertolt Brecht sought, and found, refuge in this country in 1941, he went to Hollywood "to join the sellers" on "the market where lies are bought," and wherever he went he heard the words *"Spell your name."*[2] He had been famous in German-speaking countries since the early twenties, and he did not particularly like to be unknown and poor again. In 1947, he was called before the Committee on Un-American Activities; he appeared with a ticket to Zürich in his pocket, was greatly praised for being so "co-operative," and left the country. But when Brecht tried to settle in West Germany, the military-occupation authorities refused the necessary permission.[3] This turned out to be almost equally unfortunate for Germany and for Brecht himself. In 1949, he settled down in East Berlin, where he was given the direction of a theater and, for the first time in his life, ample opportunity to watch the Communist variety of total domination at close range. He died in August, 1956.[4]

Since Brecht's death, his fame has spread all over Europe—even to Russia—and also to the English-speaking countries. With the exception of *The Seven Deadly Sins of the Petty Bourgeois*, a minor work translated by W. H. Auden and Chester Kallman (their superb translation of *The Rise and Fall of the City Mahagonny* was never published),[5] and *Galileo*, translated by Charles Laughton and Brecht himself, none of his plays and, alas, few of his poems have appeared in an English translation worthy of this great poet and playwright; nor have any of his plays—except for the *Galileo*, with Charles Laughton, that lasted six performances in New York in the late forties, and, perhaps, *The Caucasian Chalk Circle* at Lincoln Center in 1966—been given a worthy English-language production.[6] An adequate, though not very distinguished, translation of Brecht's first book of poems—*Die Hauspostille*, which appeared in 1927—by Eric Bentley, with good annotations by Hugo Schmidt, has been published by Grove Press under the title *Manual of Piety*. (I shall use this translation in some of the following.) But fame has its own momentum, and although it has sometimes been a bit difficult to understand why people who don't know a word of German should get excited and enthusiastic about Brecht in English, the excitement and enthusiasm are welcome, because they are entirely deserved. Fame has also covered up the circumstances that made it necessary for Brecht to go to East Berlin, and this, too, is welcome to anyone who thinks back to the time when second-rate critics and third-rate writers could denounce him with impunity.[7]

Still, Brecht's political biography, a kind of case history of the uncertain relationship between poetry and politics, is no slight matter, and now, when his fame is secure, the time may have come when it is possible to raise certain questions without being misunderstood. To be sure, the fact of Brecht's doctrinaire and often ludicrous adherence to the Communist ideology as such need hardly cause serious concern. In a poem written in America during the war but published only recently, Brecht himself has defined the only point of importance. Addressing his German fellow poets under Hitler, he said, "Be on your guard, you who sing this man Hitler. I . . . know that he'll soon die and that, dying, he'll have outlived his fame. But even if he made the earth unfit for habitation by conquering it, no poem praising him could last. True, too quickly does the wail of pain of whole continents die down to drown out the hymn to the tormentor. True, those who praise the outrage, they, too, have fine-sounding voices. And yet it is the dying swan's song that is held to be the most beautiful: he sings without fear."[8] Brecht was right and wrong; no poem praising Hitler or Hitler's war has survived Hitler's death, because none of the hymnists had a "fine-sounding voice." (The only German poem of the last war that will last is Brecht's own "Children's Crusade 1939," a ballad written in the moving bitter-sad tone of folk songs and telling the story of fifty-five war orphans and a dog in Poland who set out for *"ein Land, wo Frieden war"*—"a country where peace was"—and didn't know the way.) But Brecht's voice sounds fine enough in the lines to his fellow poets, and one doesn't quite see why he did not publish them—except that he might have known how a simple change of name would cause the poem to boomerang upon him: How about his ode to Stalin and his praise of Stalin's crimes, written and published while he was in East Berlin but mercifully omitted from the collection of his works? Didn't he know what he was doing? Oh, yes, he did: "Last night in a dream I saw fingers pointing at me as though I were a leper. They were worn and they were broken. 'You don't know!' I cried out, conscious of guilt."[9]

To talk about poets is an uncomfortable task; poets are there to be quoted, not to be talked about. Those whose specialty is literature, and among whom we now find the "Brecht scholars," have learned how to overcome their unease, but I am not one of them. The voice of the poets, however, concerns all of us, not only critics and scholars; it concerns us in our private lives and also insofar as we are citizens. We don't need to deal with *engagé* poets in order to feel justified in talking about them from a political viewpoint, as citizens, but it seems easier for a non-literary person to engage in this activity if political attitudes and commitments have played an all-important role in the life and work of an author, as they did in Brecht's.

The first thing to be pointed out is that poets have not often made good, reliable citizens; Plato, himself a great poet in philosopher's disguise, was not the first to be sorely worried and annoyed by poets. There has always been trouble with them; they have often shown a deplorable tendency to misbehave, and in our century their misbehavior has on occasion been of even deeper concern to citizens than ever before. We need only remember the case of Ezra Pound. The United States government decided not to put him on trial for treason in wartime, because he could plead insanity, whereupon a committee of poets did, in a way, what the government chose not to—it judged him—and the result was an award to him for having written the best poetry of 1948. The poets honored him regardless of his misbehavior or insanity. They judged the poet; it was not their business to judge the citizen. And since they were poets themselves, they might have thought in Goethe's terms: *"Dichter sündigen nicht schwer"* [Poets's sins are not grave]; that is, poets do not shoulder such a heavy burden of guilt when they misbehave—one shouldn't take their sins altogether seriously.[10] But Goethe's line had reference to different sins, light sins, such as Brecht speaks of when, in his irrepressible desire to tell the least welcome truths—which, indeed, was one of his great virtues—he says, addressing his womenfolk, "In me you have a man on whom you can't rely,"[11] knowing so well that what women want most in their menfolk is reliability—the thing that poets can afford least. They can't afford it because those whose business it is to soar must shun gravity. They must not be tied down, and hence cannot bear as much responsibility as others must.

And Brecht, it now turns out, knew this very well though he never admitted it publicly. He often had thought, he said in a conversation in 1934, "of a tribunal before which I might be interrogated. 'How is it? Are you really serious?' I should then have to admit: Entirely serious I am not. There are too many artistic matters, matters concerning the theater, I think of to be entirely serious. But having said no to this important question I would add an even more important statement, namely, that my attitude is *legitimate.*" In order to clarify what he meant he proposed the following: "Let's assume you read an excellent political novel and later learn that its author is Lenin; you would change your opinion on book and author to the detriment of both."[12] But there are sins and sins. Undeniably, Ezra Pound's sins were more serious; it was not merely a case of foolishly succumbing to Mussolini's exercises in oratory. In his vicious radio broadcasts, he went far beyond Mussolini's worst speeches, doing Hitler's business and proving to be one of the worst Jew-baiters among the intellectuals on either side of the Atlantic. To be sure, he had disliked Jews before the war and has disliked them since, and this dislike is his private affair, of hardly any political importance. It is quite another matter to trumpet this kind of aversion to the world at a moment when Jews are being killed by the millions. However, Pound could plead insanity and get away with things that Brecht, entirely sane and highly intelligent, was not able to get away with. Brecht's sins were smaller than Pound's, yet he sinned more heavily, because he was only a poet, not an insane one.[13]

For, despite the poets' lack of gravity, reliability, and responsibility, they obviously can't get away with everything. But where to draw the line we, their fellow citizens, are hardly able to decide. Villon almost ended on the gallows—God knows, perhaps rightly so—but his songs still gladden our hearts, and we honor him for them.[14] There is no surer way to make a fool of oneself than to draw up a code of behavior for poets, though quite a number of serious and respectable men have done it. Luckily for us and for the poets, we don't have to go to this absurd trouble, nor do we have to rely on our everyday standards of judgment. A poet is to be judged by his poetry, and while much is permitted him, it is not true that "those who praise the outrage have fine-sounding voices." At least, it was not true in Brecht's case; his odes to Stalin, that great father and murderer of peoples, sound as though they had been fabricated by the least gifted imitator Brecht ever had. The worst that can happen to a poet is that he should cease to be a poet, and that is what happened to Brecht in the last years of his life. He may have thought that the odes to Stalin did not matter. Weren't they written out of fear, and hadn't he always believed that almost everything is justified in the face of violence? This was the wisdom of his "Mr. Keuner," who, however, around 1930 was still a bit more fastidious in the choice of his means than his author twenty years later. In dark times, so one of the stories goes, there came an agent of the rulers to the home of a man who "had learnt how to say no." The agent claimed the man's home and food as his own and asked him, "Will you wait upon me?" The man put him to bed, covered him with a blanket, guarded his sleep, and obeyed him for seven years. But whatever he did, he never spoke a single word. After the seven years were over, the agent had grown fat with eating, sleeping, and giving orders, and he died. The man wrapped him in the rotten blanket, threw him out of the house, washed the bed, painted the walls, sighed with relief, and answered, "No."[15] Had Brecht forgotten Mr. Keuner's wisdom not to say "Yes"? In any event, what concerns us here is the sad fact that the few poems of his last years, published posthumously, are weak and thin. The exceptions are minor. There is the much-quoted witticism after the workers' rebellion of 1953: "After the rebellion of the seventeenth of June . . . one could read that the people had forfeited the government's confidence and could regain it only by redoubling their work efforts. Would it not be simpler for the government to dissolve the people and elect another one?"[16] There are a number of very touching lines in love poems and nursery rhymes. And, most important, there are praises of purposelessness of which the best sounds like a half-conscious variation on Angelus Silesius's famous "Ohne Warum."

("The rose is without why; it blooms because it blooms, / It cares not for itself, asks not if it is seen.")[17] Brecht writes:

> *Ach, wie sollen wir die kleine Rose buchen?*
> *Plötzlich dunkelrot und jung und nah?*
> *Ach, wir kamen nicht, sie zu besuchen*
> *Aber als wir kamen war sie da.*
>
> *Eh sie da war, ward sie nicht erwartet.*
> *Als sie da war, ward sie kaum geglaubt.*
> *Ach, zum Ziele kam, was nie gestartet.*
> *Aber war es so nicht überhaupt?*[18]

That Brecht could write such verses at all indicates an unexpected and decisive shift in the poet's mood; only his early poetry, in the *Manual of Piety,* shows the same freedom from worldly purposes and cares, and in the place of the earlier tone of jubilation or defiance there is now the peculiar stillness of wonder and gratitude. The one perfect product of these last years, consisting of two four-line love stanzas, is a variation on a German nursery rhyme, and therefore untranslatable.[19]

> *Sieben Rosen hat der Strauch*
> *Sechs gehör'n dem Wind*
> *Aber eine bleibt, dass auch*
> *Ich noch eine find.*
>
> *Sieben Male ruf ich dich*
> *Sechsmal bleibe fort*
> *Doch beim siebten Mal, versprich*
> *Komme auf ein Wort.*[20]

Everything indicated that the poet had found a new voice—perhaps "the dying swan's song that is held to be the most beautiful"—but when the moment came for the voice to be heard, it seemed to have lost its power. This is the only objective and therefore unquestionable sign we have that he had transgressed the rather wide limits set for poets, that he had crossed the line marking what was permitted to him. For these boundaries, alas, cannot be detected from the outside, and can hardly even be guessed at. They are like faint ridges, all but invisible to the naked eye, which, once a man has crossed them—or not even actually crossed them but just stumbled over them—suddenly grow into walls. There is no retracing of steps; whatever he does, he finds himself with his back against the wall. And even now, *après coup,* it is difficult to define the cause; our only evidence that the step was taken is supplied by the poetry, and all it tells us is the moment when it happened, when the punishment caught up with him. For the only meaningful punishment that a poet can suffer, short of death, is, of course, the sudden loss of what throughout human history has appeared a divine gift.

To Brecht the loss clearly came rather late, and hence it can teach us a lesson about the great permissiveness enjoyed by those who live under the laws of Apollo. It did not come when he became a Communist; to be a Communist in Europe in the twenties, and even the early thirties (at least for people who were not in the thick of things and could not know to what an extent Stalin had changed the Party into a totalitarian movement, ready to commit any crime and every betrayal, including the betrayal of the revolution), was no sin but merely an error. However, it did not come, either, when Brecht failed to break with the Party during the Moscow Trials, in which some of his friends were among the defendants, or during the Spanish Civil War, when he must have known that the Russians did everything they could to the detriment of the Spanish Republic, using the misfortunes of the Spanish to get even with anti-Stalinists inside and outside the Party. (He said in 1938, "Actually I have no friends there [in Moscow]; and the people in Moscow have no friends either—like the dead."[21]) And it did not come when, at the time of the Hitler-Stalin pact, Brecht failed to speak out, let alone to sever his relations to the Party; on the contrary, the years he spent in exile, first in the Danish city of Svendborg and then in Santa Monica, were creatively the best years of his life, comparable in sheer productivity only to his youth, when he was still uninfluenced by ideology and had not yet subjected himself to any political discipline. It came, finally, after he had settled down in East Berlin, where he could see, day after day, what it meant to the people to live under a Communist regime.

Not that he had wanted to settle down there; from December, 1947, until Fall, 1949, he had waited in Zürich for permission to settle in Munich,[22] and only when he had to give up all hope of getting it did he decide to go home as best he could—well provided against all hazards with a Czech passport soon to be exchanged for an Austrian one, a Swiss bank account, and a West German publisher. Up to that unfortunate moment, he had been quite careful not to come into close contact with his friends in the East. In 1933, when many of his friends foolishly believed they could find asylum in Soviet Russia, he went to Denmark, and when he fled Europe at the beginning of the war, though he came to America via Vladivostok, he hardly stopped in Moscow, never even considering Russia—this was the time of the Hitler-Stalin pact—as a possible place of refuge. Quite apart from the fact that he had never found favor with the Russian Communist Party—from beginning to end he was appreciated only by free audiences in Western countries—he must have had a foreboding that the poetic distance he had been able to keep from Communist politics even when he was most deeply committed to the "cause" (it seems he was never a member of the Party) would not withstand the onslaught of Soviet reality, as it did not withstand the infinitely less horrible onslaught of the reality of Ulbricht's Germany.[23] The element of playfulness, so important in his work, could not possibly survive in proximity with the very horrors he used to play with. It is, after all, one thing to tell your friends and acquaintances when they disagree with you, "We'll shoot you, too, when we seize power," and quite another thing to live where things worse than shooting happen to those who disagree with those who have indeed seized power. Brecht himself was not molested—not even in the years before Stalin's death. But since he was no fool, he must have known that his personal safety resulted from the fact that East Berlin was an exceptional place, the show window of the East during the fifties, and in desperate competition with the city's Western sector, just a couple of subway stops away. In this competition, the Berliner Ensemble—the repertory company that Brecht, under the aegis of the East German government, formed, headed, wrote for, and directed—was, and has remained to this day, the greatest asset of the East German regime, as it is also, perhaps, the only outstanding cultural achievement of postwar Germany. Thus, for seven years Brecht lived and worked in peace under the eyes—in fact, under the protection—of Western observers but now in infinitely closer contact with a totalitarian state than he had ever been in his life before, seeing the sufferings of his own people with his own eyes. And the consequence was that not a single play and not a single great poem was produced in those seven years, nor did he even finish the *Salzburger Totentanz,* which was begun in Zürich, and which—to judge by the fragments, which I know only in the English translation by Eric Bentley—might have become one of the great plays.[24] Brecht knew of his predicament, knew that he could not write in East Berlin. Shortly before his death, it is reported, he bought a house in Denmark and also considered moving to Switzerland.[25] No one had been more anxious to go home—"Put no nail into the wall, throw the jacket on the chair. . . . Why open the foreign grammar? The news that calls you home is written in familiar language"—and all he planned for when he lay dying was exile.

Hence, side by side with the great poet and playwright there is also the case of Bertolt Brecht. And this case is of concern to all citizens who wish to share their world with poets. It cannot be left to the literature departments but is the business of political scientists as well. The chronic misbehavior of poets and artists has been a political, and sometimes a moral, problem since antiquity. In the following discussion of this case, I shall stick to the two assumptions I have mentioned. First, although in general Goethe was right and more is permitted to poets than to ordinary mortals, poets, too, can sin so gravely that they must bear their full load of guilt and responsibility. And, second, the only way to determine unequivocally how great their sins are is to listen to their poetry—which means, I assume, that the faculty of writing a good line is not entirely at the poet's command but needs some help, that the faculty is granted him and that he can forfeit it.

II

To begin with, I must mention a few, a very few, biographical circumstances. We don't need to go into Brecht's personal life, about which he was more reticent—less willing to speak—than any other twentieth-century author (and this reticence, as we shall see, was one of his virtues, of which there were many), but we must, of course, follow the few exquisite hints in his poems. Brecht, born in 1898, belonged to what one might call the first of the three lost generations. Men of his generation whose initiation into the world had been the trenches and battlefields of the First World War invented or adopted the term because they felt that they had become unfit to live normal lives; normality was a betrayal of all the experience of horror, and comradeship in the midst of horror, that had made them into men, and, rather than betray what was most undoubtedly their own, they preferred to be lost—lost to themselves as well as to the world. This attitude, common to the war veterans of all countries, became a sort of climate of opinion when it turned out that they were succeeded by two more such "lost generations": the first, born about ten years later, in the first decade of the century, was taught, through the rather impressive lessons of inflation, mass unemployment, and revolutionary unrest, the instability of whatever had been left intact in Europe after more than four years of slaughter; the next, again born about ten years later, in the second decade of the century, had the choice of being initiated into the world by Nazi concentration camps, the Spanish Civil War, or the Moscow Trials. These three groups, born, roughly, between 1890 and 1920, were close enough together in age to form a single group during the Second World War, whether as soldiers or as refugees and exiles, as members of the resistance movements or as inmates of concentration and extermination camps, or as civilians under a rain of bombs, survivors of cities of which Brecht, decades before, had said in a poem:

> We have been living, a light generation,
> In houses that were thought beyond destruction.
> (The lanky buildings of Manhattan Island and the fine antennae
> That amuse the Atlantic Ocean are of our construction.)
>
> Of these cities will remain that which blew through them, the wind.
> The house makes the dinner guest merry. He cleans it out.
> We know we're only temporary and after us will follow
> Nothing worth talking about.

This, "On Poor B. B.," from the *Manual of Piety,* is the only poem he ever wrote that is dedicated to the subject of lost generations. The title is, of course, ironic; he says in the concluding lines that "in the earthquakes that will come I hope I won't let my cigar go out in bitterness," and, in a way, that is characteristic of his whole attitude, he turns the tables, as it were: What is lost is not merely this weightless race of men but the world that was supposed to house them. Because Brecht never thought in terms of self-pity—not even on the highest level—he cut a rather solitary figure among all his contemporaries. When they called themselves lost, they were looking upon the age and themselves with the eyes of the nineteenth century; they were denied what Friedrich Hebbel once called *"die ruhige reine Entwicklung"*—the quiet, pure unfolding of all their faculties—and they reacted with bitterness. They resented the fact that the world did not offer them shelter and the security to develop as individuals, and they began to produce their curious kind of literature, mostly novels in which nothing seems to be of interest but psychological deformation, social torture, personal frustration, and general disillusion. This is not nihilism; indeed, to call these authors nihilists would be to pay them an entirely undeserved compliment. They did not cut deep enough—they were too much concerned with themselves—to see the real issues; they remembered everything and forgot what mattered. There are two almost casual lines in another poem of the *Manual of Piety* in which Brecht said what he thought about this question of how to come to terms with one's own youth:

> *Hat er sein ganze Jugend, nur nicht ihre Träume vergessen*
> *Lange das Dach, nie den Himmel, der drüber war.*[26]

That Brecht never felt sorry for himself—hardly ever was even interested in himself—was one of his great virtues, but the virtue was rooted in something else, which was a gift and was, like all such gifts, part blessing and part curse. He speaks about it in the only strictly personal poem he ever wrote, and though it dates from the period of the *Manual of Piety,* he never published it; he did not want to be known. The poem, which belongs among his very best works, is entitled "Der Herr der Fische"[27]— that is to say, the lord and master of fishland, the land of silence. It tells how this lord comes up to the land of men, of the fishermen, rising and sinking with the regularity of the moon, a stranger and a friend to everybody (*allen unbekannt und allen nah*), and how he sits down with them, and can't remember their names but is interested in their business, in the price of the nets and the profit from the fish, in their women and their tricks of cheating the tax collector.

> *Sprach er so von ihren Angelegenheiten*
> *Fragten sie ihn auch: Wie stehn denn deine?*
> *Und er blickte lächelnd um nach allen Seiten*
> *Sagte zögernd: Habe keine.*

For a while, everything goes well. "When they ask him 'And how about your own affairs?' he smiles hesitantly: 'I have none.'" Until the day comes when they insist.

> *Eines Tages wird ihn einer fragen:*
> *Sag, was ist es, was dich zu uns führt?*
> *Eilig wird er aufstehn; denn er spürt:*
> *Jetzt ist ihre Stimmung umgeschlagen.*[28]

And he knows why their mood has changed; he has nothing to offer, and though he was welcome when he happened to come, he was never invited, for all he did was enrich their daily talk.

> *So, auf Hin- und Widerreden*
> *Hat mit ihnen er verkehrt*

Immer kam er ungebeten.
Doch sein Essen war er wert.

When they want more of him, "he will take his leave, politely, like a dismissed servant. Nothing will remain of him, no shadow, no trace. But it is with his consent and permission that somebody else, richer than he is, takes his place. Truly, he prevents no one from talking where he remains silent."

Höflich wird, der nichts zu bieten hatte
Aus der Tür gehn: ein entlassner Knecht.
Und es bleibt von ihm kein kleinster Schatte
Keine Höhlung in des Stuhls Geflecht.

Sondern er gestattet, dass auf seinem
Platz ein anderer sich reicher zeigt.
Wirklich er verwehrt es keinem
Dort zu reden, wo er schweigt.

This self-portrait, Brecht's portrait of the poet as a young man—for this, of course, is what it really is—presenting the poet in all his remoteness, his mixture of pride and humility, "a stranger and a friend to everybody hence both rejected and welcome, good only for *"Hin- und Widerreden"* ("talk and countertalk"), useless for everyday life, silent about himself, as though there were nothing to talk about, curious and in desperate need of every bit of reality he can catch, gives us at least a hint of the enormous difficulties the young Brecht must have had in making himself at home in the world of his fellow men. (There exists another self-statement, a kind of prose poem of a later period: "I grew up as a son of well-to-do people. My parents placed a collar round my neck, educated me in the habits of being waited upon, and taught me the art of giving orders. But when I had grown up and looked around me, I didn't like the people of my class, neither the giving orders nor the being waited on. And I left my class and joined the company of low people."[29] This is probably true enough, though it sounds already a bit like a program. It is no self-portrait but a stylish way of speaking about himself.) It is altogether to his credit that we can only guess at who he was in this most personal way through some lines of the early poems. Still, there were certain aspects of his later, freely acknowledged behavior that these early lines may help us to understand.

There was first, and from the very beginning, Brecht's strange inclination toward anonymity, namelessness, and an extraordinary aversion to all fuss—

to the pose of the ivory tower but also to the even more irritating bad faith of the "prophets of the people" or the "voices" of History, and to whatever else the "sale of values" (*"der Ausverkauf der Werte"* was a kind of slogan of the time) in the twenties offered its customers. But there was more to it than the natural distaste of a very intelligent and highly cultivated man for the bad intellectual manners of his surroundings. Brecht wished passionately to be (or, at any rate, to be taken for) an ordinary man—not to be marked as different by the possession of special gifts but to be like everybody else. And it is clear that these two closely connected personal dispositions—for anonymity and for ordinariness—were fully developed long before he adopted them as a pose. They predisposed him toward two apparently opposed attitudes that later played a great role in his work: his dangerous predilection for illegal work, which demands that you wipe out your traces, hide your face, blot out your identity, lose your name, "speak but conceal the speaker, conquer but conceal the conqueror, die but hide death"[30]—quite young, long before the thought of any "Praise of Illegal Work,"[31] he had written a poem on his late brother, who had died secretly and speedily disintegrated because he thought that no one saw him"[32]—and his odd insistence on collecting around him so-called "collaborators" who were often nondescript mediocrities, as though he pleaded time and again, Everybody can do what I am doing; it is a matter of learning, and no special gifts are needed, or even wanted. In a very early "Epistle on Suicide," posthumously published, he discusses the reasons one could give for the act, which should not be the true reasons, because they would look too "grand": "At any rate, it shouldn't look as though one had too high an opinion of oneself."[33] Precisely, and this is perhaps doubly true for people who, like Brecht, are tempted, not by fame or flattery but by the objective manifestation of gifts they can hardly ignore, to have a very high opinion of themselves.[34] And if he carried this attitude to absurd extremes—absurd overestimation of the illegal apparatus of the Communist Party, absurd demands upon his "collaborators" to learn what was beyond learning—it must be admitted that the literary and intellectual milieu of the twenties in Germany offered a temptation to puncture pomposity that, even without Brecht's special disposition, was difficult to resist. The bantering lines on the behavior of his fellow poets in *The Threepenny Opera* hit the nail right on the head:

> *Ich selber könnte mich durchaus begriefen*
> *Wenn ich mich lieber gross und einsam sähe*

Doch sah ich solche Leute aus der Nähe
Da sagt ich mir: Das musst du dir verkneifen.[35]

There is one more poem in which Brecht speaks explicitly of himself, and it is probably the most famous one. It belongs to the "Svendborger Gedichte," a sequence of poems written during the exile in Denmark in the thirties, and is entitled "To Those Born After Us."[36] As in the earlier "On Poor B. B.," the stress is on the catastrophes of the time in the world and on the need for stoicism with respect to everything that happens to oneself. But now that the "earthquakes to come" have arrived, all strictly biographical allusions have disappeared. ("On Poor B. B." begins and ends with the true story of his origins: "I, Bertolt Brecht, come from the black forests. My mother took me to the cities while I lay inside her. And the coldness of the forests will be with me till my dying day." His mother was from the Black Forest, and we know from posthumously published poems about her death that she was very close to him.[37]) It is the poem about those who "live in dark times," and its key lines read:

In the cities, I arrived at the time of disorder, when hunger ruled. Among men, I came at the time of upheaval, and I rebelled with them. Thus the time passed which was given me on earth.

I ate between battles, I slept among murderers, I was careless in loving, and I looked at nature without patience. Thus the time passed which was given me on earth.

When I lived, the street led to the morass. Speech betrayed me to the slaughterer. There was little I could do. But the rulers were safer without me, this I hoped. Thus the time passed which was given me on earth.

. . . You who will emerge from the flood in which we drowned remember when you speak of our weaknesses the dark time from which you escaped.

. . . Alas, we who wanted to prepare the ground for kindness could not be kind.

. . . Remember us with forbearance.

Yes, indeed, let us do that, let us remember him with forbearance, if for no other reason than that he was so much more impressed by the catastrophes of the time in the world than by anything that concerned him. And let us not forget that success never turned his head. He knew that *"wenn mein Glück aussetzt, bin ich verloren"* ("when my luck leaves me, I'm lost"). And it was his pride to rely on his luck rather than on his gifts, to believe himself lucky rather than extraordinary.[38] In a poem written a few years later, during the war, when he counted his losses in terms of friends who had died—to mention only the ones he mentioned himself, Margarete Steffin, "little teacher from the working class," whom he had loved and who had joined him in Denmark; Walter Benjamin, Germany's most important literary critic between the two wars, who, "tired of being persecuted," had taken his own life; and Karl Koch[39]—he spelled out for himself what had been implicit in an earlier poem: "I know, of course: Only through luck did I survive so many friends. But tonight in a dream I heard these friends say of me, 'Those who are stronger survive.' And I hated myself."[40] This seems to have been the only time his self-confidence was shaken; he compared himself to others, and self-confidence always rests on a refusal to indulge in such comparisons, whether they are for better or worse. But it was only a dream.

So, in a sense, Brecht, too, felt lost—not because his individual talents had failed to ripen as they should or could, or because the world had hurt him, as indeed it had, but because the task was too big. Hence, when he feels the flood rising, he does not glance longingly backward, as no one did more beautifully than Rilke in his later work, but appeals to those who will emerge from it, and this appeal to the future—to posterity—has nothing to do with "progress." What set him apart was that he realized how deadly ridiculous it would be to measure the flood of events with the yardstick of individual aspirations—to meet, for instance, the international catastrophe of unemployment with a desire to make a career and with reflections on one's own success and failure, or to confront the catastrophe of the war with the ideal of a well-rounded personality, or to go into exile, as so many of his colleagues did, with complaints about lost fame or a broken-up life. There is not a shred of sentimentality left in Brecht's beautiful and beautifully precise definition of a refugee: *"Ein Bote des Unglücks"* ("a messenger of ill tidings").[41] A messenger's message, of course, does not concern himself. It was not merely their own misfortunes that the refugees carried with them from land to land, from continent to continent—"changing the countries more often than their shoes"—but the great misfortune of the whole world. If most of them were inclined to forget their message even before they learned that no one loves the bearer of ill tidings—well, hasn't this always been the trouble with messengers?

This ingenious, more than ingenious, phrase "messengers of ill tidings" for refugees and exiles may illustrate the great poetic intelligence of Brecht, that supreme gift of condensation which is the prerequisite of all poetry. Here are a few more instances of his utterly condensed and hence very tricky way of thinking. In a poem about the shame of being a German, written in 1933:

> *Hörend die Reden, die aus deinem Hause dringen, lacht man.*
> *Aber wer dich sieht, der greift nach dem Messer.*[42]

Or in a manifesto against war addressed to all German artists and writers, West and East, in the early fifties: "Great Carthage conducted three wars. It was still a great power after the first war, still habitable after the second. It was untraceable after the third."[43] In two simple statements, the whole atmosphere of the thirties and fifties, respectively, is caught with great accuracy. And the same illuminating trickiness shows up, perhaps even more strongly, in the following story, which appeared a number of years ago in a New York magazine. Brecht was in this country at the time of the Moscow Trials, and, so we are told, paid a visit to a man who was still of the Left but was violently anti-Stalinist and had become deeply involved in the counter-trials under the auspices of Trotsky. The conversation turned on the manifest innocence of the Moscow defendants, and Brecht, after maintaining a long silence, finally said, "The more innocent they are, the more they deserve to die." The sentence sounds outrageous. But what did he really say? The more innocent of what? Of what they were accused, of course. And what had they been accused of? Of conspiring against Stalin. Hence, precisely because they had not conspired against Stalin, and were innocent of the "crime," there was some justice in the injustice. Hadn't it been the plain duty of the "old guard" to prevent one man, Stalin, from turning the revolution into one gigantic crime? Needless to say, Brecht's host did not catch on; he was outraged, and asked his guest to leave the house. Thus, one of the rare occasions when Brecht did speak out against Stalin, even though in his own teasingly cautious way, was lost. Brecht, I am afraid, might have sighed with relief when he found himself in the street: His luck had not yet left him.[44]

III

This, then, was the man: gifted with a penetrating, non-theoretical, non-contemplative intelligence that went to the heart of the matter, silent and unwilling to show himself, remote and probably also shy, at any rate not much interested in himself but incredibly curious (indeed, "the knowledge-thirsty Brecht," as he called himself in the "Solomon Song" of *The Three-penny Opera*), and, first and foremost, a poet—that is, someone who must

say the unsayable, who must not remain silent on occasions when all are
silent, and who must therefore be careful not to talk too much about things
that all talk about. He was sixteen years old at the outbreak of the First
World War and was drafted as a medical orderly in the last war year, so the
world first appeared to him as a scene of senseless slaughter, and speech appeared in the guise of ranting declamations. (His early "Legend of the Dead
Soldier"—a soldier whom a military commission of doctors arouses from
his grave and finds fit for active service—was inspired by a popular comment on draft policies at the end of the war, *"Man gräbt die Toten aus"*
["They're digging up the dead"], and has remained the only German First
World War poem worthy of being remembered.)[45] But what became decisive for his early poetry was less the war itself than the world as it emerged
from it after "the storms of steel," Ernst Jünger's *Stahlgewitter,* had done
their work.[46] This world possessed a property that is rarely taken into account but one that Sartre, after the Second World War, described with great
precision: "When the instruments are broken and unusable, when plans are
blasted and effort is meaningless, the world appears with a childlike and terrible freshness, suspended trackless in a void."[47] (The twenties in Germany
had much in common with the forties and fifties in France. What happened
in Germany after the First World War was the breakdown of tradition—a
breakdown that had to be recognized as an accomplished fact, a political reality, a point of no return—and that is what happened in France twenty-
five years later. Politically speaking, it was the decline and downfall of the
nation state; socially, it was the transformation of a class system into a mass
society; and spiritually it was the rise of nihilism, which for a long time had
been a concern of the few but now, suddenly, had become a mass phenomenon.) As it appeared to Brecht, four years of destruction had wiped the
world clean, the storms having swept along with them all human traces,
everything one could hold on to, including cultural objects and moral
values—the beaten paths of thought as well as firm standards of evaluation
and solid guideposts for moral conduct. It was as though, fleetingly, the
world had become as innocent and fresh as it was on the day of creation.
Nothing seemed left but the purity of the elements, the simplicity of sky
and earth, of man and animals, of life itself. Hence it was life that the
young poet fell in love with—everything that the earth, in its sheer there-
ness, had to offer. And this childlike, terrible freshness of the postwar world
is reflected in the horrible innocence of Brecht's early heroes—the pirates,
adventurers, and infanticides, the "enamored pig Malchus," and Jakob

Apfelböck, who struck his father and his mother dead and then went on living like "the lily of the field."[48]

In this world swept clean and fresh, Brecht was at home to begin with.
If one wished to classify him, one might say that he was an anarchist by
disposition and inclination, but it would be altogether wrong to see in
him another member of that school of decay and of morbid fascination
with death which in his generation was perhaps best represented in Germany by Gottfried Benn and in France by Louis-Ferdinand Céline.
Brecht's characters—even his drowning girls who slowly swim down the
rivers until they are taken back into nature's great wilderness of all-
encompassing peace; even Mazeppa, bound to his own horse and dragged
to his death—are in love with life and with what earth and sky have to offer, to the point where they willingly accept death and destruction.[49] The
last two stanzas of the "Ballad of Mazeppa"[50] are among the truly immortal lines of German poetry:

> Drei Tage, dann musste alles sich zeigen:
> Erde gibt Schweigen und Himmel gibt Ruh.
> Einer ritt aus mit dem, was ihm zu eigen:
> Mit Erde und Pferd, mit Langmut und Schweigen
> Dann kamen noch Himmel und Geier dazu.
>
> Drei Tage lang ritt er durch Abend und Morgen
> Bis er alt genug war, dass er nicht mehr litt
> Als er gerettet ins grosse Geborgen
> Todmüd in die ewige Ruhe einritt.

Bentley's version of these lines seems inadequate to me, and I certainly
cannot translate them properly. They speak of the end of the three days'
ride into death: into silence, the gift of the earth; into rest, the gift of the
sky. "One man rode out with the things that were most his own: with earth
and horse, with endurance and silence, then he was joined by vultures and
sky. For three days he rode, through evening and morning, until he was old
enough not to suffer anymore, when, saved and tired to death, he rode into
the great shelter, into eternal rest." There is a glorious, triumphant vitality
in this death song, and it is the same vitality—the feeling that it is fun to
be alive and that it is a sign of being alive to make fun of everything—that
makes us delight in the lyrical cynicism and sarcasm of the songs in *The
Threepenny Opera*. It was not for nothing that Brecht helped himself so
generously to a Villon translation into German—something that German

law, unhappily, called plagiarism. He is celebrating the same love of the world, the same gratitude for earth and sky, for the mere fact of being born and alive, and Villon, I am sure, would not have minded.

According to our tradition, the god of this careless, carefree, reckless love for earth and sky is the great Phoenician idol Baal, the god of the drunkards, the gluttons, the fornicators. "Yes, this planet pleases Baal if only because there's no other planet," says the young Brecht in the "Chorale of the Man Baal," of which the first and last stanzas are great poetry, especially when taken together:

> *Als im weissen Mutterschosse aufwuchs Baal*
> *War der Himmel schon so gross und still und fahl*
> *Jung und nackt und ungeheuer wundersam*
> *Wie ihn Baal dann liebte, als Baal kam.*
>
> *Als im dunklen Erdenschosse faulte Baal*
> *War der Himmel noch so gross und still und fahl*
> *Jung und nackt und ungeheuer wunderbar*
> *Wie ihn Baal einst liebte, als Baal war.*[51]

What matters, again, is the sky, the sky that was there before man was and will be there after he has gone, so that the best thing man can do is to love what for a short while is his. If I were a literary critic, I should go on from here to talk about the all-important part the sky plays in Brecht's poems, and especially in his few, very beautiful love poems. Love, in "Memory of Marie A.,"[52] is the small, pure white of a cloud against the even purer azure blue of the summer sky, blooming there for some instants and vanishing with the wind. Or, in *The Rise and Fall of the City Mahagonny,* love is the flight of the cranes veering across the sky, side by side with the cloud, the sharing of the beautiful sky by crane and cloud for a few moments of flight.[53] To be sure, in this world there is no eternal love, or even ordinary faithfulness. There is nothing but the intensity of the moment; that is, passion, which is even a bit more perishable than man himself.

Baal cannot possibly be the god of any social order, and the kingdom he rules is peopled by the outcasts of society—the pariahs who, because they live outside civilization, have a more intense, and thus a more authentic, relation to the sun, which rises and sinks with majestic indifference and shines over all living creatures. There is, for instance, the "Ballad of the Pirates," with its shipful of wild, drinking, sinning, cursing men, hell-bent for destruction.[54] There they are on the doomed ship, mad with drink, with darkness, with unprecedented rains, sick from sun and from cold, at the mercy of all the elements, hurtling to their ruin. And then comes the refrain: "O Sky, radiant, unclouded blue! Tremendous wind in our sails! Let wind and sky fly away, if only the sea will stay around [the ship] Saint Mary."

> *Von Branntwein toll und Finsternissen!*
> *Von unerhörten Güssen nass!*
> *Vom Frost eisweisser Nacht zerrissen!*
> *Im Mastkorb, von Gesichten blass!*
> *Von Sonne nackt gebrannt und krank!*
> *(Die hatten sie im Winter lieb)*
> *Aus Hunger, Fieber und Gestank*
> *Sang alles, was noch übrig blieb:*
>   *O Himmel, strahlender Azur!*
>   *Enormer Wind, die Segel bläh!*
>   *Lasst Wind und Himmel fahren! Nur*
>   *Lasst uns um Sankt Marie die See!*

I chose the first stanza of this ballad—meant to be recited in a kind of singsong, for which Brecht wrote the music—because it illustrates another element very conspicuous in these hymns to life, namely, the element of hellish pride dear to all of Brecht's adventurers and outcasts, the pride of absolutely carefree men, who will yield only to the catastrophic forces of nature, and never to the daily worries of a respectable life, let alone to the higher worries of a respectable soul. Whatever philosophy Brecht may have been born with—as opposed to the doctrines he later borrowed from Marx and Lenin—is spelled out in the *Manual of Piety,* being clearly articulated in two perfect poems, the "Grand Hymn of Thanksgiving" and "Against Temptation," which was later incorporated into *The Rise and Fall of the City Mahagonny.* The "Grand Hymn" is an exact imitation of Joachim Neander's great baroque church hymn "Lobe den Herren" [Praise the Lord],[55] which every German child knows by heart. Brecht's fifth and last stanza reads:

> *Lobet die Kälte, die Finsternis und das Verderben!*
> *Schauet hinan:*
> *Es kommet nicht auf euch an*
> *Und ihr könnt unbesorgt sterben.*[56]

"Against Temptation" consists of four five-line stanzas praising life not in spite of but because of death:

Lasst euch nicht verführen!
Es gibt keine Wiederkehr.
Der Tag steht in den Türen;
Ihr könnt schon Nachtwind spüren:
Es kommt kein Morgen mehr.
. . .
Was kann euch Angst noch rühren?
Ihr sterbt mit allen Tieren
Und es kommt nichts nacher.[57]

Nowhere else in modern literature, it seems to me, is there such clear understanding that what Nietzsche called "the death of God" does not necessarily lead into despair but, on the contrary, since it eliminates the fear of Hell, can end in sheer jubilation, in a new "yes" to life. Two somewhat comparable passages come to mind. In one, by Dostoevski, the Devil speaks in almost identical terms to Ivan Karamazov: "Every man will know that he is altogether mortal, without resurrection, and he will receive death proudly and calmly, like a god." The other is Swinburne's thanks to

Whatever gods may be
That no life lives for ever;
That dead men rise up never;
That even the weariest river
Winds somewhere safe to sea.[58]

But in Dostoevski the thought is an inspiration of the Devil, and in Swinburne, a thought inspired by weariness, a rejection of life as something that no man would wish to have twice. In Brecht, the thought of no-God and no-hereafter spells not anxiety but a liberation from fear. And Brecht must have grasped this aspect of the matter so readily because he grew up in Catholic surroundings; he obviously thought that anything would be preferable to sitting on earth hoping for Paradise and fearing Hell. What rebelled in him against religion was neither doubt nor desire; it was pride. In his enthusiastic denial of religion and his praise of Baal, the god of the earth, there is an almost explosive gratitude. Nothing, he says, is greater than life, and nothing more has been given us—and such gratitude one will hardly encounter either in the fashionable trend toward nihilism or in the reaction against it.

Yet there are nihilistic elements in Brecht's early poetry, and no one, probably, has ever been more aware of them than he was himself. Among

the posthumous poems there are a few lines entitled "Der Nachge-
borene," or "The Latecomer," which sum up nihilism better than whole
volumes of arguments could do: "I admit I have no hope. Blind men talk
of a way out. I see. When all the errors are used up, we shall be left with a
last companion across the table—nothingness."[59] *The Rise and Fall of the
City Mahagonny,* which is Brecht's only strictly nihilistic play, deals with
the last error, his own, the error that what life has to give—the great
pleasures of eating, drinking, fornicating, and boxing—could be enough.
The city is a gold-digger sort of place, erected for the sole purpose of providing fun, of catering to man's happiness. Its slogan is *"Vor allem aber
achtet scharf / Dass man hier alles dürfen darf"* ("First of all, understand
that everything is permitted here"). There are two reasons for the city's
downfall, the more obvious one being that even in the city where everything is permitted it is not permitted to lack the money to pay one's debts;
underlying this banality is the second reason—the insight that the city of
pleasure would end by creating the deadliest boredom imaginable, for it
would be the place where "nothing ever happens" and where a man might
sing, "Why should I not eat up my hat if there is nothing else to do?"[60]

Boredom, then, was the end of the poet's first encounter with the world,
the end of the marvelous, life-praising, jubilant time when he drifted
weightlessly through the jungle of what had once been one of the great
cities of Europe, dreaming of the jungles of all cities, dreaming of all
continents and the seven seas, in love with nothing but earth and sky and
trees. As the twenties came to a close, he must have begun to realize that,
not poetically but humanly speaking, this weightlessness condemned him
to irrelevance—that the world was only metaphorically a jungle and in reality a battlefield.

IV

What brought Brecht back to reality, and almost killed his poetry, was
compassion. When hunger ruled, he rebelled along with those who were
starving: "I am told: You eat and drink—be glad you do! But how can I
eat and drink when I steal my food from the man who is hungry, and
when my glass of water is needed by someone who is dying of thirst?"[61]
Compassion was doubtless the fiercest and most fundamental of Brecht's
passions, hence the one he was most anxious to hide and also was least
successful in hiding; it shines through almost every play he wrote. Even

through the cynical fun of *The Threepenny Opera* there sound the mighty, accusing lines:

> *Erst muss es möglich sein auch armen Leuten*
> *Vom grossen Brotlaib sich ihr Teil zu schneiden.*[62]

And what was sung mockingly there remained his leitmotiv up to the end:

> *Ein guter Mensch sein! Ja, wer wär's nicht gern?*
> *Sein Gut den Armen geben, warum nicht?*
> *Wenn alle gut sind, ist Sein Reich nicht fern*
> *Wer sässe nicht sehr gern in Seinem Licht?*[63]

The leitmotiv was the fierce temptation to be good in a world and under circumstances that make goodness impossible and self-defeating. The dramatic conflict in Brecht's plays is almost always the same: Those who, compelled by compassion, set out to change the world cannot afford to be good. Brecht discovered by instinct what the historians of revolution have persistently failed to see: namely, that the modern revolutionists from Robespierre to Lenin were driven by the passion of compassion—*le zèle compatissant* of Robespierre, who was still innocent enough to admit openly this powerful attraction toward *"les hommes faibles"* and *"les malheureux."* "The classics," Marx, Engels, and Lenin, in Brecht's coded language, "were the most compassionate of all men," and what distinguished them from "ignorant people" was that they knew how to "transform" the emotion of compassion into the emotion of "anger." They understood that "pity is what one does not deny those whom one refuses to help."[64] Hence Brecht became convinced, probably without knowing it, of the wisdom of Machiavelli's precept for princes and statesmen, who must learn "how not to be good," and he shares with Machiavelli the sophisticated and seemingly ambiguous attitude toward goodness which has been open to so many simple-minded and learned misunderstandings—in his case as in the case of his predecessor.[65]

"How not to be good" is the subject of *St. Joan of the Stockyards,* the marvelous early play about the Chicago girl in the Salvation Army who has to learn that on the day you must leave the world it will be of greater consequence to leave behind you a better world than to have been good. The purity, fearlessness, and innocence of Joan are matched in Brecht's plays by Simone in *The Visions of Simone Machard,* the child who dreams of Jeanne d'Arc under the German Occupation, and by the girl Grusche in *The Caucasian Chalk Circle,* where for once the whole predicament of goodness is spelled out: "Terrible is the temptation to be good" (*"Schreck-lich ist die Verführung zur Güte"*)—well-nigh irresistible in its attraction, dangerous and suspect in its consequences (Who knows the chain of events resulting from what was done on the spur of the moment? Will not the simple gesture distract him from more important tasks?), but also irrevocably terrible for him, too busy either with his own survival or with saving the world, who resists temptation: "She who doesn't listen to the cry for help but passes by with distracted ear: never again will she hear the soft call of the beloved, or the blackbird at dawn, or the happy sigh of the tired vintager when the bells toll the Angelus."[66] Whether or not one should yield to this temptation and how one is to resolve the conflicts that being good inevitably leads one into are the ever-recurring themes of Brecht's plays. In *The Caucasian Chalk Circle,* the girl Grusche yields to temptation, and everything ends well. In *The Good Woman of Setzuan,* the problem is solved by the creation of a double role: the woman, who is too poor to be good, who literally cannot afford pity, becomes a tough business-man during the day, makes a lot of money by cheating and exploiting the people, and in the evening gives the earnings of the day away to the very same people. This was a practical solution, and Brecht was a very practical man. The theme is also present in *Mother Courage* (Brecht's own interpretation notwithstanding), and even in *Galileo*. And any last doubts about the authenticity of this passionate compassion should be dispelled when we read the last stanza of the concluding song to the film version of *The Threepenny Opera:*

> *Denn die einen sind im Dunkeln*
> *Und die andern sind im Licht.*
> *Und man siehet die im Lichte*
> *Die im Dunkeln sieht man nicht.*[67]

Ever since the French Revolution, when like a torrent the immense stream of the poor burst for the first time into the streets of Europe, there have been many among the revolutionists who, like Brecht, acted out of compassion and concealed their compassion, under the cover of scientific theories and hardboiled rhetoric, out of shame. However, there have been very few among them who understood the insult added to the poor's injured lives by the fact that their sufferings remained in the dark and were not even recorded in the memory of mankind.

*Mitkämpfend fügen die grossen umstürzenden Lehrer des Volkes
Zu der Geschichte der herrschenden Klassen die der beherrschten.*[68]

This is how Brecht put it in his curiously baroque poetic version of the "Communist Manifesto," which he planned as part of a long didactic poem "On the Nature of Man," modeled after Lucretius' "On the Nature of Things," and which is an almost total failure.[69] Anyway, he understood and was outraged by not only the sufferings of the poor but their obscurity; like John Adams, he thought of the poor man as the invisible man. And it was out of this outrage, perhaps even more than out of pity and shame, that he began to hope for the day when the tables would be turned, when the words of Saint-Just—*"Les malheureux sont la puissance de la terre* [The miserable masses are the power of the earth]"—come true.

Moreover, it was out of a feeling of solidarity with the down-trodden and oppressed that Brecht wrote so much of his poetry in ballad form. (Like other masters of the century—W. H. Auden, for instance—he had the late-comer's facility in the poetic genres of the past, and hence was free to choose.) For the ballad, grown out of folk and street songs, and, not unlike Negro spirituals, out of endless stanzas in which servant girls in the kitchen lamented unfaithful lovers and innocent infanticides—*"Die Mörder, denen viel Leides geschah"* ("The murderers sorely afflicted with grief")—had always been the vein of unrecorded poetry, the art form, if such it was, in which people condemned to obscurity and oblivion attempted to record their own stories and create their own poetic immortality. Needless to say, the folk song had inspired great poetry in the German language before Brecht. The servant girls' voices sound through some of the most beautiful of German songs, from Mörike to the young Hofmannsthal, and before Brecht the master of the Moritat was Frank Wedekind.[70] Also, the ballad in which the poet becomes a storyteller had great predecessors, including Schiller and poets before and after him, and, thanks to them, had lost, together with its original crudeness, much of its popularity. But no poet before Brecht had stuck with such consistency to these popular forms and succeeded so thoroughly in gaining for them the rank of great poetry.

If we add these things up—the weightlessness and the yearning not so much for gravity as for gravitation, for a central point that would be relevant within the setting of the modern world; plus compassion, the almost natural, or, as Brecht would have said, animal-like, inability to bear the sight of other people's suffering—his decision to align himself with the Communist

Party is easy to understand, under the circumstances of the time. As far as Brecht was concerned, the main factor in this decision was that the Party not only had made the cause of the unfortunate ones its own but also possessed a body of writings upon which one could draw for all circumstances and from which one could quote as endlessly as from Scripture. This was Brecht's greatest delight. Long before he had read all the books—indeed, immediately upon joining his new comrades—he began to speak of Marx, Engels, and Lenin as the "classics."[71] But the main thing was that the Party brought him into daily contact with what his compassion had already told him was reality: the darkness and the great cold in this valley of tears.

> *Bedenkt das Dunkel und die grosse Kälte*
> *In diesem Tale, das von Jammer schallt.*[72]

From now on, he would not have to eat his hat; there was some thing else to do.

And this, of course, was where his troubles, and our troubles with him, began. He had scarcely joined the Communists before he found out that in order to change the bad world into a good world it was not enough "not to be good" but that you had to become bad yourself, that in order to exterminate meanness there should be no mean thing you were not ready to do. For—"Who are you? Sink into dirt, embrace the butcher, but change the world, the world needs change." Trotsky proclaimed even in exile, "We can only be right with and by the Party, for history has provided no other way of being in the right,"[73] and Brecht elaborated: "One man has two eyes, the Party has a thousand eyes, the Party sees seven countries, one man sees one city. . . . One man can be destroyed, but the Party can't be destroyed. For . . . it leads its struggle with the methods of the classics, which were drawn from the knowledge of reality."[74] Brecht's conversion was not quite as simple as it looks in retrospect. There were contradictions, heresies, that crept into even his most militant verses: "Let no one talk you into something, look for yourself; what you don't know yourself you don't know; examine the bill, you'll have to pay it."[75] (Hasn't the Party a thousand eyes to see what I can't see? Doesn't the Party know seven countries while I know only this city where I live?) However, these were only occasional slips, and when the Party—in 1929, after Stalin, at the Sixteenth Party Congress, had announced the liquidation of the right and left Opposition—began to liquidate its own members, Brecht felt that what the Party needed right then was a defense of killing one's own comrades and innocent people. In

Measure Taken he shows how and for what reasons the innocent, the good, the humane, those who are outraged at injustice and come running to help are being killed. For the measure taken is the killing of a Party member by his comrades, and the play leaves no doubt that he was the best of them, humanly speaking. Precisely because of his goodness, it turns out, he had become an obstacle to the revolution.

When this play was first performed, in the early thirties, in Berlin, it aroused much indignation. Today we realize that what Brecht said in his play was only the smallest part of the terrible truth, but at the time—years before the Moscow Trials—this was not known. Those who even then were bitter opponents of Stalin, both inside and outside the Party, were outraged that Brecht had written a play defending Moscow, while the Stalinists denied vehemently that anything seen by this "intellectual" corresponded to the realities of Communism in Russia. God knows, Brecht never earned less thanks from his friends and comrades than with this play. The reason is obvious. He had done what poets will always do if they are left alone: He had announced the truth to the extent that this truth had then become visible. For the simple truth of the matter was that innocent people *were* killed and that the Communists, while they had not stopped fighting their foes (this came later), had begun to kill their friends. It was only a beginning, which most people still excused as an excess of revolutionary zeal, but Brecht was intelligent enough to see the method in the madness, although he certainly did not foresee that those who pretended to work for Paradise had just started establishing Hell on earth, and that there was no meanness, no treachery they were not prepared to perpetrate. Brecht had shown the rules according to which the infernal game was being played, and, of course, he expected applause. Alas, he had overlooked a small detail: It was by no means the intention of the Party, or in the Party's interests, to have the truth told, least of all by one of its loudly proclaimed sympathizers. On the contrary, the point, as far as the Party was concerned, was to deceive the world.

Rereading this play that once caused such an uproar, one becomes conscious of the terrible years that separate us from the time it was written and first produced. (Brecht did not produce it again later, in East Berlin, and, as far as I know, it has not appeared in other theaters; however, a few years ago it enjoyed a strange popularity on American campuses.) When Stalin made ready to liquidate the old guard of the Bolshevik Party, it may have taken the foresight of a poet to know that the best elements in the movement were going to be murdered during the next decade. But what then actually happened—and today is already half forgotten, over-shadowed by even darker horrors—compared to Brecht's vision as a real storm compares to a storm in a teacup.

V

For my purpose, which is to present my thesis that a poet's real sins are avenged by the gods of poetry, *Measure Taken* is an important play. For from an artistic viewpoint this is by no means a bad play. It contains excellent lyrics, among them the "Rice Song," which was rightly famous and whose terse, hammering rhythms ring well enough even today:

> *Weiss ich, was ein Reis ist?*
> *Weiss ich, wer das weiss!*
> *Ich weiss nicht, was ein Reis ist*
> *Ich kenne nur seinen Preis.*
>
> *Weiss ich, was ein Mensch ist?*
> *Weiss ich, wer das weiss!*
> *Ich weiss nicht, was ein Mensch ist*
> *Ich kenne nur seinen Preis.*[76]

No doubt the play defends in all earnestness—not just for the fun of it, or in Swiftian sarcastic earnestness—things that are more than morally wrong, that are unspeakably hideous. And yet Brecht's poetic luck did not then forsake him, because he was still speaking the truth—a hideous truth, with which he wrongly tried to come to terms.

Brecht's sins were revealed for the first time after the Nazis had seized power and he had to confront the realities of the Third Reich from without. He went into exile on February 28, 1933, the day after the Reichstag fire. The "classics" by which he stubbornly tried to take his bearings did not permit him to recognize what Hitler actually did. He began to lie and wrote the wooden prose dialogue in *Fear and Misery of the Third Reich* that anticipates later so-called poems, which are journalese divided into verse lines. By 1935 or 1936, Hitler had liquidated hunger and unemployment; hence, for Brecht, schooled in the "classics," there was no longer any pretext for not praising Hitler. In seeking one, he simply refused to recognize what was patent to everybody—that those really persecuted were not workers but Jews, that it was race, and not class, that counted. There was not a line in Marx, Engels, or Lenin that dealt with this, and the Communists denied it—it was nothing but a pretense of the ruling classes, they said—and Brecht, stolidly refusing to "look for himself," fell into line. He wrote a few poems about conditions in Nazi Germany, all of these poems quite bad, a representative one being entitled "Burial of the Agitator in the Zinc Coffin."[77] It deals with the Nazi custom of shipping home in sealed coffins the remains of people beaten to death in concentration camps. Brecht's agitator had suffered this fate because he had preached "eating your fill, a roof over your head, feeding your children"; in short, he was a madman, for no one went hungry in Germany at that time, and the Nazi slogan of the *Volksgemeinschaft* (folk community) was by no means mere propaganda. Who would have bothered to put him out of the way? The real horror, the only point to be made, was the way this man had died, that he had to be hidden in the zinc coffin. The zinc coffin was indeed important, but Brecht did not follow up the indication of the title; in his version, the agitator's fate was hardly any worse than the fate that an opponent of any kind of capitalist government was likely to suffer. And this was a lie. What Brecht wanted to say was that there was a difference only in degree between countries under capitalist rule. And this was a double lie, for in capitalist countries opponents were not beaten to death and shipped home in sealed coffins, and Germany was not a capitalist country any longer, as the Messrs. Schacht and Thyssen were to learn, to their sorrow.[78] And how about Brecht? He had escaped from a country where everybody could eat his fill, had a roof over his head, and could feed his children. This is how it was, and this he did not dare to face. Even the anti-war poems of these years were undistinguished.[79]

However, bad as the work of this whole period was, it was not the end. The years of exile, as they went on and carried him farther and farther away from the turmoil that had been postwar Germany, had a very salutary effect upon his production. What could be more peaceful in the thirties than the Scandinavian countries? And whatever he might have said, rightly or wrongly, against Los Angeles, it was not a place famous for unemployed workers and hungry children. Although he would have denied it to his dying day, the poetic evidence is that he was slowly beginning to forget the "classics," and that his mind had started turning on themes that had nothing to do with capitalism or the class struggle. Out of Svendborg came poems like the "Legend on the Origin of the Book Tao-te Ching During Lao-tse's Journey Into Exile," which, narrative in form and making no attempt at experimenting with either language or thought, is among the stillest and—strange to say—most consoling poems written in our century.[80] Like so many of Brecht's poems, it wants to teach (in his world, poets and teachers lived close together), but this time the lesson is of non-violence and wisdom:

> *Dass das weiche Wasser in Bewegung*
> *Mit der Zeit den mächtigen Stein besiegt.*
> *Du verstehst, das Harte unterliegt.*

"That soft water in movement defeats the mighty stone in time. You understand, the tough are beaten." As indeed they were. This poem had not yet been published when, at the beginning of the war, the French government decided to put its refugees from Germany in concentration camps, but in the spring of 1939, Walter Benjamin had brought it back to Paris from a visit to Brecht in Denmark, and speedily, like a rumor of good tidings, it traveled by word of mouth—a source of consolation and patience and endurance—where such wisdom was most needed.[81] It may be of some relevance that in the sequence of the Svendborg poems the Lao-tse poem is followed by "Visit with the Exiled Poets." Dante-like, the poet goes down to the nether world and meets his dead colleagues, who were once in trouble with the powers of the upper world. Ovid and Villon, Dante and Voltaire, Heine, Shakespeare, and Euripides sit cheerfully together and give mocking advice, but then, "there came a call from the darkest corner: 'You, there, do they know your lines by heart? And those who know them, will they survive the persecution?' And Dante explained softly, 'These are the forgotten poets; not only their bodies but even their works were destroyed.' The laughter ceased abruptly. No one dared to look at the guest. He had turned white."[82] Well, Brecht didn't need to worry.

Even more noticeable than the poems were the plays he wrote during these years of exile. After the war, no matter what the Berliner Ensemble tried to do, whenever *Galileo* was staged in East Berlin, every line sounded like an open declaration of hostility to the regime, and was understood as such. Up to this period, Brecht had consciously avoided—by means of the so-called epic theater—creating characters of any individuality, but now, all of a sudden, his plays were peopled with real persons, who, if they were not characters in the old sense, were clearly unique and individual figures, such as Simone Machard, and the Good Woman of Setzuan, and Mother Courage, and the girl Grusche and Judge Azdak in *The Caucasian Chalk Circle,* and Galileo, and Puntila and his servant Matti. Today, all the plays in this group are part of the repertoire of good theater inside and outside Germany, though when Brecht wrote them they went unnoticed. No doubt this belated fame is a tribute to Brecht's own merits, and not only the merits of the poet and playwright but also those of the extraordinarily gifted theater director, who had at his disposition one of Germany's great actresses, Helene Weigel, who was his wife.[83] But this does not alter the fact that everything he staged in East Berlin had been written outside Germany. Once he was back there, his poetic faculty dried up from one day to the next. He must finally have realized that he was confronted with circumstances that no quotation from the "classics" could explain or justify. He had stumbled into a situation in which his very silence—let alone his occasional praise of the butchers—was a crime.

Brecht's troubles had started when he became *engagé* (as we would say today, for the concept did not exist then), when he tried to do more than be a voice, which was how he began. A voice of what? Not of himself, to be sure, but of the world and of everything that was real. Yet that was not enough. To be a voice of what he thought was reality had carried him away from the real; wasn't he on the way to becoming what he liked least, one more solitary great poet in the German tradition, instead of what he wanted most to be, a bard of the people? And yet, when he went into the thick of things, his remoteness as a poet was what he carried, willy-nilly, into the newfound reality, his sharp and tricky intelligence notwithstanding. It was not so much lack of courage as this remoteness from the real that caused him not to break with a party that killed his friends and allied itself with his worst enemy, and to refuse to see, for the sake of the "classics," what was actually happening in his homeland—something that in his more prosaic moments he understood only too well. In the concluding remarks to *The Resistible Rise of the Man Arturo Ui*—a satire on Hitler's "irresistible" rise to power, and not one of the great plays—he noted, "The great political criminals must be exposed by all means, and especially by ridicule. For they are above all no great political criminals but the perpetrators of great political crimes, which is not at all the same. . . . The failure of Hitler's enterprises does not mean that Hitler was an idiot, and the range of his enterprises does not mean that he was a great man."[84] This is considerably more than most intellectuals understood in 1941, and it is precisely this extraordinary intelligence, breaking like lightning through the rumble of Marxist platitudes, that has made it so difficult for good men to forgive Brecht his sins, or to reconcile themselves to the fact that he could sin *and* write good poetry. But, finally, when he went back to East Germany, essentially for artistic reasons, because its government would give him a theater—that is, for that "art for art's sake" he had vehemently denounced for nearly thirty years—his punishment caught up with him. Now reality overwhelmed him to the point where he could no longer be its voice; he had succeeded in being in the thick of it—and had proved that this is no good place for a poet to be.

~

This is what the case of Bertolt Brecht is likely to teach us, and what we ought to take into consideration when we judge him today, as we must, and pay him our respect for all that we owe him. The poets' relation to reality is indeed what Goethe said it was: They cannot bear the same burden of responsibility as ordinary mortals; they need a measure of remoteness, and yet would not be worth their salt if they were not forever tempted to exchange this remoteness for being just like everybody else. On this attempt Brecht staked his life and his art as few poets had ever done; it led him into triumph and disaster.

From the beginning of these reflections, I have proposed that we grant poets a certain latitude, such as we would hardly be willing to grant each other in the ordinary course of events. I do not deny that this may offend many people's sense of justice; in fact, if Brecht were still among us he would certainly be the first to protest violently against any such exception. (In the posthumously published book *Me-ti,* which I mentioned before, he suggests a verdict for the "good man" gone wrong. "Listen," he says after the interrogation is completed, "we know you are our enemy. Therefore we shall now put you against a wall. But in consideration of your merits and virtues, it will be a good wall, and we shall shoot you with good bullets from good guns, and we shall bury you with a good shovel in good soil.")[85] However, the equality before the law whose standard we commonly adopt for moral judgments as well is no absolute. Every judgment is open to forgiveness, every act of judging can change into an act of forgiving; to judge and to forgive are but the two sides of the same coin. But the two sides follow different rules. The majesty of the law demands that we be equal—that only our acts count, and not the person who committed them. The act of forgiving, on the contrary, takes the person into account; no pardon pardons murder or theft but only the murderer or the thief. We always forgive some*body,* never some*thing,* and this is the reason people think that only love can forgive.[86] But, with or without love, we forgive for the sake of the person, and while justice demands that all be equal, mercy insists on inequality—an inequality implying that every man is, or should be, more than whatever he did or achieved. In his youth, before he adopted "usefulness" as the ultimate standard in judging people, Brecht knew this better than anybody else. There is a "Ballad About the Secrets of Each and Every Man" in the *Manual of Piety*, whose first stanza, in Bentley's translation, reads as follows:

> Everyone knows what a man is. He has a name.
> He walks in the street. He sits in the bar.
> You can all see his face. You can all hear his voice
> And a woman washed his shirt and a woman combs his hair.
> *But strike him dead! Why not indeed*
> *If he never amounted to anything more*
> *Than the doer of his bad deed or*
> *The doer of his good deed.*

The standard that rules in this domain of inequality is still contained in the old Roman saying *"Quod licet Iovi non licet bovi,"* what is permitted to Jove is not permitted to an ox. But, for our consolation, this inequality works both ways. One of the signs that a poet is entitled to such privileges as I here claim for him is that there are certain things he cannot do and still remain who he was. It is the poet's task to coin the words we live by, and surely no one is going to live by the words that Brecht wrote in praise of Stalin. The simple fact that he was capable of writing such unspeakably bad verse, worse by far than any fifth-rate scribbling versifier who was guilty of the same sins, shows that *quod licet bovi non licet Iovi,* what is permitted to an ox is not permitted to Jove. For whether or not you can praise tyranny in "fine-sounding voices," it is true that mere intellectuals or literati are not punished for their sins by loss of talent. No god leaned over their cradle; no god will take his revenge. There are a great many things that are permitted to an ox but not to Jove; that is, not to those who are a bit like Jove—or, rather, are blessed by Apollo. Hence the bitterness of the old saying cuts both ways, and the example of "poor B. B.," who never wasted a shred of pity on himself, may teach us how difficult it is to be a poet in this century or at any other time.

Originally published in *Men in Dark Times*, 207–49. An earlier version, without notes, appeared under the title "What Is Permitted to Jove" in *The New Yorker* 42 (November 5, 1966): 68–122.

In addition to the earlier essay on Brecht included in this volume, two other sources should be mentioned: some comments she made in response to a lecture by

Walter Muschg entitled "Dichtung und Kultur" [Poetry and Culture] (*Untergang oder Übergang: 1. Internationaler Kulturkritikerkongress in München, 1958* [Munich: Banaschewski, 1959], 199–202; and a lecture Arendt delivered at Emory University on May 4, 1964. In the former she says that "the relation between poetry and politics, or more exactly, the relation of poets to politics is something I take very much to heart." She proceeds to sketch her argument concerning the one transgression Brecht committed that cost him his poetic productivity, namely, settling in the totalitarian state of East Germany. In the latter, she fleshes out her argument and produces the first draft of the essay that appeared in *The New Yorker*. In response to the publication of this essay, the literary scholar John Willett, who was co-editor of the English and American editions of Brecht's works, wrote a letter to the magazine in which he charged that Arendt had four errors: (1) Brecht never wrote any "odes" to Stalin; (2) Arendt misdated some of his earlier poems in an effort to read them as responses to the First World War; (3) Brecht was not particularly productive while he stayed in the United States; and (4) Brecht never had any desire to leave East Germany and settle in Switzerland. Because Willett did not receive a reply from the magazine, he wrote to Arendt in person about questions 1 and 4, to which she briefly replied—but did not answer his follow-up letter. Questions 2 and 3 were dropped in the course of the controversy (probably because question 2 is of no real consequence and question 3 is largely a matter of perspective). For an account of these incidents, see John Willett, "The Story of Brecht's Odes to Stalin," *Times Literary Supplement* (March 26, 1970): 334–35. The controversy was covered by *The New York Times* (March 28, 1970): 25; see also Julian Exner, "War Brecht ein Stalin-Barde?" *Berliner Tagesspiegel* (March 28, 1970), 5 (reprinted in Hannah Arendt and Uwe Johnson, *Der Briefwechsel,* ed. Eberhard Fahlke and Thomas Wild [Frankfurt: Suhrkamp, 2004], 27–29). Discussion of Arendt's replies to questions 1 and 4 can be found in the notes.

Perhaps as a result of this controversy, Arendt added a substantial bibliographical apparatus for the republication of *The New Yorker* essay in *Men in Dark Times*. But as Willett notes to his dismay, she does not alter the essay in the least. She did, however, produce a German version of the essay under the title "Quod licet Jovi . . . : Reflexionen über den Dichter Bertolt Brecht und sein Verhältnis zur Politik," *Merkur* 23 (1969): 527–42, 625–42. (The German essay varies slightly from the English in a number of places, for which I have included notes in the text.) This German version also generated a small controversy: Sidney Hook wrote a letter to *Merkur* about the passage in which Arendt discusses Hook's lack of interpretative prowess ("Was dachte Brecht von Stalin? Nochmals zu Hannah Arendts Brecht-Aufsatz," *Merkur* 23 [1969]: 1082–83); and Irving Fetscher wrote a letter to the journal in which he repeats Willett's contention that Brecht did not really write laudatory poems in favor of Stalin ("Es gibt keine Götter—auch Stalin: ein Ochs," *Merkur* 23 [1969]: 888–89). Arendt's response to Hook and Fetscher are discussed in the notes.—Ed.

§ 29 Randall Jarrell

1914–1965

I met him shortly after the end of the war when he had come to New York to edit *The Nation*'s book section while Margaret Marshall was away, and when I was working for Schocken Books. What brought us together was "business"—I had been very impressed by some of his war poems and asked him to translate some German poems for the publishing house, and he edited (translated into English, I should say) some book reviews of mine for *The Nation*. Thus, like people in business, we made it a habit of lunching together, and these lunches, I suspect but do not remember, were paid for in turn by our employers; for this was still the time when we were all poor. The first book he gave to me was *Losses,* and he inscribed it "To Hannah (Arendt) from her translator Randall (Jarrell)," reminding me jokingly of his first name which I was slow to use, but not, as he suspected, because of any European aversion to first names; to my un-English ear Randall sounded not a bit more intimate than Jarrell, in fact, the two sounded very much alike.[1]

I don't know how long it took me to invite him to our home; his letters are of no help since they are all undated. But for some years he came at regular intervals, and when he announced his next visit he would for instance write, "You could enter in your engagement book Sat. Oct. 6, Sun. Oct. 7—American Poetry Weekend." And this is precisely what it always turned out to be. He read English poetry to me for hours, old and new, only rarely his own, which, however, for a time, he used to mail as soon as the poems came out of the typewriter. He opened up for me a whole new world of sound and meter, and he taught me the specific gravity of English words, whose relative weight, as in all languages, is ultimately determined by poetic usage and standards. Whatever I know of English poetry, and perhaps of the genius of the language, I owe to him.

What originally attracted him not just to me or to us but to the house was the simple fact that this was a place where German was spoken. For

> I believe—
> I do believe, I do believe—
> The country I like best of all is German.

The "country," obviously, was not Germany but German, a language he barely knew and stubbornly refused to learn—"Alas, my German isn't a *bit* better: if I translate, how can I find time to learn German? if I don't translate, I forget about German," he wrote after my last not very convinced attempt at making him use a grammar and a dictionary.

> It is by Trust and Love and reading Rilke
> Without *ein Wörterbuch* that man learns German.[2]

For him, all things considered, this was true enough, for he had read in this way Grimm's tales and *Des Knaben Wunderhorn,* as though he was completely at home in the strange and intense poetry of German folk tales and folk songs, which are as untranslatably German as, well, *Alice in Wonderland* is untranslatably English.[3] Anyhow, it was this folk element in German poetry that he loved and recognized in Goethe and even in Hölderlin and Rilke. I often thought that the country the German language represented to him was actually where he came from, for he was, down to the details of physical appearance, like a figure from fairyland; it was as though he had been blown down by some charmed wind into the cities of men or had emerged from the enchanted forests in which we spent our childhood, bringing with him the magic flute, and now not just hoping but *expecting* that everybody and everything would come to join in the midnight dance. What I mean to say is that Randall Jarrell would have been a poet if he had never written a single poem—just as that proverbial Raphael born without hands would still have been a great painter.

I knew him best during some winter months in the early fifties when he stayed at Princeton, which he found "*much* more Princetonian than—than Princeton, even." He came to New York on weekends, leaving behind, as he described it, a whole house of undone rooms and dishes and God knows how many street cats whom he had befriended. The moment he entered the apartment I had the feeling that the household had become bewitched. I never found out how he actually did it, but there was no solid object, no implement or piece of furniture, which did not undergo a subtle change, in the process of which it lost its everyday prosaic function. This poetic transformation could be annoyingly real when he decided, as he often did, to follow me into the kitchen to entertain me while I was preparing our dinner. Or, he might decide to visit my husband and engage him in some long, fierce debate about the merits and the rank of writers and poets, and the voices of the two rang lustily as they tried to outdo and especially outshout each other—who knew better how to appreciate *Kim,* who was a greater poet, Yeats or Rilke? (Randall, of course, voting for Rilke and my husband for Yeats), and so on, for hours. As Randall wrote after one such shouting match, "it's always awing (for an enthusiast) to see someone more enthusiastic than yourself—like the second fattest man in the world meeting the fattest."

In his poem about Grimm's tales, "The Märchen," he has described the land he came from:

> Listening, listening; it is never still.
> This is the forest . . .
> where
> The sunlight fell to them, according to our wish,
> And we believed, till nightfall, in that wish;
> And we believed, till nightfall, in our lives.[4]

His was not at all the case of the man who flees the world and builds himself a dream castle; on the contrary, he met the world head-on. And the world, to his everlasting surprise, was as it was—not peopled by poets and readers of poetry, who according to him belonged to the same race, but by television watchers and readers of *Reader's Digest* and, worst of all, by this new species, the "Modern Critic," who no longer exists "for the sake of the plays and stories and poems [he] criticizes" but for his own sake, who knows "how poems and novels are put together," whereas the poor writer "had just put them together. In the same way, if a pig wandered up to you during a bacon-judging contest, you would say impatiently, 'Go away, pig! What do you know about bacon?' " The world, in other words, did not welcome the poet, was not grateful to him for the splendor he brought, seemed unneedful of his "immemorial power to make the things of this world seen and felt and living in words," and therefore condemned him to obscurity, complaining then that he was too "obscure" and could not be understood, until finally "the poet said, 'Since you won't read me, I'll make sure you can't.'" All these complaints were ordinary enough, so ordinary indeed that I at first could not understand why he bothered with them at all. Only slowly did it dawn upon me that he did not want to belong among "the happy few, who grow fewer and unhappier day by day," for the simple reason that he was a democrat at heart with "a scientific education and a radical youth," who was "old-fashioned enough to believe, like Goethe, in Progress." And it took me even longer, I must confess, to realize that his marvelous wit, by which I mean the precision of his laughter, was not the simple outgrowth of his unbelief in cheapness and vulgarity of every kind or of his belief that everybody he came in contact with had his own absolute feeling (like absolute pitch) for quality, this infallible judgment in all artistic as well as human matters, but that there was also, as he himself pointed out in "The Obscurity of the Poet," the mocking and self-mocking "tone of someone accustomed to helplessness."[5] I trusted the very exuberance of his cheerfulness, thought or hoped that it would be sufficient to ward off all dangers to which he was so obviously exposed, because I found his laughter so exactly right. How, after all, could any of the learned or sophisticated rubbish about "adjustment" hope to survive this one sentence of his (in *Pictures from an Institution*), "President Robbins was so well adjusted to his environment that sometimes you could not tell which was the environment and which was President Robbins"?[6] And if you can't laugh away the rubbish, what help is there? To disprove point by point all the nonsense our century has produced would demand ten life-spans, and in the end the disprovers would be as little distinguishable from their victims as was the College President from his environment. Randall, at any rate, had nothing to protect him against the world but his splendid laughter, and the immense naked courage behind it.

When I last saw him, not long before his death, the laughter was almost gone, and he was almost ready to admit defeat. It was the same defeat he had foreseen more than ten years earlier in the poem entitled "A Conversation with the Devil."

> Indulgent, or candid, or uncommon reader
> —I've some: a wife, a nun, a ghost or two—
> If I write for anyone, I wrote for you;

So whisper, when I die, *We was too few;*
Write over me (if you can write; I hardly knew)
That I—that I—but anything will do,
I'm satisfied . . . And yet—
      and yet, you *were* too few:
Should I perhaps have written for your brothers,
Those artful, common, unindulgent others?[7]

Originally published in *Randall Jarrell, 1914–1965,* ed. Robert Lowell, Peter Taylor, and Robert Penn Warren (New York: Farrar, Straus & Giroux, 1967), 3–9; reprinted in *Men in Dark Times,* 263–67.

Randall Jarrell (1914–1965) was an American poet. Born in Nashville and a graduate of Vanderbilt University, Jarrell studied with Robert Penn Warren and John Crowe Ransom. He entered the Air Force in 1942. Two books of his poetry, *Little Friend, Little Friend* (1945) and *Losses* (1948), revolve around his years in the armed services. He became an influential critic for *The New Republic. The Woman at the Washington Zoo* (1960) won the National Book Award. His last book of poetry is entitled *The Lost World* (1965). Near the end of his life he also wrote a number of children's books and a satirical novel about academic life, *Pictures from an Institution* (1954). He died when a car struck him while he was walking at dusk on a highway.—Ed.

§ 30 Isak Dinesen

1885–1962

Les grandes passions sont rares comme les chefs-d'oeuvre.

[Grand passions are as rare as masterpieces.]

—Balzac

The Baroness Karen Blixen, née Karen Christentze Dinesen—called Tanne by her family and Tania first by her lover and then by her friends—was the Danish woman author of rare distinction who wrote in English out of loyalty to her dead lover's language and, in the spirit of good old-fashioned coquetry, half hid, half showed her authorship by prefixing to her maiden name the male pseudonym "Isak," the one who laughs. Laughter was supposed to take care of several rather troublesome problems, the least serious of which, perhaps, was her firm conviction that it was not very becoming for a woman to be an author, hence a public figure; the light that illuminates the public domain is much too harsh to be flattering. She had had her experiences in this matter since her mother had been a suffragette, active in the fight for women's franchise in Denmark, and probably one of those excellent women who will never tempt a man to seduce them. When she was twenty she had written and published some short stories and been encouraged to go on but immediately decided not to. She "never once wanted to be a writer," she "had an intuitive fear of being trapped," and every profession, because it invariably assigns a definite role in life, would have been a trap, shielding her against the infinite possibilities of life itself. She was in her late forties when she began to write professionally and close to fifty when her first book, *Seven Gothic Tales,* appeared. At that time, she had discovered (as we know from "The Dreamers") that the chief trap in life is one's own identity—"I will not be one person again. . . . Never again will I have my heart and my whole life bound up with one woman"—and that the best advice to give one's friends (for instance, Marcus Cocoza in the story) was not to worry "too much about Marcus Cocoza," for this means to be "really his slave and his prisoner." Hence, the trap was not so much writing or professional writing as taking oneself seriously and identifying the woman with the author who has his identity confirmed, inescapably, in public. That grief over having lost her life and her lover in Africa should have made her a writer and given her a sort of second life was best understood as a joke, and "God loves a joke" became her maxim in the latter part of her life. (She loved such mottoes to live by and had started with *navigare necesse est, vivere non necesse est,* to adopt later Denys Finch-Hatton's *Je responderay,* I shall answer and give account.)[1]

But there was more than the fear of being trapped that caused her, in interview upon interview, to defend herself emphatically against the common notion of her being a born writer and a "creative artist." The truth was that she never had felt any ambition or particular urge to write, let alone *be* a writer; the little writing she had done in Africa could be dismissed, as it had only served "in times of drought" in every sense to disperse her worries about the farm and relieve her boredom when no other work could be done. Only once had she "created some fiction to make money," and though *The Angelic Avengers* did make some money, it turned out "terrible." No, she had started writing simply "because she had to make a living" and "could do only two things, cook and . . . perhaps, write." How to cook she had learned in Paris and later in Africa in order to please her friends, and in order to entertain friends and natives alike, she had taught herself how to tell stories. "Had she been able to stay in Africa, she would never have become a writer." For, *"Moi, je suis une conteuse, et rien qu'une conteuse. C'est l'histoire elle-même qui m'intéresse, et la façon de la raconter."* ("I, I am a storyteller and nothing else. What interests me is the story and the way to tell it.") All she needed to begin with was life and the world, almost any kind of world or milieu; for the world is full of stories, of events and occurrences and strange happenings, which wait only to be told, and the reason why they usually remain untold is, according to Isak Dinesen, lack of imagination—for only if you can imagine what has happened anyhow, repeat it in imagination, will you see the stories, and only if you have the patience to tell and retell them (*"Je me les raconte et re-raconte"*) will you be able to tell them well. This, of course, she had done all her life, but not in order to become an artist, not even to become one of the wise and old professional storytellers we find in her books. Without repeating life in imagination you can never be fully alive, "lack of imagination" prevents people from "existing." "Be loyal to the story," as one of her storytellers admonishes the young, "be eternally and unswervingly loyal to the story," means no less than, Be loyal to life, don't create fiction but accept what life is giving you, show yourself worthy of whatever it may be by recollecting and pondering over it, thus repeating it in imagination; this is the way to remain alive. And to live in the sense of being fully alive had early been and remained to the end her only aim and desire. "My life, I will not let you go except you bless me, but then I will let you go." The reward of storytelling is to be able to let go: "When the storyteller is loyal . . . to the story, there, in the end, silence will speak. Where the story has been betrayed, silence is but emptiness. But we, the faithful, when we have spoken our last word, will hear the voice of silence."

This, to be sure, needs skill, and in this sense storytelling is not only part of living but can become an art in its own right. To become an artist also needs time and a certain detachment from the heady, intoxicating business of sheer living that, perhaps, only the born artist can manage in the midst of living. In her case, anyhow, there is a sharp line dividing her life from her afterlife as an author. Only when she had lost what had constituted her life, her home in Africa and her lover, when she had returned home to Rungstedlund a complete "failure" with nothing in her hands except grief and sorrow and memories, did she become the artist and the "success" she never would have become otherwise—"God loves a joke," and divine jokes, as the Greeks knew so well, are often cruel ones. What she then did was unique in contemporary literature though it could be matched by certain nineteenth-century writers—Heinrich Kleist's anecdotes and short stories and some tales of Johann Peter Hebel, especially *Unverhofftes Wiedersehen* come to mind.[2] Eudora Welty has defined it definitively in one short sentence of utter precision: "Of a story she made an essence; of the essence she made an elixir; and of the elixir she began once more to compound the story."[3]

The connection of an artist's life with his work has always raised embarrassing problems, and our eagerness to see recorded, displayed, and discussed in public what once were strictly private affairs and nobody's business is probably less legitimate than our curiosity is ready to admit. Unfortunately, the questions one is bound to raise about Parmenia Migel's biography (*Titania. The Biography of Isak Dinesen,* Random House, 1967) are not of this order.[4] To say that the writing is nondescript is putting it kindly, and although five years spent in research supposedly yielded "enough material . . . for a monumental work," we hardly ever get more than quotations from previously published material drawn either from books and interviews of the subject or from *Isak Dinesen: A Memorial,* which Random House published in 1965. The few facts revealed here for the first time are treated with a sloppy non-workmanship which any copy editor should have been able to spot. (A man who is about to commit suicide [her father] cannot very well be said to have "some premonition . . . of his approaching death"; on p. 36 we are instructed that her first love should "remain nameless," but he doesn't, on p. 210 we learn who he was; we are informed in passing that her father "had sympathized with the Communards and had leftist leanings" and are told, through the voice of an aunt, that "he was profoundly saddened by the horrors he had witnessed during the Paris Commune." A disabused man, we would conclude, if we did not know from the above-mentioned memorial volume, that he had later written a book of memoirs "in which . . . he rendered justice to the patriotism and idealism of the 'communards.'" His son confirms the sympathies with the Commune and adds that "in parliament his party was the Left.") Worse than the sloppiness is the wrong-headed *délicatesse* applied to the by far most relevant new fact the book contains, the venereal infection—the husband from whom she was divorced but whose name and title she kept (for "the satisfaction of being addressed as Baroness," as her biographer suggests?) had "left her a legacy of illness"— from whose consequences she had suffered all her life. Her medical history would indeed have been of considerable interest; her secretary relates to what an extent her later life was consumed by a "heroic fight against the overwhelming odds of illness . . . like one human being trying to stem an avalanche." And worst of all is the occasional, rather innocent impertinence, so typical of the professional adorers to be found in the surroundings of most celebrities; Hemingway, who quite generously had said in his acceptance speech for the Nobel Prize that it should have been given to "that beautiful writer Isak Dinesen," "could not help envying [Tania's] poise and sophistication" and "needed to kill in order to prove his manhood, to extirpate the insecurity which he never did really conquer."[5] All this would not need saying and the whole enterprise would best be passed over in silence, if it were not for the unhappy fact that it was Isak Dinesen herself (or was it the Baroness Karen Blixen?) who had commissioned, as it were, this biography, had spent hours and days with Mrs. Migel to instruct her, and, shortly before her death, reminded her once more of "*my* book," exacting a promise that it would be finished "as soon as I die." Well, neither vanity nor the need for adoration—the sad substitute for the supreme confirmation of one's existence which only love, mutual love, can give—belongs among the mortal sins; but they are unsurpassed prompters when we need suggestions for making fools of ourselves.

No one, obviously, could have told the story of her life as she herself might have told it, and the question why she did not write an autobiography is as fascinating as it is unanswered. (What a pity that her biographer apparently never asked her this obvious question.) For *Out of Africa,* which is often called autobiographical, is singularly reticent, silent on almost all the issues her biographer would be bound to raise. It tells us nothing of the unhappy marriage and the divorce, and only the careful reader will learn from it that Denys Finch-Hatton was more than a regular visitor and friend. The book is indeed, as Robert Langbaum, by far her best critic, has pointed out, "an authentic pastoral, perhaps the best prose pastoral of our time," and because it is a pastoral and not dramatic in the least, not even in the narration of Denys Finch-Hatton's death in an airplane crash and of the last desolate weeks in empty rooms on packed cases, it can incorporate many stories but only hint, by the most tenuous, rarefied allusions, at the underlying story of a *grande passion* which was then, and apparently remained to the end, the source of her storytelling.[6] Neither in Africa nor at any other time of her life did she ever hide anything; she must have been proud, one gathers, to be the mistress of this man who in her descriptions remains curiously lifeless. But in *Out of Africa,* she admits her relation only by implication—he "had no other home in Africa than the farm, he lived in my house between his Safaris," and when he came back the house "gave out what was in it; it spoke—as the coffee-plantations speak, when with the first showers of the rainy season they flower"; then "the things of the farm were all telling what they really were." And she, having "made up many [stories] while he had been away," would be "sitting on the floor, crosslegged like Scheherazade herself."[7]

When she called herself Scheherazade in this setting she meant more than the literary critics who later followed her lead, more than mere storytelling, the *"Moi, je suis une conteuse and rien qu'une conteuse."* The Thousand and One Nights—whose "stories she placed above everything else"—were not merely whiled away with telling tales; they produced three male children. And her lover, who "when he came to the farm would ask: 'Have you got a story?',", was not unlike the Arabian King who "being restless was pleased with the idea of listening to the story." Denys Finch-Hatton and his friend, Berkeley Cole, belonged to the generation of young men whom the First World War had made forever unfit to bear the conventions and fulfill the duties of everyday life, to pursue their careers and play their roles in a society that bored them to distraction.[8] Some of them became revolutionists and lived in the dreamland of the future; others, on the contrary, chose the dreamland of the past and lived as though "theirs was . . . a world which no longer existed." They belonged together in the fundamental conviction that "they did not belong to their century." (In political parlance, one would say that they were antiliberal insofar as liberalism meant the acceptance of the world as it was together with the hope for its "progress"; historians know to what an extent conservative criticism and revolutionary criticism of the world of the bourgeoisie coincide.) In either ease, they wished to be "outcasts" and "deserters," quite ready "to pay for their wilfulness" rather than settle down and found a family. At any rate, Denys Finch-Hatton came and went as he wished, and nothing was obviously further from his mind than to be bound by marriage. Nothing could bind him and lure him back but the flame of passion, and the surest way of preventing the flame from being extinguished by time and inevitable repetition, by knowing each other too well and having already heard all the stories, was to become inexhaustible in making up new ones. Surely, she was no less anxious to entertain than Scheherazade, no less conscious that failing to please would be her death.

Hence *la grande passion,* with Africa, still wild, not yet domesticated, the perfect setting. There one could draw the line "between respectability and decency, and [divide] up our acquaintances, human and animal, in accordance with the doctrine. We put down domestic animals as respectable and wild animals as decent, and held that, while the existence and prestige of the first were decided by their relation to the community, the others stood in direct contact with God. Pigs and poultry, we agreed, were worthy of our respect, inasmuch as they loyally returned what was invested in them, and . . . behaved as was expected of them. . . . We registered ourselves with the wild animals, sadly admitting the inadequacy of our return to the community—and to our mortgages—but realizing that we could not possibly, not even in order to obtain the highest approval of our surroundings, give up that direct contact with God which we shared with the hippo and the flamingo." Among the emotions, *la grande passion* is just as destructive of what is socially acceptable, just as contemptuous of what is deemed "worthy of our respect," as the outcasts and deserters were of the civilized society they had come from. But life is lived in society, and love, therefore—not romantic love, to be sure, that sets the stage for marital bliss—is destructive of life too, as we know from the famous pairs of lovers in history and literature who all came to grief. To escape society— couldn't that mean to be granted not just passion but a passionate life? Hadn't that been the reason why she left Denmark, to expose herself to a life unprotected by society? "What business had I had to set my heart on Africa?" she asked, and the answer came in the song of the "Master" whose "word has been a lamp unto my feet and a light unto my path"—

> Who doth ambition shun
> And love to live i' the sun,
> Seeking the food he eats,
> And pleas'd with what he gets,
> Come hither, come hither, come hither:
>   Here shall he see
>   No enemy
> But winter and rough weather.
> If it do come to pass
> That any man turn ass
> Leaving his wealth and ease,
> A stubborn will to please'
> Ducdame, ducdame, ducdame:
>   Here shall he see
>   Gross fools as he,
> And if he will come to me.[9]

Scheherazade, with everything the name implies, living among Shakespeare's "gross fools" who shun ambition and love to live in the sun, having found a place "nine thousand feet up" from where to laugh down "at the ambition of the new arrivals, of the Missions, the business people and the Government itself, to make the continent of Africa respectable," intent upon nothing except preserving the natives, the wild animals, and the wilder outcasts and deserters from Europe, the adventurers turned guides and safari hunters, in "their innocence of the period before the Fall"— that is what she wanted to be, how she wanted to live, and how she appeared to herself. It was not necessarily how she appeared to others, and particularly to her lover. Tania he had called her, and then he had added

Titania. ("There is such magic in the people and the land here," she had said to him; and Denys had "smiled at her with affectionate condescension. 'The magic is not in the people and the land, but in the eye of the beholder. . . . You bring your own magic to it, Tania . . . Titania.' ") Parmenia Migel has chosen the name as title for her biography, and it wouldn't have been a bad title if she had remembered that the name implies more than the Queen of fairies and her "magic." The two lovers between whom the name first fell, forever quoting Shakespeare to each other, knew of course better; they knew that the Queen of fairies was quite capable of falling in love with Bottom and that she had a rather unrealistic estimate of her own magical powers:

> "And I will purge thy mortal grossness so
> That thou shalt like an airy spirit go."

Well, Bottom did not transform into an airy spirit, and Puck tells us what is the truth of the matter for all practical purposes:

> "My mistress with a monster is in love. . . .
> Titania wak'd and straightway lov'd an ass."[10]

The trouble was that magic once more proved utterly ineffective. The catastrophe that finally befell her she had brought about herself, when she decided to stay on the farm even when she must have known that coffee growing "at an altitude so high . . . was decidedly unprofitable," and, to make matters worse, she "did not know or learn much about coffee but persisted in the unshakable conviction that her intuitive power would tell her what to do"—as her brother, in sensible and tender reminiscences, remarked after her death. Only when she had been expelled from the land that for seventeen long years, supported by the money of her family, had permitted her to be Queen, Queen of fairies, did the truth dawn upon her. Remembering from afar her African cook, Kamante, she wrote, "Where the great Chef walked in deep thought, full of knowledge, nobody sees anything but a little bandy-legged Kikuyu, a dwarf with a flat, still face." Yes, nobody except herself, forever repeating everything in the magic of imagination out of which the stories grew. However, the point of the matter is that even this disproportion, once it has been discovered, can become the stuff for a story. Thus, we meet Titania again in "The Dreamers," only now she is called "Donna Quixota de la Mancha" and reminds the wise old Jew, who in the story plays the role of Puck, of "dancing snakes" he once saw in India, snakes that have "no poison whatever" and kill, if they kill, by sheer force of embrace. "In fact, the sight of you, un-folding your great coils to revolve around, impress yourself upon, and fi-nally crush a meadow mouse is enough to split one's side with laughter." In a way, that is how one feels when one reads on page after page about her "successes" in later life and how she enjoyed them, magnifying them out of all proportion—that so much intensity, such bold passionateness should be wasted on Book-of-the-Month-Club selections and honorary memberships in prestigious societies, that the early clear-headed insight that sorrow is better than nothing, that "between grief and nothing I will take grief" (Faulkner), should finally be rewarded by the small change of prizes, awards, and honors might be sad in retrospect; the spectacle itself must have been very close to comedy.[11]

Stories had saved her love, and stories saved her life after disaster had struck. "All sorrows can be borne if you put them into a story or tell a story about them."[12] The story reveals the meaning of what otherwise would remain an unbearable sequence of sheer happenings. "The silent, all-embracing genius of consent" that also is the genius of true faith—when her Arab servant hears of Denys Finch-Hatton's death, he replies "God is great," just as the Hebrew Kaddish, the death prayer said by the closest relative, says nothing but "Holy be His name"—rises out of the story because in the repetition of imagination the happenings have be-come what she would call a "destiny." To be so at one with one's own des-tiny that no one will be able to tell the dancer from the dance, that the answer to the question, Who are you? will be the Cardinal's answer, "Al-low me . . . to answer you in the classic manner, and to tell you a story," is the only aspiration worthy of the fact that life has been given us. This is also called pride, and the true dividing line between people is whether they are capable of being "in love with [their] destiny" or whether they "accept as success what others warrant to be so . . . at the quotation of the day. They tremble, with reason, before their fate." All her stories are actu-ally "Anecdotes of Destiny," they tell again and again how at the end we shall be privileged to judge; or, to put it differently, how to pursue one of the "two courses of thought at all seemly to a person of any intelli-gence . . . : What did God mean by creating the world, the sea, and the desert, the horse, the winds, woman, amber, fishes, wine?"

It is true that storytelling reveals meaning without committing the error of defining it, that it brings about consent and reconciliation with things as they really are, and that we may even trust it to contain eventually by implication that last word which we expect from the "day of judgment." And yet, if we listen to Isak Dinesen's "philosophy" of storytelling and think of her life in the light of it, we cannot help becoming aware of how the slightest misunderstanding, the slightest shift of emphasis in the wrong direction, will inevitably ruin everything. If it is true, as her "philosophy" suggests, that no one has a life worth thinking about whose life story cannot be told, does it not then follow that life could be, even ought to be, lived as a story, that what one has to do in life is to make the story come true? "Pride," she once wrote in her notebook, "is faith in the idea that God had, when he made us. A proud man is conscious of the idea, and aspires to realize it." From what we now know of her early life it seems quite clear that this is what she herself had tried to do when she was a young girl, to "realize" an "idea" and to anticipate her life's destiny by making an old story come true. The idea came to her as a legacy of her father, whom she had greatly loved—his death, when she was ten years old, was the first great grief, the fact that he had committed suicide, as she later learned, the first great shock from which she refused to be parted—and the story she had planned to act out in her life was actually meant to be the sequence of her father's story. The latter had concerned "*une princesse de conte de fées* whom everybody adored," whom he had known and loved before his marriage, and who had died suddenly at the age of twenty. Her father had mentioned it to her and an aunt had later suggested that he had never been able to recover from losing the girl, that his suicide was the result of his incurable grief. The girl, it turned out, had been a cousin of her father, and the daughter's greatest ambition became to belong to this side of her father's family, Danish high nobility to boot, "a race totally different" from her own milieu, as her brother relates it. It was only natural that one of its members, who would have been the dead girl's niece, became her best friend, and when "she fell in love 'for the first time and really forever,' [as] she used to say," it was with another second cousin of hers, Hans Blixen, who would have been the dead girl's nephew. And since this one took no notice of her, she decided, even at the age of twenty-seven, old enough to know better— to the distress and the amazement of everybody around her—to marry the twin brother and leave with him for Africa, shortly before the outbreak of the First World War. What then came was petty and sordid, not at all the stuff you could safely put into a story or tell a story about. (She was separated immediately after the war and received her divorce in 1923.)

Or was it? As far as I know, she never wrote a story about this absurd marriage affair, but she did write some tales about what must have been for her the obvious lesson of her youthful follies, namely, about the "sin" of making a story come true, of interfering with life according to a preconceived pattern, instead of waiting patiently for the story to emerge, of repeating in imagination as distinguished from creating a fiction and then trying to live up to it. The earliest of these tales is "The Poet" (in *Seven Gothic Tales*); two others were written nearly twenty-five years later (Parmenia Migel's biography unfortunately contains no chronological table), "The Immortal Story" (in *Anecdotes of Destiny*) and "Echoes" (in *Last Tales*). The first tells of the encounter between a young poet of peasant stock and his high-placed benefactor, an elderly gentleman who in his youth had fallen under the spell of Weimar and "the great Geheimrat Goethe," with the result that "outside of poetry there was to him no real ideal in life."[13] Alas, no such high ambition has ever made a man a poet, and when he realized "that the poetry of his life would have to come from somewhere else" he decided on the part "of a Maecenas," began to look for "a great poet" worthy of his consideration, and found him conveniently at hand in the town he lived in. But a real Maecenas, one who knew so much about poetry, could not very well be content with shelling out the money; he had also to provide the great tragedies and sorrows out of which he knew great poetry draws its best inspirations. Thus, he acquired a young wife and arranged it so that the two young people under his protection should fall in love with each other without any prospect of marriage. Well, the end is pretty bloody; the young poet shoots at his benefactor, and while the old man in his death agony dreams of Goethe and Weimar, the young woman, seeing as in a vision her lover "with the halter around his neck," finishes him off. "Just because it suited him that the world should be lovely, he meant to conjure it into being so," she said to herself. " 'You!,' she cried at him, 'You poet!' "

The perfect irony of "The Poet" is perhaps best realized by those who know German *Bildung* and its unfortunate connection with Goethe as well as its author did herself. (The story contains several allusions to German poems by Goethe and Heine as well as to Voss's translation of Homer. It could also be read as a story about the vices of *Bildung*.) "The Immortal Story," on the contrary, is conceived and written in the manner of a folk story. Its hero is an "immensely rich tea-trader" in Canton with very down-to-earth reasons for having "faith in his own omnipotence," who only at the end of his life came into contact with books. He then was bothered that they told of things that had never happened, and he got positively outraged when told that the only story he knew—about the sailor who had come ashore, met an old gentleman, "the richest man" in town, was asked by him to "do your best" in the bed of his young wife that he might still have a son, and was given a five-guinea piece for his service—"never has happened, and . . . never will happen, and that is why it is told." So the old man goes in pursuit of a sailor to make the old story, told in all harbor towns the world over, come true. And all seems to go well—except that the young sailor in the morning refuses to recognize the slightest similarity between the story and what had happened to him during the night, refuses the five guineas, and leaves for the lady in question the only treasure he possesses, "one big shining pink shell" of which he thinks "that perhaps there is not another one just like it in all the world."

"Echoes," the last one in this category, is a belated sequel to "The Dreamers" in *Gothic Tales,* the story about Pellegrina Leoni. "The diva who had lost her voice" in her wanderings hears it again from the boy Emanuele, whom she now proceeds to make into her own image so that her dream, her best and least selfish dream, should come true—that the voice which gave so much pleasure should be resurrected. Robert Langbaum, whom I mentioned before, noticed that here "Isak Dinesen pointed the finger of accusation against herself " and that the story, as the first pages suggest anyhow, is "about cannibalism," but nothing in it bears out that the singer had "been feeding on [the boy] in order to restore her own youth and to resurrect the Pellegrina Leoni whom she buried in Milan twelve years ago." (The very choice of a male successor precludes this interpretation.) The singer's own conclusion is, "And the voice of Pellegrina Leoni will not be heard again." The boy, before starting to throw stones at her, had accused her, "You are a witch. You are a vampire. . . . Now I know that I should die if I went back to you"—for the next singing lesson. The same accusations, the young poet could have hurled at his Maecenas, the young sailor at his benefactor, and generally all people who, under the pretext of being helped, are used for making another person's dream come true. (Thus, she herself had thought she could marry without love because her cousin "needed her and was perhaps the only human being who did," while she actually used him to start a new life in East Africa and to live among natives as her father had done when he had lived like a hermit among the Chippeway Indians. "The Indians are better than our civilized people of Europe," he had told his small daughter, whose greatest gift was never to forget. "Their eyes see more than ours, and they are wiser.")

Thus, the earlier part of her life had taught her that, while you can tell stories or write poems about life, you cannot make life poetic, live it as though it were a work of art (as Goethe had done) or use it for the realization of an "idea." Life may contain the "essence" (what else could?); recollection, the repetition in imagination, may decipher the essence and deliver to you the "elixir"; and eventually you may even be privileged to "make" something out of it, "to compound the story." But life itself is neither essence nor elixir, and if you treat it as such it will only play its tricks on you. It was perhaps the bitter experience of life's tricks that prepared her (rather late, she was in her middle thirties when she met Finch-Hatton) for being seized by the *grande passion* which indeed is no less rare than a chef-d'oeuvre. Storytelling, at any rate, is what in the end made her wise—and, incidentally, not a "witch," "siren," or "sibyl," as her entourage admiringly thought. Wisdom is a virtue of old age, and it seems to come only to those who, when young, were neither wise nor prudent.

Originally published in *The New Yorker* 44 (November 11, 1968): 223–36; reworked for *Men in Dark Times*, 95–109.

Isak Dinesen is the pen name of Karen Blixen, née Dinesen (1885–1962), the most widely known Danish writer of the twentieth century. In 1914 she married her cousin Baron Bror Blixen-Finecke and went with him to Kenya, where they ran a coffee plantation. They were divorced in 1921, after which Blixen ran the plantation by herself. She returned to Denmark in 1931. These years are recounted in *Out of Africa* (1938). Many of Dinesen's most famous works were written in English, including *Gothic Tales* (1932) and *Winter's Tales* (1942). Arendt's article was occasioned by the publication of the first full-scale biography of the writer, namely Migel Parmenia's *Titania: The Biography of Isak Dinesen* (New York: Random House, 1967).—Ed.

§ 31 Notes on Dostoevsky's *Possessed*

1. Every masterwork can be read on several levels, and a work is a masterwork if all the strands are so arranged that they form a consistent whole on each of the levels. This book on the lowest, but indispensable level: a key-novel, a roman-à-clef, where everything and everybody can be verified. The plot is lifted right out of the newspapers of the time, and one of the heroes is the center of the real story: Verkhovensky is Nechayev, his father a mixture of Granovsky and Kukolnik, Shatov is Dostoevsky, etc.[1]

~

2. On the second level, which is generally accepted, it is an explanation or prophecy of what actually happened: The Tsarist regime had to fall because of atheism. It undermined an authority which [existed] "by the grace of God" and lost its legitimacy when man no longer believed in God. Shatov: "If there's to be a rising in Russia we must begin with atheism." And a captain says: "If there's no God, how can I be a captain then?" (229).[2] Atheism is connected with Western ideas; the West, already corrupt, is on its way to corrupt Russia—in the form of Marxism. The Slavophils: Russia is the only hope because the Russian people still believe, even though the intellectuals don't. The very realistic description of the contempt these lovers of the people actually had for the people, and especially the Russian people.

Chief representative [of the view stated above is] Berdiaev's *Origins of Russian Communism:* the revolution first took place within and indicated the other revolution, which was on the march.[3] Since then, Dostoevsky has been granted "a gift of foresight bordering on the demonic." At least this much is true—atheism eliminates the fear of hell, and the fear of hell has been for many centuries the most potent factor to prevent people from doing evil. But the point in Dostoevsky is different: Without belief in God everything *is* permitted.

Still, the fact is that Verkhovensky-Nechayev shows a strange similarity with Stalin: "never forgets an offence," the "spying on one another" in the quintet, the "umlimited despotism" of Shigalov. The members are all potential informers—Liputin, with this marked inclination for police work, Lebyadkin, and especially Verkhovensky himself. As far as Stalin is concerned, [this would be] remarkable—if it were not for Nechayev's *Catechism,* which Stalin certainly knew, and on which he probably modeled himself.

~

3. On a third level, which was clearly Dostoevsky's own, we approach the same question of atheism, but much more seriously: The central problem in all Dostoevsky's novels is *not* the question of whether God exists but of whether man can live without belief in God. Before we discuss it: This kind of question carries doubt into belief, not from outside, as is the case in the sciences (where the answer is: the sciences neither raise nor answer this question). [This question] makes doubt rise from within: If I believe only because I can't bear *not* to believe I clearly don't believe. Dostoevsky knew that; it is his greatness. He did not believe that he or Shatov could bring salvation to Russia or mankind; this can only be done by those people who never had these thoughts, who simply believed, the feeble-minded like Marya or the Idiot.[4] The only non-feeble-minded believer is Aljosha—novel never completed.[5]

In the *Notebooks,* the urgent, most central question: Can one have faith if one is civilized, i.e., European?[6] For faith does not just mean some vague notion about a supreme being but the divinity of Christ. And this means two things, which are distinct though not quite distinct in Dostoevsky: a) Morality depends for its legitimacy upon revelation. If one part of it is destroyed, the whole of Christianity and Christian morality will collapse. If it is impossible to believe, then it is by no means inexcusable to demand total destruction. On the contrary, it is more humane: long suffering ending in death versus brief suffering and death. This side

[says]: Mankind cannot survive without faith. b) The Word became flesh in Christ, incarnation: The possibility of the divine on earth depends upon this event. It is, according to Dostoevsky, the only salvation from despair.—The representative of true non-belief is Stavrogin, the hero: who has "neither the feeling nor the knowledge of good and evil." It is precisely this indifference that is his undoing: "life bored him to the point of stupefaction." At the same time: feeling of complete freedom: Morality understood as the code of a master, the master is God, and the example is Christ. Man belongs to somebody (not to something) that is not only transcendent but superior to him.

This book [is] more explicitly concerned with this question than any other. That is, it tries to prove the disastrous consequences of losing faith. It is a negative argument, but since it is a novel, it is not [really] an argument. It is of considerable force because of the truth in the characters. Formulated as an argument: If you take away God as the one to whom man owes obedience, there is still man left, made to be a servant. Only, instead of serving God, he now serves ideas; he is no longer owned by God but possessed by ideas, which act like demons. These ideas are not something you have; [instead] the ideas have you. Stefan Trofimovitch has his whole head full of lofty and noble ideas, and not only does a son with criminal notions come out of him, he himself, in his utter thoughtlessness, borders on criminality—in the neglect and frauds against the son, in selling Fedka, the criminal, for a gambling debt. He is not evil, his ideas have only chased out of his head any ordinary thoughtfulness. Instead of being a servant of a legitimate master, man becomes a flunkey of his ideas—flunkeys of thought. (Twice by Shatov: 136 & 589.[7] The domination of phantoms [573] because there is no reality behind them.[8]) And even the noblest of these ideas, the idea of absolute freedom to be proven by suicide (Kirillov), for Kirillov is told by Verkhovensky—who incidentally is not the servant of an idea—"You haven't mastered the idea, but the idea has mastered you."

This strange possession comes about because we think ideas not just with our brains; an idea is "felt," it is "carried out in practice."

The most potent and most fascinating of these ideas which seize man is the idea of total destruction because it arises directly from the vacuum. [It is] the most powerful *inversion* of Creation. And since the vacuum is not just belief in God but the faith in incarnation—the Word became flesh—this idea, too, finds its incarnation in living men. *Notebooks:* "The idea which seizes him dominates him totally, but does not so much rule his thought as use him for its incorporation. And once *incarnated* it demands the immediate transformation into action." For "to change one's conviction is to change immediately one's whole life." This phenomenon, that an idea becomes personified and is acted out, is taken with utmost seriousness, is according to Dostoevsky what distinguishes the Russian ideologues from their Western brethren. Since they have the true faith, they become all the more dangerous when they lose it. On the other hand, the incarnation of the ideas means that their holder can become an *idol:* Stavrogin for Verkhovensky: "Without you I am a fly, a bottled idea; Columbus without America." The idol: instead of God become man, man is to become God. "One magnificent despotic will like an idol." Verkhovensky is not ruled by an idea as the others in self-deception: He does not believe in progress etc. Just as Stavrogin is not ruled by an idea because he "can never lose his reason" (a propos of Kirillov) he "cannot be interested in an idea to such a degree." Precisely for this reason he can become an idol for Verkhovensky. The true opposite of good is not evil or crime, not Fedka but Stavrogin, [but] mere indifference. The new God would be sheer indifference.

The strength [of this novel is] not in the argument but in the concrete presentation of characters and plots. But the most persuasive [argument would derive from] the thought of the incontestable grandeur of the content of beliefs as contrasted with the shallowness of these modern ideas. If men become what they think, wouldn't it be better for them to stick to the notion of Christ even if it were not the truth: Shatov to Stavrogin who had harbored this thought—the thought of an unbeliever!—"But didn't you tell me that if it were mathematically proved to you that the truth excludes Christ, you'd prefer to stick to Christ rather than to the truth?" (Strange that Dostoevsky never asked himself how people lived either before Christ or in other countries. He seems to believe that each people has its own gods and has to stick to them; to lose one's people (emigrants) means to lose one's gods. This [is] of course an entirely atheistic thought.)

⌇

4. We have left out of [this] account an altogether different story, a kind of non-plot, and its hero: Stavrogin and Kirillov. You can put the

question: What happens when atheism seizes noble natures? And the result on the plane of action is the *act gratuit*—an action which is entirely unmotivated: The Leading by the Nose; the marriage to Marya—"the shame and senseless[ness] of it reached the pitch of genius." (The fire and the murders are also called "senseless actions" but they have an aim, to compromise Stavrogin.) Finally Kirillov's suicide: "To do it without any cause at all, simply for self-will."

These are the people who want to be Gods—the sin of Superbia or pride. (Augustine: Not to serve God but to want to imitate him!) Self-will: a will that is entirely unmotivated except by itself, by affirming itself. Only this is freedom because every other act is motivated by something, hence affected by something outside itself.

Connected with atheism: "To recognize that there is no God and not to recognize at the same instant that one is God oneself is an absurdity," for the simple reason that we have such a notion as "god." This notion is inherent in life: "Man has done nothing but invent God so as to go on living, and not kill himself." Freedom means freedom from this invented master; once it is realized "man will be sovereign and . . . live in the greatest glory." There is only one hitch: even this glorious being must die. And his death is certainly not due to his self-will. If he can make himself *will* his death once, he is free. Kirillov kills himself as the savior of mankind: he is still "only a god against my will." He is still unhappy because he "is *bound* to assert my will." Once he has asserted his self-will the "physical nature of man will change" and will not need a god anymore. But one cannot say that he kills himself for any specific motives, only to assert his self-will. Absolute freedom is absolute destruction because you are bound to destroy everything that could affect and bind you. The supreme good that *binds* you is life itself. Hence, in order to be free you must destroy yourself.

This *act gratuit* is in precise connection with Stavrogin's indifference: if you take freedom to be the faculty of choosing between two alternatives, i.e., good and evil, you can never be sure that you are free: the alternative for which you decide exerts an attractive force on your will and the will is no longer free. Hence: you can show your freedom [only] by complete indifference like Stavrogin and commit suicide out of boredom and also out of pride. Out of boredom—every interest binds you, you become its servant. Or by denying life itself as the last and deepest motive force as it were. The trouble is only that once you are *free* you *are* no longer; hence, this may be noble but it means that man has lost his reason. The second hitch is in the plurality of men: if each man recognizes that he is god, then the idea is already carried to absurdity. To say: all men are gods or to say no man is God amounts to the same. How would these gods owe obedience to those who are like them? And how could absolute sovereignty be achieved? Stavrogin is aware of this absurdity. He knows that the only alternative on this level is: indifference. He does not want to be God like Kirillov. Stavrogin admires Kirillov and first does not want to commit suicide because it does not solve the absurdity of the concept of freedom: it is only a grandiose gesture. And its grandeur [consists in] the overcoming of fear. But Stavrogin does not know fear. He then takes his own life without further ado—he hangs himself, leaves no note, no testament, no confession of faith. He admits he is defeated.

~

5. That is where Dostoevsky leaves us, and I shall not try and give you solutions to the problems. (We would have to raise the question of the Will: is freedom a property of the Will?) Instead: Please be aware of the unique form of dialogue in these novels: it is as though naked soul speaks to naked soul. Intimacy approaching telepathy, i.e., the abolition of all distances: what somebody says is answered by: I knew it; if somebody arrives unexpectedly there will always be one who did expect the unexpected. [This is] the opposite of the French but also the English novel (where even the language has lost the Thou). Then the degree of intensity, of sheer passion in this intimacy. Compared with intimacy of this intensity, Western civilized society is hypocritical, full of lies; here all appearances immediately lead into the interior of the soul. The appearance is never a façade.

Most important, however, is this: the world, as an objective datum, is somehow absent. No descriptions, it is not a topic of dialogue; hence the multitude of perspectives from which you can see it (Balzac) is absent. The topic is not the world but some ultimate concern.

This intimacy can be realized only within one's own people. It is carried along by a knowledge that we find ordinarily only in certain very close family relationships. Hence, Dostoevsky's insistence that you are lost when you lose your people, that you lose God when you leave it. Separation from the people means separation from the whole world, the loss of the distinction between good and evil, along with "boredom and a tendency toward idleness."

Untitled lecture notes. The exact date is uncertain. The Library of Congress assigns it to the year 1967; but Arendt clearly draws from *The Notebooks for "The Possessed,"* which first appeared in English in 1968 (edited by Edward Wasiolek and translated by Victor Terras for the University of Chicago Press). She may have had an advance copy of the *Notebooks,* however, since she had been teaching at the University of Chicago during that time.

Arendt's lecture notes include a number of mnemonic jottings, most of which I have eliminated; I have also regularized the transcriptions of Russian names and corrected some minor spelling and grammar errors.

Dostoevsky's *Possessed* (1872), sometimes translated as *The Demons* or *The Devils,* describes the political disorder of nineteenth-century Russia, as revolutionary and anarchistic ideas become tools for the aggrandizement of sheer power.—Ed.

§ 32 Emerson Address

American Academy of Arts and Sciences
April 9, 1969

Mr. President, Mr. Trilling, Fellows of the Academy, Ladies and Gentlemen:

I thank you. It is good to be recognized, and membership in this body whose very distinction lies in its, today, almost unique combination of the arts and the sciences, means recognition that counts since it comes from one's peers. To be honored means perhaps not more, but something different. We may think that we have a claim to recognition; we earn it though we don't necessarily deserve it; but we never earn or deserve an award or an honor. These are gifts freely and gratuitously bestowed, and their meaning, at least to me, is not recognition but welcome. And if it is good to be recognized, it is better to be welcomed, precisely because this is something we can neither earn nor deserve.

To receive the Emerson-Thoreau Medal, however, has still another significance for me. Hermann Grimm once wrote to Emerson: "When I think of America I think of you, and America appears to me as the first country of the world."[1] Not only in the last century, but still in the first third of our century Emerson was one of the very few American authors with whom we, who grew up and were educated in Europe, were intimately acquainted before we came to this country. I have always read him as a kind of American Montaigne, and I discovered with great joy, only recently, how close Emerson himself felt to Montaigne.[2] When he first read him in translation, it seemed to him "as if [he] had written the book [himself] in some former life, so sincerely it spoke my thought and experience" (Journals, March 1843). What Emerson and Montaigne have most obviously in common is that they are both humanists rather than philosophers, and that they therefore wrote essays rather than systems, aphorisms rather than books. (This, incidentally, was the reason why Nietzsche, the black sheep among the philosophers, liked Emerson so much.) Both thought chiefly, exclusively, about human matters, and both lived a life of thought. "Life," said Emerson, "consists of what a man is thinking of all day." This kind of thinking can no more become a profession than living itself, hence, this is not the *vita contemplativa,* the philosopher's way of life who has made thinking his profession. Philosophers, as a rule, are rather serious animals; whereas what is so striking in both Emerson and Montaigne is their *serenity,* a serenity that is in no ways conformist or complacent—"I like the sayers of No better than the sayers of Yes," said Emerson—a cheerfulness that is pervaded by a quiet, reconciled melancholy—"Every man is wanted, and no man is wanted much." This, as it were, *innocent* cheerfulness, more innocent in Emerson than in Montaigne, is perhaps today the greatest difficulty for us. When we read in one of Emerson's best poems: "From all that's fair, from all that's foul, / Peals out a cheerful song. . . . But in the darkest meanest things / There alway, alway something sings. . . . But in the mud and scum of things / There alway, alway something sings," I am sure we feel more nostalgia than kinship. What Emerson dealt out was, as he once remarked about the "true preacher," a "life passed through the fire of thought," and whatever the fire of thought might have done to it, this life itself was still untroubled compared to ours, untroubled, more specifically, by bad thoughts.

Thus, we find in Emerson what former ages called wisdom, and that is something which has never existed in abundance or been in great demand. Embedded in this wisdom there are profound insights and observations which we have lost to our detriment, and which we may be well advised to unearth again now, when we are forced to rethink what the humanities are all about. For this great humanist, the humanities were simply those disciplines that dealt with language (which does not mean linguistics), and in the center of all thoughts about language, he found the poet, "the Namer or language-maker." Let me in conclusion read to you a few sentences which to me sound like the conclusive and still valid confession of the true humanist. The poet, he writes, names "things sometimes after their appearance, sometimes after their essence, and giving to every one its own name and not another's, [he] rejoices the intellect, which delights in detachment or boundary. The poets made all the words, and therefore language is *the archives of history,* and, if we must say it, a sort of tomb for the muses. For though the origin of most of our words is forgotten, each word was at first a stroke of genius, and obtained currency because for the moment it symbolized the world to the first speaker and hearer. The etymologist finds the deadest word to have been once a brilliant picture. Language is fossil poetry."

The untitled text reproduces a typescript Arendt wrote for her acceptance of the Emerson-Thoreau Medal awarded to her by the American Academy of Arts and Sciences on April 9, 1969.

Ralph Waldo Emerson (1803–1882) was an American philosopher and poet. Trained as a Unitarian minister, he decided against becoming a pastor. In his seminal essay "Nature" (1836), he laid the ground for American "transcendentalism." It is perhaps of some interest that Arendt mentions Henry David Thoreau (1817–1862), the philosopher and political theorist, only in conjunction with the medal she had been awarded.—Ed.

§ 33 Afterword to Robert Gilbert, *No Donkey Has Lost Me While Galloping*

Seht, da liegen die Gerühmten
Lässig in den stets beblümten
Sarkophagen Bein an Bein

Wir dagegen, Lorbeerlose,
Müssen ohne Denkmalspose
Vor Gott stehend ewig sein!

[Look at the famous ones
Lying casually and forever covered in flowers
In their caskets one by one—

But we, who are without laurels,
Must be eternal, while we stand
Before God without looking like statues!]

We are all born without laurels. We grew up without laurels, and as children, if we were lucky, we discovered something called "poesy" [*das Poetische*], which lies at the root of all poetry [*Dichtung*]. From that time—not entirely blessed, but at least not yet subject to mandatory schooling—we have managed to salvage a few things. What these things are, of course, depends on our backgrounds. But whatever else we may have retained, nursery rhymes are always among them. If one came from Berlin, as in this case, the rhymes ran: "Eene meene ming mang, / Oogen Fleesch und Beene . . . Ose pose packe dich, / eia weia weg! [Eeny, meeny, miny, moe. . . .]."[1] (In Königsberg, which is also a beautiful place,[2] the "Children's Sing-Song" sounded a little different.) The first sophisticated poems followed right on the heels of these rhymes: "Dunkel war's, der Mond schien helle / Schnee lag auf der grünen Flur, / als ein Wagen blitzesschnelle / Langsam um die Ecke fuhr [It was dark, the moon shone brightly / Snow covering the green fields, / when a car rode by very quickly / and slowly turned a corner]." Soon afterwards, when one's imagination was already being fed by the Grimm brothers' fairytales, which are also called "Grim [*Grimmige*] Fairytales," there followed one of the miracles from *The Youth's Magic Horn*, or, for some, "The Two Grenadiers," the author of which Robert Gilbert recalled so gloriously in his own "Réveil."[3] And it is not without reason that it is none other than Heinrich Heine who should have come across an entire society without laurels, which is sometimes called "the people" and which the literati of all times have always found a little questionable—Heine, who may be famous [*berühmt*] but who was hardly ever honored [*gerühmt*] and therefore remains without a monument to this day. The "Lorelei" of this German Jew could not be kept from the people, not even by the twelve-year reign of the Thousand Year Reich. Laurels could certainly be taken away from him, and the song could be said to be written by an anonymous author; but for us, a great compliment was thus paid to him, perhaps the greatest compliment that could ever be paid to a poet. It was as though they had been forced to include the Jew among the anonymous poets through whom the people—themselves bereft of laurels—had spoken: as though his poem, the product of his pen, really belonged to *The Youth's Magic Horn*.

Those who know about the poesy of childhood as the origin of all works of poetry—those who have not allowed their recollection of the primordial times in which there were no such things as laurels to evaporate into the commotion of everyday life and the inanity of career tracks—will have no difficulty recognizing Robert Gilbert as the successor of Heine whom he otherwise never really had. Heine himself knew that his "post" would be left "vacant." And one can decipher the answer to the question "But which post is it really?" in his own writing—it is the post of the good drummer and his "doctrine," which does not suit the talk of the salon:

> Schlage die Trommel und fürchte dich nicht,
> Und küsse die Merketenderin!
> Das ist die ganze Wissenschaft,
> das ist der Bücher tiefster Sinn.
>
> . . .
>
> Ich hab' sie begriffen, weil ich gescheit,
> Und weil ich ein guter Trommler bin.
>
> [Beat the drum and have no fear
> And kiss the market woman!
> That's all there is to science,
> That's the deepest meaning in books.
>
> . . .
>
> I've understood this, because I'm shrewd
> And because I'm a good drummer.][4]

Anonymity may perhaps belong to whoever takes up this post; but there is no question that the post requires a Heinean insouciance about immortality. Robert Gilbert, for one, learned early on that the price for real popularity can be a lack of widespread "name recognition." People all over Germany sang his popular hits in the 1920s and early 30s, but the author of these songs was known only to experts in the entertainment industry, which at least—after the War—provided him with something of a monopoly on the translation of the American musicals that followed upon the success of *My Fair Lady*.[5] One cannot therefore place Gilbert's work among the established literary genres. In literary terms, he belongs nowhere—least of all among those who are blessed by the light muse of a Kästner or a Tucholsky.[6] Early in his life, Gilbert said all that needs to be said about something so beloved in literary circles, namely comparison (how else, after all, could scholars write weighty tomes and thus fulfill the socially indispensable function of scholarship?):

> Nee, Heinrich Zille, nee,
> War keen Daumier.
> Er war ooch nich sein Wille.
> Er war eb'n Heinrich Zille.[7]
>
> [No, Heinrich Zille, no way
> He was no Daumier
> That was never his will
> He was just Heinrich Zille.]

Of course, his father, Jean Gilbert, had already struck it rich on the basis of popular songs ("Baby, You're the Twinkle in my Eye"), operettas, and similarly inspired spoofs, going from the position of a lowly musician in a variety show to that of a circus director who rode on the high horse in the Hagenbeck Circus, all the way to a "posh Wannsee mansion"—until the year 1933, which prepared a rather abrupt end to all this splendor.[8] What arose out of such a heritage was not Heinean popularity, however; it was only the raw talent that first makes such popularity possible, namely an uncanny facility with rhyme and a high degree of musicality.

The pop tunes of yesteryear include many genuine folk songs that have since become part of the German language. From *The White Horse Inn*: "The Love of Sailors"; "I don't have a car, don't have an estate / I've got only one thing / and that's you love"; "It must be a wonderful thing / to be loved by you"; "It only happens once, it won't happen again / it's too good to be true." Finally, the dirge of the '20s, the Eichendorffian-Berliner pop tune of the unemployed:[9]

> Keenen Sechser in der Tasche,
> bloß 'nen Stempelschein.
> Durch die Löcher der Kledasche
> Kiekt die Sonne rein.
>
> . . .
>
> Stellste dir zum Stempeln an,
> wird det Elend nicht behoben—
> wer hat der, dur armer Mann,
> abjebaut so hoch da droben?
>
> [Not a dime in my pocket
> just a card to stamp
> Through the holes in my clothes
> the sun comes shining in
>
> . . .
>
> You get in line for stamping
> that don't do nothing for your misery–
> poor fella, who's got it in
> for you high up there?]

And if the Berlin Jews had been able to emigrate as a group a few years later, and if they had still felt like singing—which is not altogether inconceivable, since Auschwitz was still far off—the song that everyone would have taken to heart was already prepared for the journey:

> Lebwohl, Berlin. Er muß geschieden sein.
> Rixdorf, ich muß dich lassen.
> Anhalter Bahnhof. Ja, da steig' ich ein
> Und zieh' dahin mein Straßen.
>
> . . .
>
> Zollrevision. Devisen. Paßkontrolle. Ach,
> Man läßt mich durch. Es ist gelungen.
> *Da murmelt noch der letzte deutsche Bach:*
> *Es ist in Ros' entsprungen.*
>
> [Goodbye, Berlin. We must part.
> Rixdorf, I must take leave.
> Anhalt Station. Yes, that's where I get on.
> to leave my streets behind.
>
> . . .

Customs. Currency. Passport check. Well,
they let me through. I made it.
While the last German brook murmurs yet:
There is a Rose in Bloom.]

Of course, on foreign streets and in foreign alleys, this farewell song stood no chance of becoming a pop tune, which is probably why it was honored by being included in the poetry anthology *The Spree Always Still Flows Through Berlin* (Blanvalet, 1971),[10] along with the Stamping Song and the Zille verses quoted above. As far as the great popular songs are concerned, everyone must really rack their brains to think of any. People in Germany still consider themselves too refined and too cultured [*gebildet*] for pop tunes and chansons, regardless of when they were written, and the same is true with respect to Yvette Guilbert and Edith Piaf.[11] These songs will have to remain all but forgotten until some young interlopers with a knack for poesy—and who had more of a knack for poesy in the poet-rich Germany of a different era than Clemens Brentano?—collect them and bestow them on their descendants in a second volume of *The Youth's Magic Horn.*

There is hardly another language in which the poesy of the people has been merged as seamlessly and effortlessly with high poetry, while still remaining true to itself, as it has been in German. This is evident in every verse here, in which lines from Hölderlin to Kafka could be inserted without effort—as quotations, of course, but without quotation marks, for they have become anonymous and without laurels, thus never in the least bit appearing epigonal. These are the broken sounds and reverberations of many melodies that naturally present themselves to the German speaker. He who masters the German language so perfectly—

Ihr sollt zusammenschlagen! Erst die Hacken.
Zweitens die Welt. Am Schluß die Hände überm Kopf

[You are supposed to bury everything! First, your heels in the ground.
Second, the world. Finally, your face in your hands.]

—to him, the status of the epigone must have been very appealing, even when the horror of the times, which should perhaps be called the negation of time [*Unzeit*], forever made it impossible for him to tread the often magically beautiful path of the latecomers, a path that Hofmannsthal, the young George and Rudolf Borchardt were still able to walk, which leads back to old ways of making it possible for poems to be eminently singable.[12] The blocking of this path was final, for "Ach, auch das Ermordern von Mördern / Bleibt ein dunkles Geschäft [Ah, even the murder of murderers / Remains a dark business]." Thus:

> Erspart uns das nachgeträufelte Labsal,
> Ihr höchlichst Erhabenen,
> Vor jedem saftig besudelten Grabmal
> Der unlängst Begrabenen.
>
> Mir ist der Weg nicht mehr gangbar
> Stelzfüßig feierlich—
> Zwischen den Liedern so sangbar
> Schrecken die Geier mich.
>
> [Spare us from belatedly sprinkled-on pleasures,
> You who are most sublime,
> Before every lushly soiled tombstone
> Of those recently buried
>
> I cannot walk this path anymore
> With properly solemn steps–
> Between those melodious songs
> The vultures frighten me.]

All of this is true enough. But what is also true is that these horrors are not enough to erase the original, marvelous wonder of being-there [*Da-sein*]:

> Nicht zu fassen
> Dort der Baum
> In dem noch Vögel flöten.
>
> [Impossible to grasp
> The tree over there
> In which birds are still warbling.]

Of course, the tree and the birds are still there, at least for a while, as is the moon, despite all efforts, and the stars, the woods, and the deer. Even

> Die Kühe glöckeln sich nachdenklich in ihr Tal
> Und alles klingt, als wär' es nie erklungen, nie
> Gesungen worden. Nicht einmal dies ein Mal.

[The cows make their bells ring thoughtfully into their valley
And everything sounds as though it had never resounded, had never
Been sung. Not even this once.]

Poesy cannot be exterminated so long as there is still the wonder we
have learned during childhood. As far as the question who really are the
poets, this can be answered, without further ado, in an unceremonious,
Berlinian style:

Denn ick bin bloß auf Besuch hier,
so von eins bis hundert—
. . .
Und wo andre längst zu Haus sind,
wo se wohl teils Mann, teils Maus sind,
steh' ick permanent verwundert
mit der Klinke in der Hand.

[For I'm just passing through
like from one to a hundred—
. . .
And while others have long since been at home,
part man, part mouse, as the case may be,
I'm permanently astonished
with the doorknob in my hand.]

The inflections of Berlin are consciously left out of this volume, and with
good reason. Unlike Northern or Southern Lower German (*Plattdeutsch* or
Alemannisch), the German of Berlin was never a real dialect. It was the
city's way of talking and thinking, and few would have thought it capable
of anything lyrical before Gilbert created a place and a rank for its poesy.
But Berlin German has by no means disappeared from those High German
poems; it has only been in a certain sense cleansed, so that it can rise into
High German, as if the Berlinian way of thinking, having lost its regional
charm, should now test itself out and see what it can do. Only a Berliner
could have experienced and described his own biography as an "Odyssey
of an Organ-Grinder."[13] And yet nowhere else does Heine rise so clearly,
"gewappnet hervor aus dem Grab [shielded from the grave in full armor],"
albeit strangely altered—still a Jew, to be sure, but now entering "ins Welt-
gebäude, / Warschauerstraße überm Pferdestall [into the cosmos, / Warsaw
Street above the stable]," while always still "foolishly" writing on—

Was nicht so unbedingt
Zwischen den Göttern und Laotse
Buchstabiert zu werden verdient

[What does not so unconditionally
Deserve to be spelled out
Between the gods and Laotse]

—forever writing on, because every moment of this, our only life demands to be recorded, but only if the recording is done in verse, for otherwise its poetic essence would be lost. Now, however, this must be done
in the mode of thought that characterizes the metropolis, in this extremely quick (Gilbert's "Odyssey" is best read in a rapid sing-song), this
not exactly intelligent but, rather, nimble-witted way of thinking that will
not let itself be fooled, least of all by itself, neither sarcastically nor hu-
morously, neither cynically nor pathetically, in this way of thinking that
always speaks up and says what it has to say. This way of thinking and
speaking—which is no less natural than the songs of birds living in the
trees and which has very unfairly been reproached for the asphalt in the
midst of which it makes its home—dates back to the times of "City air
grants freedom."[14] This way of thinking, although not the specific dialect,
could travel with its emigrants to the great cities of the Western world,
and even take on the foreign dialect of Vienna, that other German metropolis, something that could hardly have happened in a Frankfurt or a
Leipzig. The "Odyssey" tells of this migration. During this migration, the
Berlinian idiom made the transition to High German, just as other idioms have done; but its mode of thinking, its mother-wit has remained as
it was. One would hope that this way of thinking is still alive in Berlin; its
mother-wit still has some parallels in Paris and London, and even in New
York, the most threatened metropolis of them all. But who could deny
that it is now in the process of disappearing—not, to be sure, because the
"esprit sérieux" of literati and avant-gardists of all kinds could ever wipe it
out, but because the cities themselves stand defenseless against a double
threat, which strikes at the very substance of the metropolis: a rampant
consumer society and unsolvable traffic problems? The carefree liveliness,
the joy of sheer existence that pulses throughout these lines of Gilbert's
verse belongs to this substance. But so does a way of thinking in which it is
always recognized that every coin has two sides, that our *comédie humaine*
is never either all tragedy or all comedy but always and at every moment

both at the same time. Only tragicomedies can stand up to this rapid shrewdness, which is always reeling and turning—even against itself. Whatever counts as divine here is laughing and crying at once.

~

Dear reader, this is an afterword to something that does not require a commendatory preface, and it is written by a reader just like you. The lines you remember and the thoughts to which they give rise may be different ones. There are many possibilities. Perhaps the poet made you as shamelessly talkative as he did me. That would be best, for then you would write your own afterword for yourself and send it to the author.

Originally published as "Nachwort" to Robert Gilbert, *Mich hat kein Esel im Galopp verloren: Gedichte aus Zeit und Unzeit* (Munich: Piper, 1972), 133–41; translated by Martin Klebes.—Ed.

§ 34 Remembering Wystan H. Auden, Who Died in the Night of the Twenty-eighth of September, 1973

I met Auden late in his life and mine—at an age when the easy knowledgeable intimacy of friendships concluded in one's youth can no longer be attained, because not enough life is left, or expected to be left, to share with another. Thus, we were very good friends but not intimate friends. Moreover, there was a reserve in him that discouraged familiarity, not that I tested it ever; I rather gladly respected it as the necessary secretiveness of the great poet, who must have taught himself early not to talk in prose, loosely and at random, of things that he knew how to say much more satisfactorily in the condensed concentration of poetry. Reticence may be the *déformation professionnelle* of the poet. In Auden's case, this seemed all the more likely because much of his work, in utter simplicity, arose out of the spoken word, out of idioms of everyday language—like "Lay your sleeping head, my love, Human on my faithless arm."[1] This kind of perfection is very rare; we find it in some of the greatest of Goethe's poems, and it must exist in most of Pushkin's works, because their hallmark is that they are untranslatable.[2] The moment poems of this kind are wrenched from their original abode, they disappear in a cloud of banality. Here all depends on the "fluent gestures" in "elevating facts from the prosaic to the poetic"—a point that the critic Clive James stressed in his essay on Auden in *Commentary* in December 1973.[3] Where such fluency is achieved, we are magically convinced that everyday speech is latently poetic, and, taught by the poets, our ears open up to the true mysteries of language. The very untranslatability of one of Auden's poems is what, many years ago, convinced me of his greatness. Three German translators had tried their luck and killed mercilessly one of my favorite poems, "If I Could Tell You" (*Collected Shorter Poems 1927–1957*), which arises naturally from two colloquial idioms—"Time will tell" and "I told you so":

> Time will say nothing but I told you so,
> Time only knows the price we have to pay;
> If I could tell you I would let you know.
>
> If we should weep when clowns put on their show,
> If we should stumble when musicians play,
> Time will say nothing but I told you so. . . .
>
> The winds must come from somewhere when they blow,
> There must be reasons why the leaves decay;
> Time will say nothing but I told you so. . . .
>
> Suppose the lions all get up and go,
> And all the brooks and soldiers run away;
> Will Time say nothing but I told you so?
> If I could tell you I would let you know.[4]

I met Auden in the autumn of 1958, but I had seen him before, in the late forties, at a publisher's party. Although we exchanged not a word on that occasion, I had remembered him quite well—a nice-looking, well-dressed, very English gentleman, friendly and relaxed. I did not recognize him ten years later, for now his face was marked by those famous deep wrinkles, as though life itself had delineated a kind of face-scape to make manifest "the heart's invisible furies." If you listened to him, nothing could seem more deceptive than this appearance. Time and again, when to all appearances he could not cope any more, when his slum apartment was so cold that the plumbing no longer functioned and he had to use the toilet in the liquor store at the corner, when his suit (no one could convince him that a man needed at least two suits, so that one could go to the cleaner, or two pairs of shoes so that one pair could be repaired: a subject of an endless ongoing debate between us throughout the years) was covered with spots or worn so thin that his trousers would suddenly split from top to bottom—in brief, whenever disaster hit before your very eyes, he would begin to more or less intone an utterly idiosyncratic version of "Count your blessings." Since he never talked nonsense or said something obviously silly—and since I always remained aware that this was the voice of a very great poet—it took me years to realize that in his case it was not appearance that was deceptive, and that it was fatally wrong to ascribe what I saw of his way of life to the harmless eccentricity of a typical English gentleman.

I finally saw the misery, and somehow realized vaguely his compelling need to hide it behind the "Count-your-blessings" litany, yet I found it difficult to understand fully why he was so miserable and was unable to do anything about the absurd circumstances that made everyday life so unbearable for him. It certainly could not be lack of recognition. He was reasonably famous, and such ambition could anyhow never have counted for much with him, since he was the least vain of all authors I have ever met—completely immune to the countless vulnerabilities of ordinary vanity. Not that he was humble; in his case it was self-confidence that protected him against flattery, and this self-confidence existed prior to recognition and fame, prior also to achievement. (Geoffrey Grigson, in the *Times Literary Supplement,* reports the following dialogue between the very young Auden and his tutor at Oxford. "Tutor: 'And what are you going to do, Mr. Auden, when you leave the university?' Auden: 'I am going to be a poet.' Tutor: 'Well—in that case you should find it very useful to have read English.' Auden: 'You don't understand. I am going to be a great poet.'")[5] It never left him, because it was not acquired by comparisons with others, or by winning a race in competition; it was natural—interconnected, but not identical, with his enormous ability to do with language, and do quickly, whatever he pleased. (When friends asked him to produce a birthday poem for the next evening at six o'clock, they could be sure of getting it; clearly this is possible only in the absence of self-doubt.) But even this did not go to his head, for he did not claim, or perhaps even aspire to, final perfection. He constantly revised his own poems, agreeing with Valéry: "A poem is never finished; it is only abandoned."[6] In other words, he was blessed with that rare self-confidence which does not need admiration and the good opinion of others, and can even withstand self-criticism and self-examination without falling into the trap of self-doubt. This has nothing to do with arrogance but is easily mistaken for it. Auden was never arrogant except when he was provoked by some vulgarity; then he protected himself with the rather abrupt rudeness characteristic of English intellectual life.

Stephen Spender, the friend who knew him so well, has stressed that "throughout the whole development of [Auden's] poetry . . . his theme had been love" (had it not occurred to Auden to change Descartes' *"Cogito ergo sum"* by defining man as the "bubble-brained creature" that said "I'm loved therefore I am"?), and at the end of the address that Spender gave in memory of his late friend at the Cathedral in Oxford he told of asking Auden about a reading he had given in America: "His face lit up with a smile that altered its lines, and he said: 'They loved me!' "⁷ They did not admire him, they *loved* him: here, I think, lies the key both to his extraordinary unhappiness and to the extraordinary greatness—intensity—of his poetry. Now, with the sad wisdom of remembrance, I see him as having been an expert in the infinite varieties of unrequited love, among which the infuriating substitution of admiration for love must surely have loomed large.⁸ And beneath these emotions there must have been from the beginning a certain animal *tristesse* that no reason and no faith could overcome:

> The desires of the heart are as crooked as corkscrews,
> Not to be born is the best for man;
> The second-best is a formal order,
> The dance's pattern; dance while you can.⁹

So he wrote in "Death's Echo," in *Collected Shorter Poems.* When I knew him, he would not have mentioned the best any longer, so firmly had he opted for the second-best, the "formal order," and the result was what Chester Kallman has so aptly named "the most dishevelled child of all disciplinarians."¹⁰ I think it was this *tristesse* and its "dance while you can" that made Auden feel so much attracted to and almost at home in the famous Berlin of the twenties, where *carpe diem* was practiced constantly in many variations. He once mentioned as a "disease" his early "addiction to German usages," but much more prominent than these, and less easy to get rid of, was the obvious influence of Bertolt Brecht, with whom I think he had more in common than he was ever ready to admit.¹¹ (In the late fifties, with Chester Kallman, he translated Brecht's *Rise and Fall of the City of Mahagonny*—a translation that was never published, presumably because of copyright difficulties. To this day, I know of no other adequate rendering of Brecht into English.) In merely literary terms, Brecht's influence can easily be traced in Auden's ballads—for instance, in the late, marvellous "Ballad of Barnaby," the tale of the tumbler who, having grown old and pious, "honoured the Mother-of-God" by tumbling for her; or in the early "little story / About Miss Edith Gee; / She lived in Clevedon Terrace / At Number 83."¹² What made this influence possible was that they both belonged to the post–First World War generation, with its curious mixture of despair and *joie de vivre,* its contempt for conventional codes of behavior, and its penchant for "playing it cool," which expressed itself in England, I suspect, in the wearing of the mask of the snob, while it expressed itself in Germany in a widespread pretense of wickedness, somewhat in the vein of Brecht's *The Threepenny Opera.* (In Berlin, one joked about this fashionable inverted hypocrisy, as one joked about everything: *"Er geht böse über den Kurfürstendamm"*— meaning, "That is probably all the wickedness he is capable of." After 1933, I think, nobody joked about wickedness anymore.)

In the case of Auden, as in the case of Brecht, inverted hypocrisy served to hide an irresistible inclination toward being good and doing good— something that both were ashamed to admit, let alone proclaim. This seems plausible for Auden, because he finally became a Christian, but it may be a shock at first to hear it about Brecht. Yet a close reading of his poems and plays seems to me almost to prove it. Not only are there the plays *Der Gute Mensch von Sezuan* [The Good Person of Sichuan] and *Die Heilige Johanna der Schlachthöfe* [Saint Joan of the Stockyards] but, perhaps more convincingly, there are these lines in the midst of the cynicism of *The Threepenny Opera:*

> *Ein guter Mensch sein! Ja, wer wär's nicht gern?*
> *Sein Gut den Armen geben, warum nicht?*
> *Wenn alle gut sind, ist* Sein *Reich nicht fern.*
> *Wer säße nicht sehr gern in* Seinem *Licht?*[13]

What drove these profoundly apolitical poets into the chaotic political scene of our century was Robespierre's *"zèle compatissant,"* the powerful urge toward *"les malheureux,"* as distinguished from any need for action toward *public* happiness, or any desire to change the world.

Auden, so much wiser—though by no means smarter—than Brecht, knew early that, "poetry makes nothing happen."[14] To him, it was sheer nonsense for the poet to claim special privileges or to ask for the indulgences that we are so happy to grant out of sheer gratitude. There was nothing more admirable in Auden than his complete sanity and his firm belief in sanity; in his eyes all kinds of madness were lack of discipline— "Naughty, naughty," as he used to say. The main thing was to have no illusions and to accept no thoughts—no theoretical systems—that would blind you to reality. He turned against his early leftist beliefs because events (the Moscow trials, the Hitler-Stalin pact, and experiences during the Spanish Civil War) had proved them to be "dishonest"—"shamefully" so, as he said in his foreword to the *Collected Shorter Poems*,[15] telling how he threw out what he once had written:

> History to the defeated
> may say alas but cannot help nor pardon.

To say this, he noted, was "to equate goodness with success." He protested that he had never believed in "this wicked doctrine"—a statement that I doubt, not only because the lines are too good, too precise, to have been produced for the sake of being "rhetorically effective," but because this was the doctrine everybody believed in during the twenties and thirties. Then came the time when

> In the nightmare of the dark
> All the dogs of Europe bark . . .
>
> Intellectual disgrace
> Stares from every human face—[16]

the time when it looked for quite a while as if the worst could happen and sheer evil could become a success. The Hitler-Stalin pact was the turning point for the left; now one had to give up all beliefs in history as the ultimate judge of human affairs.

In the forties, there were many who turned against their old beliefs, but there were very few who understood what had been wrong with those beliefs. Far from giving up their belief in history and success, they simply changed trains, as it were; the train of Socialism and Communism had been wrong, and they changed to the train of Capitalism or Freudianism or some refined Marxism, or a sophisticated mixture of all three. Auden, instead, became a Christian; that is, he left the train of history altogether. I don't know whether Stephen Spender is right in asserting that "prayer corresponded to his deepest need"—I suspect that his deepest need was simply to write verses—but I am reasonably sure that his sanity, the great good sense that illuminated all his prose writings (his essays and book reviews), was due in no small measure to the protective shield of orthodoxy. Its time-honored coherent meaningfulness that could be neither proved nor disproved by reason provided him, as it had provided Chesterton, with an intellectually satisfying and emotionally rather comfortable refuge against the onslaught of what he called "rubbish"; that is the countless follies of the age.

Rereading Auden's poems in chronological order and remembering him in the last years of his life, when misery and unhappiness had become more and more unbearable without, however, in the least touching either the divine gift or the blessed facility of the talent, I have become surer than ever that he was "hurt into poetry" even more than Yeats ("Mad Ireland hurt you into poetry"),[17] and that, despite his susceptibility to compassion, public political circumstances were not necessary to hurt him into poetry. What made him a poet was his extraordinary facility with and love for words, but what made him a great poet was the unprotesting willingness with which he yielded to the "curse" of vulnerability to "human *un*success" on all levels of human existence—vulnerability to the crookedness of the desires, to the infidelities of the heart, to the injustices of the world.

> Follow, poet, follow right
> To the bottom of the night,
> With your unconstraining voice
> Still persuade us to rejoice;
>
> With the farming of a verse
> Make a vineyard of the curse,
> Sing of human unsuccess
> In a rapture of distress;
>
> In the deserts of the heart
> Let the healing fountain start,
> In the prison of his days
> Teach the free man how to praise.[18]

Praise is the key-word of these lines, not praise of "the best of all possible worlds"—as though it were up to the poet (or the philosopher) to justify God's creation[19]—but praise that pitches itself against all that is most unsatisfactory in man's condition on this earth and sucks its own strength from the wound: somehow convinced, as the bards of ancient Greece were, that the gods spin unhappiness and evil things toward mortals so that they may be able to tell the tales and sing the songs.

I could (which you cannot)
Find reasons fast enough
To face the sky and roar
In anger and despair
At what is going on,
Demanding that it name
Whoever is to blame:
The sky would only wait
Till all my breath was gone
And then reiterate
As if I wasn't there
That singular command
I do not understand,
Bless what there is for being,
Which has to be obeyed, for
What else am I made for,
Agreeing or disagreeing?[20]

And the triumph of the private person was that the voice of the great poet never silenced the small but penetrating voice of sheer sound common sense whose loss has so often been the price paid for divine gifts. Auden never permitted himself to lose his mind—that is, to lose the "distress" in the "rapture" that rose out of it:

No metaphor, remember, can express
A real historical unhappiness;
Your tears have value if they make us gay;
O Happy Grief! is all sad verse can say.[21]

It seems, of course, very unlikely that young Auden, when he decided that he was going to be a *great* poet, knew the price he would have to pay, and I think it entirely possible that in the end—when not the intensity of his feelings and not the gift of transforming them into praise but the sheer physical strength of the heart to bear them and live with them gradually faded away—he considered the price too high. We, in any event—his audience, readers and listeners—can only be grateful that he paid his price up to the last penny for the everlasting glory of the English language. And his friends may find some consolation in his beautiful joke beyond the grave—that for more than one reason, as Spender said, "his wise unconscious self chose a good day for dying."[22] The wisdom to know "when to live and when to die" is not given to mortals, but Wystan, one would like to think, may have received it as the supreme reward that the cruel gods of poetry bestowed on the most obedient of their servants.

Originally published in *The New Yorker* 50 (January 20, 1975): 39–40, 45–46. Reprinted in *Harvard Advocate* 108 (1975): 42–45. A slightly earlier version was published in *W. H. Auden: A Tribute,* ed. Stephen Spender (London: Weidenfeld & Nicolson, 1975), 181–87.
Wystan Hugh Auden (1907–1973) was an English poet who moved to America, where he became a citizen in 1946. He and Arendt became friends in New York in the late 1950s.—Ed.

Editorial Note:
Texts in German and English

For five of the major texts in this volume—"Stefan Zweig: Jews in the World of Yesterday," "Franz Kafka, Appreciated Anew," "Culture and Politics," and the two essays devoted to Brecht—the English and German versions differ in some significant ways:. In the first three cases, the texts have been translated from the German; in the case of the latter two, the English texts are reproduced and notes have been added that detail the changes in the respective German versions.

The essays on Zweig and Kafka were probably originally written in German, although both were first published in English. A prefatory note to an essay that appeared in the same German volume as the reflections on Zweig and Kafka indicates as much: when "Organisierte Schuld" (Organized Guilt) was originally written, Arendt insists, it would have been pointless to publish it in German (see *Sechs Essays* [Heidelberg: Schneider, 1948], 33). And the same is doubtless true of the essays on Zweig and Kafka as well. The German versions of these essays are in any case substantially different from, and considerably longer than, the English versions.

"Culture and Politics" was originally written in German for a lecture Arendt delivered at a conference on "culture critique," which was held in conjunction with the celebration of the 800th anniversary of the founding of the city of Munich. Arendt had the essay translated into English and used this translation as the basis for an English essay that appeared under the title "Society and Culture." This essay was then refashioned into "The Crisis in Culture," which forms one of the chapters of *Between Past and Future*. Whereas the English versions emphasize the relation between culture and "mass culture," the German is more directly concerned with the affinity and antagonism between the sphere of culture and the practice of politics.

Prompted by the appearance of an English edition of Brecht's poetry, Arendt wrote an essay in English on the poet in 1948. Two years later she modified and slightly expanded this essay for its German version. I have included the English version of 1948, since it includes a number of comments on the manner in which Brecht can and cannot be translated into English. The single major passage she inserted into the German version and did not then retain in her later reflections on Brecht is included in the notes. In 1964, Arendt delivered a lecture on Brecht in English at Emory University that retrieves some of the material in her earlier essay but also includes a number of further remarks that were prompted in large part by her sense that the poet's decision to reside in East Germany robbed him of his poetic productivity. This lecture served as the basis for an essay she wrote for *The New Yorker* under the title "What is Permitted to Jove," which was later reprinted, with the addition of a scholarly apparatus, in *Men in Dark Times* under the title "Bertolt Brecht, 1898–1956." Attentive to the differences between an American and German audience, she revised this essay and published it in *Merkur* in 1969 under the title "Quod licet Jovi . . . : Reflexionen über den Dichter Bertolt Brecht und sein Verhältnis zur Politik." I have decided to publish the English version of the later Brecht essay for one simple reason: it clearly captures the manner in which Arendt wanted this essay to sound in English, for there is scarcely any difference in diction between the Emory lecture, the *New Yorker* version, and the *Men in Dark Times* version. Once again, the additions she made for the German version are included in the notes. I have chosen to give the essay the title of the German version, however, since the title of the essay in *Men in Dark Times* is obviously dictated by a principle that governs this collection alone. The fact that she returned to, and added further commentary on, the title under which the essay was originally published is sufficient reason to prefer it over the others.

Notes

Introduction

1. Hannah Arendt, *Lectures on Kant's Political Philosophy,* ed. Ronald Beiner (Chicago: University of Chicago Press, 1989), 9.

2. See Arendt, *Lectures,* esp. 44–47.

3. For Benjamin's discussion of this term, which he borrowed from Brecht, see the "Epilogue" to his "Work of Art in the Age of Its Technical Reproducibility," in *Gesammelte Schriften,* ed. Rolf Tiedemann and Hermann Schweppenhäuser (Frankfurt am Main: Suhrkamp, 1972–91), 7:382; *Selected Writings,* ed. Howard Eiland and Michael Jennings (Cambridge, Mass.: Harvard University Press, 1996–2003), 4:269. A version of this Benjamin text, along with many others discussed here, can also be found in Arendt's own edition of *Illuminations,* trans. Harry Zohn (New York: Schocken, 1968).

4. Arendt, *Lectures,* 63.

5. See Arendt, *Lectures,* esp. 79–80.

6. See Arendt, "Preface: The Gap between Past and Future," in *Between Past and Future: Eight Exercises in Political Thought,* enlarged ed. (New York: Penguin, 1977), 3–15. The aphorism from Char can be found in *Feuillets d'Hypnos* (Paris: Gallimard, 1946), 49: "Notre héritage n'est précédé d'aucun testament." The aphorism from Kafka can now be found in *Gesammelte Werke,* ed. Hans-Gerd Koch (Frankfurt am Main: Fischer, 1994), 11:177. At the end of the "Thinking" section of *The Life of the Mind,* Arendt again considers "the gap between past and future" and analyzes in greater detail Kafka's fragment; see *The Life of the Mind* (New York: Harcourt, 1978), 1:202–13. It should be noted that Arendt ends this section with a quotation from W. H. Auden.

7. All quotations in parentheses refer to pages in this volume.

8. See Franz Kafka's unfinished novel, *Der Verschollene* [The One Who Is Never Heard from Again], ed. Hans-Gerd Koch (Frankfurt am Main: Fischer, 1994), 295. Max Brod (1884–1964), Kafka's friend and faithless literary executor, first published this novel under the title *Amerika* in 1927. Arendt, who struggled with Brod's editions of Kafka's diaries while working at Schocken Books, would not have been aware of the title Kafka appended to his incomplete work.

9. Günther Anders, "Kafka Pro und Contra," in *Mensch ohne Welt: Schriften zur Literatur* (Munich: Beck, 1983), 119–20. Anders is here discussing, in particular, the posthumously published story entitled "Der Dorfschullehrer" (The Village Schoolmaster) and sometimes called "Der Riesenmaulwurf" (The Giant Mole). But the point of Anders' essay is that in this story Kafka, as it were, finally plays his hand. There is no extant version of Anders' lecture, which appeared under the title "Theologie ohne Gott" (Theology without God), and one may well wonder whether the idea of "pro and contra" is not largely a response to something he only came to realize in 1946, when the written version was prepared, namely, that a Kafkean conception of punishment without guilt would be particularly amenable to a postwar German public, who could ignore the reality of what had been done in the name of Germany by celebrating the fictional work of someone who was not actually its victim. This, in any case, is what Anders emphasizes in his preface to *Mensch ohne Welt* (see especially xxxii–xxxiii); but the essay itself is much more concerned with Kafka's own apparent celebration of an authentic ur-text that, as he emphatically recognizes, is nowhere to be found. Anders, incidentally, was a distant cousin of Benjamin's, and the two seemed to have collaborated on a radio script that anticipates Anders' revised title for his Kafka paper: "La traduction pro et contre" (Benjamin, *Gesammelte Schriften,* 6:157–60).

10. Stern, *Mensch ohne Welt,* xxxiv.

11. Walter Benjamin, "Franz Kafka. Eine Würdigung," *Jüdische Rundschau* 39 (December 12, 1934): 8 and (December 28, 1934): 6. The first complete version appeared in 1955; the first English translation appeared in *Illuminations,* 111–40.

12. See especially a remark in Convolute N of the *Arcades Project.* Responding to a letter from Max Horkheimer, Benjamin writes: "The corrective to this line of thinking may be found in the consideration that history is not simply a science but also and not least a form of remembrance [*Eingedenken*]" (*Gesammelte Schriften,* 5:589; *The Arcades Project,* trans. Howard Eiland and Kevin McLaughlin [Cambridge, Mass.: Harvard University Press, 1999], 471).

13. Arendt takes issue with the idea of genius in her essay on Benjamin: "Benjamin was a case in point: his father never recognized his claims, and their relations were extraordinarily bad. Another such case was Kafka, who—possibly because he really was something like a genius—was quite free of the genius mania of his environment, never claimed to be a genius, and ensured his financial independence by taking an ordinary job at the Prague workman's compensation office. (His rela-

tions with his father were of course equally bad, but for different reasons.) And still, no sooner had Kafka taken this position than he saw in it a 'running start for suicides,' as though he were obeying an order that says 'You have to earn your grave' " (*Men in Dark Times* [New York: Harcourt, Brace & World, 1968], 180). Throughout her essay on Benjamin, she compares his situation to Kafka's.

14. See Benjamin, "Über den Begriff der Geschichte," in *Gesammelte Schriften,* 1:697–98; "On the Concept of History," in *Selected Writings,* 4:392.

15. Benjamin entrusted the manuscript to Arendt, who brought it with her to the States. When Günther Anders wrote to Arendt and told her that Adorno and Horkheimer had decided against publishing Benjamin's text, she was livid: "It is a piece of fortune in misfortune that I have it [the manuscript]. I was finally obligated to give it to them [Horkheimer and Adorno], knowing that Benji had sent them a copy that had not yet arrived. . . . I am entirely alone and in such terrible despair and anxiety that they will not have it printed. And so insanely furious that I could simply murder them" (Hannah Arendt and Heinrich Blücher, *Briefe, 1936–1968* [Munich: Piper, 1996], 127). Arendt may have decided to write her Kafka essay in part in order to get at least one fragment of Benjamin's text into print.

16. Perhaps in order to avoid this ambiguity, Arendt emphasized in the first sentence of the German version that Kafka was Jewish (94).

17. In addition to Arendt's own studies of German-Jewish infatuation with *Bildung,* beginning with her essay on the Berlin salon and continuing through her book on Rahel Varnhagen, it is worth mentioning here the work of an eminent scholar of this phenomenon, George Mosse, *German Jews Beyond Judaism* (Indianapolis: Indiana University Press, 1985). See also David Sorkin, *The Transformation of German Jewry, 1780–1840* (Oxford: Oxford University Press, 1987).

18. For Arendt's discussion of the "strata-state" (*Ständestaat*), see "Adam Müller—Renaissance?" (Chapter 4).

19. Friedrich Schiller, *On the Aesthetic Education of Man in a Series of Letters,* ed. and trans. Elizabeth Wilkinson and L. A. Willoughby (Oxford: Clarendon Press, 1967), 219. Schiller was clearly on Arendt's mind when she wrote "Culture and Politics," since she quotes from his poem "Ode to Friends."

20. Ibid., 19.

21. Ibid.

22. See Martin Heidegger, "Hölderlin und das Wesen der Dichtung," in *Erläuterungen zu Hölderlins Dichtung* (Frankfurt am Main: Klostermann, 1971), 31–45; "Hölderlin and the Essence of Poetry," in *Existence and Being,* ed. Werner Brock, trans. Douglas Scott (Chicago: Regnery, 1949), 270–91.

23. Arendt is responding to Walter Muschg's lecture entitled "Dichtung und Kultur" (Poetry and Culture), as recorded in *Untergang oder Übergang: 1. Internationaler Kulturkritikerkongress in München, 1958,* ed. Alfred Machionini (Munich: Banaschewski, 1959), 200.

24. Marcuse's comments are recorded in *Untergang oder Übergang*, 164.

25. Heine entitled the poem "Die Heimkehr" (The Homecoming) and originally dedicated it to Rahel Varnhagen; after she died the dedication was dropped. For a German-English version, see Heine, *Verse*, ed. and trans. Peter Branscombe (Harmondsworth: Penguin, 1968), 40–57.

26. See Arendt, *Lectures*, esp. 46–51.

27. In *The Life of the Mind*, Arendt places Auden and Rilke together precisely in the context of praise (see 2:92).

Note: All subsequent notes not produced by the editor are Arendt's own.

Chapter 1

1. The following discussions do not claim to produce anything more or anything other than what can be said in a line-by-line commentary. A thoroughgoing, systematic analysis would be inappropriate to the sense of the poetry.

2. Translations of the *Elegies* are based on Stephen Mitchell's translations; see Rainer Maria Rilke, *Selected Poetry*, ed. and trans. Steven Mitchell (New York: Random House, 1982). Modifications are made where a more literal translation is necessary for the quotations to cohere with Arendt and Stern's commentary, or where Mitchell's decisions entail a strong philosophical interpretation of the poem that interferes, potentially, with the surrounding discussion.—Ed.

3. Arendt and Stern engage in a play on words, which links "disjointed" (*unverbunden*) to "non-obligatoriness" (*Unverbindlichkeit*). We can follow this play in English through reference to the etymology of the Latin verb, *obligāre* "to tie to."—Ed.

4. See the absence of images in Judaism (index of the inability to localize God, or, positively expressed, God's universal presence, i.e., his non-determinability and non-representability); the determination πίστις [belief] as ἀχοή [sound] in the New Testament; and more generally the role of prayer, which does not conjure or appeal to an idol, but wants to be *heard*; and finally from Augustine, Luther, and Calvin up to Kant's secularized ethics, which still speaks of the "call" of duty. [Augustine (354–430), Bishop of Hippo, was perhaps the most important of the Church fathers in the development of Catholic doctrine. Martin Luther (1483–1546) initiated the Protestant Reformation and translated the Bible into German. John Calvin (1509–1564), who settled in Geneva, was a major Protestant theologian. Immanuel Kant (1724–1804) was the most important philosopher of the German Enlightenment and laid the foundations for both German Idealism and German romanticism. Arendt and Stern are here referring to his *Critique of Practical Reason* (1787).—Ed.]

5. The German term *Dasein* (literally, "being there") is here translated as *existence*; but it should be noted that this translation is by no means innocent.

Dasein acquires a technical sense in Martin Heidegger's *Sein und Zeit* (Being and Time, 1926), and is, for this reason, often left untranslated in English versions of this enormously influential work. Arendt and Stern had both studied with Heidegger (1889–1976), and their discussion of Rilke is clearly conscious of the correspondence between Heidegger's concept of *Dasein* and Rilke's; but it would be misleading to suggest that the two concepts were equivalent.—Ed.

6. Rilke perceives the reality of another wooing, although it is denied to human beings. This wooing no longer asks *for* something but, rather, yells "rein wie der Vogel [purely like the bird]" (7th Elegy), i.e. without care. Cf. *Sonnets to Orpheus* I, 3: "Gesang, wie du ihn lehrst, ist nicht Begehr, nicht Werbung um ein endlich noch Erreichtes; . . . In Wahrheit singen, ist ein anderer Hauch. Ein Hauch um nichts [Song, as you have taught it, is not desire, / not wooing any grace that can be achieved; . . . True singing is a different breath. / A breath about nothing]." See the interpretation of the concept of existence [*Dasein*] below.

7. While, for Kant, the realm of the beautiful is constituted through the possibility of our disinterestedness in the world, and the "stronger existence," the "sublime," is dependent upon the beautiful, here the beautiful arises only through the "stronger existence's" disinterestedness in us, and is thus derivative of the "sublime." [Arendt and Stern are here referring to Kant's *Critique of Judgment* (1790).—Ed.]

8. Rilke does, however, accord a certain kind of past, though never a future, to animals, the index of which is melancholy. For the animal is something that "fliegen muß und stammt aus einem Schoß [has to fly, and comes from a womb]" (8th Elegy). The present of the animal is therefore uncertain ("denn Schoß ist alles [for the womb is everything]"). Nevertheless, this past contains not individual or personal facts: memory does not "overwhelm," but is only the factuality cleaving to the animal of its previous lack of "distance."

9. Blaise Pascal (1623–1662) was a French mathematician and theologian, whose *Pensées* (posthumously published in 1670) has long been considered a masterpiece of philosophical-religious reflection. Søren Kierkegaard (1813–1855) was a Danish philosopher and religious thinker who exercised a strong influence on early twentieth-century German thought. Max Scheler (1874–1928) was a German philosopher who first applied the principles and techniques of phenomenological research to the fields of ethical and social relations.—Ed.

Chapter 2

1. Throughout this translation, the term *Bildung*, which gives rise to the familiar word Bildungsroman, will be left untranslated. There are two reasons for this unusual decision: first, the book under review elucidates the idea of Bildung

with reference to its German cognates and associations; second, Arendt herself at times decides against translating the term, as for instance, in her discussion of Dinesen's story "The Poet" (see Chapter 30): the story "could also be read as a story about the vices of *Bildung*" (272). Bildung can perhaps best be understood as a kind of never-ending process of education in which the educated ones, *die Gebildete,* interiorize and represent the culture of the fine arts.—Ed.

2. Johann Gottfried Herder (1744–1803) was a writer, theologian, and Protestant minister, who helped lead the fight against the principles of the Enlightenment. Anthony Ashley Cooper, 3rd Earl of Shaftesbury (1671–1713), was an English politician and philosopher, most famous for his *Characteristics of Men, Manners, Opinions, Times* (1711). Jean-Jacques Rousseau (1712–1778) exercised a profound influence over German writers and philosophers in the latter half of the eighteenth century. Wilhelm von Humboldt (1767–1835) was a Prussian diplomat, educational reformer, and linguist.—Ed.

3. The word *Innigkeit* is also left untranslated. As Arendt writes in her discussion of the artist Carl Heidenrich (Chapter 25), it is "a word impossible to translate in any other language and perhaps best described (not defined) as an intense inwardness—which inspired the very best of German lyric poetry" (203).—Ed.

4. "Inner" Bildung is thus interpreted as compensation for an "outer" state of affairs, and the direct tradition of this "inwardness," namely pietism, is, as it were, forgotten at this moment. Thus, Weil cites a letter from Humboldt to F. A. Wolf in order to show that the "'cultivated,' who were less concerned with the validity of their titles," had "to ground their validity 'deeper.'" But Humboldt describes the situation in exactly the reverse manner, namely that "the shadow of pleasure . . . to lead an active life has never so fully extinguished in me since I have become more intimate with antiquity" (235, footnote). The difference should at least have been included in the presentation. [Friedrich August Wolf (1750–1824) was one of the founders of modern philology, whose *Prolegomena ad Homerus* appeared in 1795.—Ed.]

5. The absence of a consideration of Lessing's influence on Herder and therefore on the emergence of Bildung is quite disturbing. The most striking example of this absence can be found in the passage where Weil asserts that, for Herder, "the way is considerably more significant than the goal" (50). This is derived from a "mood swing" instead of being seen, in my estimation, as a reference to the well-known dictum of Lessing: "If, while holding all truth in his right hand and holding in his left only the ever-persistent drive for truth, with the addition that I will always and forever err, God said to me 'choose,' I would fall before him in humility, choosing the left hand, and say "Father, pure truth is really for you alone!" (*Theologische Streitschriften.* Duplik I.) [Gotthold Ephraim Lessing (1729–1781), was a dramatist, critic, and theologian; he was among the foremost representatives of the German Enlightenment.—Ed.]

6. Weil is alluding to a famous manifesto of Martin Luther (1483–1546), *About the Freedom of a Christian* (1520).—Ed.

7. Friedrich Schleiermacher (1768–1834) was a major figure among German Lutherans and one of the founders of hermeneutics as an independent discipline.—Ed.

8. In this sense Herder polemicizes against all typically Enlightenment conceptions of history, which see the "goal" of history in "Enlightenment" or, as in Lessing, see history as nothing other than the "educator of the human race."

9. Caroline von Humboldt, née von Dachröden (1766–1829), married Wilhelm in 1791. A seven-volume collection of letters between herself and her husband was published in 1900.—Ed.

10. The "patriarchal stratified state [*Ständesstaat*]" was a legacy of the medieval and early modern period. The state was composed of three "estates" (*Stände*): the clergy, the nobility, and the bourgeoisie-peasantry. For a further discussion of the stratified state, see Arendt's review essay "Adam Müller-Renaissance?" (Chapter 4).—Ed.

11. Friedrich August Ludwig von der Marwitz (1777–1837) was a Prussian general and diplomat who was fiercely opposed to the Enlightenment.—Ed

Chapter 3

1. Karl August Varnhagen von Ense (1785–1858), husband of Rahel Varnhagen (see note 3 below and Chapter 5), was a political journalist who wrote portraits of various individuals, including Gentz. Gustav Schlesier published five volumes of Gentz's correspondence and papers between 1838 and 1840.—Ed.

2. Rudolf Haym (1821–1901) was a literary critic and philosopher who is most famous for his account of the romantic school.—Ed.

3. Henriette Herz, née de Lemos (1764–1847), opened one of the first salons in Berlin. Rahel Varnhagen, née Rahel Levin (1771–1834), established perhaps the most famous salon in Berlin before the Napoleonic invasion.—Ed.

4. Edmund Burke (1729–1797) was an Anglo-Irish politician, aesthetician, and orator whose *Reflections on the Revolution in France* (1790) helped establish the modern idea of political conservatism.—Ed.

5. Friedrich Wilhelm III (1770–1840) reigned as king of Prussia from 1797 to 1840.—Ed.

6. Klemens Wenzel Nepomuk Lothar Fürst (Prince) von Metternich-Winneberg-Beilstein (1773–1858) was an Austrian politician who, as one of the principal participants in the Congress of Vienna (1814–1815), helped re-create and maintain the old order of European states, following the defeat of Napoleon.—Ed.

7. Adam Müller (1779–1829) was a conservative political theorist and econo-mist, whose works were being rediscovered at this time (see "Adam Müller—Renaissance?" Chapter 4)—Ed.

8. Friedrich Schlegel (1772–1829) was among the leading figures of early Ger-man romanticism. In later life he became the secretary to Metternich.—Ed.

9. Pauline Wiesel, née César (1779–1848), was famous for, among other things, her numerous affairs, including one with Prince Louis Ferdinand of Prussia (1772–1806).—Ed.

10. Honoré Gabriel Riqueti, Comte de Mirabeau (1749–1791) was a writer, orator, and politician, who actively supported the moderate wing in the French Revolution.—Ed.

11. Karl Heinrich von und zum Stein (1757–1831) was a Prussian politician.—Ed.

12. Friedrich Schlegel's *Lucinde* (1799) was considered scandalous because of its frank depiction of sensuality.—Ed.

13. Anna Amalie von Helvig-Imhof (1776–1831) was a poet and painter who composed a hexameter epic entitled *Die Schwester von Lesbos* (The Sisters of Lesbos).—Ed.

14. Fanny Elßler (1810–1884) was an Austrian ballerina.—Ed.

Chapter 4

1. Friedrich Bülow was a Nazi apologist who followed up his edition of Müller's writings under discussion here with a pamphlet celebrating the Nazi seizure of power that was entitled *Der deutsche Ständestaat: nationalsozialistische Gemeinschaftspolitik und Wirtschaftsorganization* [The German Strata-state: Nazi Politics of Community and Organization of Economics]. The idea of a "strata-state" (*Ständestaat*) is drawn from medieval political theory and was an integral part of post-Napoleonic German conservatism.—Ed.

2. Friedrich Schelling (1775–1854) was one of the major German idealists who first developed the idea of *Naturphilosophie* (nature-philosophy).—Ed.

3. Wilhelm Meister is the eponymous hero of Goethe's paradigmatic Bil-dungsroman, *Wilhelm Meister's Years of Apprenticeship* (1795). Johann Wolfgang von Goethe (1749–1832) was, and remains, the preeminent figure in the history of modern German literature.—Ed.

4. Georg Wilhelm Friedrich Hegel (1770–1831) was one of the major repre-sentatives of German Idealism. His identification of the real with the rational can be found in the Preface to the *Grundlinien der Philosophie des Rechts* (Ele-ments of the Philosophy of Right, 1821).—Ed.

5. Jean Jacques Rousseau's *Du contrat social* (Social Contract) appeared in 1762.—Ed.

6. Heinrich von Treitschke (1834–1896) was a German historian who became one of the major exponents of Prussian conservatism in the latter half of the nineteenth century. His anti-British and especially anti-Semitic opinions were highly influential among the educated elite of Wilhemine Germany.—Ed.

7. Othmar Spann (1878–1950) was a conservative Austrian sociologist and political theorist who promoted the idea of the "corporate state."—Ed.

8. Heinrich Steffens (1773–1845) was a German romantic poet and philosopher, who, in the footsteps of Schelling, developed the idea of *Naturphilosophie.* Georg Friedrich Philipp, Freiherr von Hardenberg, pen name Novalis (1772–1801), was one of the great poets and thinkers of the romantic era.—Ed.

9. Karl August von Hardenberg (1750–1822) was the Secretary of State for Prussia. Adam Smith (1723–1790) was a Scottish philosopher and political economist.—Ed.

10. Erich Przywara (1889–1972) was a Jesuit philosopher and theologian.—Ed.

11. Thomas Hobbes (1588–1679) was a British philosopher and political theorist, most famous for his *Leviathan* (1651). Karl Marx (1818–1883) was a German philosopher and economist, most famous for his *Capital: A Critique of Political Economy* (first volume, 1867).—Ed.

12. Johann Gottlieb Fichte (1762–1814) was a major German idealist, most famous for his idea of a *Wissenschaftslehre* (theory of science). His pamphlet entitled *Der geschlossner Handelstaat* (The Closed Commercial State, 1800) advocated an end to international commerce.—Ed.

13. Ludwig Feuerbach (1804–1872) was a German philosopher who proclaimed himself a materialist and strongly influenced the young Marx.—Ed.

14. Christoph Martin Wieland (1733–1813) was an important figure in the late German Enlightenment. His novels and poems tended to satirize irrational actions and opinions, especially those of "fanatics" (*Schwärmer*). Bernd Heinrich Wilhelm von Kleist (1777–1811), who was from a distinguished Prussian military family, became a dramatist, writer, and publisher of a daily paper (among the first in Germany). The young Kleist read to the elderly Wieland a copy of his astonishing dramatic fragment, *Robert Guiscard* (1808). He thereafter produced a number of the greatest plays and stories in modern German, including the comedy *Der zerbrochene Krug* (The Broken Jug, 1811), the strange tragedy *Penthesilea* (1808), and the stories "Michael Kohlhaas" and "Die Marquise von O—" (1810).—Ed.

Chapter 5

1. Friederike von Varnhagen, née Rahel Levin (1771–1834), is the subject of Arendt's first major work (besides her dissertation on Augustine), for which the present essay is obviously a preliminary study; see *Rahel Varnhagen: The Life of a Jewess,* ed. Liliane Weisberg, trans. Richard and Clara Winston (Baltimore:

Johns Hopkins University Press, 1997). Rahel published only anonymous fragments during her tumultuous life. Before she died, she and her husband, Karl
August Varnhagen von Ense (1785–1858), who was a political journalist of sorts,
published *Rahel: Ein Buch des Andenkens für Freunde* (A Book of Remembrance
for Friends), 3 vols. (Berlin: Duncker and Humblot, 1834).—Ed.

2. Prince Louis Ferdinand of Prussia (1772–1806) was a Prussian general.—Ed.

3. On October 27, 1806, Napoleon rode through Berlin's Brandenburg Gate
in Berlin and occupied the city for two years.—Ed.

4. Friedrich II (1712–1786), Prussian king, was called "the Great" because of
his military victories. A friend of Voltaire and renowned Epicurean, he was an
advocate of religious tolerance. Even though he was himself generally antipa-
thetic to Jews, many Jewish converts of the era named themselves after him, including perhaps Rahel herself.—Ed.

5. Henriette Herz, née de Lemos (1764–1847), was married to the physician
Marcus Herz (1747–1803), who studied and corresponded with Immanuel Kant
(1724–1804). Once he established himself in Berlin, Herz opened his house to
wide-ranging discussions of Enlightenment philosophy. Henriette created one
of the first salons in Berlin on this basis. Alexander von Humboldt (1769–1859),
brother of Wilhlem, was a German naturalist, explorer, and educational reformer. Joachim Heinrich Campe (1746–1818) was an educator, who promoted
Enlightenment principles and later sought to defend the German language
against French influences. Friedrich Ferdinand zu Dohna-Schlobitten (1771–1831)
was a Prussian statesman.—Ed.

6. Carl von Laroche (1767–1839) was the son of the famous writer Sophie von
LaRoche (1731–1807). Brendel Veit (1763–1839) was the oldest daughter of Moses
Mendelssohn (1729–86). She married Simon Veit (1754–1819), a businessman
and uncle of David Veit (1771–1814). They were divorced in 1799, after which
she converted to Christianity, changed her name to Dorothea, married Friedrich
Schlegel (1772–1829), wrote a novel entitled *Florentine* (1801), and converted to
Catholicism in 1808 along with her husband. Her two sons, Johannes Veit
(1790–1854) and Philipp Veit (1793–1877), were important members of the
Nazarenes, a group of painters who revered early Italian art and emphasized
Catholic themes.—Ed.

7. Caroline von Dachröden (1766–1829) married Wilhelm von Humboldt in
1791.—Ed.

8. Gotthold Ephraim Lessing (1729–1781) was a dramatist, critic, and theologian; along with Mendelssohn and Kant, he was among the foremost representatives of the German Enlightenment.—Ed.

9. Caroline Schlegel, née Michaelis (1763–1809), was a writer who first married a physician and mining engineer and then, in 1796, Friedrich Schlegel's
brother, the literary critic and translator August Wilhelm Schlegel (1767–1845),

whom she divorced in 1803 in order to marry the German idealist philosopher Friedrich Schelling (1775–1854).—Ed.

10. Karl Gustav von Brinkmann (1764–1847) was a Swedish diplomat who also wrote poetry.—Ed.

11. Wilhelm von Burgsdorff (1772–1822) was a large landowner in Brandenburg.—Ed.

12. Peter von Gualtieri (1764–1805) was a major in the Prussian officer corps.—Ed.

13. Hans Genelli (1763–1823) was an architect. In 1818 he published a remarkable study entitled *Das Theater zu Athen* (The Theater in Athens).—Ed.

14. Frederike Unzelmann, née Flittner (1766–1815), was an actress and singer. She married her stepfather, Karl Unzelmann (1753–1832), and then Heinrich Bethmann (1774–1857); she was the lover of, among others, August Wilhelm Schlegel. Henriette Mendelssohn (1775–1831) was the daughter of Moses Mendelssohn; while a teacher in Paris, she established a relationship with Varnhagen. Countess Josephine von Pachta, née Canal Malabaila (1771–1833), moved to Berlin in 1797 in order to get away from her Bohemian husband; she lived with her son's tutor, Johann Meinert (1775–1844). Karoline von Schlabrendorff, née Kalkreuth (1761–1831), accompanied Rahel to Paris in 1795.—Ed.

15. Christiane (Christel) Dorothea Pedrillo, née Eigensatz (1781–1850) was an actress who first brought to life the character of Käthchen in Heinrich von Kleist's great play, *Prinz Friedrich von Homburg* (1809). About Pauline Wiesel, Arendt writes the following in her notes to a letter Rahel wrote to her in 1826: "Pauline Wiesel, née César, was born in Berlin in 1779; she is eight years younger than Rahel. As a very young woman, she married Wiesel, who would later become a war advisor and who, for a long time, played the role of the Enlightenment counterpart to the romantic movement in Tieck's circle. . . . Pauline Wiesel was soon separated from her husband because of her friendship with Prince Louis Ferdinand. After the latter's death, she became the lover of Friedrich von Gentz."—Ed.

16. Jean Paul is the pen name of Jean Paul Richter (1763–1825), one of the major writers in modern German literature.—Ed.

17. Schlegel's scandalous novel was addressed to Dorothea Schlegel. Schleiermacher wrote a rejoinder to its critics.—Ed.

18. Bettina von Arnim, née Brentano (1785–1853), granddaughter of Sophie de LaRoche and sister of Clemens Brentano (1778–1842), was an important figure in the romantic movement, who engaged in a famous series of correspondences with Goethe, Karoline von Günderode (1780–1806), and her brother.—Ed.

19. In Varnhagen's edition of her letter, *Rahel, ein Buch des Andenkens,* the letters to Rebecca Friedländer are identified as letters to "Frau v. F." It was Varnhagen's usual practice in his coded edition of the correspondence to equip

Jewish women as quickly as possible with a "von." Henriette Herz, for example, appears as "Frau von Bl." An even more common practice is to take excerpts from letters without indicating when or to whom the letters were written, so that words spoken in a specific, determinate situation look like "general thoughts" and give rise to a distorted image for interpretation. [Rebecca Friedländer, née Saaling-Solomon (1783–1850), was a writer who adopted the name Regina Frohberg.—Ed.]

20. From an unpublished letter to Pauline Wiesel. The correspondence with Pauline Wiesel, Rahel's only real friend, is stored unpublished in the Berlin State Library, and Varnhagen did not prepare it for publication. The reason for this cannot simply be attributed to the fact that by the 1830s, he felt that Rahel's friendship with this irresistible "apparition from the world of the Greek gods," who, despite the innumerable scandals surrounding her, remained loved by all, seemed embarrassing to the memory of Rahel, whom he was intent on putting on a pedestal; he could have coded her name, too, of course, and in fact did so in a few of the published letters. (Pauline Wiesel = Frau v. V.). A more telling reason for his suppression of these letters was that a very different Rahel appears in them, particularly in the letter from the 1820s, than the Rahel whom he wanted to present to the world. These letters also reveal that the Varnhagens' marriage did not in reality coincide with the picture of it projected in the published passages from the letters. Varnhagen proceeded here—albeit with less rigor—as he did with Clemens Brentano's letters, from which he cut everything and anything that would have thrown an unfavorable light on himself.

21. From an unpublished letter to Pauline Wiesel.

22. Friedrich August von Stägemann (1763–1840) was a poet and a Prussian Privy Councilor. Luise von Voß, née von Berg (1790–1865), was married to Count Ernst von Voß (1779–1832) and opened a salon in Berlin. Anton Heinrich von Radziwill (1775–1833) was a Prussian politician who married Princess Luise von Preußen.—Ed.

23. Ludwig Achim von Arnim (1781–1831) was a romantic writer and poet. Ferdinand von Schill (1776–1809) was a Prussian officer who died in his attempt to oust Napoleon.—Ed.

24. Reinhold Steig, *Kleists Berliner Kämpfe* (Berlin, 1901), 14. [Carl Friedrich Zelter (1758–1832) helped create and definitively established the famous Sing-Akademie in Berlin.—Ed.]

25. The Christian-German Table Society (*Christlich-deutsche Tischgesellschaft*), first established around 1811, was politically reactionary, anti-French, anti-Enlightenment, and anti-Semitic.—Ed.

26. Cf. Reinhold Steig, 21ff.

27. Brentano's essay was published in 1811 and read before the Christian-German Table Society.—Ed.

28. Friedrich Gottlieb Klopstock (1724–1803) was an important poet of the period, most famous for his *Messiah* (1748–1773). Karl Wilhelm Ramler (1725–1798) was a poet and dramaturge. Johann Heinrich Voß (1751–1826) was a poet who produced influential translations of Homer.—Ed.

29. Heinrich Heine (1797–1856) was among the greatest German poets of the nineteenth century. He converted to Christianity after receiving his law degree because, as he sardonically wrote, the baptismal certificate was the "entrance ticket" to European culture.—Ed.

30. Alexander von der Marwitz (1787–1814), brother of Friedrich August Ludwig von der Marwitz (1777–1837), engaged in a copious correspondence with Rahel, parts of which were published in 1925.—Ed.

31. In the notes to her publication of the letter from Rahel Varnhagen to Pauline Wiesel, Arendt writes the following: "Pauline Wiesel is the friend who renounced assimilation into the bourgeois order. And she did so at a time in which 'being nothing' in a social sense had already become almost impossible if one wanted to belong to society at all. To the degree that Rahel sees that her assimilation [*Einordnung*] into the order of society had gone badly—since 'everything that I should purchase with great effort *never really* exists for me'—she admires Pauline's 'courage' in remaining unassimilated, as she had always been. In this context the emphasis on remaining what one is can be understood; in it lies a perpetual cancellation of whatever she now is, namely Mrs. Varnhagen. She must now guard herself against what she is taken to be—and against being what she really is. In this struggle against social reality the only thing that helps is holding onto her youth, in other words, not-wanting-to-be-different. Pauline is a witness of this youth—all the more so because she is the only one who has not changed. She is not 'pious' (that is, Catholic), and she has not become a bourgeois." Here are the roots of the portrait that Arendt would draw of Rahel Varnhagen in the coming years.—Ed.

Chapter 6

1. Auguste Rodin (1840–1917) was a French sculptor. For a short time in 1906, Rilke was Rodin's private secretary and wrote a series of impressive letters to him.—Ed.

2. Rilke wrote a series of famous letters about the paintings of Paul Cézanne (1839–1906).—Ed.

Chapter 7

1. Thomas Mann (1875–1955) was among the most important German novelists of the twentieth century. Originally a German nationalist, he became a

leading spokesperson for a liberal German culture after the First World War.—Ed.

Chapter 8

1. The English version adds: "On the contrary, he found himself 'one rung lower,' he had 'slipped down to a lesser . . . category.'"—Ed.

2. The English version adds: "This, in his eyes, meant personal disgrace."—Ed.

3. Arendt uses *gleichgeschaltet* in the English. It refers to the Nazi policy of *Gleichschaltung* or "synchronization," in which every aspect of life was to accord with the dictates and direction of the Nazi "movement."—Ed.

4. In the English version Arendt includes the following quote from Zweig's autobiography: "the fall into the abyss . . . [and] the height from which it occurred." Charles Péguy (1874–1914) was a French writer and poet. Arendt briefly discusses him near the end of her "Preface to Bernard Lazare, *Job's Dungheap*" (Chapter 19).—Ed.

5. Arendt is quoting Hofmannsthal's "Prologue to the Book *Anatol*" (1892): "ripened early and tender and sad."—Ed.

6. Arendt adds in the English version: "Everything could go on because nobody cared."—Ed.

7. The Dreyfus Affair began when Alfred Dreyfus (1859–1935), an obscure captain in the French army was accused of espionage in 1894 and convicted because he was Jewish. The "affair" lasted for ten years and marked a major cultural moment in both modern French and modern Jewish history; see Arendt's account of Dreyfus in *The Origins of Totalitarianism*, rev. ed. (New York: Harcourt Brace, 1951), 89–120. See also Arendt's introduction to Lazare's *Job's Dungheap* (Chapter 19). Karl Lueger (1844–1910) was an Austrian politician who was a major exponent of anti-Semitism. He served as the mayor of Vienna from 1897 until his death. Georg von Schoenerer (1841–1921) was another anti-Semitic Austrian politician who was intent on creating a racist foreign policy.—Ed.

8. Theodor Herzl (1860–1904) was an Austrian-Jewish journalist and cultural editor of the *Neue Freie Presse* (New Free Press), who became one of the founders of modern Zionism with his pamphlet *Der Judenstaat* (The Jewish State, 1896).—Ed.

9. Gerhardt Hauptmann (1862–1946) was a German writer and dramatist. He won the Nobel Prize in 1912 and stayed in Germany throughout his life. The Nazis allowed his plays to be staged as a demonstration that famous members of the German cultural elite preferred to remain in Germany.—Ed.

10. Hugo von Hofmannsthal (1874–1929) was an Austrian poet, dramatist, essayist, and librettist. Arendt adds the following remark about Hofmannsthal to

the English version: "[he was] the only one of his generation who was not only cultured but, as his later work shows, came close to being a genuine poet."—Ed.

11. Arthur Schnitzler (1862–1931) was an Austrian writer, dramatist, and physician whose frank representations of sexuality were sometimes considered scandalous. Richard Beer-Hofmann (1866–1945) was a Jewish-Austrian dramatist and poet who fled from Austria in 1939 and whose work was banned under the Nazis. Peter Altenberg, pseudonym of Richard Engländer (1859–1919), was a Jewish-Austrian writer who called his brief sketches "literary pencil drawings." Franz Grillparzer (1791–1872) was an Austrian writer and dramatist who also occupied administrative posts in the Imperial bureaucracy, including finance minister.—Ed.

12. Richard Strauss (1864–1949) was a German composer and conductor who was appointed by Goebbels to the presidency of the State Music Board, from which he was forced to resign in 1935 because he included Zweig's name on the playbill for an opera (as its librettist). Karl Ernst Haushofer (1869–1946) was a German general and theoretician of war who developed the "geopolitical" idea of *Lebensraum* (life space). A friend of Rudolf Hess, he probably contributed to the writing of Hitler's *Mein Kampf.*—Ed.

13. In the English version, Arendt adds at this point: "an article that seems to me to belong with the finest of Stefan Zweig's work."—Ed.

14. The conclusion of the English version is slightly different: "For honor never will be won by the cult of success or fame, by cultivation of one's own self, nor even by personal dignity. From the 'disgrace' of being a Jew there is but one escape—to fight for the honor of the Jewish people as a whole."—Ed.

Chapter 9

1. Max Weber (1864–1920) was the founder of the modern science of sociology. In his posthumously published monograph, *Ancient Judaism* (1921), he applied the idea of a "pariah people," drawn from studies of Indian caste society, to the Jews of antiquity. The second edition of his most famous work, *The Protestant Ethic and the Spirit of Capitalism* (1905, 1920), also represented the Jews of modern Europe as a "pariah people." Arendt spoke of the pariah in connection with Judaism in a chapter of *Rahel Varnhagen: The Life of a Jewess,* 237–49.—Ed.

2. Solomon Maimon, originally Salomon Ben Joshua (1754–1800), was a philosopher who recounted his passage from a Lithuanian-Polish shtetl to Enlightenment Berlin in his *Autobiography* (1792).—Ed.

3. Bernard Lazare (1865–1903) was a French literary critic, anarchist, and Zionist; see Arendt's preface to *Job's Dungheap* (Chapter 19).—Ed.

4. Chaplin has recently declared that he is of Irish and Gypsy descent, but he has been selected for discussion because, even if not himself a Jew, he has epitomized in an artistic form a character born of the Jewish pariah mentality. [Charlie Chaplin (1889–1977) was most famous for his character of "the tramp" in numerous silent films.—Ed.]

5. Lecha Dodi: "Come, my beloved, to meet the bride; Let us greet the Sabbath-tide"—a Hebrew song chanted in the synagogue on Friday night.

6. Heinrich Heine (1797–1856) was the author of the famous lyric poem "Die Lorelei," which first appeared in his *Buch der Lieder* (Book of Songs, 1827). Because the Nazis could not expunge it from the canon of popular poetry, it was attributed to "anonymous."—Ed.

7. Benjamin Disraeli (1804–1881) was a British politician and novelist; see Arendt's depiction of him in *The Origins of Totalitarianism,* 68–79.—Ed.

8. Isaac Marcus Jost (1793–1860) was a German-Jewish historian, chiefly known for his nine-volume *History of the Israelites from the Time of the Maccabees* (1820–1829).—Ed.

9. A "Merry Andrew" is someone who amuses others by performing ridiculous stunts.—Ed.

10. Yet of all who have dealt with this age-long conflict Kafka is the first to have started from the basic truth that "society is a nobody in a dress-suit." In a certain sense, he was fortunate to have been born in an epoch when it was already patent and manifest that the wearer of the dress-suit was indeed a nobody. Fifteen years later, when Marcel Proust wanted to characterize French society, he was obliged to use a far grimmer metaphor. He depicted it as a masquerade with a death's head grinning behind every mask. [Marcel Proust (1871–1921) was a French novelist; see Arendt's account of his great work, *In Search of Lost Time* (1913–1927), in Chapter 21.—Ed.]

11. Gustav Flaubert (1821–1880) was a great French writer who helped define the realist novel with his *Madame Bovary* (1857).—Ed.

12. Ahad Ha'am, pen name of Asher Ginsberg (1856–1927), was a philosopher and Zionist.—Ed.

Chapter 10

1. Friedrich Nietzsche (1844–1900) was a major German philosopher who exercised a profound yet ambiguous influence on much of twentieth-century writing and thought. G. K. Chesterton (1874–1936) was a British writer and conservative social commentator who converted to Catholicism in 1922 and produced a series of biting critiques of modern thought.—Ed.

2. Arendt is referring to a famous dictum Heidegger first enunciated in "What Is Metaphysics?" (1929): "Nothingness nothings."—Ed.

Chapter 11

1. Hermann Broch (1886–1951) was a novelist and social thinker whom Arendt befriended. Two reflections on his work as a novelist are included in this volume (Chapters 14 and 20).—Ed.

2. Arendt adds the following reflection in *The Origins of Totalitarianism:* "Instead of inspiring humbug, Austrian bureaucracy rather caused its greatest modern writer to become the humorist and critic of the whole matter. Franz Kafka knew well enough the superstition of fate which possesses a people who live under the perpetual rule of accidents, the inevitable tendency to read a special superhuman meaning into happenings whose rational significance is beyond the knowledge and understanding of the concerned. He was well aware of the weird attractiveness of such peoples, their melancholy and beautifully sad folk tales which seemed so superior to the lighter and brighter literature of more fortunate peoples. He exposed the pride in necessity as such, even the necessity of evil, and the nauseating conceit which identifies evil and misfortune with destiny. The miracle is only that he could do this in a world in which the main elements of this atmosphere were not fully articulated; he trusted his great powers of imagination to draw all the necessary conclusions and, as it were, to complete what reality had somehow neglected to bring into full focus" (*The Origins of Totalitarianism,* 245–46).—Ed.

3. In a footnote to *The Origins of Totalitarianism,* Arendt describes the incident with the Barnabases as a "weird travesty of a piece of Russian literature": "The family is living under a curse, treated as lepers till they feel themselves such, merely because one of their pretty daughters once dared to reject the indecent advances of an important official. The plain villagers, controlled to the last detail by a bureaucracy, and slaves even in their thoughts to the whims of their all-powerful officials, had long since come to realize that to be in the right or to be in the wrong was for them a matter of pure 'fate' which they could not alter. It is not, as K. naïvely assumes, the sender of an obscene letter who is exposed, but the recipient who becomes branded and tainted. This is what the villagers mean when they speak of their 'fate.' In K.'s view, 'it's unjust and monstrous, but [he is] the only one in the village of that opinion' (*The Origins of Totalitarianism,* 246)."

4. In the Preface to *Between Past and Future,* Arendt includes a parenthetical comment that expands on the remarks made here: "The riddle of Kafka, who in more than thirty-five years of growing posthumous fame has established himself as one of the foremost writers' writers, is still unsolved; it consists primarily in a kind of breathtaking reversal of the established relationship between experience and thought. While we find it a matter of course to associate richness of concrete detail and dramatic action with the experience of a given reality and to ascribe to mental processes abstract pallor as the price exacted for their order and precision, Kafka, by sheer force of intelligence and sheer spiritual imagination, created out

of a bare, 'abstract' minimum of experience a kind of thought-landscape which, without losing in precision, harbors all the riches, varieties, and dramatic elements characteristic of 'real' life. Because thinking to him was the most vital and the liveliest part of reality, he developed this uncanny gift of anticipation which even today, after almost forty years full of unprecedented and unforeseeable events, does not cease to amaze us" (*Between Past and Future*, 10).—Ed.

5. In the original German version of the essay, the editors of *Die Wandlung* add the following note at this point: "This passage, like the essay itself, is translated from English, since unfortunately we did not have the possibility of finding the cited words. The philosopher Walter Benjamin died in emigration—by suicide, at the moment when he tried to flee from German troops who were advancing into a previously unoccupied zone of France" (*Die Wandlung* 1 [December 1946], 1056). Walter Benjamin (1892–1940) was a German philosopher and critic whom Arendt and her husband Heinrich Blücher got to know in Paris in the late 1930s. They nicknamed him "Benji" (see Hannah Arendt and Heinrich Blücher, *Briefe, 1936–1968*, ed. Lotte Köhler [Munich: Piper, 1996], 82). Arendt possessed the manuscript of Benjamin's "Über den Begriff der Geschichte" (often translated as "Theses on the Philosophy of History"); for Harry Zohn's translation of a typescript (not the manuscript in Arendt's possession), see Benjamin, *Selected Writings, Volume 4*, ed. Howard Eiland and Michael Jennings (Cambridge, MA: Harvard University Press, 2003), 389–400. It is worth noting that, except for the mimeograph booklet produced by the Institut für Sozialforschung (in Los Angeles) under the title *Walter Benjamin zum Gedächtnis* in 1942, Arendt's citation of the fragment on the angel of history represents its first appearance in print form.—Ed.

6. See Kant, *Kritik der Urteilskraft* (*Critique of Judgment*, 1790), § 49, "On the Faculty of the Mind that Constitutes Genius."—Ed.

7. See Kant, *Critique of Judgment*, § 46, "Fine Art is the Art of Genius."—Ed.

8. Arendt is referring to a chapter of Kafka's incomplete novel, *Der Verschollene* (*The One Who Is Never Heard from Again*), which was first published as *Amerika* by Max Brod. Placing this chapter fragment at the end of the novel, Brod corrected Kafka's spelling of the American state that borders on Texas and provided it with a title: "Das Naturtheater von Oklahoma" (The Nature Theater of Oklahoma). The chapter opens with Karl Roßmann, the protagonist of the novel, standing before a poster that states: "Everyone is welcome."—Ed.

Chapter 12

1. Karl Philipp Moritz (1756–1793) was a German writer, educator, and aesthetic theorist, who helped establish the idea of a *Bildungsroman* ("novel of education") with the publication of *Anton Reiser* in 1790.—Ed.

2. Arendt crossed this sentence out. Goethe's *Elective Affinities* (1807) revolves around the idea of marriage.—Ed.

Chapter 13

1. Jean-Paul Sartre (1905–1980) was a French novelist, dramatist, and philosopher. Albert Camus (1913–1960) was a French novelist and philosopher.—Ed.
2. In the Preface to *Between Past and Future,* Arendt includes some further reflections on the phenomenon of existentialism: "existentialism, at least in its French version, is primarily an escape from the perplexities of modern philosophy into the unquestioning commitment of action. And since, under the circumstances of the twentieth century, the so-called intellectuals—writers, thinkers, artists, men of letters, and the like—could find access to the public realm only in time of revolution, the revolution came to play, as Malraux once noticed (in *Man's Fate*), 'the role which once was played by eternal life': 'it saves those that make it.' Existentialism, the rebellion of the philosopher against philosophy, did not arise when philosophy turned out to be unable to apply its own rules to the realm of political affairs; this failure of political philosophy as Plato would have understood it is almost as old as the history of Western philosophy and metaphysics; and it did not even arise when it turned out that philosophy was equally unable to perform the task assigned to it by Hegel and the philosophy of history, that is, to understand and grasp conceptually historical reality and the events that made the modern world what it is. The situation, however, became desperate when the old metaphysical questions were shown to be meaningless; that is, when it began to dawn upon modern man that he had come to live in a world in which his mind and his tradition of thought were not even capable of asking adequate, meaningful questions, let alone of giving answers to its own perplexities. In this predicament action, with its involvement and commitment, its being *engagée,* seemed to hold out the hope, not of solving any problems, but of making it possible to live with them without becoming, as Sartre once put it, a *salaud,* a hypocrite" (*Between Past and Future*, 8–9). André Malraux (1901–1976) was a French writer, art critic, and diplomat.—Ed.

Chapter 14

1. David Hume (1711–1776) was a Scottish philosopher and historian.—Ed.
2. Brundisium is a harbor town on the southeastern coast of Italy.—Ed.

Chapter 15

1. Wilhelm Raabe (1831–1910) was a German novelist. When Arendt calls

Stifter a "poet" she is obviously thinking of the German word *Dichter,* which suggests a higher vocation than that of the *Schriftsteller* (writer).—Ed.

2. Rudolf Binding (1867–1938), born in Switzerland, was a German writer who glorified his experiences in the First World War and concluded his career as a writer with *Antwort eines Deutschen* (Answer of a German), which is a defense of the Nazi state against its foreign critics. Hans Carossa (1878–1956) was a German writer who specialized in his own autobiographies. Rudolf Borchardt (1877–1945) was a remarkable German poet, dramatist, and essayist, who almost completely stopped writing once the Nazis seized power. Rudolf Alexander Schröder (1878–1962), a friend of Borchardt's, was a German writer, poet, architect, and painter. Oskar Lörke (1884–1941) was a German poet. Agnes Miegel (1879–1964) was a German poet and journalist who wrote a poem in honor of Hitler that was much published before the collapse of the Nazi regime and suppressed thereafter. Albrecht Schaeffer (1885–1950) was a German writer who immigrated to the United States in 1939.—Ed.

3. Eduard Friedrich Mörike (1804–1875), a German poet and novelist, is often considered the last of the great German romantic writers. Hans Blüher (1888–1955) was a German writer who celebrated male homosexual desire and whose most famous work is the three-volume *Wandervogel: Geschichte einer Jugendbewegung* (Wandervogel, History of a Youth Movement).—Ed.

Chapter 16

1. Detlev von Liliencron (1844–1909) was a German poet. Arno Holz (1863–1929) was a German poet and dramatist.—Ed.

Chapter 17

1. George Bernard Shaw (1856–1902) was a major Anglo-Irish dramatist and one of the founders of Fabianism.—Ed.

2. Richard Hillary (1919–1943) was a British pilot and author.—Ed.

3. Thomas Edward Lawrence (1888–1935) was a British officer, diplomat, and author, whose masterpiece, *The Seven Pillars of Wisdom,* appeared in two versions (1922 and 1926).—Ed.

4. Patroclus and Thersites are characters in Homer's *Iliad:* the former was a hero who was killed by Hector, the latter a coward.—Ed.

Chapter 18

1. Christian Friedrich Hebbel (1813–1863) was a major Austrian dramatist, whose conception of theater is very unlike Brecht's.—Ed.

2. From Brecht, "An die Nachgeborenen" (To Posterity).—Ed.

3. Friedrich Hölderlin (1770–1843) is arguably the greatest lyric poet in modern German literature.—Ed.

4. Compare Hays's translation of "Concerning Poor B. B." and "Legend of the Dead Soldier" with the prose translation by Clement Greenberg in a remarkably good essay on Brecht, in *Partisan Review* (March/April 1941). Greenberg is never forced into such serious distortions as the following: The first line of "Poor B. B." mentions "black forests" and not the "Black Forest," a mountain range in southern Germany. The second line, "Meine Mutter trug mich in die Städte hinein," Hays translates as "My mother carried me to town," thereby sacrificing the subject of the poem, which treats of cities, to the English idiom. In the third stanza, Brecht is "zu den Leuten freundlich," which indicates aloofness and does not mean "I make friends with people"— Greenberg says, correctly, "I am friendly with people." Difficult to understand, moreover, is why "Litany of Breath" and "Grand Chorale of Thanksgiving" were included at all. The poetic effect of both depends upon the reader's knowing by heart certain well-known German verses ironically quoted in an incongruous context. [Clement Greenberg (1909–1994) was an important American art critic.—Ed.]

5. Gottfried Benn (1886–1956), a physician by profession, was one of the leading expressionist poets in Germany. In 1933 he wrote essays in favor of the Nazis and considered his re-enlistment into the German army in 1935 as an "aristocratic form of emigration." Occasionally Arendt compares the relation between Benn's engagement with the Nazis and Brecht's association with communism; see especially her comments in response to Walter Muschg's lecture, "Dichtung und Kultur [Poetry and Culture]," recorded in *Untergang oder Übergang*, 199–202. Louis-Ferdinand Destouches, pen name Céline (1894–1961), also a physician by profession, was a French novelist. After briefly associating himself with communism, he reversed his political allegiances and became a militant anti-Semite, as evinced in, for example, *Bagatelles pour un Massacre* (Bagatelles for a Massacre, 1937).—Ed.

6. From Brecht, "Ballade von den Abenteurern" (Ballad of the Adventurers).—Ed.

7. From Brecht, "Großer Dankchoral" (Great Thanksgiving Chorale).—Ed.

8. Both of the quotations from Goethe derive from one of his most often-recited poems, "Wandrers Nachtlied II" (Wayfarer's Night Song, II).—Ed.

9. Martin Greenberg, the brother of Clement, worked with Arendt as a reader at Schocken Books. Arendt and Martin Greenberg together translated the second volume of *The Diaries of Franz Kafka* (New York: Schocken, 1949).—Ed.

10. In the German version of this essay Arendt is much more expansive at this point: "This motif from *The Three-Penny Opera* is a sort of *Leitmotiv*

appearing throughout Brecht's work. And it makes an especially beautiful reappearance in the 'Ballade vom Wasserrad' (Ballad of the Waterwheel), which stems from *Die Rundköpfe und die Spitzköpfe* (Roundheads and Pointyheads): 'Von den großen dieser Erde / Melden uns die Heldenlieder: / Steigend auf so wie Gestirne / Gehn sie wie Gestirne nieder. / Das klingt tröstlich und man muß es wissen. / Nur: für uns, die wir sie nähren müssen / Ist das leider immer ziemlich gleich gewesen. / Aufstieg oder Fall: wer trägt die Spesen? // Freilich dreht das Rad sich immer weiter, / Daß, was oben ist, nicht oben bleibt. / Aber für das Wasser unten heißt das leider / Nur: daß es das Rad für ewig treibt.' [The heroic songs tell us of the great men of this earth: Rising up like stars, they fall down like stars. That sounds comforting and is something you should know. Only: for us, who have to feed them, that has sadly never really mattered. Rise or fall: at whose expense? The wheel always keeps turning, of course, so that what's on top doesn't stay on top. But sadly what that means for the water below is only this: that the wheel goes round forever.] The 'philosophy of history' suggested by this poem has nothing to do with either socialist realism or proletarian poetry. It deals with something much more general, which is at the same time something much more precise, namely the production of a world in which all people are equally visible, and the planning of a history that is not remembered by a few and forgotten by many, that doesn't induce forgetfulness under the pretense of remembering, that doesn't involve some while making others the instruments of history."—Ed.

Chapter 19

1. Stéphane Mallarmé (1842–1898) was one of the major French poets of the nineteenth century and an English teacher by profession.—Ed.
2. Georges Ernest Boulanger (1837–1891) was a reactionary French general who failed to initiate a coup aimed at toppling the Third Republic. The Panama Scandal took place in 1889 when the joint-stock company formed to dig a cross-oceanic canal went bankrupt.—Ed.
3. Georges Clémenceau (1841–1929) was a French publisher and one of the dominant politicians of the era. Émile Zola (1840–1902) was a major French novelist and activist journalist who published his famous defense of Dreyfus under the title *J'Accuse* (I Accuse) in a newspaper published by Clémenceau. Jean Jaurès (1859–1914) was the leader of the French socialists who was assassinated on the eve of the First World War.—Ed.
4. Arendt briefly describes the life of Charles Péguy near the end of this preface.—Ed.
5. Max Nordau, originally Simon Maximilian Südfelt (1849–1923), was a Zionist leader and social critic.—Ed.

6. Georges Sorel (1847–1922) was a French syndicalist and political theorist, most famous for his *Réflexions sur la violence* (Reflections on Violence, 1908).—Ed.

7. Henri Bergson (1859–1941) was a French philosopher who contrasted true time, understood as "duration," from spatialized time, which is quantified and measured.—Ed.

8. Romain Rolland (1866–1944) was a French novelist, dramatist, essayist, and well-known pacifist. Daniel Halévy (1872–1962) was a French historian, essayist, and biographer. Rosa Luxemburg, originally Luksemburg (1870 or 1871–1919), was a leader of the German Communist Party and a Marxist political theorist. Arendt's portrait of Luxemburg can be found in *Men in Dark Times*, 33–56.—Ed.

Chapter 20

1. In Goethe's famous conversations with the German poet Johann Peter Eckermann (1792–1854), he defines the novella as an "unheard-of incident that nevertheless took place" (29 January 1827). For Walter Benjamin's discussion of the relation between stories and advice, see his essay "Der Erzähler: Betrachtungen zum Werk Nikolai Lesskows" (The Storyteller, Reflections on the Work of Nicolai Leskov), esp § 4.—Ed.

2. William Faulkner (1897–1962) was among the most important American novelists of the twentieth century. Arendt's *Denktagebuch* (*Thought Diary*) includes a number of reflections on Faulkner, including the following: "Faulkner's pride is the pride of endurance, the only legitimate one: 'If happy I can be I will, if suffer I must I can' " (*Denktagebuch*, ed. Ursula Ludz and Ingeborg Nordmann in conjunction with the Hannah-Arendt-Institute in Dresden [Munich: Piper, 2002], 525). James Joyce (1882–1940) was an Irish novelist who exercised a broad influence on twentieth-century literature. When Broch was imprisoned by the Nazis after the annexation of Austria in 1938, a group of his friends, including Joyce, helped facilitate his release. Arendt wrote the following untitled preface to a collection of Broch's reflections on Joyce's own achievement: "This essay was published in 1936 by Herbert Reichner Verlag and was originally subtitled: 'Address on the Occasion of Joyce's 50th Birthday.' The second part of the essay was delivered as a talk at the Vienna Institute for Continuing Education. It may perhaps be worth noting that Broch himself also turned fifty when the essay was published. // Kafka was without a doubt the contemporary author that Broch appreciated the most, and against whom he secretly measured all contemporary writing. The fact that Broch only rarely talked about Kafka and never wrote about him is no evidence to the contrary; it is, rather, the very demonstration of a method evident in his work more generally; according to this method, everything that is said is organized around a

center—by no means empty but deliberately left unspoken—that is not only a center but also a yardstick. This technique is most conspicuous in his study of Hofmannstahl, where everything is measured against Hofmannstahl's *The Tower* [a play from the mid-1920s that takes Calderon's *Life Is a Dream* as its model], and all remarks about his work are centered on *The Tower,* but hardly anything is said about the tower itself. With respect to Kafka, about whom Broch never wrote but against whom he still measured all of his contemporaries, it was probably neither accidental nor unconscious that Broch attributed to him the only self-interpretive statement of a purely personal nature about which we are aware. // The contemporary author, however, whose work influenced Broch's work the most, and most directly, is Joyce; Broch most likely read *Ulysses* immediately after the completion of *The Sleepwalkers,* and thus at a time when he was more than skeptical about the genre of the novel as a form of art. What he praises in Joyce is the courage to describe '16 hours of a life in 1200 pages, which makes 75 pages per hour, more than a page for every minute, almost a line for every second' (p. 28). Joyce's purpose in doing this, namely to catch on, as it were, to the everyday life of the people, was of no importance to Broch. He cared only about the method whereby one could 'unify the sequential, force the sequence of events back into the unity of simultaneity' (p. 35). *Ulysses* gave him the courage, so to speak, for *The Death of Virgil,* in which 24 hours are likewise described on 533 pages, albeit not those of a regular day but of the most irregular of all human days—the day of dying" (Hermann Broch, *James Joyce und die Gegenwart: Essays* [*James Joyce and the Present*] [Frankfurt am Main: Suhrkamp, 1972], 5–7; translated by Martin Klebes). Arendt doubtless directs the reader's attention to Hofmannstahl's *Tower* in response to Broch's own *Hugo von Hofmannsthal und seine Zeit,* the original version of which includes an afterword by Arendt that is excerpted from the essay that was later translated as "Hermann Broch, 1886–1951" in *Men in Dark Times,* 111–51.—Ed.

3. Adalbert Stifter's last novel, *Witiko* (1865–1867), is set in twelfth-century Bohemia.—Ed.

4. Baruch de Spinoza (1632–1677), the descendent of a Sephardic Jewish family, was a Dutch philosopher whose magnum opus, *The Ethics* (1677), argued that "God or nature" was the one and only substance.—Ed.

Chapter 21

1. Walter Benjamin (1892–1940) wrote a sketch of his massive *Arcades Project* under the title "Paris, Capital of the Nineteenth Century." A translation can be found in volume 3 of *Selected Writings, 1935–1938,* ed. Howard Eiland and Michael Jennings (Cambridge, MA: Harvard University Press, 2002), 32–44.—Ed.

2. For Arendt's analysis of the Dreyfus Affair, see *The Origins of Totalitarianism,* 89–120.—Ed.

3. Yves Simon, *La Grande Crise de la République Francaise,* Montreal, 1941, p. 20: "The spirit of the French Revolution survived the defeat of Napoleon for more than a century. . . . It triumphed but only to fade unnoticed on November 11, 1918. The French Revolution? Its dates must surely be set at 1789–1918."

4. The fact that certain psychological phenomena did not come out as sharply in German and Austrian Jews may partly be due to the strong hold of the Zionist movement on Jewish intellectuals in these countries. Zionism in the decade after the First World War, and even in the decade preceding it, owed its strength not so much to political insight (and did not produce political convictions) as it did to its critical analysis of psychological reactions and sociological facts. Its influence was mainly pedagogical and went far beyond the relatively small circle of actual members of the Zionist movement.

5. Compare the interesting remarks on this subject by E. Levinas, "L'Autre dans Proust" in *Deucalion,* No. 2, 1947.

6. J. E. van Praag, "Marcel Proust, Témoin du Judaisme déjudaizé" in *Revue Juive de Genève,* 1937, Nos. 48, 49, 50. A curious coincidence (or is it more than a coincidence?) occurs in the moving-picture *Crossfire* which deals with the Jewish question. The story was taken from Richard Brooks's *The Brick Foxhole,* in which the murdered Jew of *Crossfire* was a homosexual. [Richard Brooks (1912–1992) was a novelist, screenwriter, and producer. *The Brick Foxhole* (1947), adapted as *Crossfire,* was his first novel.—Ed.]

7. For the following see especially *Cities of the Plain,* Part I, pp. 20–45.

8. *Cities of the Plain,* Part II, chapter iii.

9. Ibid.

10. Ibid.

11. *The Guermantes Way,* Part I, chapter i.

12. Ibid.

13. Ibid.

14. *Within a Budding Grove,* Part II, "Placenames: The Place."

15. Ibid.

16. *Cities of the Plain,* Part II, chapter iii.

17. *The Guermantes Way,* Part II, chapter ii.

18. Ramon Fernandez, "La vie sociale dans l'oeuvre de Marcel Proust," in *Les Cahiers Marcel Proust,* No. 2, 1927.

19. "But this was the moment when from the effects of the Dreyfus case there had arisen an antisemitic movement parallel to a more abundant movement towards the penetration of society by Israelites. The politicians had not been wrong in thinking that the discovery of the judicial error would deal a

fatal blow to antisemitism. But provisionally at least a social antisemitism was on the contrary enhanced and exacerbated by it." See *The Sweet Cheat Gone,* chapter ii.

Chapter 22

1. In his *Reflections on the Revolution in France* (1791) Edmund Burke makes the following pronouncement, to which Arendt refers: "The power of the House of Commons, direct or indirect, is indeed great; and long may it be able to preserve its greatness, and the spirit belonging to true greatness, at the full; and it will do so, as long as it can keep the breakers of the law in India from becoming the makers of the law for England" (paragraph 73). Henry John Temple, Viscount Lord Palmerston (1784–1865), is generally considered the one who quipped that the British Empire was created "in a fit of absent-mindedness."—Ed.

2. Rudyard Kipling, "The First Sailor," in *Humorous Tales,* 1891.

3. Cecil Rhodes (1853–1902) was a British imperialist and largely unsuccessful business magnate. Lord George Curzon (1859–1925) was a British politician and writer.—Ed.

4. In *The Day's Work,* 1898.

Chapter 23

1. The text refers to a poem by Rilke on art which, under the title "Magic," describes this transfiguration. It reads as follows: "Aus unbeschreiblicher Verwandlung stammen / solche Gebilde—: Fühl! und glaub! / Wir leidens oft; zu Asche werden Flammen, / doch, in der Kunst: zur Flamme wird der Staub. / Hier ist Magie. In das Bereich des Zaubers / scheint das gemeine Wort hinaufgestuft- . . . / und ist doch wirklich wie der Ruf des Taubers, / der nach der unsichtbaren Taube ruft" (in *Aus Taschen-Büchern und Merk-Blättern* [1950]). [Rilke's poem, which was written in 1924, can be roughly translated as follows: "From indescribable transformation stem / such image-formations—: feel and believe! / We suffer it often; flames turn into ashes, / yet in art: dust turns into flame. / Here is magic. In the domain of magic the common word appears upgraded . . . / and is still really like the calls of the deaf man [*Tauber*], / who calls after the invisible pigeon [*Taube*]."—Ed.]

2. The idiomatic "make a poem" or *faire des vers* for the activity of the poet already relates to this reification. The same is true for the German *dichten,* which probably comes from the Latin *dictare:* "das ausgesonnene geistig Geschaffene niederschreiben oder zum Niederschreiben vorsagen" (Grimm's

Wörterbuch); the same would be true if the word were derived, as is now suggested by the *Etymologisches Wörterbuch* (1951) of Kluge/Götze, from *tichen,* an old word for *schaffen,* which is perhaps related to the Latin *fingere.* In this case, the poetic activity which produces the poem before it is written down is also understood as "making." Thus Democritus praised the divine genius of Homer, who "framed a cosmos out of all kinds of words"—*epeōn kosmon etektēnato pantoiōn* ([Hermann] Diels, [*Die Fragmente der Vorsokratiker: Griechisch und Deutsch* (Berlin: Weidmannsche Buchhandlung, 1906–1907)], B 21). The same emphasis on the craftsmanship of poets is present in the Greek idiom for the art of poetry: *tektōnes hymnōn.* [Democritus (460 B.C.E.?–370 B.C.E.?) was a Greek philosopher, especially well-known for his atomism.—Ed.]

3. Protagoras (490 B.C.E.?–420 B.C.E.?) was among the original Greek sophists, whose most famous dictum Arendt here quotes: "man [*ho anthrōpos*] is the measure of all things."—Ed.

Chapter 24

1. In "The Crisis in Culture" Arendt prefaces her remarks on culture with a discussion of "mass culture" and includes a description of the origin of the novel: "Good society, as we know it from the eighteenth and nineteenth centuries, probably had its origin in the European courts of the age of absolutism, especially in the court of Louis XIV, who knew so well how to reduce French nobility to political insignificance by the simple means of gathering them at Versailles, transforming them into courtiers, and making them entertain one another through the intrigues, cabals, and endless gossip which this perpetual party inevitably engendered. Thus the true forerunner of the novel, this entirely modern art form, is not so much the picaresque romance of adventurers and knights as the *Mémoires* of [Louis de Rouvroy, Duc de] Saint-Simon [1675–1755], while the novel itself clearly anticipated the rise of the social sciences as well as psychology, both of which are still centered around conflicts between society and the 'individual.' "—Ed.

2. Clemens von Brentano (1778–1842), a German poet and writer, wrote a pamphlet entitled "Philistines Before, In, and After History" in 1811. In "The Crisis in Culture" Arendt is a little more expansive on this point: "The charge the artist, as distinguished from the political revolutionary, has laid to society was summed up quite early, at the turn of the eighteenth century, in the one word which has since been repeated and reinterpreted by one generation after the other. The word is 'philistinism.' Its origin, slightly older than its specific use, is of no great significance; it was first used in German student slang to dis-

tinguish between town and gown, whereby, however, the Biblical association indicated already an enemy superior in numbers into whose hands one may fall."—Ed.

3. When Arendt first delivered a lecture based on this paper, these remarks generated a number of objections. In reply to her critics, especially Hermann Kesten, who accused her of a certain "hostility to life" (*Lebensfeindschaft*), she said the following: "I have opposed the world to life, and because we live in a time in which there has been, and still is, an enormous overestimation of life, I have perhaps overdone the theme of love for the world, which belongs to culture as such. I do not think that I am hostile to life. Life is a magnificent thing but it is not the highest good. Whenever life is considered the highest good, life is just as soon whisked away. In our society there is a dangerous estrangement from the world and, alongside this, a terrible inability of human beings to love the world" (*Untergang oder Übergang*, 165–66).—Ed.

4. Arendt is here alluding to the title of a famous monograph written by the founder of psychoanalysis, Sigmund Freud (1856–1939), *Das Unbehagen in der Kultur* (Uneasiness with Culture, 1929; usually translated as *Civilization and Its Discontents*).—Ed.

5. Theodor Mommsen (1817–1903) was a highly influential historian of Roman antiquity. Gaius Terentius Varro was a Roman general during the Second Punic War.—Ed.

6. Arendt is quoting from the second Choral Ode of Sophocles's *Antigone;* she quotes the Greek below (see 195).—Ed.

7. Phidias (500 B.C.E.?–432 B.C.E.?) was a Greek sculptor.—Ed.

8. Thucydides (460 B.C.E.?–400 B.C.E.?) was an Athenian general and one of the founders of historiography; his *History of the Peloponnesian Wars* paints a vivid yet ambiguous portrait of Pericles (495 B.C.E.?–429 B.C.E.), the leader of Athens during the zenith of its power.—Ed.

9. Arendt is quoting from Pericles's funeral oration, as it is recounted in Thucydides's *History of the Peloponnesian Wars* (book 2, chapter 40). In "The Crisis of Culture" Arendt offers the following, as a rough translation: "We love beauty within the limits of political judgment, and we philosophize without the barbarian vice of effeminacy" (*Between Past and Future*, 214).—Ed.

10. Arendt is quoting from Friedrich Schiller's "An die Freunde" (Ode to Friends). A dramatist, poet, and aesthetic theorist, Schiller (1759–1805) and Goethe are often paired as the twin pillars of modern German culture.—Ed.

11. Arendt is alluding to the title of a polemic written by Julian Benda (1867–1956), whose treatise, *La Trahison des clercs* (The Treason of the Intellectuals, 1928) attacked intellectuals who abandoned reasoned argumentation in favor of political propaganda.—Ed

12. Arendt is again quoting from the second Choral Ode of Sophocles's *Antigone;* for a translation, see 185 above.—Ed

13. For further development of the paragraphs below, see Arendt, *Lectures on Kant's Political Philosophy.*—Ed

Chapter 25

1. Caspar David Friedrich (1774–1840) is generally considered one of the major German painters of the romantic era. Lovis Corinth (1858–1925) was a German painter who experimented in numerous media. Emil Nolde, originally Emil Hansen (1867–1956), was a German painter who is best known for his watercolors.—Ed.

2. José Victoriano González-Pérez, otherwise known as Juan Gris (1887–1927), was a Spanish painter and sculptor who became one of the original cubists.—Ed.

3. Amedeo Clemente Modigliani (1884–1920) was an Italian painter and sculptor.—Ed.

Chapter 26

1. Maximilien Marie Isidore de Robespierre (1758–1794) was a French lawyer and revolutionary, who, as leader of the Committee of Public Safety, established the "Reign of Terror" (June 1793–July 1794). He was guillotined along with many of his associates at the end of July 1794.—Ed.

2. For Rousseau, see *Discours sur l'origine de l'inégalité parmi les hommes* (1755), translated by G. D. H. Cole, New York, 1950, p. 226. Saint-Just is quoted from Albert Ollivier, *Saint-Just et la force des choses,* Paris, 1954, p. 19. [Antoine Louis Léon de Richebourg de Saint-Just (1767–1794), dubbed "St. John of the Messiah of the People," was among the leaders of the French Revolution and was guillotined with Robespierre.—Ed.]

3. R. R. Palmer, *Twelve Who Ruled: The Year of the Terror in the French Revolution,* Princeton, 1941, from which the words of Robespierre are quoted (p. 265), is, together with Thompson's biography, mentioned earlier, the fairest and most painstakingly objective study of Robespierre and the men around him in recent literature. Palmer's book especially is an outstanding contribution to the controversy over the nature of the Terror.

4. Quoted from Zoltán Haraszti, *John Adams and the Prophets of Progress,* Harvard, 1952, p. 205. [John Adams (1735–1826) was a leader of the American Revolution and the second president of the United States.—Ed.]

5. See *Genesis* 4:1.—Ed.

Chapter 27

1. Vladimir Nabokov (1899–1977) was a Russian novelist who wrote his most famous works in English. Evelyn Waugh (1903–1966) was an English novelist. André Gide (1869–1951) was a French novelist, whose *Les Faux-monnayeurs* (*The Counterfeiters*) appeared in 1926.—Ed.

2. Honoré de Balzac (1799–1850) was a French novelist, most famous for his multi-volume series entitled "The Human Comedy." Marie-Henri Beyle, otherwise known as Stendhal (1783–1842), was a French novelist and essayist, whose novel *Le Rouge and le noir* (*The Red and the Black*, 1830), includes two characters to which Arendt later refers in this essay, Julien Sorel and Mme. de Rênal.—Ed.

3. August Strindberg (1849–1912) was a Swedish novelist and dramatist who helped create the modernist idea of the theater. Later in the essay Arendt quotes the following line from Strindberg's *A Dream Play* (1902), "Oh, for the pity of men."

4. Mary McCarthy (1912–1989), a close friend of Arendt's, was an American writer, critic, and political activist.—Ed.

5. See Franz Kafka's story "Die Verwandlung" (The Transformation, 1915), which tells the story of a young man who wakes up to find himself turned into a bug.—Ed.

Chapter 28

1. From W. H. Auden, "The Cave of Making," a section from a longer cycle entitled "Thanksgiving for a Habitat," *Collected Poems,* ed. Edward Mendelson (New York: Vintage, 1991), 691–96. For a discussion of Arendt's relation to Auden (1907–1973), and for Arendt's comparison of Auden to Brecht, see "Remembering Wystan H. Auden" (Chapter 34).—Ed.

2. Almost all of Brecht's poems exist in several versions. Unless otherwise noted I shall quote from the Collected Works published since the late nineteen-fifties by Suhrkamp in West Germany and the Aufbau-Verlag in East Berlin. The first two quotations are from "Hollywood" and "Sonett in der Emigration," *Gedichte 1941–1947,* vol. VI. The first two stanzas of the "Sonnet in the Emigration" are noteworthy because they contain a personal complaint—something very rare in Brecht's poetry.

> Verjagt aus meinem Land muss ich nun sehn
> Wie ich zu einem neuen Laden komme, einer Schenke
> Wo ich verkaufen kann das, was ich denke.
> Die alten Wege muss ich wieder gehn

Die glatt geschliffenen durch den Tritt der Hoffnungslosen!
Schon gehend, weiss ich jetzt noch nicht: zu wem?
Wohin ich komme hör' ich: Spell your name!
Ach, dieser "name" gehörte zu den grossen!

(Hunted out of my country, I now must see how to open a new shop, some place where I can sell what I think. I must take the old paths, worn smooth by the steps of the hopeless ones! Already on my way, I don't know yet: to whom am I going? Wherever I come, I hear: Spell your name! Oh, this "name" was one of the great ones.)

3. Martin Esslin, author of *Brecht: The Man and His Work* (Anchor Books, 1961), stated recently that Brecht "could have gone back into Germany whenever he wanted . . . ; what was difficult at that time was for Germans to *leave* Germany, not to get in." ("Brecht at Seventy," in *tdr*, Fall 1967.) This is an error; but it is true that Brecht "wanted non-German travel documents precisely to keep his line of retreat open."

4. In the corresponding German edition of this essay, she adds at this point: "only a few months before the outbreak of the Hungarian Revolution."—Ed.

5. This translation first appeared as *The Rise and Fall of the City of Mahagonny*, trans. W. H. Auden and Chester Kallman (Boston: D. R. Godine, 1976).—Ed.

6. Charles Laughton (1899–1962) was a British actor and director.—Ed.

7. To avoid misunderstandings, Brecht fared no better with Communist literary critics, and what he said about them, in 1938, applies equally to "anti-Communists": "Lukács, Gabor, Kurella . . . are enemies of production. Productivity makes them suspicious. It is unreliable, it is unpredictable. You never know what is going to happen with productivity. And they themselves don't want to produce. They want to play at being *apparatchiks*, to have control over others. Each of their criticisms contains a threat." (See Walter Benjamin, "Gespräche mit Brecht," in *Versuche über Brecht*, Frankfurt, 1966.) [Some of the conversations between Benjamin and Brecht can be found in volume 2 of Benjamin's *Selected Writings*, ed. Michael Jennings, Howard Eiland, and Gary Smith [Cambridge, MA: Harvard University Press, 1999], 783–91.—Ed.]

8. "Briefe über Gelesenes," *Gedichte*, vol. VI.

9. "Böser Morgen," *Gedichte 1948—1956*, vol. VII. Brecht's praise of Stalin has been carefully eliminated from his *Collected Works*. The only traces are to be found in *Prosa*, vol. V, the posthumously published *Me-ti* notes (see note 44). There Stalin is praised as "the useful one" and his crimes are justified (pp. 60ff. and 100f.). Immediately after his death, Brecht wrote that he had been "the incarnation of hope" for "the oppressed of five continents." (*Sinn und Form*, vol. 2, 1953, p. 10). Cf. also the poem in *op. cit.*, II, 2, 1950, p. 128. [Arendt's claim that Brecht had written "odes to Stalin" prompted the co-editor of his English and American

works, John Willett, to demand that she either produce the odes in question or is-sue a retraction. Upon reading the text in the East German journal *Sinn und Form* to which Arendt points, Willett makes the following response: "I wouldn't have thought that calling Stalin 'the useful one'—which incidentally, like the other ref-erence is about as low on the scale of Stalin-flattery as one can get—constituted praise of his crimes" (Willett, "The Story of Brecht's Odes to Stalin," *Times Liter-ary Supplement* [March 26, 1970]: 335.) A similar remark is made by Irving Fetscher in his "postscript" to Arendt's essay. After quoting a poem by Brecht entitled "Ansprache eines Bauern an seine Ochsen" (Address of a Peasant to His Ox): "Stalin as ox—that is not only meant as a thoroughly polemical contrast to the de-ification of Stalin; an ox is also a useful animal, and Brecht had elsewhere made the suggestion that Stalin be called 'the useful one' rather than 'the great'" (Fetscher, "Es gibt keine Götter—auch Stalin: ein Ochs," *Merkur* 23 [1969]: 888). Arendt ap-parently did not respond to Willett, perhaps because of his tone; but she did write the following in response to Fetscher's "postscript": "I am thankful to Irving Fetscher for drawing my attention to the Stalin-ox poem. It does not, however, have anything to do with my ox [i.e., the animal in the Latin proverb "what is per-mitted Jove is not permitted to an ox"]. Fetscher judges Brecht's 'sins' in a more friendly fashion than I do. Would he think the same thing if he were a Russian, or if Hitler were called 'the useful one'? For, after all, the controversial point here is not the so-called usefulness of Stalin but that he was a murderer like Hitler and, incidentally, an even worse one. And that Brecht, in contrast to Fetscher, had every opportunity to know this" ("Was dachte Brecht von Stalin? Nochmals zu Hannah Arendts Brecht-Aufsatz," *Merkur* 23 [1969], 1084).—Ed.]

10. In the German essay on Brecht from 1950 Arendt adds the following: "Any editor who, appealing to their thirst for fame, convinces them [poets] that they ought to write differently has an easier time corrupting them than did the much-maligned annual salary once lent to Heine by the French government. In the latter case, the artist alone is compromised when he (to remain with the same example, which is admittedly rather antiquated) takes his governmental paymas-ters seriously, and fulfills his duties with the same gleeful sense of responsibility as any government employee. But in the former case, it's all over: the artist no longer paints but, instead, daubs some hackneyed material; the poet no longer writes poetry but, instead, bangs out some battle songs, which usually fare worse than the current propaganda. Money and political conviction—which are gener-ally called corruption—have nothing to do with this. The really fatal thing for the artist is to take political advice seriously." While exiled in Paris, Heine was given some financial support by the royalist government of France. Heine, who prided himself on his oppositional stance and his republican attitudes, was em-barrassed when this support became a matter of public knowledge.—Ed.

11. "In mir habt ihr einen, auf den könnt ihr nicht bauen," in "Vom armen B. B.," the last poem of the Hauspostille, *Gedichte 1918–1929,* vol. I.

12. Walter Benjamin, *op. cit.,* pp. 118–19. [In the German version of the essay Arendt is more expansive at this point, perhaps because she could expect that her readers would know of Benjamin: "In a conversation with Benjamin, he said, 'I often think about a tribunal before which I would be examined. "How is it? Are you really serious about it?" Then I would have to admit: I'm not entirely serious about it. I think about too many artistic matters, about what's good for the theater, for me to be able to be entirely serious about it. But when I've answered this important question in the negative, then I'll add an even more important claim: that my behavior is *permitted.'* And in order to clarify how we should imagine these poets who aren't entirely serious about it, he begins with a story about how Confucius wrote a tragedy, or how Lenin wrote a novel. 'Say you read an excellent political novel, and later learn that it's by Lenin; your opinion about both would be changed, and in both cases for the worse. Nor could Confucius get away with writing any of Euripides' works; one would see that as being beneath him. But these aren't his analogies.' "—Ed.]

13. In the German version Arendt also considers the case of T. S. Eliot (1888–1965), an American-British poet and critic who helped define the idea of literary modernism: "If one compares Brecht and Pound, the communist and the fascist, then there is no question that Pound's behavior was considerably worse than Brecht's. The essential consideration is not that Mussolini's oratory was able to persuade him, but that he actually went far beyond this oratory in his radio addresses during the war, above all with regard to Hitler's policy concerning the Jews. Among renowned writers there was hardly anyone apart from Céline, who matched him in stirring up hatred against the Jews in the most malignant manner. The fact that he could never stand Jews does not enter into it. He shares this aversion with T. S. Eliot, for whom it is a private matter without political significance. In contrast to Eliot, however, who very wisely ceased to speak publicly about this question after Hitler's seizure of power, Pound thought it advisable to make himself one of the most prominent spokesmen of anti-Semitism during the years of the Jewish massacre; and that, God knows, is an entirely different matter. But it is also a fact that Pound, a great poet, was presumably mentally ill for a time, and that he also wasn't very worldly-wise. Thus he could get away with things that the very healthy and clever Brecht, as we will see, could not just get away with."—Ed.

14. François Villon, whose birth name is much disputed (1431?–1474?), was a French poet and vagrant who was imprisoned for unknown crimes and who achieved lasting fame with his *Grand testament* (1461).—Ed.

15. In the "Geschichten vom Herrn Keuner," *Versuche 1–3,* Berlin, 1930.

16. *Gedichte,* vol. VII, entitled "Die Lösung."

17. Angelus Silesius, *Cherubinischer Wandersmann* (1657), Book I, 289, in *Werke*, München, 1949, vol. III. [Angelus Silesius, pen name of Johannes Scheffer (1624–1677), was a German physician and mystic poet whose *Cherubinischer Wandersmann* (The Cherubic Pilgrim) is considered among the classics of Christian mysticism.—Ed.]

18. "How, oh how can we account for the little rose? Suddenly dark red and young and near? Oh, we didn't come to visit her, but when we came she was there. // Before she was, she wasn't expected; when she appeared she was hard to believe in. Oh, something arrived that had never been started. But is that not the way it has always been?" In *Gedichte*, vol. VII.

19. Ibid., p. 84.

20. Despite Arendt's warning, here is a literal translation: "The bush has seven roses / Six belong to the wind / But one remains, so that / I, too, may find one. // Seven times I'll call you / Six times, stay away / But promise, the seventh time, / To come my way."—Ed.

21. Benjamin, *op. cit.*, p. 133.

22. Esslin, *op. cit.*, points out that "in the official East German version, Brecht's return to East Berlin is usually dated October 1948; at that time Brecht did indeed visit East Berlin, but he returned to Zürich again," and it was only "toward the end of 1949 [that] Brecht agreed to go to East Berlin." In October of that year, he still wrote: "I have no official function or obligation of any kind in East Berlin and receive no salary."

23. Walter Ulbricht (1893–1973) was the leader of the German Communist Party who became the deputy premier of the German Democratic Republic (East Germany).—Ed.

24. In *The Jewish Wife and Other Short Plays*, Evergreen Paperbacks.

25. See Marianne Kesting's monograph *Bertolt Brecht*, Hamburg, 1959, p. 155. [Arendt must have meant page 161 of Kesting's biography: "Brecht bought a house on the Danish coast where he could retreat to write." John Willett pointed out that Kesting says nothing about moving to Switzerland; but as an addendum to his declaration that he knew of no such plans, he sent the following letter to *TLS*: "The source [on which Arendt drew], I now see, must have been a sentence in Max Frisch's obituary article 'Brecht ist tot' in the Zürich *Weltwoche* in August, 1956, which describes the two men's last meeting a year earlier, when Brecht, a tired man, 'confined himself to a question in connexion with a quiet house on Lake Geneva.' Frederic Ewen took this up in his biography, but in neither case was there any implication that Brecht meant to leave East Germany for good, and I have since learned that he had been playing with the idea of having a number of minimal establishments in different countries where he could isolate himself in order to write" (*Times Literary Supplement* [December 18, 1970], 1493). It is unclear whether Arendt read this paragraph, but if she had, she might

have been quite amused, for it substantiates the basic thesis of her essay—that, as a consequence of settling in a totalitarian state Brecht lost his poetical talent. Whether he wanted to remain in Switzerland or move from country to country, in search of a place to write is strictly irrelevant.—Ed.]

26. "Forgotten his whole youth but not its dreams, long forgotten the roof but never the sky above it." See "Ballade von den Abenteuern," *Gedichte,* I, 79.

27. Ibid., p. 42.

28. "One day one of them will ask him, 'And why, please, do you come to us?' He will get up in a hurry, knowing that their mood has changed."

29. "Verjagt mit gutem Grund," in *Hundert Gedichte,* Berlin, 1951.

30. "Aus einem Lesebuch für Städtebewohner" (1930), in *Gedichte,* vol. I.

31. In *Gedichte 1930–1933,* vol. III.

32. The poem "Meines Bruders Tod," certainly written before 1920, in *Gedichte 1913–1929,* vol. II.

33. The "Epistel über den Selbstmord," ibid.

34. At this point in the German version Arendt adds the remarkable comment: "Above all, therefore, no pompous self-importance [*Wichtigtuerei*]!" The last word is difficult to capture in English, and she may have dropped the comment for this reason.—Ed.

35. "I too could understand myself quite well if I preferred to look great and solitary; but I saw such people rather close by and said to myself: This is not for you."

36. The whole cycle, including "An die Nachgeborenen," in *Gedichte 1934–1941,* vol. IV.

37. See the two poems "Von meiner Mutter" and "Meiner Mutter," in *Gedichte,* vol. II.

38. In the German version this sentence is slightly more emphatic: "His pride demanded precisely that he *not* take himself to be a "great man" or an exception, and to praise Fortuna rather than himself."—Ed.

39. "Die Verlustliste," in *Gedichte,* vol. VI. [Margarete Steffin (1908–1941) was an actress and writer who was a companion of Brecht's. Carl Koch (1901–1940) was a German filmmaker and cartoonist.—Ed.]

40. "Ich, der Überlebende," ibid.

41. In "Die Landschaft des Exils" in *Gedichte,* vol. VI.

42. From "Deutschland," *Gedichte,* vol. III. "Hearing the speeches that ring from your house, the whole world laughs. But whoever sees you reaches for his knife."

43. See M. Kesting, *op. cit.,* p. 139.

44. See Sidney Hook, "A Recollection of Bertolt Brecht," in *The New Leader,* October 10, 1960.—According to Benjamin (*op. cit.,* p. 131), Brecht was well informed of everything Trotsky wrote during the thirties; he said that these writings proved the existence of a justified suspicion that demanded a skeptical view

of Russian developments. Should the suspicion prove true one would have to turn against the Russian regime *publicly,* but "fortunately or unfortunately, as you please," the suspicion was not yet a certainty. An interesting record of Brecht's desperate attempts to come to terms with Stalin's rule can now be found in an odd little volume of aphorisms, written chiefly during the thirties and found among his papers after his death. It was edited by Uwe Johnson and published in 1965 under the title *Me-ti, Buch der Wendungen,* which M. Esslin rightly translates "Book of Twists and Turns." [Uwe Johnson (1934–1984) was a German novelist and writer who befriended Arendt while they were neighbors on the Upper West Side of New York City. Sidney Hook (1902–1989) was an American academic philosopher who produced an influential book on Marxism in the early 1930s, opposed Stalinism both before and after the Second World War, became a professor at NYU, and joined the Hoover Institution in 1973. In response to the German version of Arendt's essay on Brecht, Hook declared that her "mode of reading is a fantastic, demonstrably false interpretation of Brecht's words. Hannah Arendt is in error about the time and the occasion of Brecht's meeting with me. Brecht, she says, 'was in America during the time of the Moscow trials.' His meeting occurred in 1935, therefore *before* the Moscow trials. She is in error about who were then the victims of the arrests. She does not know with what charges the Soviet presses accused the prisoners. The charge was not that they had 'conspired against Stalin' but, rather, that they were foreign spies who were in service to Hitler and planned the dismemberment of the nation. Only one word describes Hannah Arendt's attempt to explain away Brecht's remark and to turn it into an index for his anti-Stalinistic sentiment: shamelessness. . . . With this unscrupulous apology for Brecht's inhumanity Hannah Arendt has not only done herself a disfavor but also—and this is much worse—the truth" ("Was dachte Brecht von Stalin? Nochmals zu Hannah Arendts Brecht-Aufsatz," *Merkur* 23 [1969]: 1083). Arendt replied by questioning whether Hook could be sure, twenty-five years after the fact, that the conversation took place in 1935 rather than 1936, but "if the meeting did in fact take place before 1936, then it can only have concerned the victims who immediately followed in the wake of the Kirov murder, and these would not have been accused of being Gestapo or Hitler spies. Stalin used to accuse his opponents of what he had done or planned to do. . . . Perhaps it has escaped the hair-splitting "acumen" [*Scharfsinn*] of Sidney Hook that behind the constantly changing and arbitrarily exchangeable official accusations in the Stalin trials—accusations that no one in any case believed—the accusation against the old guard was always that they conspired against Stalin. This alone in any case played a role in the debates among the left about the guilt or innocence of the accused. That Hook, after so many years, can only remember a single word of Brecht's—and this, a word spoken as he was closing the door—is comprehensible. Less comprehensible is that it never occurred to him, in his aggressively aggravated vanity, to ask for an explanation. . . . It is always the same: the pleasure of argumentation, of attacking, and of confirming one's own acumen has little in common with thinking. This is not a bad example of what results from all of this—when, instead of thinking about things in a calm and therefore non-aggressive manner, one simply spews out words in the face of one's opponent" (*Merkur* 23 [1969]: 1083–84).—Ed.]

45. "Die Legende vom toten Soldaten," in *Gedichte,* vol. I.

46. Ernst Jünger (1895–1998) was a German soldier and writer. His account of life on the front lines in World War I, *Im Stahlgewitter* (Storms of Steel, 1920), was enormously successful and made him into a major representative of the radical Right in Weimar Germany.—Ed.

47. As Arendt elsewhere notes, this passage comes from Sartre's "Qu'est-ce que la littérature?" (What Is Literature?).—Ed.

48. All these in the *Hauspostille,* now vol. I of *Gedichte.*

49. In the German version Arendt expands on this thought: "Brecht's human figures from this time—the fallen and drowned maidens who drift slowly down the river, like Ophelia, until seaweed and algae, plants and animals take their bodies up into the uncomplaining peace of nature, untouched by humankind; the friends in the jungle ('wie zwei Kürbisse . . . verfault, doch an einem Stil [like two pumpkins . . . rotten, but on one stem]'); his adventurers ('von Sonne krank und ganz von Regen zerfressen / Geraubten Lorbeer im zerraulten Haar [Sick from the sun and consumed by the rain / Plundered laurel-leaf in disheveled hair]'); the 'Mörder, denen viel Leides geschah [murderers who have suffered much pain]'; and even Mazeppa on his death-ride ('mit eigenem Strick verstrickt dem eigenen Pferde [tied up with his own rope to his own horse]')—they all remain loyal to life and are willing to endure and to enjoy whatever heaven and earth have to offer, both the beginning and the end."—Ed.

50. Ibid.

51. "Der Choral vom Grossen Baal," ibid. The translation of the first and last stanzas: "When Baal grew up inside the white maternal womb there was the sky, great and still and pale, young and naked and immensely wondersome, as Baal then loved it when Baal came // When Baal was left to rot inside the earth's dark womb, there still was the sky, great and still and pale, young and naked and immensely wonderful, as Baal had loved it when Baal was."

52. "Erinnerung an die Marie A.," in *Gedichte,* vol. I.

53. "Die Liebenden," in *Gedichte,* vol. II.

54. The "Ballade von den Seeräubern" of the *Hauspostille,* in *Gedichte,* vol. I.

55. Joachim Neander (1650–1680) was a German hymnist.—Ed.

56. "Grosser Dankchoral," ibid. "Praise ye the cold, the darkness, and the ruin. Look up to the skies: You do not matter and you may die without fear." According to Hugo Schmidt's notes to Eric Bentley's translations of the *Hauspostille* under the title *Manual of Piety*, its English version, "Praise ye the Lord the Almighty, the King of creation," is known from the Presbyterian Hymnal.

57. "Gegen Verführung," ibid. "Do not let them tempt you! There is no recurrence of life. Day stands in the doors; the night wind blows through them: there will be no morrow. . . . How can fear still touch you? You die together with all animals, and there will be nothing thereafter."

58. Algernon Charles Swinburne (1837–1909) was an English poet who is often associated with "decadence." Arendt's quote is drawn from the penultimate stanza of "The Garden of Proserpine" (1866).—Ed.

59. In *Gedichte*, vol. II.

60. "Aufstieg und Fall der Stadt Mahagonny," now in *Stücke (1927–1933)*, vol. III.

61. In "An die Nachgeborenen," *op. cit.*

62. "First it must be possible even for poor people to cut their slice from the great bread of life." From the song "Denn wovon lebt der Mensch?" in *Gedichte*, vol. II.

63. "To be good! Yes, who wouldn't want that? To give your possessions to the poor, why not? When all are good His kingdom is not far. Who wouldn't sit with pleasure in His light?" From "Über die Unsicherheit menschlicher Verhältnisse," ibid.

64. The quotations are from *Me-ti, Buch der Wendungen*.

65. In chapter 15 of *The Prince* (1513) the Italian political philosopher Niccolò Machiavelli (1469–1527) argues that rulers should learn how not to be morally good.—Ed.

66. *Der Kaukasische Kreisekreis*, written 1944–45, in *Stücke*, vol. X.

67. "For some are in darkness, and others stand in the light. And you see those in the light, those in darkness are not seen." *Gedichte*, vol. II.

68. "The great subversive teachers of the people, participating in its struggle, add the history of the ruled class to that of the ruling classes." In "Das Manifest," *Gedichte*, vol. VI.

69. Titus Lucretius Carus (99 B.C.E.?–55 B.C.E.) was a Latin poet and philosopher whose masterpiece, *De rerum natura* (On the Nature of Things), presents a materialist account of the cosmos.—Ed.

70. Frank Wedekind (1864–1918) was a major German dramatist and poet in the years before the First World War, most famous perhaps for the cycle of plays that involve the *femme fatale* named Lulu. A moritat is a barrel organ player; as a lyric genre, it refers to a popular, often satirical, and generally life-affirming ballad that was adapted for the cabaret at the end of the nineteenth century.—Ed.

71. In Benjamin, *op. cit.*, one reads with pleasure that Brecht had his doubts. He compares the Marxist theoreticians with the clerics (*Pfaffen*) whom he hates with a deep-rooted hatred, inherited from his grandmother. Like the priests, the Marxists will always form a camarilla; "Marxism offers too many opportunities of interpretation."

72. "Think of the darkness and the great cold in this valley that rings with wails." From the "Schlusschoral" of the *Dreigroschenoper,* in *Gedichte,* vol. II.

73. Arendt is quoting Trotsky's speech before the Thirteenth Party Congress in 1924.—Ed.

74. I quote from the songs of *Die Massnahme,* the only strictly Communist play Brecht ever wrote. See "Ändere die Welt: sie braucht es" and "Lob der Partei," in *Gedichte,* vol. III.

75. "Lob des Lernens," *ibid.*

76. "Do I know what rice is? Do I know who knows it! I don't know what rice is, I only know its price. / Do I know what man is? Do I know who knows it! I don't know what man is, I only know his price." From "Song von der Ware," ibid.

77. "Begräbnis des Hetzers im Zinksarg," in *Gedichte,* vol. III.

78. Hjalmar Schacht (1877–1970) and Fritz Thyssen (1873–1951) were German financiers who provided money for the Nazis. Schacht was sent to a concentration camp in 1944. Thyssen emigrated in 1939 and dictated a book entitled *I Paid Hitler* to an American journalist.—Ed.

79. It appears that Brecht had second thoughts about the matter. In an article entitled "The Other Germany: 1943" and published by CAW (an SDS [Students for a Democratic Society] publication) in February 1968 without indication of source, he tried to explain why the German working class supported Hitler. The reason is that "unemployment was done away with [by the Third Reich] in short order. Indeed the speed and scope of the abolition were so extraordinary that it seemed like a revolution." The explanation, according to Brecht, was war industry, and "the truth is that war is in [the workers'] interest so long as they cannot or will not shake off the system under which they live." "The regime had to choose war because the whole people needed war only under this regime and therefore have to look for another way of life."

80. "Legende von der Entstehung des Buches Taoteking auf dem Weg des Laotse in die Emigration," in *Gedichte,* vol. IV.

81. In the German version Arendt presents this thought in quasi-religious terms: "The poem was not yet published, when at the beginning of the war the French government interned Hitler's refugees in concentration camps, but Walter Benjamin had taken it back to Paris with him after visiting Brecht in early 1939. The poem spread like wild-fire in the camps, passed from mouth to mouth like a Gospel, which God knows was needed nowhere more urgently than on those straw-mats of hopelessness." Arendt was herself one of the victims of the

French decree about which she here writes; see the description of Arendt's deportation to Gurs in Elisabeth Young-Bruehl, *Hannah Arendt: For Love of the World* (New Haven, CT: Yale University Press, 1982), esp. 152–53.—Ed.

82. "Besuch bei den verbannten Dichtern," ibid.

83. Helene Weigel (1900–1971) often played the principal female characters in Brecht's plays, including *Mutter Courage und ihre Kinder* (Mother Courage and Her Children). Along with Brecht she was the director of the Berlin Ensemble, which was founded in 1949. Brecht and Weigel had two children.—Ed.

84. The remarks *"Zu der Aufhaltsame Aufstieg des Arturo Ui,"* in *Stücke*, vol. IX.

85. In the German version, as a subtle commentary on the epigraph to the essay, Arendt adds the following: "Auden occasionally remarked on the case of Brecht in a very similar fashion. He would have put him up against the wall, but not without first having served him the most magnificent dinner with the choicest wines." Auden's name also enters into the controversy over Arendt's remarks about Brecht and Stalin. The following is drawn from the editors' commentary in the *Times Literary Supplement:* "[In an unpublished letter to *TLS*] Miss Arendt contends other points as well [which the editors do not reproduce], but she concludes by starting an altogether new and, one would have imagined, rather broken-winded hare. 'May I add what seems to me the only important issue in this matter.' Those of us who hoped that this issue was the one of scholarly accuracy were very wide of the mark: Miss Arendt's final stand is taken not on her own behalf at all, but on that of W. H. Auden, whose admirable translations from Brecht have not brought any invitation 'to help in the publication of Brecht's collected works in English under the editorship of Mr. Willett' " (*Times Literary Supplement* 69 [April 9, 1970]: 384. John Willett responds, via a published letter in *TLS*, by insisting that he has tried to interest Auden in doing some of the translations for his edition of selected poems "but so far without success. Quite apart from my own feelings about his poetry, which are akin to Miss Arendt's, he is the one poet whom Brecht's wife, son and daughter have all at different times told me they would like to see translate Brecht's verse" (*Times Literary Supplement* 69 [April 16, 1970]: 430).—Ed.

86. For Arendt's reflections on forgiveness, see especially *The Human Condition* (Chicago: University of Chicago Press, 1958), 236–43.—Ed.

Chapter 29

1. Randall Jarrell, *Losses: Poems* (New York: Harcourt Brace, 1948).—Ed.

2. From Jarrell, "Deutsch Durch Freud," in *The Complete Poems* (London: Faber & Faber, 1971), 266ff.—Ed.

3. The philologists and critics Jacob Grimm (1785–1863) and his brother Wil-

helm (1786–1859) collected (or invented) the fairy tales with which their names have since been associated. *Des Knaben Wunderhorn* (The Youth's Magic Horn, 1805–1808) is a collection of German folk poems undertaken by Achim von Arnim (1781–1831) and Clemens von Brentano (1778–1842). *Alice in Wonderland* (1865) was written by Lewis Carroll, the pseudonym of Charles Lutwidge Dodgson (1832–1898).—Ed.

4. From Jarrell, "The Märchen (Grimm's Tales)," in *The Complete Poems,* 82.—Ed.

5. Jarrell, "The Obscurity of the Poet," in *Poetry and the Age* (London: Faber & Faber, 1986), 27.—Ed.

6. Jarrell, *Pictures from an Institution: A Comedy* (1954, reprint: Chicago: University of Chicago Press, 1986), 11.—Ed.

7. From Jarrell, "A Conversation with the Devil," in *The Complete Poems,* 29.—Ed.

Chapter 30

1. Denys Finch-Hatton (1887–1931) was a British officer who often visited Africa and for a time lived with Karen Blixen.—Ed.

2. Johann Peter Hebel (1760–1826) was a German writer and poet who collected the stories and anecdotes he published as part of his yearly almanacs under the title *Schatzkästlein des rheinischen Hausfreundes* (Treasure Chest of the Rhenish Friend of the House, 1811). One of the stories included in this collection is "Unverhofftes Wiedersehen" (An Unhoped-for Return), which revolves around the death of a bridegroom in a mine and the reappearance of his body fifty years later. Walter Benjamin also referred to this story in his famous essay, "Der Erzähler: Betrachtungen zum Werk Nikolai Lesskows" (The Storyteller: Reflections on the Work of Nikolai Leskov), which Arendt included in her edition of *Illuminations*; see esp. 94–95.—Ed.

3. Eudora Welty (1909–2001) was a southern American writer. Arendt is quoting from Welty's memorial essay for Dinesen in *Isak Dinesen: A Memorial,* ed. Clara Svendson (New York: Random House, 1964), 94.—Ed.

4. See Parmenia Migel, *Titania: The Biography of Isak Dinesen* (New York: Random House, 1967). Blixen requested that Migel not visit Africa to conduct research, and she complied; furthermore, Migel never gained access to Blixen's letters.—Ed.

5. Ernest Hemingway (1899–1961) was an American writer who was awarded the Nobel Prize in 1954.—Ed.

6. Arendt is referring to Robert Langbaum, *The Gayety of Vision: A Study of Isak Dinesen's Art* (London: Chatto & Windus, 1964). Parts of this study are included in *Isak Dinesen: A Memorial,* to which Arendt refers above.—Ed.

7. In the story that frames *A Thousand and One Nights* Scheherazade is the bride of the Persian king Shahryar, who beheads his wives after their first night of marriage. In order to postpone her fate, she recounts each night a story that will leave the king in suspense. In the end, Shahryar allows her to live.—Ed.

8. Berkeley Cole (1882–1925) was a friend of Karen Blixen who died in Africa of heart failure.

9. Blixen draws this quote from Shakespeare, *As You Like It,* Act 2, Scene 5.—Ed.

10. From Shakespeare, *A Midsummer's Night Dream,* Act 3, Scene 1.—Ed.

11. The quotation from William Faulkner (1897–1962) stems from his novel, *The Wild Palms* (1939).

12. This quotation, attributed to Dinesen, does not appear in any of the author's published works. The probable source is a telephone interview published in *The New York Times Book Review* on November 3, 1957, in which Dinesen is quoted as saying, "One of my friends said about me that I think all sorrows can be borne if you put them into a story or tell a story about them, and perhaps this is not entirely untrue." For a discussion of Arendt's (mis)quotation, see Lynn R. Wilkinson, "Hannah Arendt on Isak Dinesen: Between Storytelling and Theory," *Comparative Literature* 56 (winter 2004): 77–98.—Ed.

13. Johann Wolfgang von Goethe (1749–1832) was a "Privy Counselor" (*Geheimrat*) to Charles Augustus, Duke of Saxony-Weimar.—Ed.

Chapter 31

1. Sergey Gennadiyevich Nechayev (1847–1882) was a Russian revolutionary whose *Catechism of a Revolutionary* (1869) begins by declaring that "the revolutionary is a doomed person" and includes the statement, "The ends justify the means." Nestor Kukolnic (1809–1868) was a Russian poet and dramatist. Timofei Nikolaevich Granovsky (1813–1855) was an important liberal scholar and historian of the era. At this point in the text, Arendt includes a number of additional notes about Nechayev's doings at this time. I have eliminated them, because they are a series of sentence fragments clearly written to remind Arendt of the historical background for Dostoevsky's novel.—Ed.

2. Arendt is drawing her quotations from Fyodor Dostoevsky, *The Possessed,* trans. Constance Garnett (New York: Random House, 1963).—Ed.

3. Nicolas Berdiaev (1874–1948) was a Ukrainian social philosopher who taught at the University of Moscow but was forced to leave the Soviet Union because of his opposition to the Bolsheviks. An English translation of his *Origins of Russian Communism* appeared in 1960.—Ed.

4. Arendt is referring to Prince Myshkin, the protagonist of Dostoevsky's novel *The Idiot* (1868).—Ed.

5. Aljosha is one of the Karamazov brothers, in the novel by the same name.—Ed.

6. See Dostoevsky, *Notebooks for "The Possessed,"* ed. and intro. Edward Wasiolek, trans. Victor Terras (Chicago: University of Chicago Press, 1968).—Ed.

7. "'Men made of paper! It all comes from flunkeyism of thought,' Shatov observed calmly" (*The Possessed,* 136). "'Marie, Marie,' said Shatov, turning to her . . .'The enemies of all true life, out-of-date Liberals, who are afraid of their own independence, the flunkeys of thought" (*The Possessed,* 589).—Ed.

8. "If anyone doubts that such fantastic incidents occur in everyday Russian life, even now, let him look into the biographies of all the Russian exiles abroad. Not one of them escaped with more wisdom or real justification. It has always been the unrestrained domination of phantoms and nothing more" (*The Possessed,* 573).—Ed.

Chapter 32

1. Hermann Grimm (1822–1901), an admirer of Emerson, was a writer and critic who helped edit the philological work of his father Wilhelm (1786–1859) and his uncle Jacob (1785–1863).—Ed.

2. Michel Eyquem de Montaigne (1533–1592) was a French philosopher and writer who achieved enormous influence with his wide-ranging *Essays* (first edition, 1580).—Ed.

Chapter 33

1. Throughout this translation, no attempt is made to render Gilbert's poetry into corresponding English verse.–Ed.

2. Arendt grew up in Königsberg, the old capital of East Prussia, now the isolated Russian port city of Kaliningrad.–Ed.

3. Heine's "Die Grenadiere" can be found in his *Buch der Lieder* (Book of Songs, 1827) and has often been set to music (by Robert Schumann, among others).—Ed.

4. From Heine's poem "Doktrin," which first appeared in *Neue Gedichte* (New Poems, 1844).—Ed.

5. In her rejoinder to a critical comment made in response to her essay "Politics and Culture," Arendt says the following: "I must confess that I was very amused by *My Fair Lady.* And in general I am not at all against entertainment and the entertainment industry, if only they really entertain people. There is a difference between entertainment and joy" (*Untergang oder Übergang,* 166).—Ed.

6. Erich Kästner (1899–1974) was a German poet, novelist, and journalist

who is probably best known for his children's book *Emil und die Detektive* (Emil and the Detectives, 1928). He wrote popular light verse. Kurt Tucholsky (1890–1935) was a German journalist and satirist who is best known for his cabaret lyrics.—Ed.

7. Heinrich Zille (1858–1929) was a German artist, especially well-known for his satirical drawings, including his scandalous *Hurengespräche* (prostitute dialogues) of 1913.—Ed.

8. Wannsee is a wealthy neighborhood in the southwest corner of Berlin, near Potsdam. It was the scene of—among other things—Heinrich von Kleist's suicide in 1811 and the conference of Nazi officials in 1943 that initiated the "final solution" of "the Jewish question."—Ed.

9. Joseph Freiherr von Eichendorff (1788–1854) was a German poet and novelist who belonged to the second generation of romantics.—Ed.

10. See Robert Gilbert, *Durch Berlin fließt immer noch die Spree* (Berlin-Wannsee: Blanvalet, 1971).—Ed.

11. Yvette Guilbert (1867–1944) was a popular French singer and actress. Edith Piaf (1915–1963) was the iconic French singer of her generation.—Ed.

12. Stefan George (1868–1933) exercised a powerful influence over early twentieth-century German poetry and thought; a group of poets and intellectuals ("the George circle") gathered around him. Arendt is alluding to the subtitle of Gilbert's volume: "Gedichte aus Zeit und Unzeit." The word *Unzeit* is formed on the model of *Unding,* which derives from the word "thing" (*Ding*) and means "monster." *Unzeit* means "out of season" and suggests that this "untimeliness" has its origin in something monstrous.—Ed.

13. "Odyssey of an Organ-Grinder" (*Leierkastenodysse*) is a thirty-nine-part poem in which Gilbert recounts his life; it concludes *No Donkey Has Lost Me While Galloping.*—Ed.

14. The phrase "Stadtluft macht frei" refers to medieval common law, according to which a serf who had escaped from his feudal lord to the city would be considered a free citizen after a year and a day.—Ed.

Chapter 34

1. From "Lullaby," in W. H. Auden, *Collected Poems,* ed. Edward Mendelson (New York: Vintage, 1991), 157–58.—Ed.

2. Aleksandr Sergeyevich Pushkin (1799–1837) is generally regarded as the greatest Russian poet of the nineteenth century.—Ed.

3. See Clive James, "Auden's Achievement," *Commentary* 56 (December 1973), 563.—Ed.

4. Auden, "If I Could Tell You," in *Collected Poems,* 314.—Ed.

5. Geoffrey Grigson, "A Meaning of Auden," in *W. H. Auden: A Tribute,* ed. Stephen Spender (London: Weidenfeld & Nicolson, 1975), 15. Geoffrey Grigson (1905–1985) was the editor of *New Verse* from 1933 to 1939, where he published many of Auden's early poems.—Ed.

6. In his "Foreword" to *Collected Shorter Poems,* Auden writes: "I agree with Valéry: 'A poem is never finished; it is only abandoned' " (*Collected Shorter Poems: 1927–1957* [London: Faber & Faber, 1966], 16). Paul Valéry (1871–1945) was a highly influential French poet and essayist.—Ed.

7. Stephen Spender, "Valediction" (Address given on October 27, 1973 at Auden's memorial service in Christ Church), in *W. H. Auden: A Tribute,* 247–48. Stephen Spender (1909–1995) was an English poet and essayist, who was a close friend of Auden's.—Ed.

8. Here, as elsewhere, Arendt inconspicuously inserts an autobiographical reference. Three years before his death, Auden had approached Arendt with a proposal of marriage, which she refused. The day after he died, she wrote a letter to Mary McCarthy, in which she revealed the personal origins of some of the reflections published here: "I'm still thinking of Wystan, naturally, and of the misery of his life, and that I refused to take care of him when he came and asked for shelter. Homer said that the gods spin ruin to men that there might be song and remembrance. . . . Well he was both the singer and the tale" (Arendt and McCarthy, *Between Friends: The Correspondence of Hannah Arendt and Mary McCarthy, 1949–1975,* ed. Carol Brightman [New York: Harcourt Brace, 1995], 343–44). Arendt's writings display an almost singularly consistent reticence regarding details of her personal life—details that nevertheless seem to haunt much of her prose. From her early reflections on acculturated German Jews (and the outrage that so insignificant a phenomenon as anti-Semitism could play such a decisive role in the machinery and ideology of Nazi power), through her reference to the French government's decision to intern its German refugees (344), to the melancholy remembrance recorded here, Arendt refrains from revealing events from her own life. We may find a clue for her reserve first, in the imperative with which she describes the best element of Brecht's character ("Above all, therefore, no pompous self-importance!" [339]), and second, in her discussion of Gilbert ("every moment of this, our only life demands to be recorded, but only if the recording is done in verse. . . ." [292]). The latter may suggest one of the reasons for Arendt's lifelong interest in the work of poets. And all of the reflections contained in this volume on literature and culture may provide clues to the moments Arendt was incapable of putting into verse.—Ed.

9. From "Death's Echo," in Auden, *Collected Poems,* 152–54.—Ed.

10. Chester Kallman (1921–1975) was a poet, librettist, and translator. He was Auden's lover for a time, and the two exchanged marriage vows in 1939. After

the dissolution of their sexual partnership, the two remained life companions and collaborated on a number of libretti and translations. Kallman lived with the poet intermittently from 1939 until Auden's death in 1973.—Ed.

11. Bertolt Brecht (1898–1956) was a German poet and dramatist who is often the subject of Arendt's reflections on modern literature (see Chapters 18 and 28).—Ed.

12. From "Ballad of Barnaby," in Auden, *Collected Poems,* 824–27; from "Miss Gee," in *Collected Poems,* 158–61.—Ed.

13. Roughly translated: "To be a good man! Yes, who wouldn't like to be one? / To give his goods to the poor, why not? / If everyone is good, His kingdom is not far. / Who would not like to sit happily in his light." (From "Erstes Dreigroschen-Finale: Über die Unsicherheit menschlicher Verhältnisse [On the insecurity of human relationships], in Bertolt Brecht, *Gesammelte Werke* [Frankfurt am Main: Suhrkamp, 1967], 2:430).—Ed.

14. From "In Memory of W. B. Yeats (d. January 1939)," in Auden, *Collected Poems,* 247–49.—Ed.

15. See the "Author's Forewords" in *Collected Poems,* xxv-xxvii. Auden is quoting lines from his 1937 poem, "Spain"; see *Selected Poems,* ed. Edward Mendelson (New York: Vintage, 1979) 51–55—Ed.

16. From "September 1, 1939," in *Selected Poems,* 86–89.—Ed.

17. From "In Memory of W. B. Yeats," in *Collected Poems,* 247–49.—Ed.

18. Ibid.—Ed.

19. Arendt is referring to a famous phrase of Gottfried Wilhelm von Leibniz (1646–1716), a German philosopher who solved the problem of theodicy (his own neologism) by means of "optimism," i.e., the thesis that this is the best of all possible worlds, and God is therefore justified in having created it under the condition that a world should be created at all.—Ed.

20. From "Precious Five," in Auden, *Complete Poems,* 587–91.—Ed.

21. From "The Truest Poetry Is the Most Feigning," in Auden, *Complete Poems,* 619–21.—Ed.

22. Spender, "Valediction," 248.—Ed.

Index

abandonment, 180; by God and world, xiv, 23; Rilke's abandonability, 12–16. *See also* loss; love; world

actor, 46; authenticity of, 118; Jews, and fame, 63–64; and society, 162. *See also* fame; vice

Adams, John, 210, 247, 333n4

aesthetic state, xiii, xxiv–xxv

Ahad Ha'am, 89, 320n12

Anders, Günther, xiv, xix–xxi, xxvii, 23, 306n9, 307n15

angel, xiv, xxvii, 2–3, 5–9, 210; of history, xxi, 102, 322n5 (*see also* Benjamin, Walter)

animal, 10, 19–21, 118, 173, 176, 267, 309n8, 341n49

anti-Semitism, 52, 62; Brecht against, 141; Ezra Pound's, 226, 337n13; French, 144–45; Nazi version, 165. *See also* Dreyfus Affair; Jewishness; Nazism

aristocracy, 30; and bourgeois, 46; and culture, 163–64 (*see also* Bildung); loss of, 29–30; the nobleman, 41; and romanticism, 51–52. *See also* strata-state (*Ständestaat*)

Aristotle, xxiv, 130, 186

Arnim, Achim von, 39, 51, 316n23, 345n3; *The Youth's Magic Horn (Des Knaben Wunderhorn),* 258, 285–86, 289, 345n3

Arnim, Bettina von, 58, 315n18

artist, 64, 124, 155, 175, 197; becoming an, 264; compromise of, 336n10; Greek conception of, 187, 189, 192; production of culture, xxiv–xxvi; Roman conception of, 185–186; task of, 331n2. *See also* culture; pariah; poet

artwork, 189–91, 308; permanence of, 172–78; purpose of, 196. *See also* poetry

Auden, W. H., xi, xxviii–xxxi, 224, 294–302, 357n1; Arendt's friendship with, 294–7, 302, 334n1; "Ballad of Barnaby," 297; Brecht's influence on, 297–98, 344n85; "The Cave of Making," 223; "Death's Echo," 297, 350n9; "If I Could Tell You," 295, 349n6; "In Memory of W. B. Yeats," 19, 300, 349n17; and love, 297; poetry and politics, 298–99; praise in, 300; "Precious Five," 301, 350n20; "September 1, 1939," 299, 350n16; "The Truest Poetry Is the Most Feigning," 301

authorship: and women, 262–63

autonomy. *See Bildung*

tradition: break in, xvi, 139–40. *See also* history; loss
transcendence, 5–6, 8, 13, 177
Treitschke, Heinrich von, 41, 62, 313n6
Trotsky, Leon, 238, 248, 339n44, 343n73
Tucholsky, Kurt, 287, 348n6

Ulbricht, Walter, 230, 338n23
Unzelmann, Frederike, 49, 315n14
utilitarianism, 175–77, 192–93

Valéry, Paul, 296, 349n6
Varnhagen von Ense, Karl August, 31, 311n1, 314n1
Varnhagen von Ense, Rahel, xxiii, 31, 33–6, 46–48, 52–53, 58, 73, 307n17, 308n25, 311n3, 313n1, 315n19, 316n20, 317nn30,31
Varro, Marcus Terentius, 185, 332n5
Veit, Brendel. *See* Schlegel, Dorothea
Veit, David, 48, 314n6
Verlassenheit, Verlassbarkeit. See abandonment
vice, xvii, 156–66, 207–9. *See also* evil; goodness
Villon, François, 227, 240–41, 252, 337n14
violence, xxiv–xxv, 185, 192–94, 210, 213
Voltaire (François-Marie Arouet), 52, 252
Voß, Countess Luise von, 51, 316n22
Voß, Johann Heinrich, 52, 272, 317n28

Waugh, Evelyn, 214, 334n1
Weber, Max, 70, 319n1
Wedekind, Frank, 247, 342n70
Weigel, Helene, 253, 344n83

Weil, Hans: *The Emergence of the German Principle of "Bildung,"* 24–30
Welty, Eudora, 264, 345n3
Wiesel, Pauline, 33, 49–50, 53, 312n9, 315n15, 316n20, 317n31
Willet, John, 256n, 336n9, 338n25, 344n85
Winterfeld, Robert. *See* Gilbert, Robert
women: in the intelligentsia, xxii, xxiii, 47–49, 315n19 (*see also* salons)
world: being-in-the-world, 10; changing the world, 245–46, 248; in common, 222; and compassion, 212; and culture, 182–83; destruction of, 108–9; estrangement from, 6–8, 12–13, 17–23, 118–19, 180; future world, 122; mastery of, 169; is not life, 332n3; permanence of, 172–78; production of, 185, 189–91, 193–97, 326n10; taking part in, 36; and taste, 200; "terrible freshness" of, 139, 239–40; unwelcoming to poets, 259–60; worldliness and inwardness, 24–25; of yesterday, 58–68. *See also* fame; pariah

Yeats, William Butler, 259, 300

Zelter, Carl Friedrich, 316n24
Zille, Heinrich, 287, 348n7
Zionism, 318n8, 329n4; Kafka's, 89; Lazare's, 145–46. *See also* Herzl, Theodor
Zionist Actions Committee, 146
Zola, Emile, 145, 326n3
Zurishaddai, Shelumiel ben, 71
Zweig, Stefan, xxiii, 68; "The Great Silence," 67–68; *The World of Yesterday: An Autobiography,* 58–68

Crossing Aesthetics

Jean Genet, *Fragments of the Artwork*

Shoshana Felman, *The Scandal of the Speaking Body: Don Juan with J. L. Austin, or Seduction in Two Languages*

Peter Szondi, *Celan Studies*

Neil Hertz, *George Eliot's Pulse*

Maurice Blanchot, *The Book to Come*

Susannah Young-ah Gottlieb, *Regions of Sorrow: Anxiety and Messianism in Hannah Arendt and W. H. Auden*

Jacques Derrida, *Without Alibi*, edited by Peggy Kamuf

Cornelius Castoriadis, *On Plato's 'Statesman'*

Jacques Derrida, *Who's Afraid of Philosophy? Right to Philosophy 1*

Peter Szondi, *An Essay on the Tragic*

Peter Fenves, *Arresting Language: From Leibniz to Benjamin*

Jill Robbins, ed. *Is It Righteous to Be?: Interviews with Emmanuel Levinas*

Louis Marin, *Of Representation*

J. Hillis Miller, *Speech Acts in Literature*

Maurice Blanchot, *Faux pas*

Jean-Luc Nancy, *Being Singular Plural*

Maurice Blanchot / Jacques Derrida, *The Instant of My Death* / Demeure: *Fiction and Testimony*

Niklas Luhmann, *Art as a Social System*

Emmanuel Levinas, *God, Death, and Time*

Ernst Bloch, *The Spirit of Utopia*

Giorgio Agamben, *Potentialities: Collected Essays in Philosophy*

Ellen S. Burt, *Poetry's Appeal: French Nineteenth-Century Lyric and the Political Space*

Jacques Derrida, *Adieu to Emmanuel Levinas*

Werner Hamacher, *Premises: Essays on Philosophy and Literature from Kant to Celan*

Aris Fioretos, *The Gray Book*

Deborah Esch, *In the Event: Reading Journalism, Reading Theory*

Winfried Menninghaus, *In Praise of Nonsense: Kant and Bluebeard*

Giorgio Agamben, *The Man Without Content*

Giorgio Agamben, *The End of the Poem: Studies in Poetics*

Theodor W. Adorno, *Sound Figures*

Louis Marin, *Sublime Poussin*

Philippe Lacoue-Labarthe, *Poetry as Experience*

Ernst Bloch, *Literary Essays*

Jacques Derrida, *Resistances of Psychoanalysis*

Marc Froment-Meurice, *That Is to Say: Heidegger's Poetics*

Francis Ponge, *Soap*

Philippe Lacoue-Labarthe, *Typography: Mimesis, Philosophy, Politics*

Giorgio Agamben, *Homo Sacer: Sovereign Power and Bare Life*

Emmanuel Levinas, *Of God Who Comes To Mind*

Bernard Stiegler, *Technics and Time, 1: The Fault of Epimetheus*

Werner Hamacher, *pleroma—Reading in Hegel*

Serge Leclaire, *Psychoanalyzing: On the Order of the Unconscious and the Practice of the Letter*

Serge Leclaire, *A Child Is Being Killed: On Primary Narcissism and the Death Drive*

Sigmund Freud, *Writings on Art and Literature*

Cornelius Castoriadis, *World in Fragments: Writings on Politics, Society, Psychoanalysis, and the Imagination*

Thomas Keenan, *Fables of Responsibility: Aberrations and Predicaments in Ethics and Politics*

Emmanuel Levinas, *Proper Names*

Alexander García Düttmann, *At Odds with AIDS: Thinking and Talking About a Virus*